T0314058

REINVENTING BANKRUPTCY LAW

A History of the *Companies' Creditors Arrangement Act*

REINVENTING BANKRUPTCY LAW

A History of the *Companies'*
Creditors Arrangement Act

VIRGINIA TORRIE

UNIVERSITY OF TORONTO PRESS
Toronto Buffalo London

ISBN 978-1-4875-0642-1 (cloth)
ISBN 978-1-4875-3413-4 (EPUB)
ISBN 978-1-4875-3412-7 (PDF)

Library and Archives Canada Cataloguing in Publication

Title: Reinventing bankruptcy law : a history of the Companies' Creditors
Arrangement Act / Virginia Torrie
Names: Torrie, Virginia, author.
Description: Includes bibliographical references and index,
Identifiers: Canadiana (print) 20200179969 | Canadiana (ebook) 20200179977 |
ISBN 9781487506421 (cloth) | ISBN 9781487534134 (EPUB) |
ISBN 9781487534127 (PDF)
Subjects: LCSH: Canada. Companies' Creditors Arrangement Act. |
LCSH: Bankruptcy – Canada – History.
Classification: LCC KE1518.C6 T67 2020 | LCC KF1544 .T67 2020 kfmod |
DDC 346.7107/8–dc23

This book has been published with the help of a grant from the Federation
for the Humanities and Social Sciences, through the Awards to Scholarly
Publications Program, using funds provided by the Social Sciences and
Humanities Research Council of Canada.

University of Toronto Press acknowledges the financial assistance to its
publishing program of the Canada Council for the Arts and the Ontario Arts
Council, an agency of the Government of Ontario.

 Canada Council   Conseil des Arts
for the Arts   du Canada

 ONTARIO ARTS COUNCIL
CONSEIL DES ARTS DE L'ONTARIO
an Ontario government agency
un organisme du gouvernement de l'Ontario

Funded by the   Financé par le
Government   gouvernement
of Canada   du Canada

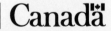 Canadä

This book is dedicated to my maternal and paternal grandmothers:
to
Maryke Y. Young
who wholeheartedly encouraged my pursuit of higher education,
delighting in seeing me take up an opportunity that
had not been available to her;
and
in memory of
Beverley A. Torrie
who always supported my education and
who set an example as a businesswoman, which is a
continuing source of inspiration.

Time is the dimension in which ideas and institutions and beliefs evolve.
Douglass North, In Anticipation of the Marriage of
Political and Economic Theory

Contents

Contents

Figures and Table

Figures

Table

Foreword

In this book, Professor Torrie sets out to demonstrate that contemporary courts' interpretation of the *Companies' Creditors Arrangement Act* (CCAA) is at odds with the early history of the statute. Specifically, the statute started life as a form of secured creditor remedy, but in the later part of the twentieth century, it was transformed, by a process of expansive judicial interpretation, into a measure aimed at rescuing insolvent debtors from liquidation. As part of this process, the underlying policy focus shifted from creditor protection to debtor protection, with debtor protection including the protection of the debtor's stakeholders (employees, trade suppliers, and others dependent on the debtor for their own financial well-being). Professor Torrie explains how this shift occurred, with reference to changes in social and political factors, lending patterns, and approaches to statutory interpretation.

But, more ambitiously, Torrie seeks to locate these changes within a socio-political framework based on the twin ideas of "historical institutionalism" and "recursivity of law." As she explains, "historical institutionalism" is a social sciences approach that examines "the influence of institutions on social, political or economic regimes over time" (page 11), while "recursivity of law" refers to the idea that "law not only flows from the books to legal practice, but that legal practices also shape formal law" (page 14). At this deeper level, the author's concern is with the evolution of ideas in a legal context and how factors such as accidents of timing and path dependency shape legal outcomes.

On both levels, the book is a *tour de force*. On the first level, the book explodes the conventional wisdom surrounding the CCAA's underlying policy objectives, and it exposes the historical errors in the more recent case law to devastating effect. In this connection, the work has important things to say about the evolution in methods of statutory interpretation, judicial method, and the relationship between courts

and the legislature. On the second level, the author uses the history of
the CCAA as a vehicle for exploring the dynamics of legal change.

The conventional wisdom in insolvency law circles is that the
CCAA's purpose has always been to facilitate corporate restructurings
with a view to protecting both debtors and their stakeholders and that
the courts correctly interpreted the statute to achieve this purpose. The
book contradicts both these claims, arguing, in effect, that, contrary to all
established rules of statutory interpretation, the courts read the statute
expansively to implement a policy that they themselves had invented.
In summary, the courts took over the role of the legislature which, for
its part, acquiesced in this usurpation of its function by standing by
and letting it happen. Passive acquiescence later morphed into positive affirmation when the legislature adopted some of the key judicial
innovations as statutory amendments. In these respects, as Professor
Torrie persuasively argues, the history of the CCAA demonstrates the
triumph of commercial pragmatism over the rule of law. Time will tell
whether Canada's judicially created Chapter 11 has come at too great a
price on this account.

These are all challenging claims, and so the book will no doubt be
read with great interest by practitioners and scholars working in the
insolvency field. But the readership will extend beyond insolvency law
circles. For the reasons indicated above, the book will appeal to readers
interested in statutory interpretation, judicial method, the relationship
between courts and legislatures and, at the broadest level, the history of
ideas and the dynamics of change. In short, the book makes an important contribution to legal theory that extends beyond the immediate
context of Canadian insolvency law.

Anthony Duggan
Hon. Frank H. Iacobucci Chair
Faculty of Law
University of Toronto

Acknowledgments

I was fortunate to have the encouragement and advice of many people over the course of this project. I am very grateful for their support, which helped make this book possible.

This book developed out of a PhD thesis completed at Kent Law School, University of Kent in 2016. The thesis was subsequently refined, enhanced, and edited into book form. Accordingly, I wish to thank Lynn Risbridger, Dylan Williams, and Karen Finch of the Kent Law School Postgraduate Office, and Ben Watson at the University of Kent Library for his assistance in obtaining many of the historical materials for this research. I wish to thank my supervisors at the University of Kent: Iain D.C. Ramsay, Paddy Ireland, and Iain Frame. I am especially grateful to Iain D.C. Ramsay, who was my principal supervisor throughout this project, and who guided me through the research and writing process. His advice helped me produce a scholarly product that exceeded my own expectations; for that I am profoundly grateful.

As an historically oriented project, I consulted and received much help from librarians and archivists at a number of institutions in Canada and England in the course of this research. I wish to thank the librarians and archivists at the following institutions for their support and assistance: York University Libraries, University of Toronto Libraries, Toronto Public Library, University of Manitoba Libraries, Library and Archives Canada, Supreme Court of Canada Records Centre, Bibliothèque et Archives nationales du Québec, Provincial Archives of New Brunswick, British Library, and University of London Libraries.

My family and friends have been a tremendous support over the course of this project. In particular, I would like to thank my parents and my sister for their love and patience throughout this process. I am also grateful for the ongoing support and encouragement I received from friends in Canada and England.

I also benefitted from conversations with numerous people as this project developed. I presented early versions of this research at several conferences in Canada and England, including the Queen Mary Postgraduate Legal Research Conference (London), University of British Columbia Graduate Law Student Conference (Vancouver), INSOL Europe Academic Forum Conference (Nottingham), King's College London International Graduate Legal Research Conference (London), Social Science History Association (Montreal), INSOL International Academics' Colloquium (London). I am grateful to the delegates of those conferences for their feedback. In addition, I would like to thank Rosa Lastra (Queen Mary University of London) and Hester Lessard (University of Victoria) for taking the time to chat with me about different aspects of this research. These conversations helped me to refine my understanding of key issues. I also wish to thank colleagues at the Faculty of Law, National University of Singapore and Faculty of Law, University of Manitoba for their encouragement as I prepared the final manuscript for publication.

A number of people read sections of this thesis at various stages in the process and provided valuable feedback. In particular, I would like to thank Thomas G.W. Telfer, Karen Martin, Anna Lund, Georgina Garrett, Stephanie Ben-Ishai, and Vern W. DaRe for their comments and suggestions. I am also grateful to Bryan Cragg, Samuel Thomson, Mark Ginsberg, Anna Tourtchaninova, Tyson Bannatyne, and Jennifer Bisch for their assistance with sorting and cataloguing data for this project, editing and formatting the citations, and tracking down various bits of information in the final stages of this project.

I am grateful to the staff of the University of Toronto Press, particularly Len Husband who served as editor for this project. I also wish to thank two anonymous peer reviewers for generously taking the time to read the draft manuscript and offer detailed comments and suggestions. This feedback was essential to enhancing and refining the final manuscript into publishable quality.

The financial support provided by the Social Sciences and Research Council of Canada through the Doctoral Fellowships Program, the Federation of Humanities and Social Sciences through the Awards to Scholarly Publications Program, the Legal Research Institute of the University of Manitoba, and the Manitoba Law Foundation are all gratefully acknowledged.

Finally, I wish to thank Stephanie Ben-Ishai for encouraging me to do a PhD in the first place, which in turn led to this monograph.

Winnipeg, Canada
November 2019

Abbreviations

Bankruptcy Act of 1919	*Bankruptcy Act of 1919*, SC 1919, c 36
BIA	*Bankruptcy and Insolvency Act*, RSC 1985 c B-3
CBCA	*Canada Business Corporations Act*, RSC 1985, c C-44
CCAA	*Companies' Creditors Arrangement Act*, SC 1933, c 36
DIP	Debtor-in-Possession
DMIA	Dominion Mortgage and Investments Association
JCPC	Judicial Committee of the Privy Council
LAC	Library and Archives Canada, Ottawa
OSB	Office of the Superintendent of Bankruptcy
SCC	Supreme Court of Canada

REINVENTING BANKRUPTCY LAW

A History of the *Companies' Creditors Arrangement Act*

1

Historical Institutionalism and the Recursivity of Law

An effect created by causes at some previous period [can become] ... *a cause of that same effect in succeeding periods.* In such arguments, the problem of explanation breaks down into two causal components. The first is the particular circumstances that caused a tradition to be started. The second is the general process by which social patterns reproduce themselves.[1]

Arthur Stinchcombe, *Constructing Social Theories*

1 Why Was Corporate Restructuring Added to Federal Insolvency Law?

In the worst year of the Great Depression in Canada, parliament enacted the *Companies' Creditors Arrangement Act* (CCAA).[2] Debates on the new statute took up roughly six pages of Hansard. No parliamentarian objected and the bill, which was twenty provisions long, passed into law in just over one month's time. Commentators and the press scarcely took notice of these events, yet the enactment of the CCAA marked a significant milestone in Canadian legal history: for the first time, bankruptcy and insolvency law established a federal authority to bind secured creditor claims.

The act was met with stunned reactions from the legal community. Lawyers refused to recommend the law to their clients because they believed it was an unconstitutional exercise of federal jurisdiction. According to prevailing views of Canadian federalism, only the provinces could regulate secured creditor rights, irrespective of the debtor's insolvency. Sooner or later an arrangement under the new statute would surely provoke a legal challenge from an unhappy creditor, and once that happened the court would be compelled to declare the act ultra vires, which lawyers feared would dissolve any restructuring already carried out under the CCAA.

The act's framers anticipated that the uncertainty around the new act would prompt a constitutional challenge, but instead it caused major bondholders to shy away from using the CCAA. This ultimately prompted the Conservative government of R.B. Bennett to send its own statute for constitutional reference. The Committee of the Privy Council, Canada, submitted a question to the Supreme Court of Canada (SCC) concerning the legal scope and authority of the CCAA, and the SCC unanimously ruled that the act was intra vires.[3] This decision astonished the legal community. But in its short judgment the SCC downplayed the most controversial aspect of the legislation – the act's facility for binding secured creditors to a compromise or arrangement. As a result, uncertainty persisted until a 1937 Judicial Committee of the Privy Council (JCPC) reference decision on a similar statute upheld this feature of insolvency legislation as a valid exercise of federal jurisdiction.[4]

After the Great Depression, the CCAA slipped into obscurity, and ongoing confusion surrounding the objects of the skeletal act led to several calls for its repeal. Along with limited parliamentary debate and scanty scholarly commentary, the act lacked a preamble or other clear policy statement. But instead of repealing the act or issuing policy guidance, parliament amended the CCAA in 1953 by adding a provision that limited its application to companies with outstanding issues of bonds or debentures issued under a trust deed and running in favour of a trustee.[5] All restructurings carried out under the CCAA had to include a compromise or arrangement with respect to these claims. Nevertheless, due to continued disuse, by the early 1980s commentators, quite reasonably, thought the statute was a dead letter.

Beginning in the late 1980s and early 1990s case-driven developments brought the CCAA into legal and public consciousness. Relying on liberal interpretations of the statute, judges and counsel used the act to facilitate a number of large, high-profile reorganizations. At the time the act was still the only insolvency statute that could compulsorily bind secured claims.[6] Judges, counsel, academics, and the press spun a new public interest narrative around the CCAA, which included a prominent public role for the concerns of stakeholder groups, such as organized labour. Relying on arguments put forward by counsel, judges read new social policy considerations into the statute and outwardly refashioned an obscure and antiquated act into a versatile and modern debtor-in-possession restructuring regime. During this period the CCAA came to be regarded as a functional equivalent to the American restructuring law, Chapter 11,[7] and this characterization helped guide the direction of judicial interpretation. In the process, courts relegated the CCAA's few textual provisions to a supporting role in increasingly expansive exercises of judicial discretion.

This sketch of CCAA history raises several questions. Why did parliament unanimously pass a (supposedly) unconstitutional statute with so little discussion? How did a dead letter act come to represent Canada's major corporate restructuring regime? What drove these developments? And how might this historical account contribute to broader understandings of corporate insolvency law and cycles of legal change?

Although the act is over eighty years old, it has attracted significant scholarly attention in just the last thirty years or so. Since the 1980s and 1990s a number of commentators and scholars have published journal articles on corporate reorganization law under the act. Janis Sarra's book *Creditor Rights and the Public Interest,* based on her SJD thesis, examines contemporary CCAA law.[8] Sarra has also written a text for practitioners on CCAA law and practice, which is now in its second edition.[9] Aside from the sketches of the act's history contained in Sarra's books and in several journal articles,[10] there has not yet been a systematic, historical study of CCAA law or a comparison of historical company reorganization with contemporary practices.

Accordingly, this book offers a socio-legal history of CCAA over the twentieth century. The theoretical approach relies on the twin lenses of legal history and socio-legal studies, and therefore the scope of the work has been intentionally limited to the twentieth century, where these two approaches can be applied in tandem. While the socio-legal analysis could potentially be brought up to the present day, doing so would take the book out of the legal history literature. At the time of this writing, twenty-first-century developments are too recent for an historical analysis. Nevertheless, readers familiar with CCAA law will note that some of the socio-legal dynamics captured in this analysis continue to prevail in early twenty-first-century developments, reinforcing the thesis and themes of the book. Indeed, section 3 (below) and the chapters that follow endeavour to outline *why* and *how* the history of corporate restructuring matters for readers today.[11]

2 Rehabilitating Debtor Companies: Public Policy or Private Interests?

Terminology

Before proceeding, a few definitions of the technical terminology involved in Canadian corporate reorganization are in order. "Bankruptcy" refers to a legal process that involves the liquidation of the debtor's assets and distribution of the proceeds to creditors, usually on a pro rata basis.[12] "Insolvency" is a financial state of affairs where the debtor is unable to pay their debts as they become due.[13] Thus, a person may be insolvent without being bankrupt.

The terms "reorganization" and "restructuring" are used interchangeably. These are commercial terms that lack a legal definition.[14] A restructuring is generally understood to mean rehabilitation of the debtor in the sense that the debtor company will stay in business. However, the specifics of the restructuring may involve selling off profitable divisions of the company, or amalgamating it with another company, such that the one that emerges from restructuring looks quite different from before. Thus, corporate reorganization generally refers to the resolution of the company's insolvency without resorting to bankruptcy proceedings. However, it may involve recourse to other legal regimes relating to insolvency[15] or corporate law,[16] for example.

"Receivership" is a secured creditor remedy[17] that often coincides with the insolvency of the debtor, but it is not necessarily predicated on a situation of insolvency. Pursuant to the terms of the lending agreement or a court order, a creditor may institute receivership proceedings, in which they take over the business operations of the debtor.[18] The creditor (through its representative, a "receiver") may then decide to sell part of the debtor's business or assets, or sell the entire business as a going concern. The proceeds realized from the sale are applied toward the debts owed to the creditor. Receivership often operates in tandem with bankruptcy proceedings. Bankruptcy is a remedy of last resort for unsecured creditors, while receivership is the ultimate remedy for secured creditors. The debtor's assets that are subject to security interests are allocated to secured creditors, with any additional assets being subject to the claims of unsecured creditors.

The term "debtor-in-possession" (DIP) in relation to restructuring indicates that the debtor (or its management team) is allowed to stay in charge of the company. This is exceptional because creditors usually exercise their legal rights to assert control over insolvent companies. For instance, as part of bankruptcy proceedings, control of the debtor company is turned over to the bankruptcy trustee, which acts for the benefit of unsecured creditors. Similarly, when secured creditors place a company in receivership their representative (a receiver) takes control of the firm.

Contemporary Narratives

In the modern context, rehabilitation of debtor companies is generally equated with the promotion of broad public policy objectives, such as preserving the jobs of workers and promoting economic activity in cities and regions.[19] Therefore, as a matter of policy, the contemporary view posits that corporate insolvency legislation should encourage the rehabilitation of debtor firms where possible. Although debtor rehabilitation can have positive outcomes for these stakeholder groups, this approach tends to obscure the interests and motivations of powerful creditors. For instance, it glosses over the fact that contemporary debtor rehabilitation regimes require a majority of creditors to vote in favour of a reorganization plan.[20]

As this historical study shows, debtor rehabilitation was often creditors' remedy of choice when large debtors encountered financial difficulty. In an era before reorganization became a policy goal of insolvency law, large creditors had established methods of restructuring debtor firms. Motivated by self-interest, these creditors used private ordering and the creditor remedy of receivership to reorganize debtor companies. Modern theorists posit that the insolubility by private parties of the collective action problem[21] and common pool problem[22] to which insolvency gives rise justify a legislative response.[23] The history of corporate reorganization in Canada, however, confutes this assumption by demonstrating not only that private parties *can* overcome these problems without insolvency law, but also that their self-interest motivates them to do so. Thus, as a matter of history, the role of debtor rehabilitation in promoting broad public policy objectives is somewhat ambiguous. However, individual cases of debtor rehabilitation certainly advance the interests of the private parties that supported the restructuring.

Private Interests as Public Policy

This historical study demonstrates that the CCAA extended bondholder-led receivership reorganizations into federal bankruptcy and insolvency law. It argues that parliament intended the CCAA to be a secured creditor remedy carried out by a trustee or receiver rather than a debtor-in-possession restructuring statute. Furthermore, the historical record shows little regard for contemporary public interest considerations. The impetus for this federal statute was to help prevent large bondholders (financial institutions) from failing, by allowing them to restructure debtors (read: restructure losses) and so return these companies (read: investments) to profitability. Leading up to the 1920s and 1930s, many Canadian companies omitted majority provisions from their trust deeds in order to attract American investors. "Majority provisions" refers to a term included in the bondholders' lending agreement (a "trust deed"), which allowed a majority of bondholders to bind a dissenting minority for the purpose of effecting changes to the lending agreement. (Although the US *Trust Indenture Act of 1939* prohibited the use of majority provisions, these provisions were not used extensively in the United States before then.[24]) Changes commonly brought about under majority provisions included alterations to repayment schedules, which often formed part of a plan to restructure the debtor company. Without majority provisions, there was no mechanism for restructuring bondholder claims. Thus, the broad policy underlying the CCAA was to help ensure stability in the Canadian financial system by preventing failures of large financial institutions that may have resulted from shutting down many large debtors during the Great Depression. The weightiness of this policy rationale – with the social, economic, and political ramifications that financial instability entails – better counterbalances the constitutional risk that the CCAA represented in 1933.

The historical narrative goes on to interpret later CCAA law developments in the 1980s and 1990s in light of the act's early history, as well as significant social, economic, and political changes that took place in Canada after the 1930s. By the 1980s and 1990s, the prevailing social, political, and economic backdrop, as well as new approaches to statutory interpretation, led Canadian courts to re-interpret the CCAA as a debtor remedy on an essentially a priori basis. This modern assumption influenced the way later actors interpreted historical records, and in so doing obscured the origins of the act. The very presence of the act on the statute books came to stand for an implicit policy purpose: encouraging corporate reorganizations for the wider public interest; but this broader objective, as it is now understood, is actually a recent addition to CCAA law.

Nevertheless, interpretation of the CCAA as a debtor remedy in the 1980s and 1990s occurred with the support of large secured lenders, which were primary beneficiaries and proponents of these changes. Secured lending practices changed leading up to the recessions of the 1980s and 1990s, without corresponding changes in lender remedies. Thus, during these downturns, large secured lenders found themselves without effective methods of reorganizing debtors, echoing the situation of large bondholding interests in the 1930s. Once again, within the setting of an economic recession, large secured lenders wished to reorganize some of their largest debtors but did not always have the legal tools to do so. Unlike the 1930s, however, in the 1980s and 1990s courts – rather than parliament – facilitated legal change so that large secured lenders could effect reorganizations of corporate debtors.

Although stalled bankruptcy reform contributed to the lack of effective reorganization tools in the 1980s and 1990s, it is the active role of the courts that stands out in this period of legal change. The fact that such legal changes *could* come through the courts illustrates how far judicialization had advanced in Canada in just fifty years; judge-driven reforms of this nature would have been hard to imagine in the 1930s. By the end of the twentieth century, courts adopted liberal, policy-focused interpretations of the CCAA and drew on contemporary ideas about the public policy benefits of corporate reorganization. In so doing, they applied a public interest gloss to a secured creditor remedy – reinvented the statute as a debtor remedy – and broke with traditional explanations for company restructuring, which were rooted in the property rights of large secured creditors.

Departing from lender-remedy justifications for corporate reorganization and relying on broad statements of the public interest for policy guidance led to inconsistencies. For instance, both debtors and creditors have unilateral access to the CCAA, and there is no provision for pushing through a plan against the wishes of the majority of creditors. This leaves large secured creditors among the few with an effective veto over reorganization attempts. Although debtor-in-possession case law and statutory amendments have accreted onto CCAA law over the past thirty years, the act still functions as a secured lender remedy. So contemporary case law illustrates (apparently) conflicting uses for the act. For example, use of the CCAA to liquidate companies is at odds with the statute's implicit policy purpose of effecting going-concern reorganizations. A debtor-remedy view of the act cannot account for the trend toward using the CCAA to liquidate (as opposed to restructure) firms (a proceeding known as a "liquidating CCAA"). A lender-remedy perspective, however, offers a robust explanation for these types of trends.

This historical account illustrates how ideas, law, and institutions can change from the ground up to become quite different over time. CCAA history showcases how practices on the ground can influence formal lawmaking. For several decades parliament made no substantive changes to the act; nevertheless, practices under the statute changed dramatically. Yet periods of formal stasis do not always generate changes in practice. For example, although the *Bankruptcy Act* of the 1930s also went decades without substantive reforms, no similar judge-made law occurred under that statute. This demonstrates that the factors that lead to conditions that are ripe for the kind of judicial changes that occurred under the CCAA are more complex than a mere lack of parliamentary action.

3 Stasis and Change in Legal Regimes: Historical Institutionalism and the Recursivity of Law

This book forms part of a growing body of scholarly literature about institutions and the law, and is one of the first full-length studies to apply these concepts to the study of insolvency law. It dovetails with the work of American scholars on developments in contemporary corporate insolvency law in the United States, the United Kingdom, China, Indonesia, and Korea.[25] It also complements a recently published book about personal insolvency systems in the United States and several European countries, which similarly employs ideas from modern institutionalism. [26]

This book employs a socio-legal analysis within a broader and longer institutionalist view of history to explore the factors that spur cycles of legal change and to assess the ways in which changes unfold. This approach reveals that cycles of legal change usually do not begin with a clean slate. Indeed, we find that trends and themes emerge through successive rounds of lawmaking. By adopting a long and broad view of history that considers the political-economic and socio-legal contexts of reorganization, we can identify continuities and ruptures in CCAA law over time.

The ideas that influenced corporate reorganization policy in the 1980s and 1990s and the mechanisms through which legal changes occurred bear little resemblance to the 1920s and 1930s. On the importance of an historical approach to understanding developments in US bankruptcy law, David A. Skeel Jr notes that scholarship which "focus[es] solely on the process that led to the 1978 reforms ... cannot provide a full explanation why the 1978 Code so thoroughly repudiated the existing approach to corporate reorganization."[27] Accounts of developments in Canada during the 1980s and 1990s give rise to a similar problem. They tend not to recognize that these cases represented a distinct break with earlier approaches to corporate restructuring, nor do they explain why they occurred.

A longer view of history and of the way changes in practice factor into formal legal changes illustrates the role of large secured creditors as key drivers and beneficiaries of corporate restructuring law, and underscores the importance of restructuring as a secured creditor remedy. Twice during the twentieth-century, economic downturns showcased secured creditors' need for (and lack of) effective legal mechanisms for restructuring debtors. These were rare yet significant events in the development of Canadian corporate restructuring law. Concepts from historical institutionalism help explain why things developed the way they did, and they shed light on the enduring legacy of the "restructuring crises" that these two economic downturns precipitated. A recursivity-of-law analysis illuminates the substance of the restructuring solutions to which each crisis gave rise, as well as the mechanisms by which solutions from legal practice shaped subsequent changes to formal law.

A recursivity-of-law analysis illustrates the way in which practices on the ground shape more formal legal developments, as well as the way in which professionals and courts help mediate the application of law on the books into practice. This approach factors in the importance of ideas, interest groups, and the relative political and legal strength of the parties into distinct cycles of legal change. Such an analysis sheds light on periods of stability and change in CCAA law and provides a systematic account of the mechanisms by which changes occurred at key points in time.

An historical institutionalism and recursivity-of-law framework together illustrate how gradual changes in financing practices led to circumstances that were ripe for legal change and were likely to have a profound and enduring impact on the law and practice of Canadian corporate reorganization. Looking forward from the 1920s, very little about these historical events unfolded the way one might have expected.

Historical Institutionalism

"Historical institutionalism" is a social sciences research approach that examines the influence of institutions on social, political, or economic regimes over time. Many authors have used this research orientation to study a variety of subjects and contexts.[28] The historical institutionalism ideas employed in this book are drawn primarily from political scientists, particularly the work of Paul Pierson, who builds on the work of modern institutionalists such as Douglass North.[29] This book uses a broad definition of the term "institution," which may be used to describe a formal institution, such as the Office of the Superintendent of Bankruptcy (OSB), as well as less formal institutional arrangements, such as the practice of restructuring companies under trust deeds. It also adopts an interdisciplinary historical approach, similar to one used by bankruptcy historians David A. Skeel Jr[30] and Thomas G.W. Telfer,[31] which situates legal developments within their historical, political, and economic context.

Pierson's conception of "positive feedback" and "path dependence" are used to help account for the stickiness of institutional arrangements and their tendency to become more resilient in the face of change over time, even to be able to withstand attempts at repeal. "Positive feedback" refers to a process by which "each step along a particular path produces consequences that increase the relative attractiveness of that path for the next round."[32] This concept is used to identify when things changed and when existing arrangements were reaffirmed, as well as when things did *not* change[33] and when there was no evidence of self-reaffirming processes.

The term "path dependence" is used to mean that "once ... started down a track, the costs of reversal are very high. There will be other choice points, but the entrenchments of certain institutional arrangements obstruct an easy reversal of the initial choice."[34] "Sequencing" is significant in path-dependent processes because "outcomes of early events may be amplified [through positive feedback], while the significance of later events or processes is dampened."[35] Thus, "*when a particular event in a sequence occurs will make a big difference.*"[36]

Path-dependent processes often unfold over long periods of time, and early historical events tend to put these processes on a certain path. But positive feedback, or self-reinforcement, does not necessarily involve the recreation of those same early events, as Arthur Stinchcombe explains:

> An effect created by causes at some previous period [can become] ... *a cause of that same effect in succeeding periods*. In such arguments, the problem of explanation breaks down into two causal components. The first is the particular circumstances that caused a tradition to be started. The second is the general process by which social patterns reproduce themselves [emphasis in original].[37]

Hence, Pierson observes that "explanation requires the examination of considerable stretches of time." This study therefore adopts a longer view of business reorganization than the lifespan of the CCAA in order to identify longer-term processes, or reorganization "traditions," which predate formalization in federal insolvency law.

The institutionalist ideas used in this book focus on the increasing resilience of institutions to withstand or adapt to change the longer they have been in place.[38] Due to the tendency of institutions, particularly "parchment institutions" such as legislation, to be longstanding[39] and even to outlast certain interest groups, institutionalism provides a broader picture of developments over time than do analyses of interest groups alone. It also captures the phenomenon of new interest groups forming around old institutions.

When reform efforts face off against a longstanding institution, "institutional resilience" may lead to "layering" or "institutional conversion" rather than broad or overt institutional change. "Layering" refers to "the partial renegotiation of some elements of a given set of institutions while leaving others in place."[40] It may also "involve the creation of parallel or potentially subversive institutional tracks."[41] "Institutional conversion" describes a situation where "existing institutions are redirected to new purposes, driving changes in the role they perform and/or the functions they serve."[42]

One phenomenon that can contribute to institutional resilience is "asset specificity." In this discussion, "asset specificity" refers to the result of various actors coordinating around existing institutional arrangements in a way that is not easily transferable to new or different arrangements.[43] In other words, the arrangements or coordination (the assets) are specific to a certain institution. In this case, the uses and applications of the act created, over time, a body of legal interpretation and a valued legal instrument that would have made its transfer to other arrangements improbable. Thus, where actors have coordinated around institutional arrangements in this way, asset specificity suggests that these actors will be inclined to oppose institutional change.[44]

Identifying "critical junctures" is one way of identifying significant instances of change. The term "critical juncture" in historical institutionalism literature refers to periods of significant institutional change. It is the window of time in which an equilibrium or period of stasis is "punctuated" by change.[45] Pierson describes these junctures as "critical" because "they place institutional arrangements on paths or trajectories, which are then very difficult to alter."[46] As Jacob Hacker notes, path dependence helps explain "the *reproduction* of a critical juncture's legacy ... [and] suggests why the effects of critical junctures are so profound and enduring."[47]

Literature on critical junctures, however, has a difficult time explaining what causes them in the first place; they are often attributed to "big, exogenous shocks."[48] To capture gradual processes that may help bring institutional arrangements to the brink of critical junctures, this book employs a socio-legal historical approach that takes account of changes in practice, which sometimes precede formal changes.

Recursivity of Law

"Recursivity of law" is a socio-legal analytical framework formulated by Terence C. Halliday and Bruce G. Carruthers[49] to study developments in bankruptcy and insolvency law. These authors argue that law

Figure 1.1 Recursive Cycles of Bankruptcy Lawmaking

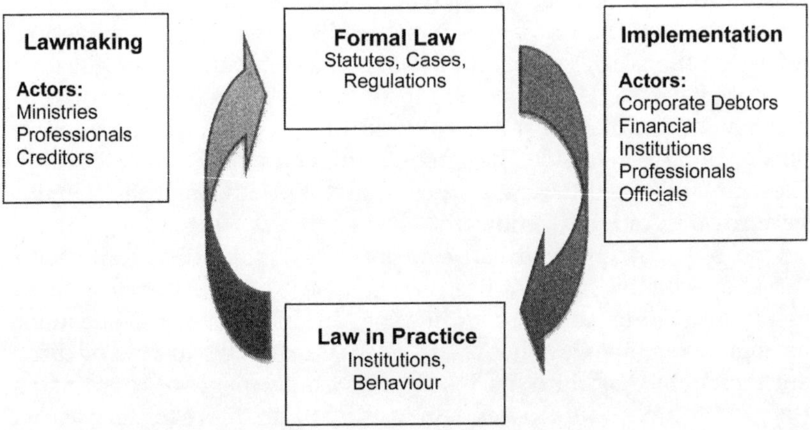

Note: This is a simplified version of the figure that appears in Halliday and Carruthers, "The Recursivity of Law," 1147.

not only flows from the books to legal practice, but that legal practices also shape formal law, through the involvement of professionals in law reform, for instance.[50] Their approach takes account of the fact that formal laws, which tend to be mediated through professionals, are further shaped and interpreted in the course of being implemented into practice. Halliday and Carruthers use the term recursivity of law to refer to the process of law on the books influencing law in practice and vice versa.

The theory of recursivity is one of legal change in which the unit of change studied is the cycle that holds law on the books and law in practice in dynamic tension.[51] This cycle is illustrated in figure 1.1, above. "Law on the books" is defined as law that is "binding in form or effect, most often by a sovereign authority."[52] "Law in practice" is "behavior and institutions that constitute and enact law as it actually is experienced by those it regulates."[53] Hence, law in practice is effectively law to those it regulates, but is understood in the context of law on the books.[54]

Drawing on the concept of "punctuated equilibrium," originated by Frank Baumgartner and Bryan D. Jones,[55] Halliday and Carruthers note that law reform often proceeds in cycles in which periods of equilibrium are punctuated by periods of change. These authors observe that years or decades may pass in which no significant changes occur in formal law or in legal practice – periods of equilibrium.[56] Cycles of law reform often begin with a build-up in pressure for legal change during such periods of stasis,[57] followed by a political opportunity to effect change, and ending when "contradictions are resolved, or consensus is reached or legal meanings settle, or an underlying cause fades away"[58] – in essence, when a new equilibrium is reached. Halliday and Carruthers further posit that legal change can occur even though formal law remains static,[59] and thus attention to possible developments in legal practice may reveal that cycles of legal change are occurring despite the appearance of a formal equilibrium.

As a sociological theory, recursivity pays close attention to the role and influence of legal actors and institutions – including lawyers, judges, professional associations, and courts – at both the lawmaking and implementation stages.[60] In periods of formal law reform, these legal actors and institutions have often been influential[61] and, as Halliday and Carruthers note, lawyers' creativity has sometimes appropriated formal law for purposes other than those originally intended.[62] Powerful legal institutions may also modify law so much in practice that they effectively create their own "law."[63] In addition, formal law reform tends to institutionalize new legal concepts in statute.[64] As a result, the subjects of the law often view their problems through the lens of these (new) legal concepts.[65] In practice, these legal concepts may also be "amplified, distorted, and creatively reinterpreted."[66]

Cycles of recursivity of law occur in varying degrees of complexity. A rather straightforward cycle is one in which a law is enacted to respond to a particular problem. Once enacted, however, new problems may arise. For example, actors try to circumvent the law, and so lawmakers may amend the law or enact a new one to respond to the new problems. This cycle may then repeat many times through numerous iterations of law.[67] In more complex cycles of recursivity of law, several patterns may be at play. For instance, ambiguities in the law may lead actors to bring questions before courts, where judges may clarify matters, a process known as "settling."[68] Ambiguity can therefore help drive cycles of reform. Alternatively, subsequent court decisions may substantially deviate from what was intended by legislators, which can lead legislatures to respond through new legislation, in order to override the courts' decisions.[69]

Lauren B. Edelman's theory of endogeneity of law[70] refers to a recursive cycle in which law arises more from the practices of private parties in carrying out broad legal policies or mandates, than from formal lawmaking bodies.[71] Where the substance of formal law is broad or open-ended, the substantive aspects of private attempts to implement that law in practice can become institutionalized in case law over time.[72] These ideas relate to a further feature of the recursivity-of-law framework, which pays special attention to the *form* of law, which influences its interpretation and signals its relative degree of authority.[73]

Gregory C. Shaffer notes that recursivity of law is particularly helpful for explaining processes that involve cooperation and coordination problems.[74] Building on Edelman's theory of endogeneity of law, this study shows that recursivity is especially useful in contexts where there is a significant amount of professional input at the stage of applying the law. One example of this is court-driven insolvency procedures where professionals craft a tailor-made solution, such as a restructuring plan, under a fairly broad legal architecture. As described by Jérôme Sgard, English business reorganization was historically conducted outside of formal bankruptcy law or statutes, through trust deeds, for instance.[75] As a result law in practice formed the basis for formal law when business reorganization provisions were later added to English *Companies Acts*, and eventually to insolvency statutes. The Anglo-Canadian legal tradition bears out a similar pattern.[76]

4 Research Sources and Methods

This book relies primarily on qualitative methods to answer the questions that this study addresses. The historical component of this research draws mainly from case law, legal facta, legislation, news sources, scholarly writing (published and unpublished), trade journals and pamphlets, histories, parliamentary materials (published and unpublished), and archival materials. This historical narrative benefits from several historical sources not available to earlier scholars, including legal facta for the CCAA reference, parliamentary committee minutes concerning a 1938 CCAA repeal bill, and an unpublished parliamentary sessional paper from 1938.

Where available, quantitative data is incorporated to add texture to the historical narrative and to supplement the qualitative analysis. This data includes historical figures on the number of Dominion companies in bankruptcy or receivership, frequency of commercial failures, and the number of filings under the CCAA, all of which were listed in parliamentary materials. As quantitative data, these figures are limited in several ways. For example, in some instances it only includes information on federally incorporated companies, and does not provide details for companies incorporated under provincial legislation. Nevertheless, this data helps to illustrate general trends, and thus is a useful part of the qualitative analysis (see appendices 1, 2, and 3).

Some quantitative data was also compiled for this project, with the first set consisting of reported cases that reference the CCAA from 1933 to 2017 inclusive. This information, compiled from consulting the print edition of the *Canadian Statute Citations* (CSC) and supplements, illustrates a sharp increase in reported decisions around the late 1980s and early 1990s. If a single case was listed more than once in the CSC, it was recorded as just one datum. Data was sorted on reported cases by the year in which they were reported. If there was any disparity between different law reporters in terms of publication year, the case was allocated to the year in which the court rendered its decision.

In addition, available information was compiled on the number of CCAA applications in the 1930s and 2000s. This data is neither complete nor exhaustive for the years prior to 2010. However, it does provide a rough contrast between the numbers of applications made in the 1930s as opposed to the 2000s. CCAA filing data from the 1930s only refers to applications filed in Montreal and comes from statistics presented by the Montreal Board of Trade to the 1938 parliamentary committee. The Montreal Board of Trade relied on notices in trade publications to compile information on CCAA applications, which gave an under-inclusive picture of 1930s applications rates. In the third quarter of 2009, the OSB began keeping records on CCAA applications, and this information was relied upon to compile data on applications from this point through to the end of 2017. Accordingly, these more recent filing rates provide an accurate picture of the number of CCAA applications throughout Canada.

These two quantitative data sets are relied upon to illustrate general trends. As parliamentary records and academic commentary demonstrate, and as comparing these two sets of quantitative data confirms, the vast majority of early CCAA cases went unreported. In the 1930s, applications under the act far outpaced reported decisions. Conversely the number of reported decisions mentioning the act eclipses more recent filing rates. It is important to note that cases that reference the CCAA do not necessarily have to do with restructuring. For instance, a number of cases simply discuss the SCC's ruling on the constitutionality of the act. Furthermore, contemporary reorganizations under the act tend to produce multiple reported decisions of judicial rulings on various aspects of the same restructuring. This phenomenon amplifies the appearance of a sharp upturn in reported cases beginning in the 1980s and 1990s, as does the general growth of law reporting in Canada since the 1930s along with the advent of electronic legal research sources, such as Westlaw and Quicklaw, in the latter years of the twentieth century.

Despite its limitations as a quantitative data set, this information is still useful to a qualitative understanding of CCAA history. Judges and counsel in the 1980s and 1990s looked primarily to reported cases to get a sense of the history of the act and the frequency with which it was used, so the small number of early decisions they found factored into their narrative of the statute. Since no formal records were kept on the CCAA until autumn 2009, reported decisions also informally (and often tacitly) served as a rough proxy for the frequency of CCAA applications. The appearance of exponential growth in reported decisions in the past few decades thus serves as part of the contextual backdrop for much conventional wisdom concerning the act.

5 Overview of the Book

The rest of the book is structured as follows. Chapter 2 describes the development of corporate restructuring practices under lending agreements (trust deeds) and the creditor enforcement remedy of receivership. It traces the adoption of English restructuring traditions into the Canadian context in the late nineteenth and early twentieth centuries, and highlights the factors that were beginning to create pressure for formal legal changes by the 1920s.

This sets the stage for chapter 3, which provides an historical account of the enactment of the CCAA. Although the Great Depression provided the impetus for passing the act, this historical analysis brings to light the gradual changes that contributed to the need for a statutory scheme for restructuring secured debt and the way that the act attempted to address this need. Chapter 3 shows that the CCAA was a continuation of longstanding receivership reorganization practices under provincial law, which large bondholding interests (financial institutions) routinely carried out under private agreements.

Chapter 4 critically analyses the constitutional reference decision that upheld the CCAA and argues that it represented a distinct break with conventional interpretations of the division of powers. This decision thus redrew the dividing line between provincial and federal jurisdiction over secured creditor rights, which facilitated the addition of corporate reorganization to federal bankruptcy and insolvency law.

Chapter 5 considers the controversy that the CCAA sparked in the legal community and among trade creditor groups, which led to several repeal bills. This chapter shows how secured creditor representatives argued successfully against the repeal bills and proposed, instead, a restrictive amendment to address trade creditor concerns. This amendment passed into law in 1953 and limited the application of the act to restructurings involving bondholder oversight, which greatly reduced the number of restructurings under the statute.

Chapter 6 describes changes to the corporate lending landscape in the 1970s and 1980s. It tracks the entry of new lending institutions into the long-term secured lending market and the introduction of new financing documents, alongside stalled bankruptcy reform efforts. Taken together, this mixture of stasis and change laid the groundwork for another "restructuring crisis" with the onset of the recessions of the 1980s and 1990s.

Chapter 7 sheds light on how courts reinterpreted the CCAA during the 1980s and 1990s. It highlights how judges fleshed out the anemic act and repurposed it into a debtor remedy. This chapter offers a critical analysis of the role of purposive statutory interpretation and treatment of historical sources in court. It argues that judicial repurposing of the CCAA into a debtor remedy turned the policy of the act on its head.

Chapter 8 examines the judicial sanction of "tactical devices," which debtors used to gain access to the act. It argues that by allowing the use of tactical devices, judges effectively repealed the restrictive amendment added to the CCAA in 1953. This ensured that the act was no longer solely a bondholder remedy and opened the door to debtor-led restructuring efforts.

Chapter 9 draws together the preceding three chapters to describe how changes in CCAA law were formalized into a modern debtor-in-possession restructuring narrative. This chapter applies theoretical ideas from historical institutionalism and the recursivity of law to describe the impetuses and mechanisms of these changes. It also highlights the role of judges and courts and the influence of ideas in the transformation of CCAA law into a modern corporate restructuring regime.

Chapter 10 concludes by synthesizing the discussion and analysis of the previous chapters. By adopting a longer view of history that is attuned to socio-legal mechanisms of change, this chapter offers insight into the underlying factors that have contributed to periods of stability and change in restructuring law and practices over time. It brings to light several long-term trends in this area of law to show the explanatory power of the research approach of this project.

PART ONE

Traditions and Emerging Practices, 1920s–1950s

2

Corporate Restructuring as a Bondholder Remedy

Fortunately we have long followed the practice of the English conveyancers of including in trust deeds the so-called majority clauses, which permit bondholders' meetings to pass resolutions binding on all the bondholders, and both before and since the passing by Parliament of the Companies' Creditors Arrangement Act, important reorganizations have been satisfactorily brought about in our country in this way.[1]

Fred R. MacKelcan, K.C., *Canadian Bar Review*

1 Receivership Reorganizations

English Practices

Corporate restructuring initially evolved outside bankruptcy and insolvency law because legislators were suspicious of the potential abuses and frauds that could be perpetrated by debtors if business restructuring were permitted.[2] In nineteenth-century England, trust deeds were commonly used to facilitate the reorganization of large, important companies.[3] A "trust deed" is a financing instrument used by bondholders to secure bonds against assets of the company, and the business itself, through fixed and floating charges.[4] In 1887, Baron Bowen, a legal scholar and a Lord Justice in the Court of Appeal in England, wrote:

> The important insolvencies which had been brought about by pure mercantile misfortune were administered to a large extent under private trust deeds and voluntary compositions, which, since they might be disturbed by the caprice or malice of a single outstanding creditor, were always liable to be made the instruments of extortion.[5]

Even after adding reorganization provisions to English bankruptcy legislation in 1825, legislators made restructuring so difficult to complete that these statutes were little used.[6] So trust deeds were well-established instruments of restructuring in company law before effective reorganization provisions were added to English bankruptcy or insolvency statutes.

Measures for compromises between debtor companies and their creditors were added to English legislation as early as 1862. The *Companies Act, 1862* allowed businesses undergoing voluntary winding-up proceedings to make binding arrangements with their creditors, subject to three-fourths majority creditor approval and sanction by an extraordinary resolution of the company.[7] An "extraordinary" or "special" resolution is a decision that is passed by a high-threshold majority of shareholders (usually two-thirds or three-fourths).[8]

A few years later, the English parliament enacted the *Joint Stock Companies Arrangements Act, 1870* specifically "to facilitate compromises and arrangements between creditors and shareholders of Joint Stock and other Companies in Liquidation."[9] The 1870 act expanded the possibility of creditor-debtor arrangements set out in the *Companies Act, 1862* to include compromises between companies and their shareholders, and companies undergoing court-supervised winding-up, allowing the substitution of "a living company for a receivership and a liquidation."[10] These English statutes were early iterations of what is known as a "scheme of arrangement" or "scheme."

Six decades later, the CCAA continued the English approach of restructuring companies through a stand-alone statute. The substance and framing of the CCAA resembles that of the 1870 act, including its use of the clunky appellation "companies arrangement act."[11] In Canada, these restructuring plans were usually referred to as "arrangements," rather than "schemes," although both short forms are derived from the long form: "scheme of arrangement." Common law tests used in CCAAs – such as compliance with all statutory requirements and the fairness and reasonableness of the plan – were originally developed by English courts overseeing restructuring proceedings under the 1870 act.[12]

The addition of reorganization provisions to English companies legislation extended the application of trust-deed-like reorganization practices to all companies and their creditors. This avoided drafting inadequacies that could thwart restructuring attempts under a trust deed and helped standardize English reorganization practice. These provisions were passed down through companies legislation and were eventually enumerated in section 153 of the English *Companies Act,*

1929.[13] By the time the CCAA was before parliament, in the 1930s, reorganization under the *Companies Act, 1929* was the preferred means of restructuring in England.[14]

Canadian Approaches

The CCAA bill, enacted in 1933, imported the substance of section 153 of the English *Companies Act, 1929* to Canada. Charles H. Cahan (MP, Conservative) characterized the CCAA as basically an amendment to the federal *Companies Act*,[15] linking it to English reorganization practice.[16] Thus, company restructuring in the Anglo-Canadian context has a long history and was not initially an aspect of bankruptcy or insolvency law.[17]

In Canada, the division of legislative powers between the provinces and the federal government posed challenges to wholesale adoption of the English approach to company reorganization. Nevertheless, before the enactment of the CCAA, legal practices existed to effect company restructurings outside of insolvency law, borrowing from English techniques.[18]

Bondholder reorganizations, conducted through the provisions of a governing trust deed, were the most prevalent and important form of restructuring in the early twentieth century.[19] Modeled on English trust deeds, the Canadian versions usually provided that a stated majority of bondholders could compel the minority to accept a modification of their rights as bondholders, thereby avoiding the problem of holdout creditors.[20] From this early date bondholders used the private architecture of trust deeds to solve collective action problems concerning their rights and remedies as creditors.

The contemporary English academic Jennifer Payne notes that the statutory majority provisions of the *Joint Stock Companies Arrangement Act, 1870* were enacted in part as a response to problems with small creditors derailing compromises and arrangements.[21] Majority provisions were also useful where it was not practicable to track down all creditors for the purposes of voting on a restructuring plan. This could occur when, for instance, the bondholders were widely dispersed or because the company had an outstanding issue of bearer bonds.[22] "Bearer bonds" are unregistered debt instruments in respect of which no records are kept concerning ownership or transactions involving ownership. Although bearer bonds are largely of historical significance, these debt instruments sometimes formed part of the capital structure of Canadian companies, for example with Dome Petroleum, into the 1980s.[23]

Majority clauses gave rise to some concern that they could be used to the detriment of minority bondholders. In Canada and England, however, practitioners regarded these provisions as necessary to prevent obstructive tactics by minority bondholders and to facilitate action by bondholders as a class.[24] Where the majority of bondholders exercised its power unfairly or oppressively, the court could, at least theoretically, grant relief to the minority.[25]

Floating Charges

In England and Canada, the floating charge gave rise to bondholder reorganizations.[26] In late nineteenth- and early twentieth-century Canada, bond issues were the main form of long-term commercial financing,[27] and bondholder reorganizations were the primary method of business restructuring. As historian Michael Bliss notes, it was easier for Canadian corporations to obtain capital through bond issues as opposed to commercial bank loans.[28] The key elements of bondholder floating charges under Canadian trust deeds were the long-term nature of the credit arrangement and the charge on the business undertaking as part of the security for the loan. These features gave bondholders an interest in the long-term success of the company, which somewhat resembled that of shareholders. As a result, the presumptive response to debtor failure by bondholders during this period was to restructure the enterprise.

The origins of the English floating charge shed light on the restructuring incentive it created for Canadian and English bondholders. According to Robert Pennington, an English solicitor and Reader at the Law Society's School of Law, nineteenth-century English courts recognized that the floating charge was a means of obtaining capital for companies, which faced a scarcity of *equity* investment.[29] By their long-term nature and charge on the business undertaking of the company, bondholders' floating charges contemplated a situation in which there were inadequate assets to secure the loan – intrinsically a situation of under-security. The floating charge holder whose security included future profitability of the business undertaking took security, in part, against the anticipated success of the company – likely because this was the only security that the company had left to offer.

Since a significant portion of the security for long-term credit issued under a floating charge included the earning power of the business, the ongoing operation of the enterprise was the ultimate creditor remedy. In 1952, Canadian lawyer Fred MacKelcan wrote that the only cases in which bondholders would *not* attempt to restructure the debtor were where "the company's business had ceased to be carried on or plainly could not be further continued."[30] In such cases, the company usually wound up in liquidation or bankruptcy, with a receiver acting for bond-holders. According to MacKelcan, the importance of the floating charge was "that it enables a remedy [reorganization] to be applied which will preserve the going concern value of the debtor company's business and its future earning power ..."[31]

Shortly after recognizing the floating charge, English courts accepted a new equitable remedy that responded to the particular interests of floating charge holders in restructuring debtor companies. Where the floating charge secured the enterprise in favour of bondholders, the courts allowed for the right of the bondholders to appoint a receiver-manager under the terms of the trust deed.[32] At law, reorganizations were technically actions by mortgagees to enforce their security, which was made possible by the court's characterization of the charge over the debtor's business as a proprietary rather than a contractual right.[33]

In the rare cases where the business undertaking was not charged in favour of the bondholders, only a receiver could be appointed.[34] A receiver was responsible for taking possession of the secured assets and selling them for the benefit of bondholders, after payments to any pri-ority creditors. A receiver-manager, however, had the additional duty of preserving the going-concern value and the goodwill associated with the enterprise until the company was restructured or sold, usually with the sanction of the court.[35]

It is worth mentioning that Canadian chartered banks of the nine-teenth and early twentieth centuries were mainly engaged in short-term business loans and seasonal farm credit, and thus they were not bondholders. As described by Canadian academic William Moull, an initial objective of the Bank Act of 1870 was to keep banks liquid.[36] To this end, banks were generally deterred or prohibited by law from lend-ing against fixed and non-negotiable assets. Parliament relaxed these prohibitions over time, and by the 1920s and 1930s section 88 of the Bank Act allowed banks to take charges on certain forms of security from eligible borrowers. However, the Bank Act in force at that time still restricted banks to lending on a short-term basis and barred them from mortgage lending until 1967.[37] With a few exceptions, such as for accounts receivable financing, banks were further limited to taking security in the form of fixed charges.[38] Banks could lend against certain security, such as accounts receivable, using floating charges;[39] however, these differed from bondholder floating charges in that they were short-term, or revolving in nature, and did not amount to a charge on the undertaking or future profitability of the business.

Floating Charge Holder Remedies

Under the terms of the trust deed, bondholders could appoint a receiver-manager to restructure the company if their security was in jeopardy.[40] "Jeopardy" referred to any situation where the bondholders' security would likely be depreciated. It did not require the debtor to have actually defaulted on its obligations, violated the terms of the trust deed, or be considered insolvent.[41] Rather, it was based on the principle that secured creditors should not have to watch passively as unsecured creditors enforced their claims against the company's assets,[42] and jeopardy was therefore the most common trigger for the appointment of a receiver or receiver-manager.[43] This concept is retained in modern provincial *Personal Property Security Acts*, which allow for the inclusion of acceleration clauses in financing agreements where there is reasonable cause to believe that the collateral is, or is about to be, in jeopardy.[44] Since appointment of a receiver-manager could negatively affect a company's goodwill (and going-concern value) bondholders were inclined to forgive the occasional missed payment. Thus, although jeopardy allowed bondholders to institute receivership proceedings proactively – before a company was in serious financial trouble – bondholders' commercial interest in the success of the company meant that they were inclined to exercise forbearance for minor repayment issues.

As a practical matter, technical insolvency was probably not a useful benchmark for initiating receivership or reorganization proceedings by floating charge holders. Courts recognized the floating charge over the business enterprise in the first place because companies had inadequate security to offer as collateral for long-term financing.[45] A floating charge over the debtor's business enterprise meant that the company could be balance-sheet insolvent as soon as it spent the loan on something not covered by the creditors' security, such as employee wages.

As the company's financial situation worsened, bondholders could act to crystallize their floating charge, which would effectively bar unsecureds from enforcing or enhancing the priority of their claims through execution.[46] "Execution" refers to the enforcement of a debt through a court order. This process can elevate the priority of an unsecured claim by securing it against some of the debtor's assets.[47] Thus, in effect, an execution order can turn an unsecured claim into a type of secured claim. As a general matter, unsecured creditors ranked behind floating charge holders unless they could complete an execution order before crystallization of the floating charge. Often this was practically impossible because the financial difficulty of the company, which would prompt execution orders, usually also triggered crystallization of the bondholders' floating charge. Since almost all of the company's assets were secured under the floating charge, this left little or nothing for a bankruptcy distribution to unsecured creditors. So the crystallization of the bondholders' floating charge provided a de facto stay of proceedings against all other creditors.

Jeopardy thus provided an advantageous point to initiate floating charge holder remedies. Once the security was in jeopardy, bondholders could pursue reorganization or liquidation, depending on which remedy was expected to result in higher recoveries.[48] Reorganizing the debtor could potentially benefit the company's shareholders as well as other stakeholders, such as employees, who otherwise would receive little or nothing in liquidation.[49] This is similar to the trickle-down benefits that can accrue to junior creditors and stakeholders in a modern debtor-in-possession restructuring.[50]

Bondholder reorganizations relied broadly on the framework of receivership law to effect restructurings, meaning that reorganizations operated almost solely within provincial jurisdiction.[51] The CCAA continues to reflect this basis in receivership by looking to receivership case law for guidance on asset sales, for example.[52] Early CCAA guidance on the fairness and reasonableness of plans also came from case law on earlier shareholder and creditor reorganizations under company law, further indicating that some restructuring mechanisms and principles already existed by the time the CCAA was enacted.[53]

Creditor Control versus Debtor-in-Possession

There are interesting similarities between historical and contemporary restructurings in the mechanisms used to finance reorganization efforts. The practice of issuing receiver's certificates in historical bondholder reorganizations parallels the contemporary practice of granting super-priority to debtor-in-possession financing under CCAA law. In his 1971 PhD thesis on finance, Jean Pierre Garant stated that a receiver-manager acting for floating charge holders had authority to raise money for carrying on the business in a bondholder reorganization by issuing receiver's certificates that ranked ahead of bonds.[54] According to Garant and lawyer Winslow Benson, this was an essential power for completing restructurings since most receivers were appointed in situations where there was a lack of working capital.[55] According to Garant, the effectiveness of this method of secured financing and corporate restructuring is illustrated by the fact that

it is often the firm that requests receivership when working capital is lacking. Such a request, apart from allowing for working capital to be raised, protects the firm through crystallization against a rush of unsecured creditors with execution orders. At the same time, it protects shareholders' value, especially when it is recalled that bondholders may modify their rights such as to payments of interest and principal for the purpose of placing the reorganized company on a sound basis.[56]

In these respects, the practice and outcome of bondholder reorganizations parallels modern debtor-in-possession restructurings.

Junior and unsecured creditor rights were usually disregarded in bondholder reorganizations. In Canada, where unsecured creditors could petition a company into bankruptcy, there was typically nothing in the estate to satisfy their claims since all of the company's assets were secured by the bondholders' fixed and floating charges.[57] According to William Kaspar Fraser, an expert in company law, unsecured creditors could "be disregarded or given only such terms as the reorganization committee deems expedient on business grounds."[58] However, the necessity and desirability of honouring junior and unsecured creditor claims in whole or in part probably arose more frequently than Fraser indicated.[59]

MacKelcan noted that bondholders typically negotiated bank claims since financing from the bank was often needed to continue operating the business as a going concern during and after reorganization.[60] From the bank's perspective, it might be impossible to collect receivables that were assigned to it by the debtor without the ongoing operation of the plant and equipment, which was typically secured in favour of bondholders. Consequently, trust deeds usually included a provision giving the company's bank priority for money lent and secured under section 88 of the *Bank Act*.[61] Therefore, bondholders were inclined to forgive minor defects in payments, since otherwise the company would likely borrow from the bank to meet bond payments, thereby burdening its working capital with more loans, which would rank ahead of bondholder claims.[62]

George F. Curtis, the founding Dean of Law at the University of British Columbia, noted several other specific types of debt that courts had held ranked ahead of bondholder claims, including garnishee orders, solicitors' and vendors' liens, and purchase money.[63] Due to the lack of records, it is not clear to what extent these kinds of priorities were invoked during this period.

Bondholder reorganizations frequently took the form of a sale from the old company to a newly formed one for non-cash consideration in the form of new securities. Such transactions could require court approval if the province had enacted bulk sales legislation or a *Judicature Act*.[64]

This form of reorganization eliminated unsecured claims. In effect, it discharged these debts as far as the new company was concerned. Where unsecured creditors were likely to attack the plan, Fraser recommended that bondholders obtain court approval, which would bind all other interested parties to the terms of the (bondholders') reorganization plan.

Court approval was typically obtained by converting a private receivership into a court-appointed receivership, sometimes also called an equity receivership. While a private receivership arises from contractual provisions in a financing agreement, such as a trust deed, a court appoints a receiver in an equity receivership.[65] Writing in 1943, MacKelcan noted that the majority of receiverships in which National Trust Company, one of the largest trust companies in Canada, was involved were ones in which it acted as indenture trustee and had obtained court appointment as receiver.[66] Garant wrote that court approval was recommended in bondholder reorganizations due to the fact that floating charge security did not charge specific assets, suggesting that court-appointed receiverships were used by bondholders to obtain broader or stronger powers than those provided through private receivership alone.[67] Garant wrote that it was nevertheless legal for the trustee to seize and sell corporate assets if such powers were conferred in the trust deed.

MacKelcan and Fraser both reported that the Ontario *Judicature Act* was used to facilitate bondholder reorganizations.[68] That act, like its English counterpart,[69] provided for the court appointment of a receiver as an equitable remedy.[70] Over time, some equitable remedies, such as receivership, were enumerated in Canadian statutes, although these remedies also continue to exist under common law. Canadian equity receiverships resulted from the court appointment of a receiver, which could be based on statutory provisions or common law principles.[71]

Under a court-appointed receivership a court could approve the plan or compromise based on its statutory or equitable jurisdiction, which would bind non-bondholder parties to the plan. This allowed bondholders to have the best of both private and equitable receivership. They used private receivership to work out a compromise that advanced their interests, and then converted the process into an equitable receivership to obtain court approval, which would bind other interested parties to the plan. In effect, equitable receiverships were used as a judicial rubber stamp for private restructuring plans. This practice parallels modern pre-packaged insolvencies, in some respects. [72] In a pre-packaged insolvency, the major parties invoke insolvency law with a restructuring plan already in hand, which provides judicial imprimatur for privately negotiated agreements.

In contrast with the United States, unsecured creditors in Canada could not initiate receivership proceedings, which were a common means of reorganizing American corporate bond issues in this period.[73] Courts in the United States also refused to recognize a floating charge over a debtor's property.[74] Accordingly, creditor remedies developed under the floating charge, such as the doctrine of jeopardy, majority provisions in trust deeds, and private receiverships, were not used in the United States, where creditors used different remedies under equity receiverships, the *Bankruptcy Code*, and secured lending laws.[75] Canadian practitioners maintained that Anglo-Canadian bondholder reorganizations offered a more flexible procedure for the benefit of bondholders, which they regarded as an advantage over the American approach.[76]

In Canada reorganization proceedings with respect to unsecured creditor claims were available to companies in liquidation under the *Winding-up Act* (WUA) where court leave was obtained. These reorganizations were also usually conducted by way of a "sale by the liquidator to a new company in consideration of the shares and securities to be delivered under the plan."[77] Where a three-fourths majority in value of the company's creditors, according to class, approved a compromise or arrangement, sections 63 and 64 of that act provided that the court could sanction the plan.[78] Fraser notes that this method of reorganization did not apply to bondholders, whose claims could only be restructured under a trust deed.[79] Therefore this unsecured creditor remedy was rather ineffectual as a matter of practice, and the WUA was not frequently used for this purpose. However, compromises under the WUA could be used to enhance the bondholder remedy of reorganization where it was desirable (for business purposes) to effect a compromise with unsecured creditors. Fraser stated that bondholders could generally carry out a restructuring more effectively and efficiently through an action to enforce their security, than could unsecured creditors via insolvency legislation – an argument that is still made in relation to administrative receivership in England.[80] From a bondholder perspective, liquidation proceedings were best avoided in any event since they often prompted unsecureds to organize and "attack the bond mortgage on technical grounds, such as defective registration," which was a nuisance to bondholders.[81]

While the *Bankruptcy Act of 1919* included provision for a company to make a composition with its unsecured creditors, the act was not widely used for this purpose.[82] Once a company was in bankruptcy, the administrative workings were so slow that virtually all goodwill eroded long before meaningful restructuring negotiations could take place.[83] The slow-moving statutory process was intended to prevent abuses by debtors. As a debtor remedy, reorganization gave rise to concerns that companies would use bankruptcy compositions to avoid paying debts that they were in fact able to pay.[84] The same concerns did not arise in bondholder reorganizations. As a creditor remedy in which the creditors exercised control through a receiver-manager, a solvent debtor was unable to use the proceedings to avoid paying its debts.

Shareholder reorganizations were also fairly common in the 1930s. These reorganizations proceeded under the company legislation applicable to the company in question, such as the Dominion *Companies Act*, with the requisite majority approval of the shareholders and the court.[85] Fraser discussed several examples of shareholder restructurings, which, he wrote, were also usually conducted by way of a sale of the old company's assets to a newly formed company.[86] In extraordinary cases provinces enacted special legislation to confirm a scheme of arrangement and to make it binding on all persons affected.[87]

Creditor versus Debtor Remedy

The differing attitudes toward reorganization, depending on its characterization as a creditor or debtor remedy, are evident in the early use of the CCAA. The act attracted no criticism when deployed as a bondholder remedy since the receiver-manager's control of the business prevented strategic behaviour by the debtor. Use of the act as a bondholder remedy essentially paralleled bondholder rights outside of insolvency legislation, and so invoking the act did not change creditor priorities, which may have led adversely affected creditors to object. When the company or its junior creditors used the CCAA to advance their interests, however, it gave rise to concerns that the act was being abused.[88] With no provision for third-party oversight, there was no check on strategic behaviour by debtors or junior creditors absent the bondholders' receiver or trustee.

Company reorganizations of this period were heavily weighted in favour of bondholders' interests and held clear advantages for other senior secured creditors, the debtor company, and its shareholders. How employees and management were likely to fare depended on the circumstances. In a restructuring that only involved adjusting bondholder claims, employees and management likely were unaffected. In a complete company restructuring, employees might lose their jobs and some management positions would probably also disappear. If trade creditors were important to the ongoing operation of the company, they likely fared reasonably well in the restructuring. Otherwise, junior creditors could expect to recover little or nothing of whatever they were owed. In this regard, junior creditors helped finance many corporate restructurings, along with bondholders who often forgave minor defects in interest payments and subordinated their claims to fresh financing. Unlike bondholders, however, the junior creditors who helped finance the restructuring often did so involuntarily and without sharing in the long-term advantages of having rehabilitated, rather than liquidated, the debtor firm.

2 Catalysts for a Coordinated Statutory Framework

Canadian corporate reorganization in the 1920s entailed navigating a complex framework of legislation, case law, and business practices. Bondholder reorganizations of this period operated both outside the realm of insolvency law and the federal jurisdiction generally, based on the terms of privately drafted trust deeds and provincial legislation. To effect a complete reorganization of a company's debt and equity, a firm would need to negotiate different compromises with all of its debt and equity holders, with no one arrangement guaranteeing that others would follow. Furthermore, provincial jurisdiction over bondholder reorganizations meant that recourse was to the superior court in the province where the assets or company were situated. This could necessitate bringing actions in the courts of multiple provinces if corporate assets and operations were spread throughout the country. By the 1920s, the general lack of coordination in Canadian business reorganization law frustrated some restructuring attempts and acted to undermine creditor confidence in other instances, contributing to the failure of viable restructuring plans.[89]

The multi-pronged approach to Canadian business reorganization up to the early 1930s stemmed from the division of legislative powers contained in the *Constitution Act, 1867*. Section 92(13) made secured creditor rights the purview of the provinces, while section 91(21) gave the Dominion responsibility for bankruptcy and insolvency law.[90] The Dominion and provinces also shared legislative power with respect to company law and shareholders under sections 91(2) and the residuary clause, and 92(11), respectively.[91] The JCPC generally interpreted these provisions as discrete divisions of legislative power and held that legislation affecting secured creditor rights was outside of federal jurisdiction, even in cases of bankruptcy or insolvency.[92] Parliamentary boldness in the face of the Great Depression and the constitutional references in the 1930s would change this interpretation and, with it, the legal landscape of commercial reorganization.[93]

Table 2.1 Sales of Canadian Corporate Bonds

Period	Total Millions $	Sold in Canada %	Sold in US %	Sold in UK %
1904–14	2186	17.7	9.1	73.2
1915–20	3428	67.0	29.6	3.4
1921–30	5491	57.6	40.6	1.8
1931–9	6314	83.3	13.5	3.2
1940–5	16577	98.3	1.7	—
1946–50	9031	93.2	6.8	—

Adapted from table 14.4, "Foreign Investment in Canada and Domestic and Foreign Sales of Canadian Bonds, 1900–1970," in Neufeld, *The Financial System of Canada*, 492–3.

During the late 1920s and early 1930s, two major catalysts contributed to the coordination of the legal framework governing bondholder reorganizations. First, corporate reorganization legislation was increasingly necessary by the 1930s in order to attract US capital.[94] In the 1920s, Canadian firms came to rely more on American rather than British investment finance. Following the First World War, interest rates in Britain rose faster than in Canada, increasing the cost of bond financing for Canadian companies.[95] American interest rates, while also rising, were lower than those in both Canada and Britain.[96] Additionally, in this period the United States transitioned from being a debtor to a creditor nation, releasing a lot of investment capital for foreign borrowers. Therefore, Canadian corporations increasingly placed bonds with American investors. Statistical evidence collected by the Canadian economist E.P. Neufeld illustrates that in the period 1915–20, American investment replaced British investment as the main source of new issue bond financing for Canadian companies.[97] Over the decade that followed, from 1921 to 1930, American purchases of Canadian new bond issues accounted for 40.6 per cent of total purchases.[98] See table 2.1, above.

American preferences influenced the form of Canadian financing agreements.[99] American investors were suspicious of the majority provisions in Canadian trust deeds, which they thought negatively affected the negotiability and integrity of the securities.[100] In the United States, the actions of a majority of bondholders acting under a trust deed were curtailed by legislation with a view to protecting minority bondholders.[101] Furthermore, the New York Stock Exchange was reluctant to list securities with majority clauses, which they framed as an issue of bond "negotiability."[102] This deterred large issuers and underwriters from proposing and underwriting bonds with majority provisions in the American securities market.[103] Consequently, trust deeds governing bonds placed with American investors, who invested heavily in the Canadian forestry and mining industries, for example, usually omitted majority provisions.[104] American influence, however, should not be overstated since majority provisions, as well as floating charges, remained standard features of Canadian trust deeds well beyond the 1930s.[105]

Second, economic downturns in the 1920s were significant catalysts for changes in Canadian corporate reorganization practices. The difficulties that beset the pulp and paper industry in the mid-1920s illustrate the challenges that many companies faced. But pulp and paper was the most important industry in Canada at that time, and the largest of its kind in the world. The sector had expanded rapidly in the decade before by issuing bonds, but by the late 1920s the market faced overcapacity and falling prices.[106] By the 1930s, Abitibi Power and Paper, Price Brothers, Great Lakes Paper, and Fraser Companies were all in receivership.[107]

The conditions at Abitibi Power and Paper were extraordinary: Their receivership lasted for fourteen years, from 1932 to 1946 – a product of the economic downturns that began after the First World War, which were then followed by the onset of the Great Depression.[108] In 1928 Abitibi began to experience financial difficulty. In 1932 the company defaulted on bond interest payments and was placed in receivership by its bondholders.[109] Abitibi was one of many large corporations in receivership in 1933, when parliament passed the CCAA and, like many others, the company was eventually reorganized under the act.

Three main factors contributed to the length of Abitibi's financial difficulties. First, their receivership coincided with the expiration of leases for its timber concessions from the Ontario government, the renewal of which was necessary for a viable reorganization plan.[110] Initially Premier Mitchell Hepburn (Liberal) refused to extend the leases until the receivership was over; however, he eventually agreed to restore the concessions if the courts and his cabinet approved the reorganization plan.[111] Second, it was very difficult to garner majority bondholder support for a restructuring plan: More than thirty-two plans were proposed and rejected between 1932 and 1936 alone.[112] The parties involved generally sought to advance their interests by taking hardline positions in negotiations, such as the bondholders' insistence on receiving the full value of their claims under any proposed restructuring.[113] Third, when a plan was finally put forward for approval under newly enacted Ontario legislation in 1938, the court's analysis of the division of powers led it to hold that the provincial act could not be used to restructure an insolvent company and thus the company would have to restructure under the CCAA instead.[114] It took several more years and a Royal Commission before another restructuring plan was concluded under the CCAA.

The financial problems of the pulp and paper industry worsened during the Great Depression, which began in 1929. Further corporate failures highlighted the fact that corporate reorganization practices had not yet adapted to meet the requirements of American investors and illustrated the inadequacy of existing legislation for conducting complete company reorganizations.[115] Bondholder reorganizations could not be conducted without adequate trust deed provisions since the uncoordinated legislative landscape in Canada was not equipped to handle the restructuring of secured credit.[116] Furthermore, majority provisions provided no basis for adjusting unsecured or shareholder claims. This led to difficult and sometimes futile attempts to conduct complete reorganizations of a company's debt and equity, using the bondholders' trust deed and applying provincial or federal legislation as it pertained to other creditors and shareholders.[117]

While earlier recessions and depressions also led to corporate bankruptcies, and even to the collapse of small financial institutions, the Great Depression was different in that the failure of private ordering (bondholder reorganizations under trust deeds) converged with the deepest economic crisis in Canadian history. This plunged large Canadian concerns into receivership and threw the solvency of their largest creditors into question as well. The magnitude of potential losses facing financial institutions would, in all likelihood, have had significant ramifications for the stability of the Canadian financial system. Straitened federal finances,[118] the near bankruptcy of several provinces, and the lack of a Canadian central bank[119] meant that bailouts, or direct financial backstopping of financial institutions, were probably not realistic options.

The spectre of large failures due to the Great Depression necessitated a legislative response to the restructuring crisis facing Canadian companies and their bondholders. It is worth underscoring the fact that it was not corporate failures per se that led to the enactment of the CCAA, but the precarious financial position of major creditors (institutional bondholders such as life insurance companies) if they could not recoup their investments in viable business debtors. For example, by 1931, Sun Life, one of the largest Canadian financial institutions at the time, was insolvent.[120] Other insurance companies and trust and loan companies also faced the prospect of failing by the early 1930s. The

Canadian financial community was concerned that the large number of corporate insolvencies would trigger insurance company defaults as well, and thus these financial institutions supported the idea of drafting legislation like the CCAA.[121]

Despite the seriousness of the situation facing the Canadian government, the division of legislative powers challenged the adoption of reorganization provisions into companies legislation. This was probably the main reason Canada did not earlier adopt reorganization provisions based on the English *Companies Acts* of the nineteenth and early twentieth centuries. The restructuring crisis of the 1920s and 1930s prompted Canadian lawyers and legislators to look for a new legislative approach to company reorganization, which would provide for compromises with secured and unsecured creditors as well as shareholders – complete company reorganization.

The English *Companies Act, 1929* provided the inspiration. As lawyer Harold E. Manning wrote, "Many schemes of compromise or arrangement which could not be worked out under the powers in the instrument creating the charge [a trust deed], [were] possible under [that] Act."[122]

As the Depression wore on, it became increasingly clear that Canada needed a statutory scheme in order to deal with many large, impending corporate reorganizations.[123] Finally, in 1933, parliament adopted the restructuring provisions of the English *Companies Act, 1929* into the CCAA bill.[124] By that time, despite the constitutional difficulties, there was a general consensus that federal action was necessary, at least to coordinate the multiple restructuring regimes, either through a single federal statute or cooperation with the provinces.[125]

3 Historical Institutionalism and Recursivity of Law

The early part of the twentieth century was a period of much informal change in Canadian corporate debt financing, both in terms of financing sources and in practices. Canadian companies increasingly relied on American rather than British investors to purchase corporate bonds, and tailored the terms of trust deeds to reflect American preferences. A recursivity of law analysis shows that law in practice increasingly omitted majority provisions from Canadian trust deeds – especially in industries with heavy American investment, such as pulp and paper. These changes occurred incrementally, on a company-by-company basis until a new, practical norm was established: Canadian corporate trust deeds no longer tended to provide for restructuring bondholder claims.

These changes in commercial practices occurred without changes to formal law. Most law on company reorganization in Canada came from private agreements (such as trust deeds) operating alongside the creditor remedy of receivership – secured creditor remedies that dated from the nineteenth century. What is most significant about this period in terms of company restructuring is that the main method of reorganizing companies in Canada – a private, secured creditor remedy – was essentially taken off the table by the private parties themselves. Once majority provisions were removed from Canadian trust deeds, private parties could not fix this deficiency since majority provisions were the mechanism by which bondholders ordinarily carried out amendments to trust deeds.

It seems that no Canadian trustee or corporate manager at the time realized the potentially significant problem this created, despite the fact that a contemporary English commentator wrote: "the draftsman who omits to insert [majority provisions] runs the risk of being accused of neglecting the best interest of the debenture [holder]."[126] While companies operated at a profit, the new trust deeds produced no changes in business operations. However, economic downturns, which began with the pulp and paper industry in the late 1920s and that affected conditions generally by the start of the Great Depression, called attention to the significance of this oversight. By the early 1930s, many companies were in receivership. Yet, without majority provisions there was often no way to restructure these firms as going concerns – the preferred remedy of bondholders. Incremental changes in practice, combined with the triggering events of economic downturns (big exogenous shocks), led to a critical juncture for Canadian corporate reorganization law and practice. This restructuring crisis among Canadian corporations threatened the solvency of financial institutions and necessitated significant institutional changes because traditional, private, restructuring mechanisms were no longer available. Since receivership provided a de facto stay of proceedings against junior creditor claims, it served as a holding pattern for insolvent companies and their bondholders until new legislation was enacted to facilitate restructuring.

How Canada resolved this issue of facilitating corporate reorganizations for the benefit of bondholders in the 1930s would have potentially long-lasting implications for the law and practice of corporate restructuring. What made this juncture particularly critical was that problematic institutional arrangements concerning bond financing intersected with the worst economic depression in Canadian history, dramatically highlighting the flaws of the new trust deeds. The solution would probably have to come through legislation, thereby adding a statutory, public flavour to the longstanding private practice of bondholder reorganizations. Whatever approach was adopted was likely to generate a significant amount of positive feedback, as bondholders acted to restructure hundreds of struggling companies, thereby entrenching the new approach to restructuring. Therefore, the solution to this problem, adopted during the Great Depression, would likely set corporate restructuring on a new path.

4 Conclusion

Canadian bondholder reorganizations were principally creditor remedies that grew out of commercial financing practices and receivership law, and these approaches were later enshrined and perpetuated in federal insolvency law. The policy and practice of bondholder reorganizations of the 1930s were conducted with little regard for the interests of other creditors or stakeholders, which generally held weak legal rights in relation to bondholders' all-encompassing floating charge.

As a secured creditor remedy, bondholder reorganizations operated as the presumptive response to a large firm's financial distress during the early twentieth century. Even significant procedural difficulties did not cause bondholders to shy away from restructurings. Instead large bondholding interests adopted (or co-opted) more cumbersome methods of restructuring, such as court-appointed receiverships; they went to provincial or federal governments for political and financial assistance, and even obtained enabling legislation.

3

Enshrining a Bondholder Remedy in Federal Legislation

It was never the intention under the Act, I am convinced, to ... permit the holders of junior securities to put through a scheme ... amounting to confiscation of the vested interest of the bondholders.[1]

Kingstone J., *In re Wellington Building Corporation Limited, 1934*

On 20 April 1933, Conservative Member of Parliament Charles H. Cahan introduced Bill No. 77 – an act to facilitate compromises and arrangements between companies and their creditors – in the House of Commons by stating:

At the present time some legal method of making arrangements and compromises between creditors and companies is perhaps more necessary because of the prevailing commercial and industrial depression ...[2]

In the Senate the Right Honourable Arthur Meighen (Conservative) stated that the Depression prompted the CCAA bill:

The depression has brought almost innumerable companies to the pass where some such arrangement is necessary in the interest of the company itself, in the interest of its employees ... and in the interest of the security holders ...[3]

Since the CCAA bill was based on the single provision of the English *Companies Act* concerning reorganizations, it was quite brief.[4] It even lacked a preamble. The CCAA provided that an insolvent company or one of its creditors could make an application under the act to restructure both the unsecured and secured debt of the firm.[5] This initial application was made in the relevant court in the province or territory in question.[6] The act could be conjointly applied with the relevant companies legislation to restructure equity holdings in the debtor company.[7] Upon the application by an interested party in respect of a company that had filed under the CCAA, the court could stay all claims and proceedings against the debtor, including those under the *Bankruptcy Act* and the WUA.[8] It is not clear to what extent parties relied on a broad or general stay of proceedings, which became the common practice in the 1980s and 1990s. Historical documents suggest that court involvement was minimal and served as judicial rubber stamp for essentially private arrangements worked out under the statute.[9] The CCAA required the support of a majority of a company's secured and unsecured creditors, which were divided into classes based on the similarity of their claims. The act required the support of three-fourths of each class of creditors, present and voting, before a plan could be put before the court for consideration.[10] If the plan was "fair and reasonable," the court would sanction the plan for implementation.

Debate on the new bill was limited, taking up roughly six pages of Hansard, and the bill had the support of both the Conservative and Liberal parties.[11] No figures or statistics on bankruptcy or business failure were cited. Rather, it appears there was a tacit understanding of the seriousness of the Depression as well as circumstances in struggling industries, such as pulp and paper. Bankruptcy and liquidation statistics for Dominion companies compiled by the Secretary of State indicate that business failure rates were very high in this period, as illustrated in appendices 1 and 2 – a fact which parliamentarians were likely aware of, and which came out in debates on other bills from that period. The lack of discussion in parliament can also be explained by the fact that the CCAA essentially harmonized existing practices and legislation to the extent possible under the Canadian constitution.

1 Interest Groups

Politicians

The personal interests of parliamentarians may have helped prompt the reform of business reorganization practices and thus garner support for the CCAA bill. For instance, Senator Meighen personally held a considerable number of bonds in Ontario Power Service (OPC), a subsidiary of Abitibi.[12] When Abitibi and OPC defaulted in 1932, Meighen and other financiers successfully appealed for government intervention when their bonds lost over two-thirds of their face value, without disclosing their interests in the distressed companies – information that only came out later.[13] Additionally, Prime Minister Richard B. Bennett (Conservative) had already established a reputation as a "millionaire businessman" when he was elected Prime Minister in 1930, so he too may have held some of the affected bonds.[14] The personal interests of parliamentarians might help explain the multi-partisan support for the CCAA bill and might account for the limited discussion recorded in the debates in the House of Commons and Senate.

Prime Minister Bennett's experiences and ideology also help shed light on the policy behind the CCAA as an insolvency statute that promoted financial interests. He possessed a driving ambition for success, and as a partner in a Calgary law firm in 1897 he represented many corporate clients, including railroads, retail businesses, banks, loan and insurance companies, as well as farmers and ranchers.[15] This law partnership was dissolved after twenty-five years, and then Bennett became a founding partner in a new firm, now known as Bennett Jones LLP.[16] He also served as president of the Canadian Bar Association from 1929 to 1930, the years immediately preceding his election as prime minister of Canada.[17] As a lawyer, businessman, and politician, Bennett was a strong advocate for large corporations and financial firms, and he possessed a vision of promoting capital expansion and development in Canada.[18] This experience and ideology fit well with the underlying purposes of the CCAA.

Bondholders

The major beneficiaries of the CCAA were large bondholding interests – namely, life insurance companies and trust and loan companies.[19] These were essentially the same financial interests that benefitted from the *Farmers' Creditors Arrangement Act* (FCAA), which provided a similar insolvency law mechanism for restructuring secured farm debt.[20] Yet, significantly, this same interest group derided the provincial debt adjustment legislation, enacted by Alberta's Social Credit government, as fundamentally anti-capitalist.[21]

The fact that large financial interests supported the CCAA and FCAA indicates that the federal legislation was different: It advanced the interests of this group in ways that the Social Credit legislation did not. The provincial legislation concerning debt adjustment contemplated downward adjustments on capital owed to creditors as part of a fundamental shift in debtor-creditor relations, which would curtail the rights of creditors.[22] Large secured creditors did not support legislative efforts to diminish their rights as secured creditors; however, they were not altogether opposed to debt adjustment since moderate legislative intervention could serve their long-term interests.[23] For example, in the 1930s, farming operations in the Prairies had been hit hard by the deep financial crisis, along with a long-lasting drought that came to be known as the "Dust Bowl."[24] To work through these challenging conditions, mortgage loan companies favoured adjustments to interest payments or time frames for repayments, which could be negotiated on a farmer-by-farmer basis.[25] These kinds of arrangements preserved the creditors' bargaining power and prevented the need to seize and sell illiquid assets, such as farmland, on a mass scale. Mortgage loan companies and other secured creditor interests, such as the Dominion Mortgage and Investment Association (DMIA), also supported "emergency" legislation like the FCAA, which was temporary in nature and allowed for case-by-case negotiation of debt.[26] Public funding of the administration of the FCAA also reduced adjustment costs for creditors and farmers alike.[27]

Interest groups representing secured creditors did not make submissions to parliament about the CCAA bill. Indeed, DMIA and other trade groups were not even directly consulted about the original bill. DMIA learned about the draft legislation through one of its members, and then circulated the details to other trade groups, including the Canadian Life Insurance Officers Association, the Canadian Manufacturers Association, and the Canadian Bankers Association.[28] However, parliament passed the CCAA bill so quickly that these trade groups did not have time to study the bill and make submissions.[29]

DMIA, which supported the new legislation, reported to its members that it thought it "inadvisable to make representations to the Government respecting the unconstitutionality of the [CCAA] Bill."[30] This group, representing life insurance companies, supported the objectives of the CCAA bill but thought it raised serious federal-provincial jurisdictional issues. DMIA expressed concern that defeat of the CCAA bill on jurisdictional grounds might close the door to further attempts to pass effective legislation, but welcomed the idea of consultations about the proposed legislation with the federal Department of Justice and the provinces, especially Ontario and Quebec.[31] For members of this interest group, the stakes were high. The fate of some life insurance companies depended on getting new creditors' arrangement legislation of this kind.

The CCAA extended, rather than limited, bondholder rights by facilitating company reorganization where bondholders' interests were better served by restructuring than by liquidation. In describing the bill to its members, DMIA highlighted language in the bill that stated its provisions were "in extension" to existing provisions, demonstrating to its members that the CCAA bill was intended to be a creditor remedy.[32]

In effect, the CCAA strengthened bondholder rights in certain ways by diminishing the already weak rights of unsecured creditors. CCAA applications could formally stay all proceedings against the debtor, including those under the *Bankruptcy Act*. Unsecured creditors, who already had very weak rights vis-à-vis bondholders, might have no method of enforcing their claims once the CCAA was invoked. Even then, the extent of remedies for unsecured creditors under the CCAA was limited to the right to vote on a plan, if a plan was proposed with respect to unsecured claims.

The CCAA did not provide for the appointment of an official such as a bankruptcy trustee to oversee the process.[33] In its brevity, the act provided almost no guidance on the administration of proceedings under the statute, aside from a few requirements concerning meetings and creditor voting.[34] This contrasted with the more rules-based restructuring procedure in the US *Bankruptcy Act*, which similarly was enacted during the Great Depression and adopted the practice of American equity receivership reorganizations into bankruptcy law.[35] In Canada, the lack of guidance can be explained by the act's function as an extension of bondholder remedies; a CCAA restructuring would be worked out under the legal architecture of receivership under a trust deed – something which was expressly allowed for by the fact that the act was "in extension, and not in limitation, of the provisions of any instrument now or hereafter governing the rights of creditors."[36] This was apparently so obvious at the time that it required no explanation.

The FCAA, by contrast, spelled out an administrative framework for farmer-creditor compromises,[37] suggesting that that act did something more novel in the Canadian context. Prior to 1935, there was no federal administrative regime for facilitating compromises on farm debt,[38] and thus it was necessary for parliament to establish procedures for debt adjustment under the FCAA. This was not necessary under the CCAA, since company reorganization was already the subject of a long body of English and Canadian case law by the 1930s. The CCAA merely added supplemental, harmonizing provisions to overcome specific difficulties encountered by bondholders in conducting company reorganizations.

The fact that the CCAA was justified as federal insolvency legislation is significant, although it led to confusion about the essential character of the statute, including the act's original purposes. The majority decision of the SCC in the 2010 *Century Services* case captures the conventional thinking on the CCAA:

> The purpose of the CCAA – Canada's first reorganization statute – is to permit the debtor to continue to carry on business and, where possible, avoid the social and economic costs of liquidating its assets.[39]

Early commentary and jurisprudence also endorsed the CCAA's remedial objectives. It recognized that companies retain more value as going concerns while underscoring that intangible losses, such as the evaporation of the companies' goodwill, result from liquidation. Reorganization serves the public interest by facilitating the survival of companies supplying goods or services crucial to the health of the economy or saving large numbers of jobs. Insolvency could be so widely felt as to impact stakeholders other than creditors and employees.[40]

Contemporary scholars have inferred that the mention of employees when the CCAA bill was introduced in parliament demonstrates that parliamentarians had a broader public interest in mind when enacting the CCAA.[41] This is unlikely in view of the broader context of the act. Other than this sole remark in parliament, employees and public interest considerations are not mentioned in any of the CCAA materials from the 1930s located in the course of this study. The earliest mention of the public interest value of CCAA reorganizations appears to be in 1947, when Winslow Benson suggested that a bondholder reorganization may be "in the interest of the community, for the continuance of the enterprise concerns employees, suppliers, and the whole economy."[42] But he offers no evidence to support this view, which instead appears to be a throwaway line. In a *Canadian Bar Review* article published the same year, Stanley Edwards advocated that judges should proactively reshape CCAA law along these lines.[43] By contrast, the FCAA, which extended debt relief to distressed farmers, entailed extensive discussions in parliament and the press concerning public policy rationales for keeping farmers on their land.[44]

It is also difficult to reconcile the CCAA's purported policy goal of advancing the public interest through restructuring large, important firms with the fact that the act excluded from its scope the institutions that were arguably of the greatest national and public interest in the 1930s. Subsection 2(b) of the CCAA excluded banks, railway companies, telegraph companies, insurance companies, trust companies, and loan companies from the definition of "debtor company" for the purposes of the act.[45] Writing in 1932, bankruptcy lawyer Lewis Duncan noted that these were institutions that provided "essential services," and hence supervision of such private concerns was necessarily a "feature of the modern State."[46] Rather than leave the fate of these firms to receivership or business insolvency legislation,[47] their national and public importance warranted more direct government assistance in the face of insolvency.

An historical analysis shows that the CCAA was intended as a bondholder remedy to cover drafting defects in trust deeds that did not make adequate provision for reorganizations. The public interest value of individual bondholder-led reorganizations under the CCAA (if any) was incidental to the use of reorganizations as a bondholder remedy for large, secured lenders. Accordingly, the significant public policy aspect of the CCAA was geared toward preventing collapses of large Canadian financial institutions, rather than saving more labour-intensive, non-financial companies. The benefits that may have accrued to junior creditors or other stakeholders were by-products of this main purpose. Unlike bankruptcy law,[48] the CCAA was not designed as a collective process and did not advance the bankruptcy notion of creditor equality. The reason that the CCAA was made applicable to insolvent corporations – technically making it insolvency law – was because it was the only (potentially) constitutionally valid method for the federal government to enact a company restructuring law that would apply throughout Canada.

Significantly, the enactment of the CCAA made restructuring insolvent companies the exclusive domain of the federal government. This was dramatically affirmed in 1938 by the Abitibi case, where the Ontario Court of Appeal refused to approve a judicial sale under the *Judicature Act, 1935* that would have restructured claims against the company and ended the Abitibi receivership.[49] The Ontario Court of Appeal upheld the lower court holding that because Abitibi was insolvent, the Ontario legislation could not be applied, and any restructuring attempt would need to proceed under the CCAA.[50]

The rationale for attempting to restructure under the Ontario Act in the Abitibi case is nevertheless noteworthy. Under the *Judicature Act, 1935*, the court could approve a judicial sale even where the plan did *not* have majority creditor approval – in essence, a minority could force a restructuring plan on the dissenting majority.[51] This provision was added by the Ontario legislature in 1935 specifically because of the Abitibi insolvency and the difficulty of marshaling the majority support needed to proceed under the CCAA.[52] As the *Judicature Act, 1935* shows, even after the enactment of the CCAA, practitioners did not regard restructuring as primarily an insolvency law matter.[53] From a bondholder perspective, the CCAA modestly addressed through insolvency law what was a much broader secured credit and company law issue.

The relative flexibility and utility of the CCAA for completing bondholder reorganizations was further curtailed by the courts' strict interpretation of the statute. In contrast to recent CCAA case law, 1930s decisions held the following:

- A debtor company could make only one CCAA application. If the plan failed, or the company ran into further financial difficulties after implementing the plan, it had no further recourse to the act.[54]
- Only one vote was held with respect to a proposed CCAA plan. There was no provision for redrafting plans and holding new votes as part of further negotiations.[55]
- The act did not bind Crown claims; however, this did not preclude government involvement in plans.[56] For instance, the Ontario (Liberal) government instituted a Royal Commission to inquire into the Abitibi insolvency and passed an amendment to the *Judicature Act* to help that company restructure.[57]
- The court was not prepared to approve the use of a "convenience class" for the purpose of obtaining majority creditor support for a plan.[58] (A "convenience class" refers to creditors with relatively small claims against the debtor, which are paid out in full as a matter of administrative convenience. This avoids the necessity of winning the votes of many small creditors.)
- The debtor company had to be technically insolvent at the time of a CCAA application.[59] This is quite unlike the modern *Stelco* case, in which the court held that a company that was nearing insolvency qualified as insolvent for CCAA purposes.[60]

Beginning in the 1980s and 1990s, these decisions were overturned in favour of more "liberal" interpretations of the act, based on a conception of the CCAA as primarily an insolvency statute that encouraged businesses to reorganize, instead of liquidating or winding up. The implicit reasoning is that such an interpretation is necessary to achieve the act's (purported) policy goals. For instance, in the 1993 case *Re Lehndorff General Partner Ltd.*, Farley J. held:

> The CCAA is intended to facilitate compromises and arrangements between companies and their creditors as an alternative to bankruptcy and, as such, is remedial legislation entitled to a liberal interpretation.[61]

Liberal interpretations of the CCAA facilitating reorganizations are justified on the basis that the ongoing operation of the company benefits a wider constituency of unsecured creditors and stakeholders, in addition to the major secured creditors.[62] The early history of the act shows, however, that the CCAA was principally a bondholder remedy, and was not based on a normative policy of encouraging company reorganization to promote broader stakeholder interests.[63] Thus, the policy justification given for liberal interpretations of the CCAA finds little basis in the origins of the statute. Since business reorganization was the presumptive response to a firm's financial difficulties where bondholders were involved, there was no need to create an incentive for this group of creditors. The general lack of interest in promoting business reorganization – even of just unsecured creditor claims – through the *Bankruptcy Act* is more indicative of the state of normative policies and attitudes concerning business rehabilitation under insolvency law at this time.[64]

Furthermore, early CCAA case law demonstrated strong pro-bondholder sentiments, which do not accord well with conceptions of bankruptcy as a collective process amongst different classes of creditors. In the 1934 case of *Re Wellington Building Corp.*, for example, when deciding a creditor classification issue, Kingstone J. held:

> It was never the intention under the Act, I am convinced, to deprive creditors in the position of these bondholders [holders of first mortgages] of their right to approve as a class by the necessary majority a scheme propounded by the company which would permit the holders of junior securities to put through a scheme inimicable to this class and amounting to confiscation of the vested interest of the bondholders.[65]

In refusing to approve the CCAA plan, Kingstone J. further remarked:

> I do not think the statute should be construed so as to permit holders of subsequent mortgages power to vote and thereby destroy the priority rights and security of a first mortgagee ...
>
> I am of the opinion that the scheme as propounded and which this Court is asked to approve is unfair to the bondholders ...[66]

Early business reorganizations and CCAA law allowed senior bondholders to work out arrangements that effectively diminished junior creditor rights, as noted above. As expressed by Kingstone J., the judiciary was not prepared to allow lower priority creditors to use the act to impose a plan that was to the detriment of bondholders. This essentially paralleled bondholder rights and remedies outside of the CCAA.

Case law from the 1930s also indicates that the *Bankruptcy Act* was not considered the proper place to look when determining the nature of creditor claims for CCAA purposes.[67] As legislation that was "separate and distinct" from the *Bankruptcy Act*, claim priorities in CCAA cases were established with reference to provincial law.[68] Contrary to present-day conceptions of the act as the first Canadian debtor-in-possession restructuring statute, secured creditors were actually in control of a company undergoing reorganization through a receiver-manager.[69] So negotiations under the act took place in the shadow of provincial debtor-creditor laws, rather than with a view to proceedings under the *Bankruptcy Act*.

In the 1930s and 1940s companies without outstanding bond issues did resort to the Act – a fact that is reflected in the case law – and thus controlled the proceedings without the oversight of a receiver-manager.[70] This practice was the source of many complaints that the act was being used to further the interests of debtors, and led to repeal efforts just five years after its enactment.[71] As a matter of history, the CCAA was not a manifestation of a policy that favoured debtor-in-possession reorganization proceedings. This was actually an unanticipated side effect of the legislation and was remedied by an amendment in 1953.[72] The CCAA permitted the debtor to initiate proceedings in order to accommodate receiver-led applications under the act, since at law private receivers were considered agents of the debtor, although they were appointed by secured creditors.

The fact that the CCAA was essentially a private bondholder remedy helps to explain why there was little administrative support and no formal record keeping by the Department of the Secretary of State, which had responsibility for the act in the 1930s and 1940s.[73] The Department did not keep specific records on restructurings completed under the Dominion *Companies Act* either, which contained provisions that facilitated shareholder restructurings. Writing in 1927, Fraser makes no mention of records being kept on bondholder reorganizations, which was likely due to the multiplicity of legislation and mechanisms used to complete such reorganizations.[74] Despite the institution of the Dominion Bureau of Statistics in 1918, even that organization did not track business failures directly, relying instead on data published in *Dun's Statistical Review* or *Bradstreet's*, which it reprinted in its *Monthly Review of Business Statistics*.[75] Additionally, the term "business failure" was not defined for the purposes of these statistics.

A similar rationale explains why judges typically did not provide written reasons when ruling on CCAA matters. Each plan was tailored to the circumstances at hand, and the details were not regarded as having precedential value. As Fraser noted, "In Canada as elsewhere it is difficult to indicate any general principles applicable to reorganizations as the specific provision made for bondholders depends on many variable factors."[76]

The fact that the CCAA was enacted as a separate statute – distinct from the *Bankruptcy Act* – is also explained by the fact that it was essentially a bondholder remedy. The composition provisions of the *Bankruptcy Act* only bound unsecured creditor claims, for which that act operated as a final debt enforcement mechanism. Bondholders on the other hand had historically used provincial laws to redress situations of debtor default, which kept bondholders, instead of a bankruptcy trustee, in control of the proceedings. In the early 1930s there were also ethical concerns about bankruptcy trustees. Leading up to the 1932 *Bankruptcy Act* amendments, essentially anyone could call themselves a bankruptcy trustee – there were no required qualifications or regulatory oversight – which led to widespread abuses.[77] This provided a further reason for bondholders to avoid turning over responsibility and control of fragile reorganization proceedings to a bankruptcy trustee. In Canada, where corporate law federalism meant that new reorganization provisions could not simply be added to the relevant Companies Acts, the result was a stand-alone statute, purportedly justified as insolvency law, but which operated in practice like a secured creditor remedy under receivership or company law rather than bankruptcy proper.

Labour

In light of this historical background, it is not surprising that vocal stakeholder groups in modern restructurings, such as labour, were not active in insolvency policy-making in the 1930s. This study did not locate any mention of employee claims or collective bargaining agreements in business reorganizations from this period.[78] This reflects the fact that the CCAA was a bondholder remedy, highlighting the relatively weak rights of employee claims under provincial legislation of the time and the fact that labour was not yet a strong political force in Canada.

In his study *Canadian Labour in Politics*, Gad Horowitz notes that labour movements faced numerous obstacles to political organization in the early 1900s.[79] Among other things, the number of industrial labourers in Canada in the 1920s was still relatively small, and farmers and middle-class Canadians outnumbered labourers in the coalition that formed the Co-operative Commonwealth Federation (CCF).[80] A political party along the lines of the British Labour Party was therefore not practicable in 1930s Canada. A third-way political party would need to form an alliance of farmers, labour, socialists, and other Canadians if it was to pose a challenge to the well-established and well-financed Liberal and Conservative parties. Horowitz notes that it was not until the mid-1940s that labour began to wield more influence through political channels, but even then this was through the CCF, which remained more of a farmer- than a labour-based political party.[81]

Other Secured Creditors

While bondholders supported the new legislation, the CCAA's purported adjustment of secured creditors rights was heavily criticized by others who also appear to have represented the interests of secured creditors.[82] Critics of the CCAA, such as Manning, might have had in mind non-bondholder secured creditors with relatively small stakes in a given company, who were unable to influence the drafting of the plan of arrangement, or to veto the plan when it came time to vote. This might have included creditors with security interests in specific pieces of equipment, for instance. Duncan cited the necessity of an officer similar to a trustee in bankruptcy to look after the interests of those creditors who were not in a position to look after their own interests, either because they held small stakes in the company or were scattered throughout the country.[83] For this type of creditor, who otherwise enjoyed rights untouched by bankruptcy, the CCAA was a "definite retrogression," as Duncan declared in 1933.[84] As an extension of bondholder remedies, the CCAA did not conform to the conventional view of bankruptcy as a collective process, and as bankruptcy legislation the act left much to be desired.

Nevertheless, it is not clear to what extent these non-bondholder secured creditor rights were affected in any given reorganization. For instance, fixed charges under the *Bank Act* were often afforded priority by bondholders under the terms of the trust deed.[85] This arrangement was the result of business negotiations and, therefore, the extent to which such terms were routinely included in trust deeds is not clear.[86] It is also possible that business negotiations resulted in other trust deed provisions or reorganization plans that afforded priority to other secured or unsecured creditors on business grounds.[87] It is probably safe to assume that larger, more powerful creditors fared better than smaller, weaker ones, and that business negotiations reflected the relative bargaining power of the parties.

2 Historical Institutionalism and Recursivity of Law

Despite the novelty of the *form* that legal reform efforts took in respect of company restructuring, the *substance* of formal law came from the longstanding practice of bondholder reorganizations under majority provisions. The CCAA addressed the lack of majority provisions in many Canadian trust deeds by enshrining boilerplate majority provisions into a skeletal statute, which was designed to apply alongside the governing trust deed. As recorded in Hansard, the CCAA was based on a single provision of the English *Companies Act, 1929*,[88] which was in turn based on majority provisions in earlier English trust deeds. Large bondholding interests were the major beneficiaries of these changes, and saw their preferred, private, contractual remedies enshrined into legislative form. Law in practice informed and gave shape to law on the books.

In this way, the CCAA can be regarded as a manifestation of the institutional resilience of nineteenth-century bondholder reorganization practices. By giving legislative form to what had long been law in practice for bondholders, the act continued longstanding institutional arrangements concerning restructuring and created a "parchment institution." In large part because these institutional arrangements were put in parchment form, bondholder reorganization "law" endured and helped shape Canadian restructuring law several decades later, despite the preponderance of new forms of corporate financing and security, and re-characterization of the act as a debtor remedy. It is in large part due to the endurance of parchment institutions[89] that nineteenth-century bondholder reorganization forms the skeleton on which modern Canadian debtor-in-possession restructuring law is based.

3 Conclusion

As matter of history, the CCAA was not intended to promote the public interest, as that term is now understood. The public interest value of the CCAA (if any) was its design and implementation as a secured creditor remedy to prevent financial institution failures during the Great Depression. Accordingly, the public interest value of individual CCAA reorganizations should be evaluated in light of the benefits these arrangements also convey to large creditors.

Over 200 companies restructured under the CCAA in the first few years it was on the statute books[90] – a figure that exceeds conventional accounts of its usage as well as contemporary filing rates under the act.[91] This data in turn provides a basis for comparison and analysis with contemporary CCAA filing rates, which is the subject of recent scholarly writing.[92] It also dispels the assumption that CCAA applications only took off in the late 1980s, and points to other factors that may have influenced CCAA popularization and filing rates over time, such as economic and bankruptcy trends and increasingly liberal interpretations of the act.

This history of the CCAA therefore brings to light several novel findings with implications for current scholarship on corporate reorganization law in Canada. As a bondholder remedy based in receivership law, separate and distinct from the *Bankruptcy Act*, the CCAA relied on the fine distinction between insolvency and bankruptcy for both its validity and efficacy. The early history of the act helps explain the foundation and development of modern Canadian business reorganization under insolvency law.

4

Constitutional References and Changing Conceptions of Federalism, 1934–1937

It is believed that Parliament under the head of bankruptcy and insolvency has no power to legislate so as to enable secured creditors to be bound by the will of a majority in respect of the administration of their security.[1]

Harold E. Manning, *Fortnightly Law Journal*

In 1933, there was widespread doubt about whether the federal power to legislate on bankruptcy and insolvency could validly interfere with secured creditor rights.[2] This led to much uncertainty concerning the vires of the federal CCAA. In parliament, no objections were raised about the bill, and it passed into law with unanimous support. But this fact disguised the concern that existed about the act. While a few commentators spoke out against the constitutional validity of the CCAA, others who shared their views kept quiet. Over time, this silence obscured the constitutional controversy that the CCAA sparked in the legal community, as well as the way in which this statute shifted the boundaries between provincial and federal jurisdiction. The impetus to make changes to bankruptcy law is explained by the desperate need for restructuring legislation, the expediency of a federal approach, and the perceived risk that federal failure would jeopardize any future restructuring legislation – whether enacted by the provinces or parliament.

Parliamentarians knew that compulsorily binding secured claims under federal bankruptcy and insolvency law would likely provoke constitutional challenges, so they drafted the CCAA bill as tightly as possible to try to fit it within the federal lawmaking power. An early draft of the bill would have omitted any substantive provision affecting secured claims in favour of a section that would have harmonized the operation of the act with provincial legislation for adjusting secured debts, such as the Ontario *Judicature Act*. Writing about this draft bill, one lawyer stated:

> In so far as property rights of secured creditors were concerned, the draft [CCAA] bill was prepared upon the view that such rights, being property of creditors duly conveyed to them and established under Provincial law, no *ex post facto* event ... could deprive such property owners of their vested rights and those rights were not property of the debtor divisible amongst his creditors and were not subject to the legislative interference of Parliament under the head of Bankruptcy and Insolvency.[3]

The final version of the CCAA, however, provided for federal adjustment of both secured and unsecured claims.

In Canada, due to corporate law federalism, it was not possible for parliament to provide general restructuring legislation simply by adding a provision to corporate law, as England had done with the *Companies Act, 1929*. This approach would only allow parliament to provide restructuring legislation for federal companies, leaving the restructurings of provincially incorporated companies, such as Abitibi Power and Paper, outside of federal jurisdiction. As a fallback position, however, the Attorney General for Canada argued that, at minimum, the CCAA was valid in respect of Dominion companies under parliament's company law jurisdiction.[4]

In the Depression years, several provinces enacted laws relating to debt adjustment for farmers or individuals, including Ontario, Alberta, Saskatchewan, and Manitoba.[5] Such piece-meal solutions were considered inadequate to address the widespread economic crisis. Furthermore, much of the provincial legislation favoured debtors at the expense of large, secured creditors, which concerned members of DMIA and similar associations.[6]

The Bennett government proceeded alone with its CCAA bill, just as it did with much of its social reform legislation.[7] The CCAA did not fully address the need for effective business restructuring law; it did not apply to technically solvent companies, and this attracted criticism.[8] But the act did provide a national law for restructuring both federally and provincially incorporated companies, provided the debtor company was insolvent. The coordinating provisions of the CCAA provided a solution to the problem of complete company reorganization by incorporating the relevant companies legislation governing shareholder restructurings, and allowing all restructurings to proceed in a single forum.

1 The Great Depression and Legislative Experiments

Developments in the 1920s and early 1930s provided commercial and economic impetus for a coordinated statutory framework that would overcome inadequate provisions in trust deeds and establish a mechanism for adjusting both secured and unsecured debt. Rising federalism alongside deteriorating economic conditions and the inadequacy of existing reorganization practices played important roles in mustering the political will to pass the CCAA and other Canadian New Deal legislation.

This section situates the CCAA within this broader economic and political context, and illustrates the novelty and boldness of this new federal approach to corporate reorganization. Contrasting the outcome of the CCAA reference with those of the other New Deal references demonstrates the marked shift in the constitutional dividing line between federal and provincial jurisdiction over secured creditor rights. This expansion of the federal power would have significant ramifications for Canadian insolvency law over time, and helped prepare the way for the corporate restructuring developments of the 1980s and 1990s.

Canadian bankruptcy reform has tended to follow periods of recession or depression, and the 1930s reforms fit this pattern. An important difference, however, is that two of the significant bankruptcy and insolvency reforms of the 1930s were designed for the benefit of secured creditors – a first in Canadian history. The severity of the Great Depression prompted federal attempts to justify secured creditor remedies under insolvency law. In this context, the interests of bondholder interest groups, including life insurance companies and trust and loan companies, held particular sway with the Bennett government, leading to the proclamation of both the CCAA and FCAA.

For certain significant industries in Canada, economic conditions began to deteriorate before the Great Depression. The pulp and paper industry was in serious financial difficulty by the late 1920s, as epitomized by the Abitibi receivership. In the Canadian Dust Bowl, drought and falling prices for staple crops such as wheat led to the insolvencies of many farmers.[9] In the shipping industry, Canada Steamship Company faced severe financial difficulties, and eventually restructured under the CCAA.[10] The Depression also hit the Canadian steel industry particularly badly. By the 1930s, the two leading iron and steel firms – Algoma and Besco – were in receivership.[11] Stelco, the third leading iron and steel firm, fared relatively well through the Depression and did not reorganize.[12]

In an era where the term restructuring amounted to job losses in public parlance, the Bennett government intervened directly in such notable insolvencies as Algoma Steel and the Canadian National Railroad (CNR).[13] Algoma was too important an employer in Northern Ontario, and the CNR too large an employer, to leave the fate of these firms up to their creditors to decide.[14] For instance, the large number of layoffs associated with the private restructuring efforts of the CNR led the Bennett government to subsidize that railroad, essentially as part of its public works program.[15]

The depth and length of the Depression drained municipal and provincial resources through relief payments, and underscored the inability of these governments to deal with a crisis of such magnitude without federal assistance.[16] Many Canadian municipalities defaulted on their debts, which caused further financial difficulties for trust, loan, and insurance companies, which were large investors in bonds issued by all levels of government.[17] British Columbia, Alberta, Saskatchewan, and Manitoba were all in danger of default by the mid-1930s.[18] This prompted a significant shift toward greater federalism in Canada, essentially because the Dominion was the only level of government that could keep up relief payments as the Depression dragged on.

Prime Minister Mackenzie King (Liberal) was in office at the time of the 1929 stock market crash, but he lost the 1930 election to R.B. Bennett (Conservative), largely due to a widespread popular perception that he did not do enough to respond to the deepening Depression.[19] King saw the early stages of the economic downturn as a natural swing in business cycles, which helps explain his inaction in the first months of the crisis.[20] In contrast, the incoming Bennett government intervened to assist the struggling provinces by enacting social legislation and channelling relief funds to the Prairie provinces in particular.[21]

Initially federal relief efforts were not a straightforward matter. JCPC decisions, construing the division of powers as "watertight" compartments, left little room for direct federal involvement.[22] Leading up to the 1930s, JCPC decisions also provided wide interpretations of "property and civil rights in the province," which expanded provincial legislative powers at the expense of federal jurisdiction.[23] With few exceptions the JCPC adhered to a narrow interpretation of the federal legislative power, holding that the Dominion could only legislate on those subjects specifically enumerated under section 91.[24] However, the Depression, New Deal legislation, and Canadian constitutional references striking down relief efforts prompted renewed interest in the interpretation of the division of powers and Canadian federalism.[25]

The prospect of political alternatives further contributed to rising federalism. The Social Credit government in Alberta, elected in 1935, enacted a series of laws aimed at regulating banking, finance, and currency, but the measures overstepped the province's legislative powers. These statutes were either refused royal assent, disallowed, or struck down as unconstitutional.[26] In Saskatchewan, discontent with mounting farm debts leading up to the 1934 provincial election prompted the Bennett government to enact a federal farm debt adjustment statute – the FCAA – in order to stave off more radical provincial legislation.[27] The governments of both Bennett and King saw increased centralization as the best means of preventing the spread of anti-capitalist threats, which were generally regional in their base and focus.[28] Even more moderate political alternatives, such as the CCF and United Farmers, provided impetus for the Liberal and Conservative parties to find ways to address the deepening Depression in order to prevent electoral defeat.

Against this backdrop Bennett enacted a series of statutes, which were dubbed the Canadian "New Deal," to help address the growing crisis.[29] In his radio speeches introducing the legislation, Bennett asserted that the era of individualism was past and now government regulation and cooperation would carry the day.[30] Tellingly, his efforts attracted two main criticisms from the Liberal and CCF parties, as well as individual politicians, lawyers, and scholars: They overstepped the federal legislative power,[31] and their practical benefit as social legislation was minimal because they changed little about the status quo – in effect, they failed to live up to the promise of a New Deal.[32] The fact that commentators saw the New Deal legislation as both beyond the powers of the Dominion and ineffectual underscores the difficult constitutional balance Bennett tried to strike in order to provide Depression relief at the federal level.

The Liberal and CCF parties criticized the New Deal legislation for essentially supporting big business.[33] For example, it was in part the prospect of the financial failures of loan companies that prompted parliament to introduce the FCAA bill in 1934.[34] Although the preamble to the FCAA framed the act as a temporary Depression measure and emphasized its social policy purpose of helping farmers, these outcomes were ancillary to its purposes of staving off a more radical provincial alternative, and giving mortgagees a means of restructuring secured debt – something that was not possible under other federal legislation.[35] Concern for lenders was further reflected by the fact that the bill made no provision for "hopelessly insolvent farmers" – who could neither make a reasonable proposal under the act, nor discharge their debts in bankruptcy – despite the concerns raised about these farmers in the House of Commons.[36] When the FCAA was later upheld on constitutional reference, it made the more farmer-friendly provincial debt adjustment regimes ultra vires insofar as they applied to insolvent farmers.[37]

The CCAA was not officially part of the New Deal legislation and had little in the way of window dressing to support a view that it advanced a public or social policy objective.[38] The majority provisions enshrined into the CCAA advanced the interests of large security holders without meaningful safeguards for other creditors or stakeholders.[39] Furthermore, the CCAA was enacted to help large financial interests – bondholders who needed a way to reorganize faltering companies.

Academics and the media focused on the social reform aspects of the New Deal statutes, while the changes to these bankruptcy and insolvency laws went nearly unnoticed.[40] The constitutional references that struck down most of the New Deal legislation – provoking the ire of many Canadian commentators – upheld the FCAA, and reaffirmed the CCAA reference decision, with significant ramifications for the interpretation of the division of powers concerning bankruptcy and insolvency and property rights.

2 Constitutional Interpretation and Legal Change

Up until 1986 and 1992, respectively, English and Canadian bankruptcy legislation generally did not compulsorily bind secured creditor claims. The CCAA and FCAA were singular exceptions. Even today, secured claims are only bound under certain insolvency restructuring regimes, whereas they are unaffected in traditional bankruptcy proceedings. Thus, a key advantage of securing one's claim – then as now – is that it allows creditors to exercise debt enforcement remedies irrespective of whether the debtor is in bankruptcy.

Taking security elevates one's claim over unsecured creditors because, instead of pro rata sharing through bankruptcy, secured creditors are entitled to recover against the security for up to the full value of their claim. In England and Canada, the distinction between secured and unsecured creditors is a fundamental concept of commercial law. The strength of the secured creditor's claim stems from their proprietary interest in the collateral provided by the debtor, and this collateral, in turn, is specifically excluded from the debtor's estate in the event of the debtor's bankruptcy.[41]

At a conceptual level there are important differences between unsecured and secured creditor remedies. Bankruptcy was a remedy of last resort for unsecured creditors in the event that the debtor absconded or became insolvent. The stay of proceedings imposed by bankruptcy law and pro rata sharing of the bankrupt estate addressed the issue of a creditors' race to enforce their claims against the debtor's pool of dwindling assets. This solved a collective action problem among unsecured creditors. In contrast, bondholders had long provided for collective action through majority provisions in their governing trust deed. As described by bankruptcy historian Thomas G.W. Telfer, Canada's first permanent bankruptcy law was in large part the product of lobbying efforts by trade groups representing unsecured creditors.[42] Thus, both in principle and in practice, bankruptcy is fundamentally an unsecured creditor remedy.

The ultimate remedies for secured creditors, on the other hand, were seizure of collateral or receivership, neither of which is predicated on a situation of insolvency. A missed payment can trigger enforcement efforts by a secured creditor, even though the debtor may be considered solvent. What differentiates secured from unsecured lending arrangements is the degree of control that the secured creditor contracts for ex ante. Secured creditors often include clauses that impose restrictions on the business (commonly known as restrictive covenants), in addition to taking a proprietary interest in the debtor's collateral. In other words, secured creditors proactively use contracts to establish remedies that are stronger than those afforded by bankruptcy law and, in so doing, contract out of being compulsorily bound to bankruptcy law.

These two conceptual paradigms imbued the Canadian division of legislative powers as they applied to debtor-creditor relations. While most debtor-creditor relationships are governed pursuant to the provinces' jurisdiction over property and civil rights,[43] the federal bankruptcy and insolvency power is more circumscribed. The *Constitution Act, 1867* gives parliament the express and exclusive jurisdiction to legislate in cases of bankruptcy or insolvency. Since bankruptcy was, both conceptually and practically, an unsecured creditor remedy, it followed that parliament could not rely on its bankruptcy and insolvency law power to validly adjust secured creditor rights. Thus, the rights of secured creditors remained within provincial jurisdiction, whether or not the debtor was insolvent. Over time, this view ossified into a traditional interpretation of sections 91(21) and 92(13), which was so pervasive it tended to go without saying. This in turn lent constitutional significance to the distinction between secured and unsecured credit in Canada.

Within this context, the CCAA and FCAA were bold pieces of legislation. By binding secured creditor claims, these statutes departed from the English and Canadian experience of bankruptcy and insolvency legislation. They plainly overstepped parliamentary jurisdiction over bankruptcy and insolvency, as it was then understood. To the minds of many lawyers, they were clearly ultra vires parliament. Yet the presence of these two statutes on the books carried potentially significant implications for the provinces due to the negative implication that there "shall not be any other legislation on a concurrent subject by a province."[44] Unless the CCAA and FCAA were struck down as unconstitutional, provincial jurisdiction over secured creditor rights could henceforth be limited, in effect, by federal insolvency legislation.

Doubt about the constitutional validity of the CCAA caused many prominent restructuring lawyers to refuse to recommend it to their clients.[45] They were justifiably concerned that an unhappy creditor would be able to successfully challenge a CCAA restructuring on constitutional grounds, making efforts to use the new statute risky, and probably futile. This skepticism within the legal community prompted the Bennett government to refer the CCAA to the SCC for a ruling on its constitutional validity. [46] On 18 January 1934, Minister of Justice Hugh Guthrie submitted a report to the Office of the Privy Council, indicating that "[s]everal opinions of leading counsel have been given to the effect that parliament did exceed its power [in enacting the CCAA]," and stating "that it is essential for the satisfactory enforcement of [the CCAA's] provisions that any doubts should be set at rest."[47]

The CCAA and FCAA implicitly rested on a broader conception of bankruptcy and insolvency than earlier English and Canadian statutes. Instead of drawing the conceptual (and hence constitutional) dividing line between secured and unsecured claims, these statutes proposed that the dividing line be drawn between solvent and insolvent debtors. Thus, both acts contemplated a significant expansion of the federal insolvency power as it was then understood. The constitutional references that followed served as judicial referenda for this new conception of insolvency and its implications for interpreting the division of legislative powers.

The facta filed in connection with the CCAA reference discussed the issue of jurisdiction over secured creditor rights. The Attorney General for Quebec submitted that the CCAA did not conform to the definition of "bankruptcy" as established in *RBC v Larue*.[48] Furthermore, the CCAA did not provide for a rateable distribution of the debtor's assets among its creditors.[49] Although the act purported to provide for a scheme of arrangement for the general benefit of creditors, it contained none of the safeguards used in the *Bankruptcy Act* to protect the general body of creditors.[50]

The Attorney General for Canada submitted that the CCAA was valid federal legislation in relation to bankruptcy and insolvency. The federal government asserted that parliament had ample power to legislate respecting secured creditors under insolvency legislation.[51] In particular, they submitted that parliament may validly interfere with and modify civil rights in the case of a bankrupt or insolvent, and that doing so necessarily involved infringing on the provincial power over property and civil rights.[52] They also noted that determining priorities among creditors was part of every bankruptcy system.[53] The Attorney General for Canada submitted that it was within federal jurisdiction to provide that secured creditors shall be bound by any composition or arrangement that was approved by three-fourths of their number and by the court.[54] In essence, the Attorney General for Canada invited the court to extend by analogy the parliamentary ability to re-adjust unsecured creditor claims in cases of insolvency, to cover secured creditor claims as well.

In the alternative, the Attorney General for Canada submitted that, in so far as the CCAA related to Dominion companies, it was valid federal legislation in relation to companies with other than provincial objects.[55] This fallback position is telling for illustrating a degree of federal uncertainty about the validity of the CCAA as insolvency legislation, as well as connecting the objects of the act to the English practice of restructuring companies through corporate law. Had the CCAA been upheld as part of parliament's legislative jurisdiction over Dominion companies, it likely would have produced a fragmented landscape of federal and provincial restructuring regimes, similar to the field of securities regulation.[56] In that case, federal jurisdiction over corporate restructuring legislation would have stemmed, rather bizarrely, from parliament's power to legislate for the "peace, order and good government" of Canada.[57] The constitutional dividing line between federal and provincial jurisdiction would have been clearer and firmer by virtue of being tied to the company's jurisdiction of incorporation. In the event, the federal *Companies Act* had contained provisions to facilitate shareholder compromises and arrangements with those of creditors under the *Winding-up Act* from as early as 1923.[58] In 1934, parliament extended these harmonizing provisions to companies undergoing restructuring under the CCAA as well.[59]

The SCC decision did not directly address the constitutional issue surrounding secured creditor rights, nor did it construe the CCAA as part of federal companies legislation. Instead, in its short judgment the court focused on whether compositions or arrangements were a valid part of bankruptcy and insolvency law.[60] Citing examples of composition and arrangement provisions in various bankruptcy and insolvency laws enacted before and after Confederation, the SCC unanimously upheld the CCAA as intra vires the legislative power of parliament. The court noted that it was valid for parliament to legislate in respect of companies that were insolvent, but not yet in bankruptcy proceedings, with a view to financially rehabilitating the debtor.[61] Such a scheme could benefit creditors as a group, even if not all creditors were treated in exactly the same way, and may also benefit the company's share-holders.[62] The court allowed that there may be a double aspect to such rehabilitation schemes, but stated that "when treated as matters pertaining to bankruptcy and insolvency they clearly fall within the legislative authority of the Dominion."[63]

Due to its silence on the issue of secured creditor rights, the SCC decision did little to allay concerns about the constitutional validity of the CCAA. Following release of the SCC decision the Deputy Attorney General for Ontario, I.A. Humphries, wrote to his opposite number in Quebec, stating, "I feel quite strongly with regard to the Court's decision in the Companies' Creditors Arrangement Act as, to my mind, this is a direct interference of property and civil rights."[64] In his reply, the Deputy Attorney General for Quebec, Charles Lanctot, wrote that he was "greatly surprised and disappointed at the [judgment] … the course of the argument seemed favourable to us and I do not see what could have impressed their Lordships to such an extent."[65]

The *CCAA Reference* represented such a change in thinking about the division of powers as it related to secured credit that there was a general view that it would be overturned if ever challenged before the JCPC.[66] The omission of a substantive discussion of the constitutional issue around secured creditor rights led Manning to argue in 1935 that the act may still be invalid in this respect.[67] Following the *CCAA Reference* decision in 1934, efforts to address the restructuring crisis shifted to provincial legislatures. Most notably, Ontario amended its *Judicature Act* to facilitate bondholder restructurings of companies such as Abitibi. According to Stanley Edwards, it was the constitutional reference concerning the FCAA in 1937, in which the JCPC specifically upheld parliament's jurisdiction to adjust secured creditor rights through insolvency legislation, which finally brought closure to this issue.[68]

In the FCAA reference, the SCC found the act intra vires by a majority of 4 to 1 (Cannon J. dissenting.)[69] The majority decision, written by Duff, C.J.C., acknowledged the court was bound to accept the validity of compositions or arrangements as a component part of bankruptcy and insolvency legislation based on its decision in the *CCAA Reference*.[70] The SCC next considered whether the legislation was intra vires the legislative power of parliament, insofar as it prevented secured creditors from exercising their ordinary remedies and purported to adjust their claims as part of a composition or arrangement.[71] Relying on Lord Selborne's broad characterization of "bankruptcy and insolvency" in the 1875 case of *L-Union St. Jacques de Montreal*, the majority held that parliament had wide discretion to legislate with respect to bankruptcy and insolvency, which was "not necessarily limited in the exercise of that discretion by reference to the particular provisions of bankruptcy legislation in England prior to the date of *The B.N.A. Act*."[72]

The SCC acknowledged that bankruptcy legislation had not typically deprived mortgagees of their right to resort to their security.[73] However, in the court's view, this aspect of historical bankruptcy legislation did not justify the conclusion that parliament could not exercise its discretion to adjust secured creditor rights as part of "a system for the administration of the estates of insolvents."[74] It was, therefore, within the discretion of parliament to adjust secured creditor rights in insolvency legislation, even in instances where the secured creditor did not assent to a compromise.[75]

These decisions represented a break with the rationales underpinning earlier cases, such as *L-Union St. Jacques de Montreal* and *Atty-Gen of Ontario v Atty-Gen for Can*.[76] Despite characterizing "bankruptcy and insolvency" in broad terms, the *L-Union St. Jacques de Montreal* case actually upheld Quebec legislation to prevent the "financial embarrassment" (read: insolvency) of a benevolent society. In this case the JCPC found the provincial legislation was valid on the grounds that it related to "a matter merely of a local or private nature in the province" within the meaning of section 92(16) of the *Constitution Act, 1867*.[77] In *Atty-Gen of Ontario v Atty-Gen for Can*, the JCPC upheld the validity of the Ontario *Assignments and Preferences Act* on the basis that voluntary assignments to postpone judgments and executions were "ancillary" to bankruptcy and insolvency law.[78] Although these cases made passing reference to the potentially broad construction of the federal bankruptcy and insolvency law power, they actually stood for broad interpretations of provincial jurisdiction. The SCC thus appeared to reference these cases to connect its broad construction of section 91(21) in the CCAA and FCAA references, with earlier mention of the potentially broad, yet unrealized, scope of parliament's bankruptcy and insolvency power.

The provinces also challenged the legitimacy of the FCAA's provisions adjusting the claims of a province as a creditor of the estate.[79] In response to this argument the majority of the SCC held that federal bankruptcy and insolvency law could validly take away Crown privilege and treat these claims as ordinary creditor claims.[80] This was another significant departure from what was customary for Canadian bankruptcy law at that time. In point of fact, it was not until 1992 and 1997, respectively, that most Crown claims were bound by the BIA and CCAA.[81] The significance of this constitutional ruling increased over the twentieth century because of the growth of income taxation as a financial obligation on individuals and companies and the corresponding importance of tax monies as a source of government revenue.[82]

The FCAA and other New Deal references were all subsequently appealed to the JCPC, which handed down its decisions in 1937. The SCC's decision in the FCAA reference was upheld in a unanimous judgment, written by Lord Thankerton, which held that secured creditor rights could be validly adjusted through federal bankruptcy and insolvency legislation.[83] On the other hand, the JCPC struck down almost all the other New Deal statutes as beyond the legislative powers of parliament.[84]

The narrow construction of the Canadian division of powers adopted by the SCC and JCPC made the decisions on the constitutionality of the CCAA and FCAA – both of which were held intra vires in their entirety – all the more significant. These decisions established a new area of exclusive federal jurisdiction. For the first time in Canadian history, the provinces were barred from adjusting secured creditor rights in cases of insolvency – an area that had been, until then, exclusively within provincial jurisdiction[85] – and, by virtue of negative implication, provincial debt adjustment legislation enacted in response to the Depression became ultra vires insofar as it applied to insolvent companies or farmers.[86] The courts' broad construction of the federal bankruptcy and insolvency law power remains difficult to reconcile with its decisions in the other New Deal references.

The CCAA and FCAA judgments were watershed moments in the development of Canadian insolvency law. There was little public interest in the CCAA reference, which was the subject of only a handful of journal articles and trade publications. On the other hand, the farming crisis in the Canadian prairies received international public attention.[87] Nevertheless, legal commentators tended to focus on the JCPC decisions that struck down much of the Canadian New Deal and focused less on the FCAA. Those who did discuss the FCAA usually approved of the court's decision.[88] In defending all of the JCPC's New Deal decisions, the British scholar A. Berriedale Keith considered the FCAA "unassailable" as bankruptcy and insolvency legislation, as did Canadian authors such as Frank Scott who criticized the other New Deal decisions.[89]

The fact that constitutional law commentators agreed with the CCAA and FCAA references is astonishing. One is left with the impression that they did not really understand commercial law. The adjustment of secured creditor rights contemplated by both the CCAA and FCAA was a marked departure from prevailing conceptions of bankruptcy and insolvency law and the traditional interpretation of sections 91(21) and 92(13). Criticism of this interpretation of the division of powers seems to have come almost exclusively from the corporate and commercial bar.[90] To the minds of these lawyers, the CCAA and the FCAA did not pass the "pith and substance" test as federal insolvency legislation. Taken together, this gives the discomfiting impression that the courts did not appreciate the significant change in constitutional interpretation that their decision would bring about.

In effect, the CCAA enshrined a longstanding secured creditor remedy into federal law. By upholding the constitutional validity of this statute, the court justified this exercise of parliamentary jurisdiction and for the first time legitimized the financial condition of insolvency as a dividing line between federal and provincial jurisdiction. Consequently, this significantly expanded the federal bankruptcy and insolvency law power. Due to the doctrine of negative implication, the corollary of expanding federal jurisdiction in this area would be a corresponding contraction of provincial jurisdiction over secured creditor rights.

In the years following these constitutional decisions, legal debates moved beyond the question of whether or not federal insolvency law could validly affect secured creditor rights. Debates shifted to other issues surrounding the treatment of secured claims under insolvency law,[91] with one noteworthy exception. In 1986, J. Murray Ferron, Registrar in Bankruptcy and Master of the Supreme Court of Ontario, argued in the *Canadian Bankruptcy Reports* that the FCAA – by then a dead letter – was unconstitutional for purporting to adjust property rights in the absence of majority creditor support.[92] The author's argument, however, reveals the shift in constitutional interpretation that the CCAA and FCAA references brought about. Ferron was advocating for a majority voting requirement in order to establish the vires of a federal regime for adjusting secured debts. He did not suggest that the adjustment of secured creditor rights in insolvency was beyond parliament's jurisdiction altogether.

Notwithstanding its constitutional validity, the CCAA was still regarded with skepticism by many lawyers, unsecured creditors, trade groups, and lawmakers. This was fuelled in large part by confusion about its objects and its widespread, but unintended, use by debtor companies to restructure their unsecured and trade debts only. Although intended to be a secured creditor remedy, this purpose was downplayed due to concerns about the act's constitutional validity. The CCAA reference decision further obscured this purpose by emphasizing the potential benefits of restructuring for all kinds of creditors and avoiding the thorny issue of secured creditor rights. This contributed to a general impression that the act was a debtor remedy, a view that was reinforced by its use by hundreds of companies for this purpose.

Broad dissatisfaction with the CCAA in particular, and resistance to the idea of restructuring as a debtor remedy more generally, led to repeated repeal efforts. The first repeal bill was introduced to parliament in 1938, one year after the JCPC conclusively upheld the validity of federal bankruptcy and insolvency law to adjust secured creditor claims.

3 Historical Institutionalism and Recursivity of Law

Once the CCAA was enacted and affirmed by constitutional reference, it set debt reorganization on a distinct path that became increasingly difficult to alter over time, despite the unpredictability and unlikelihood of this outcome from a pre-1930s viewpoint. Since the CCAA and FCAA were constitutional, provincial attempts to enact similar legislation were ultra vires by implication – due to the doctrine of negative implication and the JCPC's view of the division of powers as "watertight" compartments. To overturn the JCPC decisions on this point would require a constitutional amendment or a subsequent appeal to the court of last resort in which the JCPC overturned its earlier decision. Both of these possibilities were unlikely. Furthermore, due to the nature of case law precedent, lower courts were bound to follow the JCPC's decision, as illustrated in the 1938 Ontario Court of Appeal's decision concerning the Abitibi restructuring.[93] Accordingly, the JCPC's view of where debt reorganization fell in the division of powers reproduced itself in subsequent judicial decisions, particularly concerning the constitutionality of provincial legislation to effect debt compromises, such as *Re Orderly Payments*.[94] The interpretation of the division of powers from the CCAA and FCAA references on this point was thus further entrenched through case law with the passage of time.

Both the CCAA and FCAA quickly generated positive feedback in terms of hundreds and tens of thousands of debt compromises carried out in the 1930s under each act, respectively. Whatever practitioner views of the CCAA were, these actors still coordinated the act as a restructuring mechanism after it was upheld, essentially because it was the only viable restructuring option. When attempts were made to restructure insolvent companies under provincial legislation, as with Abitibi, the courts ruled that the new federal act had to be used instead. It is fair to assume that many companies that needed restructuring – particularly in pulp and paper – were already insolvent by the time the CCAA was enacted in 1933. The numerous uses and applications of the act led to a high degree of asset specificity, reinforced by further positive feedback, thereby contributing to path dependence of the CCAA, and federal insolvency law, as mechanisms for restructuring the debts of insolvent companies and farmers. Institutional arrangements concerning corporate reorganizations were thus formally adopted into the federal sphere of legislative power. These decisions set in motion a centralizing trend in Canadian debt reorganization legislation.

Since early federal efforts to deal with the corporate restructuring crisis of the 1930s helped place reorganization on a distinct path, it is worth briefly considering a counterfactual scenario. What might have happened if provincial legislation, such as the Ontario *Judicature Act Amendment Act, 1935* had been enacted *prior to* the CCAA? Many practitioners at the time favoured a provincial approach, which would not be limited to technically insolvent companies or subject to constitutional uncertainties. Had the Ontario legislation been enacted first, it likely would have generated positive feedback and asset specificity, just as the CCAA did. The existence of this provincial legislation may have altered the outcome of the CCAA reference, as the CCAA may have appeared to be trenching on an existing exercise of provincial legislative power. It is worth emphasizing the fact that up until the CCAA, bondholder reorganizations had always been carried out under provincial law. Thus there was a longstanding exercise of provincial jurisdiction in this area. In the result, however, the constitutionality of the CCAA led to the curtailment of subsequent provincial restructuring legislation, which thereafter had to be confined to solvent companies only. Had the Ontario legislation been enacted first, however, the result may have been quite the opposite, with the CCAA being struck down in favour of a provincial approach. This outcome would have been more in keeping with the traditional interpretation of sections 91(21) and 92(13). This counterfactual scenario illustrates the importance of the sequencing of events in positive feedback processes, where the early head start of one approach (such as the CCAA) may be amplified, rather than cancelled out over time.

A further ramification of the CCAA constitutional reference and subsequent Ontario legislation is that it helped lay the groundwork for a paradigm of restructuring as a solution for insolvency, by virtue of drawing insolvency as the dividing line between federal and provincial jurisdiction. The solvency or insolvency of a company was not a particularly important consideration in bondholder reorganizations prior to the 1930s. Bondholders did not need to, nor did they want to, wait until the company was technically insolvent in order to restructure bond repayments. Bondholders often carried out reorganizations to *prevent* a situation of technical insolvency. Moreover, since secured creditor remedies generally fell within provincial jurisdiction, bondholder remedies were found in provincial law irrespective of the debtor's financial picture prior to 1933. After this point, however, constitutional references, positive feedback, and path dependence helped establish restructuring parameters such that *effective* legislation for conducting complete company reorganizations usually *only* applied to insolvent enterprises. This facilitated construction of a de novo legal concept in which restructuring was cast as a remedy for company insolvency, and this framed the way future parties interpreted their issues in relation to restructuring legislation.[95]

The historical reasons for this are largely due to the fact that provincial legislation – when it existed at all – did not necessarily provide for complete restructuring prior to 1933. And after 1933, provincial legislation effectively *could not* provide for complete restructuring of insolvent enterprises due to the CCAA and FCAA reference decisions. Hence, provincial legislation such as the Ontario *Judicature Act Amendment Act* probably had limited application during the Great Depression, since many companies were insolvent by the time Ontario enacted this legislation in 1935. As illustrated by the high-profile Abitibi case, the enormous cost and uncertainty created by having to re-do a restructuring plan under federal legislation if, by the time it came to applying for judicial approval, the debtor was technically insolvent, likely deterred parties from using provincial reorganization legislation.

4 Conclusion

The enactment of the CCAA represented a significant development in Canadian insolvency and restructuring law. By compulsorily adjusting secured creditor rights, this coordinating act was the first insolvency statute capable of effecting complete company reorganization. Like the other New Deal statutes, the CCAA represented a novel exercise and extension of parliament's legislative power, as it was then understood. Unlike most of the New Deal legislation, the CCAA and FCAA were both declared intra vires. As a result, compulsory adjustment of secured creditor rights became a valid part of bankruptcy and insolvency law based on a very broad conception of federal jurisdiction by the JCPC of the 1930s. This paved the way for a migration of company and debt reorganization into the sphere of insolvency law.

5

Efforts to Repeal the *Companies' Creditors Arrangement Act*, 1938–1953

It appeared that the *Companies' Creditors Arrangement Act* was passed without too careful regard for the protection of the trade creditors of mercantile concerns ... since the arrangements under the *Companies' Creditors Arrangement Act* were not in the hands of an official trustee as under the *Bankruptcy Act*, it was found in a number of cases that the trade creditors' interests were frequently and seriously prejudiced.[1]

Hon. Stuart S. Garson (Minister of Justice, Liberal),
Debates of the House of Commons, 23 January 1953

1 Calls for Repeal

By 1938 there were two chief complaints against the CCAA: It was being widely abused by insolvent companies to reorganize unsecured and trade debts only;[2] and the act was an emergency measure, which was no longer warranted due to the improving economic situation. In 1938, Ernest Bertrand (Liberal) tabled a private member's bill to repeal the CCAA.[3] Parliamentary discussion of the bill revealed a third issue: a potential loophole that could facilitate fraudulent claims. Around the same time, reform efforts were also underway in the United States, with a view to instituting more oversight and preventing abuses in reorganization proceedings.[4] A few years later, England conducted an inquiry into the actions of protective committees and trustees in bondholder reorganizations, which resulted in amendments to the *Companies Act* in 1947.[5] Similar concerns about the actions of trustees and bondholder protective committees arose in Canada in the 1940s, and represented a fourth complaint about the CCAA. In all three countries, reform efforts centered on real as well as perceived abuses of business reorganization legislation. Unlike the United States and England, however, Canada's efforts to reform insolvency legislation by repealing the CCAA did not come to fruition, and parliament did not pass significant amendments to the act until 1953.

Three of these four issues are discussed here. The second complaint – the assertions that the CCAA was emergency legislation and that the Canadian economy had sufficiently recovered – was inaccurate. Historical evidence shows that the CCAA was not enacted as a temporary measure in response to the Depression – something that Cahan (MP, Conservative) raised in the House debates over the repeal bill – although the Depression was a catalyst for its enactment.[6] Furthermore, by 1938, Canada was in a recession, as was the United States.[7] While conditions in 1936 and part of 1937 showed signs of rapid recovery, by mid-1937 economic activity in Canada dropped off sharply, the wheat crop failed, and in early autumn the stock market collapsed.[8] The economy did not pick up again until the start of the Second World War, in 1939.

Evidence presented at the House of Commons Standing Committee on Banking and Commerce raised serious concerns over abuse of the CCAA to adjust unsecured and trade claims. Uncontested statistics presented by the Montreal Board of Trade showed that the act was resorted to frequently, and was used to restructure over 200 companies in Montreal between 1933 and 1938.[9] A separate historical document affirms that a large number of CCAA applications were made in Montreal during this time. In a 1935 memorandum to the Honourable E.N. Rhodes (Minister of Finance), H.F. Gordon (Department of Finance) advised that he had learned that filing fees collected by Quebec for CCAA applications made in Montreal amounted to over $20,000 per year.[10] Most of these reorganizations were thought not to have involved bondholder oversight, although no evidence was offered in support of this view. Lacking any administrative structure, such as that provided under the FCAA or *Bankruptcy Act*, many complaints arose that debtors had used the act to force unfair plans on their unsecured creditors.[11] In effect, a CCAA application barred unsecureds and junior creditors from petitioning the company into bankruptcy or suing for recovery of debts.[12] Unsecureds had no control over the debtor's property, no access to the company's financial statements, and no third-party to verify the debtor's representations.[13] Thus, unsecured and trade creditors were at the mercy of debtor companies that invoked the act.

As submitted by the Montreal Board of Trade, the central issue surrounding the CCAA was "the fact that the debtor may control both its own affairs and the machinery for considering a proposal."[14] In contrast, use of the CCAA to effect bondholder reorganization raised no complaints, and was supported even by those who complained of the act's use by companies to restructure unsecured debt. Thus, complaints stemmed from the fact that the CCAA was designed as an extension of receivership proceedings and lacked the safeguards needed in the absence of oversight by a trustee or receiver. In essence, the abuse complained of was the use of the act as a debtor-in-possession restructuring mechanism.

2 Interest Groups

Politicians

The Conservatives and Liberals agreed on the passage of the CCAA in 1933, and reached a consensus again about the importance of retaining the act in 1938. The Conservatives, who introduced the bill in 1933, generally favoured greater federal intervention to coordinate existing restructuring procedures. Prime Minister Bennett was interested in getting provincial support for the CCAA and New Deal legislation, which would test the limits of the federal legislative power.[15] However, when that support was not forthcoming, he proceeded with the new legislation anyway.[16] Moreover, in 1935 Bennett himself – along with King and the general concurrence of the House of Commons – favoured constitutional amendments to give Canada the power to amend its constitution in order to get around the JCPC's narrow interpretation of the federal legislative power.[17] Bennett saw constitutional amendment as a means of conferring on the federal government the power to enact social legislation to deal with Depression conditions. It appears that the Conservative government itself doubted the constitutional validity of much of its New Deal reform package. Bennett's stance is perhaps explained by a combination of factors: The Tories were inclined to favour government intervention; difficult economic circumstances warranted urgent action; the dire conditions sparked renewed interest in federalism; and the government was eager to bolster waning political support ahead of an impending election.[18]

The Liberal position is harder to account for because subsequent Liberal governments adopted different positions toward the CCAA. While there was no Liberal opposition in either the House of Commons or Senate when the CCAA was enacted in 1933, Prime Minister King's government viewed the New Deal legislation, including the FCAA, as largely unconstitutional outside of a situation of national emergency.[19] While not opposed to the New Deal legislation in principle, King favoured an approach that would put the entire agenda on sounder constitutional footing. Accordingly, the Liberals favoured either a constitutional amendment giving the federal government authority to act, or a legislative framework that would work by coordinating with provincial legislatures.[20] Thus, Liberal support for the 1933 CCAA bill probably stemmed from the fact that it was largely harmonizing legislation, which would operate alongside other provincial and federal laws.

Bennett originally approached the problem of implementing social legislation with the idea of "legislative coordination"; however, the idea of provincial-Dominion conferences to consider the problem met with a cold response from the provinces.[21] Bennett's government also favoured constitutional amendment, but efforts in that regard were mired in provincial-federal controversy and made little progress.[22] Thus, while the Liberal position on this point sounded good in theory, there is reason to doubt whether it would have worked in practice.

Efforts to repeal the CCAA in 1938 ultimately failed in part because the issue was folded into a substantial overhaul of all Canadian bankruptcy and insolvency statutes. That project was to have taken place in 1939 and would have incorporated a company reorganization element into the *Bankruptcy Act*.[23] In 1939, however, bankruptcy reform was not taken up, possibly due to the outbreak of the Second World War, and it was not until 1946 that the idea of repealing the CCAA resurfaced in parliament.[24] Committee Minutes from 1938 show that Liberals MPs, including the Liberal MP who introduced the 1938 repeal bill, were amenable to a CCAA-type scheme, provided that there was secured creditor support and that abuses of unsecured creditor rights by debtor companies could be satisfactorily prevented.

Montreal and Toronto Boards of Trade

The Montreal and Toronto Boards of Trade[25] represented distinct interest groups with stakes in business reorganizations. The Montreal Board of Trade spearheaded efforts to repeal the CCAA in 1938, and their representative presented extensive evidence to demonstrate the abuses of that act by companies seeking to reorganize unsecured debt only.[26] The Toronto Board of Trade's representative, however, highlighted the usefulness and necessity of retaining the act for bondholders.[27] The minutes of the meeting indicate that the two organizations had conferred beforehand and had agreed on a compromise that would address both positions: limiting the CCAA to companies with outstanding bond issues under a trust deed and running in favour of a trustee.[28] This amendment would mean that the CCAA could only be used in cases with bondholder oversight. This would ensure that companies could not use the act to take advantage of their junior and unsecured creditors, but would retain the CCAA for bondholder-led reorganizations of both secured and unsecured debt.

The proportion of secured and unsecured creditor interests represented by the Montreal and Toronto Boards of Trade helps explain their respective stances on the CCAA repeal bill. In the 1930s, the Montreal Board of Trade represented a significant number of companies that held unsecured claims or small non-bondholder secured claims in an insolvency scenario, such as trade creditors. Accordingly, in 1938, this interest group voiced its general concern that the CCAA facilitated fraud and abuse of unsecured creditor rights by giving companies the ability to implement debt adjustment plans. The Montreal Board of Trade believed that most instances of the act's use involved compromises of only unsecured debt – a point that was not disputed.[29] All groups represented at the committee meeting agreed that there was no evidence of complaints about the use of the CCAA by secured creditors.[30]

By the early 1900s Toronto was a large industrial, commercial, and financial centre in Canada and began to rival Montreal as the economic centre of the country.[31] Toronto businesses were more heavily concentrated in financial services than those in Montreal, and were therefore more likely to be bondholders – the primary beneficiaries of CCAAs.[32] Insurance companies were key figures in CCAA reorganizations in the 1930s, as they typically had large bondholdings in Canadian corporate securities. Toronto was the headquarters of a number of large insurance companies, such as Canada Life, which invested heavily in Canadian bonds and mortgages.[33] Sun Life, headquartered in Montreal, was also a large Canadian insurer and investor at this time; however, during the 1920s it invested more heavily in the United States than in Canada, and in stocks rather than bonds.[34] Accordingly, the CCAA was not as important to Sun Life as it was to other Canadian insurance companies, which had a larger proportion of their investments in Canadian bonds. Thus, the Toronto Board of Trade represented major Canadian bondholder interests, for which the CCAA provided a useful reorganization tool.

Dominion Mortgage and Investments Association

The DMIA represented "important insurance companies and loan and trust companies throughout Canada," and it was often called on to advise and render opinions on possible reorganization plans, including those conducted under the CCAA.[35] Given the membership of DMIA, it is unsurprising that the organization favoured retaining the CCAA, which provided a valuable restructuring tool for its members.

DMIA became aware of unsecureds' dissatisfaction with the CCAA in June 1937, prior to Ernest Bertrand introducing his repeal bill. At that time DMIA was asked to join other interested groups to consider the problem.[36] DMIA formed a sub-committee to study the matter, consisting of representatives of member companies interested in corporate bonds. This sub-committee recommended addressing the unsatisfactory features of the act with rules and restricting the application of the CCAA to companies that had issued securities, whether secured or unsecured, in favour of a trustee.[37] For companies without such an issue of securities, the committee recommended making provision for their restructuring under the *Bankruptcy Act*, where a bankruptcy trustee could oversee the process.[38] Thus, DMIA was prepared to make submissions by the time Bertrand introduced his bill in parliament to repeal the CCAA in 1938.

When the bill was referred to the House of Commons Banking and Commerce Committee, DMIA retained William Kaspar Fraser, a Toronto lawyer, to make representations on its behalf.[39] Fraser explained the importance of retaining the act and presented the suggestions formulated by the association's sub-committee, which persuaded Bertrand to withdraw his repeal bill.[40]

According to DMIA, the CCAA filled a gap in Canadian legislation by providing a mechanism whereby a reorganization could be effected without a traditional receivership, liquidation, or a realization sale – all of which led to a deterioration of the credit, securities, and standing of the company in question.[41] According to DMIA's representative, the slightest prospect of a company entering bankruptcy acted to deter security holders from pursuing reorganization.[42]

In addition, many issues of Canadian bonds did not have adequate majority provisions for effecting bondholder reorganizations under the governing trust deed. Fraser stated that this omission was necessary in order to placate investors in the United States, where such provisions were not generally used.[43] Americans adopted an alternate approach to bondholder reorganizations. Fraser provided a brief sketch of the American approach under section 77B of the US *Bankruptcy Act*, which essentially provided a CCAA-like procedure.[44] The key differences were that section 77B required only a two-thirds majority, and instead of holding a meeting, creditors provided their vote in writing.[45]

Like the other interest groups represented at the meeting, DMIA agreed that the act should be restricted to companies with outstanding trust deeds, as suggested by the Montreal and Toronto Boards of Trade, since this would preserve its use for restructuring corporate securities.[46]

Labour

The concerns of labour were not represented in the early commentary or government material on the CCAA, nor did the 1938 Committee consider labour-related issues. The only reference to labour is the single remark in the Debates of the Senate of Canada by Senator Meighen (Conservative) in 1933.[47] This study found no other historical evidence to show that labour was consulted or involved in CCAAs, or bondholder reorganizations more broadly during this period, or that this group benefitted through ongoing employment, despite the fact that by 1937 unemployment had contributed to increasing labour disputes.[48] While later usage of the CCAA has given rise to labour concerns and participation in negotiations, this was absent from the policy and practice of early CCAA law.

Canadian Credit Men's Trust Association

The Canadian Credit Men's Trust Association (CCMTA) was a national organization that generally represented the interests of unsecured creditors.[49] It acted both as a trustee in bankruptcy and occasionally as a representative of its members' claims in bankruptcy proceedings.[50] Accordingly, the CCMTA was concerned about the protection of unsecured creditor rights in CCAA proceedings and agreed with the Toronto Board of Trade's suggestions for amendments in this regard.[51] Lee Kelley, the CCMTA's representative, closed his submissions by stating, "My whole position can be summed up by saying that we are backing up the position that we have worked out with the Toronto Board of Trade."[52]

As evidenced by the committee minutes, the Toronto Board of Trade and DMIA, representing the interests of bondholders, were successful in rallying support for keeping the CCAA. They did this by suggesting amendments to protect unsecured creditors from debtor-led CCAAs by ensuring bondholder oversight of restructuring efforts. In essence, this reaffirmed and entrenched bondholders' power over reorganization proceedings.

Office of the Superintendent of Bankruptcy

In 1938, the Superintendent of Bankruptcy, William Reilley, represented a distinct point of view in insolvency law debates. The OSB was established in 1932 as part of reforms to the *Bankruptcy Act*, and Reilley served as the first Superintendent.[53] Reilley noted that he had received many complaints concerning the abuses that had arisen under the CCAA as well as the WUA, both of which were outside of the OSB's jurisdiction.[54] Accordingly, he argued that parliament should review the piecemeal approach to Canadian insolvency legislation with a view to consolidating the statutes into one act, overseen and administered by the OSB.[55] (Parliamentarians and academics have advocated for this position at various points over the past eighty years, but to little avail.[56]) Reilley's position held sway with the committee. Since *Bankruptcy Act* amendments were outside its remit, the committee agreed to go back to parliament to try to secure a general reference so that it could investigate the *Bankruptcy Act*, CCAA, and WUA together.[57]

Lawyers

Lawyers did not form a united interest group with respect to stances taken on the CCAA, and they were not represented at the 1938 meeting. The interests of their clients probably influenced the opinions of individual lawyers. For instance, Fraser was in favour of keeping the CCAA, which benefited the clients he represented. Manning thought the act was ultra vires the federal government, a view shared by other reputable lawyers, who refused to recommend the CCAA to their clients.[58] But despite these concerns, by the time Edwards wrote his LLM thesis on the CCAA in 1947, the act was an established piece of the insolvency law framework in Canada.[59] Commenting on Manning's 1935 article, Edwards stated, "However reasonable his doubts may have appeared at that time, it is now clear that the Act is valid in its entirety."[60]

American Investors

Although American investors were not an organized interest group in discussions about the CCAA, concern over American investment in Canadian bond issues was a significant matter in 1938. This helped prompt parliament to abandon its bill to repeal the CCAA. It is ironic that by 1940–5 American investors had almost entirely abandoned the Canadian corporate bond market.[61] Following the corporate failures of the Great Depression – including many financed through trust deeds that contained no majority provisions, and thus encountered great difficulty restructuring – Canadian corporations largely returned to the practice of including majority provisions in trust deeds.[62] It is possible that the long drawn-out restructurings of companies such as Abitibi also deterred American investors from purchasing Canadian bonds in favour of investing in shares. Canadian equity investments could be restructured relatively easily under corporate law statutes, which, due to the CCAA, could be combined into a single proceeding with debt restructurings.[63]

By the time parliament finally closed the debtor-in-possession loophole in the CCAA in 1953 – in a move to restrict the act to bondholder-led restructurings – the most compelling rationale for retaining the act was no longer a major issue. By including majority provisions in trust deeds, Canadian companies sacrificed access to US debt markets, in order to secure increased flexibility with respect to bondholder restructurings. This underscores the fact that the CCAA was enacted to overcome drafting deficiencies in Canadian trust deeds. Into the 1950s and beyond, most bondholders preferred to restructure privately or through receiverships.[64]

3 An "Open Door to Fraud"

Ernest Bertrand highlighted a concern about the operation of the CCAA, specifically with subsection 11(2) of the act, arguing that it was an open invitation for fraud by company management or the receiver-manager, and a departure from English restructuring practice.[65] Subsection 11(2), which remains part of the CCAA to this day,[66] allows debtors to "accept any claims for the purpose of voting and reject those claims after that when they have settled with the creditors."[67] The possibility for fraud arises in the event that a debtor strategically admits false claims in order to secure the votes needed for plan approval, thereby forcing a plan on its real creditors even if the majority of those creditors do not support the restructuring. After voting, the debtor can then contest the false claims to eliminate them from the plan and any distribution.

According to the committee minutes, this provision had not arisen as an issue in the context of bondholder-led reorganizations, as represented by the Toronto Board of Trade and DMIA.[68] Despite its presence on the statute books for over eighty years, this study found no instances of judicial or scholarly attention focused on this subsection.[69]

An historical analysis suggests that this provision simply provides a distinction between voting claims and admitting them as legitimate in order for the CCAA to operate in a timely way. The subsection allows voting to go ahead even if the debtor or receiver-manager has not examined all claims in detail, and may later want to contest their legitimacy. If the vote is successful, contested claims can (theoretically) be submitted to the court for a ruling. The provision appears to provide no ex ante safeguard against abuse. However, if the company had to scrutinize all claims before ever getting to a vote, it would probably slow down the operation of the act to the point where it could be entirely ineffective – essentially causing the CCAA to operate like the composition provisions of the *Bankruptcy Act of 1919.*[70]

In the 1930s and today, judges have been asked to re-examine CCAA plan votes in light of facts that arise later, with a view to obviating the need for a further vote.[71] In such instances judges determine how the vote would have been decided if certain claims had, or had not, been counted as claims ex ante, in order to decide whether the requisite majority creditor approval has been met ex post. This approach offers fewer safeguards, but is arguably necessary in a non-bankruptcy statutory restructuring regime.

4 Vulture Capitalism

The final issue surrounding the CCAA was the use of the statute to confirm plans that furthered the interests of aggressive investors, known today as "vulture capitalists." The predatory practices of bondholder protective committees (BPCs), complained of by 1940,[72] appear to have escaped the notice of the 1938 parliamentary Standing Committee on Banking and Finance.[73] Bertrand's concern over other possible abuses of the CCAA suggests that he was unaware of the practices of vulture capitalists, which he likely would have raised otherwise. This practice has echoes in current insolvency issues such as distressed debt trading, vulture capitalism, and the role of creditor committees, with which contemporary scholars, judges, and practitioners now grapple.[74]

The predatory investors in bondholder reorganizations during the 1930s essentially operated as follows: Small groups of individuals purchased distressed bonds with a view to seizing control of the reorganization.[75] After purchasing the bonds, the vultures established a BPC and, through advertisements, convinced other bondholders to deposit their bonds with the BPC – turning over their voting rights in the bargain – rather than with the bondholder committee established by the trustee under the governing trust deed.[76] The advertisements claimed that the bondholders would fare badly under the plan proposed by the bondholder committee, and urged them instead to support the BPC, which would secure a better plan.[77] Ordinarily bondholders had a right to appoint a BPC to represent their interests and act as a "strong, organized creditor group" in restructurings, which is how the vultures' BPC garnered support from bondholders.[78] In some cases the same trustee acted as depository for both committees, contributing to bondholder confusion and leading to allegations of deception and fraud.[79] The vultures sought control of the proceedings and the firm in order to ensure that they received higher-ranking, and higher-value, securities in the reorganization than the other bondholders.[80] As a matter of practice, the restructurings were usually completed by way of a sale under either the CCAA or the Ontario *Judicature Act*.

This phenomenon raises a concern with respect to creditor voting that the 1938 committee did not address. Under the 1933 version of the CCAA, a creditor stake as small as 25 per cent in a given class amounted to a veto in a plan vote.[81] Distressed-debt traders were more inclined to exercise veto power than the original claim holders when their immediate interests were not advanced.[82] Since vultures acquired their bonds at a discount after the company was in financial difficulty, they had less to lose if the restructuring failed. In effect, this meant that a BPC only needed to secure 25 per cent of claims of a given class in order to block a plan put forward by the bondholder committee, which is what occurred, for instance, in the *Wellington* case.[83] The court in that matter, looking narrowly at the issue of creditor classification, seems to have been unaware of the different objectives of the respective committees. Without any concerted inquiry beyond the bare voting provision, the court sided with the BPC over the bondholder committee.[84]

The uncovering of this "racket" years after the fact led to criticism, especially of the professionals involved.[85] This was all the more troubling because trustees were supposed to look out for the rights of bondholders, with the courts acting as a final layer of oversight.[86] The BPCs of the 1930s illustrate that abuses can take place inside and outside insolvency legislation, and that professional or judicial oversight is no panacea.

5 Historical Institutionalism and Recursivity of Law

By enshrining majority provisions into statute, parliament inadvertently opened the door to early debtor-in-possession restructuring attempts under the CCAA. Since the act did not include any provision limiting its application to companies in receivership, debtor companies that were not subject to receiver or trustee oversight could invoke it. As a result, many companies in the 1930s filed under the CCAA in order to restructure trade creditor and unsecured claims only. This practice was widely regarded as an abuse of the legislation, since there was no mechanism for requiring the debtor to disclose its financial information, nor any official oversight to ensure disclosures were accurate. Debtor-in-possession restructurings of this nature thus led directly to two early repeal bills – in 1938 and 1946 – both of which were introduced as private members' bills.

The use of the CCAA as a debtor-in-possession restructuring statute in the 1930s and 1940s represents an unsuccessful attempt at layering by debtor companies. While debtor-in-possession restructurings were never the intent of the legislation, debtors exploited a loophole in order to redirect the act for new purposes. This attempt at layering was met with opposition by various interest groups, including those representing unsecured creditors and bankruptcy officials. No organized group at that time supported the use of the act as a debtor remedy, nor did any group oppose its use as a bondholder remedy. This in turn accounts for the fact that interest groups and parliamentarians charged with reviewing the repeal bills both times reached a consensus that the act should be restrictively amended in order to preserve the statute as a bondholder remedy, and prevent further debtor-in-possession reorganizations.

Despite the fairly large role played by interest groups in these two CCAA repeal attempts, the resulting 1953 amendment was not primarily driven by professional self-interest. Instead it was motivated by a desire to maintain the status quo concerning bondholder reorganizations. This underscores the resilience of these nineteenth-century institutional arrangements. These efforts ultimately led to the 1953 trust deed amendment, which limited the application of the act to compromises involving bondholders, thereby closing the loophole contained in the original legislation and ending further layering attempts for the time being. This amendment is therefore an example of a straightforward recursive cycle in which a law was enacted to respond to a particular problem.

The 1953 amendment thus marked the formal end of a cycle of legal change that began in roughly the 1910s, with the gradual elimination of majority provisions from trust deeds governing bonds placed with US investors. This cycle of legal change saw nineteenth-century bondholder reorganization practices enshrined into federal insolvency legislation, affirmed as constitutional by the court of last resort, and then limited to restructurings involving bondholders. In a highly recursive process, law trickled up from practices employed by bondholders under private agreements into the public arena of legislation.

Even after creating significant problems by omitting majority provisions from trust deeds, bondholders successfully availed themselves of the legislative process to patch over defects in trust deeds, demonstrating the significant influence of this creditor group in lawmaking. Bondholders played a major role in this cycle of legal change, through organizations such as the DMIA and the Toronto Board of Trade.

They saw their longstanding lender remedy of corporate reorganization enshrined into insolvency legislation and prevented repeal of the CCAA some years later. Bondholder success in this regard was both significant and longstanding.

Retaining the CCAA or a similar act on the statute books was essential after 1938 in order to allow Canadian corporate bonds to be listed on the New York Stock Exchange. Pursuant to the US *Trust Indenture Act of 1939*, trust deeds governing bonds listed in the United States could not contain majority provisions, and so a statutory mechanism was needed to effect any potential compromises or arrangements affecting these bondholders. The CCAA was therefore necessary after 1938 to facilitate access to US debt markets.

Ironically, legislative efforts to facilitate reorganizations of companies with US bondholders and allow Canadian companies ongoing access to US debt finance through the CCAA were followed by a return to the use of majority provisions in Canadian trust deeds. In the 1930s, bondholders used the CCAA to reinsert majority provisions into their governing trust deeds. The remarkable result was that Canadian companies forewent access to US debt markets, and for the next fifteen years new bond issues were placed almost exclusively with Canadian investors.[87] This appears to indicate that despite the extension of bondholder reorganizations into insolvency law traditional bondholder reorganizations under trust deeds constituted a deeper equilibrium.

The influence of this deep equilibrium may help account for why contingent events surrounding the enactment and endurance of the CCAA on the statute books, from 1933 to 1953, came out the way they did. The early resilience of the CCAA to repeal attempts was no doubt aided by the fact that the act itself was a continuation of existing practices, and hence was more resilient to repeal than an entirely new restructuring regime likely would have been. As Pierson defines institutional resilience, "all other things being equal, an institution will be more resilient, and any revisions more incremental in nature, the longer the institution has been in place."[88] The enshrining of bondholder reorganizations into insolvency law was a superficial change to a longstanding institution. Early efforts to repeal the CCAA – despite the changes it brought about in terms of the formal appearance of bondholder reorganizations, and the co-opting of the act by debtors – were actually facing off against an institutional equilibrium that was sixty or seventy years old and already extended through provincial law. The early history of the CCAA led to a new equilibrium by entrenching the practice of bondholder reorganizations in federal insolvency law and, in that regard, it and the subsequent return to majority provisions bear out the inflexibility of positive feedback processes, illustrating that "particular courses of action, once introduced, can be virtually impossible to reverse."[89]

These theoretical approaches to interpreting CCAA history offer greater explanatory power than do interest group analyses alone. They account for the fact that the CCAA long outlasted (by over forty years) its strongest early proponent, DMIA.[90] DMIA defeated repeal bills in 1938 and 1946, and proposed the only substantial amendment made to the CCAA in its first fifty-nine years on the statute books.

The new equilibrium introduced by the CCAA in 1933, and affirmed by the 1953 amendment, was one in which nineteenth-century bond-holder remedies were extended into the federal jurisdiction via insolvency law and made the exclusive purview of parliament when the debtor company was insolvent. Positive feedback and institutional resilience of bondholder reorganization practices help account for the enactment and continued endurance of this bondholder remedy on the statute books, despite a significant element of contingency in the events surrounding the enactment of the CCAA, its constitutional reference, and early repeal attempts.

6 Conclusion

Despite achieving a consensus on CCAA reforms to address abuses of the act raised by the lack of oversight, nothing came of the 1938 parliamentary committee meeting, and the CCAA process remained in the hands of bondholders or company management until the trust-deed amendment of 1953.[91] This was partly due to misperceptions of the CCAA evident in parliamentary debates. For example, by 1938 the originally disconcerting aspect of the CCAA – the power it conferred to adjust secured creditors rights – was absent from the list of complaints put before the House of Commons Committee. By that time concern was for the interests of unsecured and junior creditors in debtor-led CCAAs. The adjustment of secured creditor rights was a settled feature of insolvency law by 1938, even though it was widely regarded as unconstitutional just a few years prior. From 1938 onward, parliamentarians generally construed the CCAA as a debtor-remedy insolvency law geared toward rehabilitating distressed firms, a purpose for which the statute was unsuited, and this accordingly provoked complaints and recurring calls for repeal.[92]

Canadian developments came at the same time as significant changes were made in American bankruptcy law, which introduced Chapter 11 and imported receivership practices into the US *Bankruptcy Code*.[93] As in Canada, by 1938 there were concerns over the abuse of bankruptcy law in the United States, which led to an investigation by the Securities and Exchange Commission (SEC). Reforms in the United States instituted an independent trustee to take a supervisory role in reorganization proceedings.[94] In Canada the bondholders' trustee or receiver-manager supposedly fulfilled this function in the course of CCAA reorganizations, although this was not always true in practice.

In early 1939, DMIA took part in a series of conferences with other interested organizations to discuss strategies for addressing the abuses experienced in the operation of the CCAA.[95] These conferences resulted in proposals for regulations under the act, which were presented to the Department of the Secretary of State for adoption by the Governor-General in Council.[96] Writing in 1940, DMIA noted that the matter was still awaiting action by the Department of the Secretary of State.[97] It appears that this action was never taken.

The endurance of the CCAA on the statute books is linked to stalled attempts at Canadian bankruptcy and insolvency law reform. Reform efforts often included repeal of the CCAA as part of amendments to the *Bankruptcy Act* adding or expanding a section on company reorganization. This historical study reveals that the CCAA was a relatively open-ended, bondholder-controlled remedy, in contrast to the rules-based, third-party-supervised processes under the *Bankruptcy Act*. From a bondholder standpoint, there was no advantage to consolidating the two acts, which could only reduce bondholder control and discretion over reorganizations. In light of the introduction of more oversight in CCAA proceedings over the past thirty years, path dependence sheds light on subsequent failed attempts to consolidate Canadian bankruptcy and insolvency statutes – sometimes resulting in duplicative amendments to the CCAA and *Bankruptcy and Insolvency Act*[98] – despite persuasive efficiency arguments for unifying these two insolvency regimes.[99]

PART TWO

Transforming CCAA Law, 1970s–2000s

6

New Lenders, New Forms of Lending, and Stalled Bankruptcy Reforms, 1970s–1980s

"The attitude of leaving something for the shareholders and management is new," says Peter Perdue [of TD Bank] ... "The old approach was to say 'why worry about them? We rank ahead.' Now we leave something in it for everyone – management, shareholders, and the bank."[1]

Peter Perdue, *The Financial Post*

1 Stasis and Change

From the 1950s up to the recession of the early 1980s, the Canadian economy enjoyed strong growth[2] and lenders seldom resorted to the CCAA.[3] Parliament made no substantive amendments to the act, except for the 1953 trust deed amendment – the overdue brainchild of the DMIA. Despite notable efforts to modernize Canada's bankruptcy laws,[4] parliament did not pass major business bankruptcy reforms until 1992[5] – after the 1980s recession and mid-way into the 1990s recession. But limited activity in the area of bankruptcy and insolvency law during this period belies considerable commercial and legislative activity in the areas of credit and debt. From the 1950s to the 1980s, many provinces enacted legislation concerning credit, debt, and over-indebtedness.[6] Liberalization of the federal *Bank Act* in 1967 paved the way for chartered banks to become major providers of long-term secured credit.[7] Coupled with the introduction of *Personal Property Security Acts* (PPSAs) by the provinces, this led to declining use of trust deeds to secure long-term corporate loans. Without trust deed financing, neither lenders nor corporate borrowers had recourse to the enabling provisions of the CCAA after the 1953 trust deed amendment.

Canadian companies increasingly turned to banks rather than capital markets to raise long-term debt finance.[8] The size and increased lending facilities of chartered banks made these institutions one-stop shopping for many corporate borrowers. Unlike widely dispersed bondholders, chartered banks had no reason to concern themselves with majority provisions to coordinate internally in response to debtor default. Much like earlier bondholders, chartered banks relied on the priority and strength of their security vis-à-vis other secured and unsecured creditors, and displayed little interest in coordinating with smaller creditors in cases of debtor default. In the midst of several decades of strong economic growth, it appears that neither banks nor parliament concerned themselves with the particular issues raised by widespread defaults associated with a general economic downturn. Bondholder reorganizations and the circumstances that gave rise to the corporate restructuring crisis of the 1920s–30s, as well as the CCAA, were essentially forgotten.

These changes significantly altered the secured lending landscape, with untested implications for lenders and borrowers during subsequent economic recessions. Changes to secured lending arrangements ex ante would prove significant for approaches to debtor default and reorganization ex post. When combined with the 1980s and 1990s recessions, these would precipitate another restructuring crisis.

The political, legal, and social backdrop of the recessions of the 1980s and 1990s, however, was much changed from that of the 1930s. Fifty years on, Canadian labour was an organized interest group with legal rights, and it had acquired a political voice in the New Democratic Party (NDP).[9] The growth of environmental concerns similarly resulted in new legal rights, through legislation to hold firms accountable for clean-up costs, for example.[10] Labour and environmental constituencies did not exist as such in the 1930s, but they could not be disregarded in the restructuring crises of the 1980s and 1990s.[11] Accordingly, these decades would see a public relations gloss applied to Canadian corporate reorganization law, and an antiquated secured creditor remedy would be recast in the public interest.

Important changes within the legal profession in Canada helped to facilitate this transformation. First, Canadian courts were far more policy-conscious and even activist by the 1980s and 1990s than they were in the 1930s.[12] This change came about gradually and over many years as a result of various factors. A touchstone for the new approach of Canadian courts to judging can be found in the approach taken by the SCC under Chief Justice Bora Laskin, from 1973 to 1984. Chief Justice Laskin transformed the SCC into a modern, policy-conscious institution that assumed a far greater role in *developing* Canadian law rather than merely settling disputes.[13] Due to the operation of legal precedent, this affected the way lower courts decided matters as well. In addition, the 1982 proclamation of the *Canadian Charter of Rights and Freedoms* led to increased judicial review of legislation in Canada more generally.[14]

Second, Canadian approaches to statutory interpretation changed between the time of the CCAA's enactment and its revival in the 1980s and 1990s. In the late 1970s and 1980s the SCC and lower courts adopted Elmer Driedger's "modern principle of statutory interpretation," first published in 1974,[15] as the preferred approach. Driedger's principle placed greater emphasis on the policy behind legislation and the intention of parliament than earlier approaches to statutory construction. Thus, while the CCAA remained more or less the same for over fifty years, approaches to interpreting it and the institutions charged with doing so changed significantly.

As a result of this unique mixture of stasis and change, the CCAA was deployed in new ways within completely different social, political, and economic circumstances, compared to conditions that existed at the time of its enactment. The stasis of the CCAA during this period, and in federal bankruptcy and insolvency law more generally, tends to obscure the many contextual factors that had changed dramatically since the 1930s. These factors influenced the way that lawyers, courts, managers, and other stakeholders approached and interpreted the CCAA in the 1980s and 1990s; this, in turn, led to some erroneous conclusions about the origins of the CCAA, many of which continue to circulate as received wisdom. This broad, contextual paradigm shift thus helps explain *why* a secured creditor remedy from the 1930s was, fifty years later, regarded as a debtor remedy on essentially an a priori basis.

2 The 1980s and 1990s Recessions: Another "Restructuring Crisis"

By the 1980s, changes in legislation and commercial practices had largely disconnected the CCAA from the 1930s context of secured lending laws and institutions. Chartered banks, rather than life insurance companies, were major lenders to large Canadian corporations, and often used new forms of lending under the *Bank Act* and PPSAs. By not securing corporate loans with trust deeds,[16] banks did not have access to the CCAA. Additionally, the detailed restructuring provisions typically contained in corporate trust deeds were largely lost or forgotten in the transition to much shorter statute-based security agreements. This period thus marked a slow-moving but distinct rupture in the history of Canadian corporate reorganization practices. Bondholder reorganizations, which were standard practice for roughly one century, fell out of use. As a result, at the onset of the recessions in the 1980s and 1990s, large secured lenders lacked effective tools to restructure corporate debtors (again).

The recessions of the 1980s and 1990s hit the Canadian economy and financial institutions particularly hard, compared to earlier economic downturns. Many companies, including large Canadian concerns, such as Dome Petroleum, Daon Development, and Olympia and York, encountered severe financial difficulty. This in turn led to large losses for their creditors, the largest of which were often chartered banks. These were the first economic recessions that Canadian chartered banks experienced as major providers of long-term secured credit. In some instances, the size of the losses incurred by Canadian financial institutions led to concern about the financial soundness and stability of these institutions themselves.[17]

In 1982, a parliamentary review revealed that several Canadian banks were overextended, and some had very large exposure to a single, large corporate borrower.[18] According to testimony provided by Canadian banks to the House of Commons Standing Committee on Finance, Trade and Economic Affairs, inflation-generated uncertainty in the early 1980s limited bond and stock financing for Canadian companies, increasing reliance on bank funds, and increasing bank exposure in the bargain.[19] The size of the potential write-offs made liquidation of debtor companies an unattractive option for banks. The scale of losses to the big banks potentially placed their own solvency in jeopardy, at a time when many other Canadian financial institutions, including three chartered banks[20] and three life insurance companies,[21] were falling into receivership or were being taken over by regulators.[22]

The public failure of a Big Five bank would have been economically costly and politically undesirable.[23] For reasons of market integrity and public confidence in financial institutions, states try to avoid these sorts of bail outs.[24] This may be especially so in more recent recessions, as indicated by the careful characterization of high-profile CCAAs as "private solutions," despite critical government funding.[25] Nevertheless, during the 1980s and 1990s recessions, both provincial and federal governments in Canada were prepared to assist to some extent in preventing the failure of any one of the Big Five banks, and offered funding for large restructurings to which those banks were significantly exposed. During the 1980s recession, courts, banks, and the provincial and federal governments effectively (re)affirmed corporate reorganization through insolvency law and receivership as a commercially and politically desirable response to the insolvency of large firms.

The CCAA was an anachronism in the commercial landscape by the 1980s, which proved important. This ambiguity contributed to the possibility that the act would be interpreted by later actors in a manner that conformed to contemporary conceptions of corporate insolvency law.[26] In fact, contextual changes necessitated reinterpretation in order to use the act to restructure companies by the 1980s. The skeletal provisions of the statute, which courts took to confer much scope for judicial discretion, aided the CCAA's reinvention. This transformation was also spurred by the lack of another effective mechanism to facilitate complete corporate restructurings (largely due to stalled bankruptcy reform efforts), and by the fact that large secured lenders (such as banks) supported reorganization in principle as a creditor remedy in large insolvencies. With their largest creditors "on side," there was no organized group to oppose the idea of restructuring in principle.

Although the 1980s and 1990s ushered in a new, debtor-centred interpretation of the CCAA (borrowing from narratives surrounding US Chapter 11), the act was (and is) still used to advance the interests of large secured creditors such as banks and life insurance companies. The following section explores how secured lenders initially grappled with reorganizing large, struggling companies during this period and illustrates how and why banks in particular played a major role in driving legal changes in this area.[27]

Restructuring as a Remedy for Large Secured Creditors

During the 1980s and 1990s recessions, large secured lenders in Canada supported restructurings of large corporate debtors as a potential creditor remedy, whether inside or outside insolvency law. Bank support for debtor restructuring in principle does not amount to universal support for all restructurings. But large secureds and corporate debtors both see reorganization as a desirable response to a firm's financial difficulties, where reorganization is expected to result in higher returns than liquidation.

Large secured creditor (or finance creditor) support for *insolvency* restructurings in Canada stems in part from constitutional constraints under the division of legislative powers as between the provinces and parliament. The constitutional references concerning the CCAA and FCAA meant that federal insolvency law jurisdiction superseded provincial restructuring regimes once the debtor was insolvent. This pushed Canadian capital and business restructurings under the heading of bankruptcy and insolvency law in order to effect complete reorganizations of insolvent firms. (Court-appointed receiverships remain useful, however, since they do not require the debtor to be technically insolvent.) The fact that this shift took place in the 1930s was the product of Canadian federalism and constitutional interpretation rather than a reflection of normative or popular ideas about insolvency or corporate restructuring. In England, by contrast, Westminster only added provision for company reorganization to its insolvency laws in 1986.[28] If not for Canada's provincial-federal division of powers, parliament similarly might not have added provisions for complete company reorganizations to insolvency law until the 1980s or 1990s – after ideas about corporate insolvency had started to shift toward the normative desirability of encouraging companies to reorganize. The tendency in England for legal changes to come through formal legislative reform also contributes to somewhat greater clarity about the debtor- and lender-remedy functions of specific restructuring regimes in that jurisdiction.

Even outside of the CCAA, banks preferred to reorganize rather than liquidate a number of large companies in the 1980s and 1990s. Peter Farkas, an insolvency professional at a firm frequently retained by banks as receivers, reported that by 1992 his work consisted of approximately 80 per cent restructuring and 20 per cent liquidation – the opposite of what it was in the early 1980s.[29] Despite the revival of the CCAA in the 1980s[30] and the addition of commercial reorganization provisions to the BIA in 1992, secured creditors continue to resort to mechanisms such as receivership to deal with debtor default, often with a view to effecting a going-concern sale of the business.[31] Corporate failures from the 1980s and 1990s demonstrate that large insolvencies spurred restructuring efforts on a largely commercial basis, which in turn prompted counsel to seek out effective mechanisms for conducting and implementing reorganization plans.

Dome Petroleum: A Case Study

The 1980s insolvency of Dome Petroleum is a good case study of a large secured creditor-supported reorganization that took place outside of insolvency law. This restructuring sheds light on the interests of several creditor and stakeholder groups and illustrates their (typical) respective interests in an insolvency scenario. Some of the key themes in this restructuring were concerns for lender solvency, which prompted government help with restructuring; preferences among different types of creditors for different outcomes, which led actors to maneuver strategically within the legal landscape; and expectations for a restructuring plan that was justified based on the wider public interest, but the outcome of which is of questionable public interest value.

Dome began to encounter severe financial difficulty in 1982, due to the collapse of world oil prices.[32] Collectively, Bank of Montreal, Canadian Imperial Bank of Commerce, Toronto-Dominion Bank, and Royal Bank of Canada held approximately $2 billion of Dome's $6.2 billion in outstanding debt.[33] Management as well as the federal government and major secured creditors thought the underlying business was viable and that the company could be turned around if Dome's debt load was reduced.[34]

Dome's collapse, along with other large insolvencies of the period, prompted fears that corporate failures might bring down heavily exposed Canadian banks as well. This prompted Prime Minister Pierre Trudeau's Liberal government to offer financial assistance to help keep the company afloat as part of a debt-rescheduling plan put forward by the banks.[35] Concern for the solvency of large Canadian lenders in the 1980s and 1990s thus provided significant impetus for secured creditors and politicians to effect reorganizations of important firms. Worries for the solvency of financial institutions in the 1980s and 1990s echo the 1920s and 1930s in this regard. But by the 1980s and 1990s the notion of corporate restructurings as a debtor remedy was widely seen as legitimate,[36] and even in the public interest – a first in Canadian history – and this framed the way parties approached the issue of debtor insolvency.

In contrast to the position adopted by Canadian banks, a few European banks, with fairly small, secured positions in the Dome insolvency, threatened to put the company into bankruptcy over delays in repayment.[37] This illustrates that factors such as the size of a creditor's stake may significantly influence the remedies sought. It also parallels the differing approaches of bondholders and other secured creditors in earlier CCAA restructurings. In the early twentieth century, bondholders were generally inclined to forgive missed payments in order to help reorganize a struggling debtor, whereas secured creditors with smaller stakes in the company tended to favour enforcing their security.

In response to the prospect of creditor-initiated bankruptcy or receivership, Dome threatened these European banks with a CCAA application, which would stay all proceedings against the company.[38] This threat received much media attention.[39] The Dome insolvency showed that the CCAA could be used as a shield against receivership and bankruptcy. It also underscored the utility of the CCAA to stay junior secured creditor claims in particular, which may stand to gain less in a restructuring than other groups,[40] and so may oppose restructuring efforts altogether.

In 1988 Dome concluded a $5.5 billion debt compromise by way of sale of the company to Amoco Canada Limited, using only the *Canada*

Business Corporations Act (CBCA).[41] This was within the constitutional purview of parliament, since Dome was incorporated under the CBCA, and thus fell under both the federal corporate law and bankruptcy and insolvency law powers.[42] Although Dome could have qualified for CCAA protection,[43] it opted to use the arrangement provisions of the CBCA instead. Janis Sarra notes that one of the rationales for filing under the CBCA was to preserve shareholder equity in Dome since debt-for-equity swaps between Dome and its bankers featured in the plan of arrangement.[44]

Since shareholder claims rank behind unsecured claims, shareholder value is usually wiped out in a corporate bankruptcy. Therefore, the preservation of shareholder value in this case, and other large reorganizations in the 1980s and 1990s, poses challenges for public interest accounts of corporate restructuring that have to do with junior creditor and employee interests, especially where junior creditors were not made whole or employees were laid off. In cases like Dome, the most senior debt was usually converted into equity, existing shareholder value was (partly) preserved, and junior debt holders took the largest write-downs in proportion to the size of their claims.[45] In other words, the weakest and most junior creditors helped fund a reorganization that tended to benefit the most senior and sophisticated creditors and shareholders.

On its face, such an arrangement seems to go against the public interest. Although there is no precise definition of this term, courts have generally held that it means inter alia "allowing the corporation to carry on business in a manner that causes the least possible harm to employees and the communities in which it operates."[46] Preserving shareholder value is not necessarily in the public interest, especially if this is accomplished by compromising claims of more vulnerable creditor or stakeholder groups. In addition, the legitimacy of preserving equity claims when shareholders are already shielded from debt liabilities through limited liability requires justification. Using the public interest rationale to protect shareholder claims in insolvency serves as a check against the complete loss of their investment.

There is a conflicting understanding of expectations between public interest discourses surrounding CCAA restructuring and the substance of many of the plans that are carried out under this statute, as well as the CBCA. The substance of many of these restructurings echo bondholder reorganizations of the 1920s and 1930s, in that they are focused on restructuring the corporation's capital (debt and equity) rather than on junior creditor claims or the interests of the community at large. In theory, these latter groups are the beneficiaries of the intrinsic trickle-down benefits of restructuring. The problem in practice, however, is that there is little empirical evidence to show these groups actually benefit in the way that they are supposed to.[47]

Public Interest Rationales

During the 1980s and 1990s, preserving shareholder value was often publicly characterized as being "in the public interest." In a *Financial Post* article that summarized a number of debtor restructurings conducted by Canadian banks, Dunnery Best reported:

> One constant theme through each of these arrangements is that the banks have left real value in the hands of shareholders, even though they rank after unsecured creditors in the event of a collapse.
> The TD seems to have gone the farthest in this regard.
> "We'd rather a smaller portion in something better, than a larger chunk of something weak," says TD's Perdue. "We didn't take stock as cheap as possible. That made it better for existing shareholders – and us, over the longer term."[48]

In several cases in the 1980s, chartered banks accepted equity in exchange for their secured claims, swelling their balance sheets with shares in large companies such as Daon Development and Nu-West.[49] Thus, it was in the banks' self-interest to keep share prices high. These debt-for-equity exchanges usually required special permission from the Inspector-General of Banks and the Minister of Finance, since they frequently gave banks more than a 10 percent stake in the debtor company, which was ordinarily prohibited under the *Bank Act*.[50] According to John Clarke, vice president of Royal Bank:

> Our goal is not to make a huge profit on the restructurings ... Our main goal is to try to get our money back, compensate us for our risk, and still be fair to the client.[51]

Banks understood that even distressed debt could be profitable – an example of enlightened self-interest in an insolvency scenario.

The business press sometimes described bank involvement in high-profile insolvencies in terms of benevolent concern for stakeholders, such as shareholders and employees. According to an article in the *Financial Post*, banks sacrificed immediate debt enforcement, instead of seizing and liquidating everything to satisfy their claims, so that a wider constituency of stakeholders could benefit:

"The attitude of leaving something for the shareholders and management is new," says Peter Perdue, assistant general manager of corporate banking with Toronto Dominion Bank in Toronto, recently returned from several years in the work-out trenches in Calgary. "The old approach was to say 'why worry about them? We rank ahead.' *Now we leave something in it for everyone – management, shareholders, and the bank.*" [Emphasis added.][52]

This paints a pleasing image of corporate insolvency, but the plans of arrangement advanced bank interests first and foremost. The support of the company's largest creditors (banks) was essential for a restructuring plan to succeed. While some members of more vulnerable groups, such as employees, did benefit from certain restructurings, this was largely a by-product of the use of restructuring as a remedy for the company's largest creditors. Furthermore, sophisticated and powerful groups, such as shareholders, who usually do not recover anything in a bankruptcy, also gained by the reorganization of insolvent firms. Setting aside the public relations gloss, the outcomes of many corporate reorganizations from the 1980s and 1990s paralleled the bondholder reorganizations of the early twentieth century.

Interestingly, parties did not particularly emphasize the benefits accruing to employees in bank-led restructurings in the early 1980s, and reporters rarely addressed employee issues in the attendant press coverage. In the one major case from the 1980s where employee concerns were discussed, it was to justify government sponsorship of the CCAA plan. In the restructuring of United Co-operatives of Ontario (UCO),[53] approximately 600 (about one-third) of employees were laid off to reduce operating expenses.[54] The preservation of the remaining 1,300 jobs formed part of the justification for a provincial loan to assist the restructuring effort.[55]

The few other CCAAs from the 1980s that mention employee claims contain little substantive discussion about the treatment of the employees in insolvency proceedings. Employees did not feature as the prototypical, sympathy-evoking creditors they so often are in contemporary CCAAs. In some cases, employee claims did not form part of the proposed CCAA plan at all.[56] In other instances company spokespersons simply said that employees fared better in a restructuring than they would in a liquidation, and lumped employee interests in with those of other creditors and shareholders.[57] Wider concern for employee claims in business restructuring appears to have begun in 1990s corporate insolvencies, which were often spearheaded by corporate managers. High profile cases such as Algoma Steel and Anvil Range Mining were among the first to deal substantively with these issues under the CCAA.[58]

By the end of the 1980s, practitioners saw the lack of statutory wage protections in corporate insolvencies as a deficiency of the CCAA, which they expected the 1992 bankruptcy reforms to address.[59] Since these amendments essentially retained the CCAA as is, the practical effect of the business reorganization provisions added to the BIA were curtailed insofar as large corporations continued to file under the CCAA, and in increasing numbers.[60] The enactment of the BIA provisions on business reorganization, however, did at least provide a benchmark other than liquidation with which to compare a proposed plan of arrangement under the CCAA. It is unclear to what extent this translated into meaningful improvements for workers in corporate insolvencies.

The fact that employees fare better by at least the prospect of keeping their jobs (through reorganization) than by losing their jobs (through liquidation) essentially justifies any restructuring attempt based on employee interests. One could make the same argument in respect of shareholder interests in the insolvent undertaking, although it would likely not play well in the polity. There are other methods open to government to help protect employee interests, such as employment insurance, skills training, and preference to employee claims in insolvency and liquidation. Therefore, employee interests alone are a weak justification for promoting business rehabilitation under an insolvency statute that does not substantively address labour issues. Something as simple as employee wage claim reforms could at least ensure a higher baseline for the treatment of employee claims in insolvency, thereby providing this interest group a better bargaining position in restructurings.[61]

Labour interests made significant advances in Canadian politics and law between the Great Depression and the recessions of the 1980s and 1990s, which are important for understanding CCAA history. For example, in 1940 the federal government under Prime Minister King (Liberal) enacted the *Unemployment Insurance Act*, which provided a financial assistance to laid-off workers.[62] The formation of the NDP in 1961, Canada's first labour-based political party, gave labour interests a stronger political voice.[63] In 1980 the government of Ontario Progressive-Conservative Premier Bill Davis established the Pension Benefits Guarantee Fund (PBGF) to guarantee pension benefits to workers whose workplace pension plans were underfunded.[64]

The timeline of these developments suggests that labour's progress in politics and law *outside* insolvency legislation facilitated an active voice for labour as a stakeholder in corporate reorganizations by the 1990s. For instance, Sarra credits the success of the Algoma restructuring in 1991–2 in large part to the active involvement of the Ontario government in that insolvency. In Sarra's view, Premier Bob Rae's NDP political affiliation and the fact that the debtor was a large regional employer help explain his interest in seeing Algoma reorganize.[65] Sarra also notes that the likely prospect of the Premier Mike Harris's Progressive-Conservative government being held liable for roughly $650 million in pension shortfalls through the PBGF may have been what prompted his eventual support for the Algoma restructuring in 2001.[66] The growth of labour rights and political power outside insolvency legislation by the 1990s also helps account for the fact that Algoma's importance as a regional employer led Prime Minister Bennett to prohibit the company from restructuring in the 1930s, but paradoxically led later NDP and Conservative premiers to support Algoma's reorganization efforts. This underscores how changing ideas about corporate reorganization were interrelated with the growth of stakeholder rights and political voice between the Great Depression and the 1980s and 1990s.

Job losses, wage issues, and underfunded pensions are not sui generis to the field of corporate insolvency, but these issues are often raised to help justify corporate restructurings based on labour concerns. The restructuring versus liquidation (read: job retention versus job loss) dichotomy tends to obscure other, non-insolvency options and to imply that one need look no further than insolvency law for answers to labour issues that exist in an insolvency setting. The problem with this is that substantive insolvency law barely addresses labour concerns. Since labour's influence in an insolvency setting generally comes from outside insolvency law, it makes sense to look beyond insolvency law (and the spectre of liquidation) to gain perspective on how well, or to what extent, CCAAs advance social policy concerns relative to other policy options.

3 Historical Institutionalism and Recursivity of Law

Following the 1953 amendment, during a period in which the act was little used, significant changes occurred in the field of secured lending, while the CCAA remained substantially unchanged. Increasingly, new financial institutions entered the long-term, secured lending market and used financing instruments other than trust deeds. The act fell into further disuse, and up until the 1980s commentators, quite reasonably, thought the CCAA would become a dead letter.

Substantial liberalization of the *Bank Act* in 1967 allowed Canadian chartered banks to lend on a long-term, secured basis, and thus compete with life insurance companies in this area. During this period most provinces also enacted PPSAs, modernizing chattel security regimes and replacing floating and fixed charges with generic "security interests." These changes significantly altered the corporate lending environment. Banks, rather than life insurance companies, became major sources of corporate debt financing, and loans were increasingly secured using fixed charges, under relatively brief security documents pursuant to the *Bank Act* or PPSAs, rather than through floating charges under trust deeds with their especial provision for conducting restructurings. These changes produced both actor discontinuity and reorganization procedure discontinuity within the Canadian secured lending landscape.

With a single entity – a bank – as the only secured lender under a corporate loan, there was also little need for majority provisions or the restructuring practices they had facilitated in respect of bondholder claims. Additionally, since banks did not always use a trust deed to secure corporate loans, they did not necessarily have recourse to the CCAA, which could mean that they effectively had no method of compulsorily binding other creditors to a debt compromise in respect of a debtor company.[67] As a result, there was (again) effectively no way to carry out full reorganizations of many Canadian companies – something that did not greatly matter while the economy was growing and few companies faced financial difficulty.

During this period of formal stasis in respect of restructuring law, ideas and discourses surrounding bankruptcy and creditor rights evolved, particularly in the United States, with ramifications for ideas and developments in this field in Canada. During this period the US *Bankruptcy Code* underwent significant reforms, culminating in amendments in 1978, which introduced a DIP business restructuring mechanism in Chapter 11.[68] Shortly thereafter, American legal scholars such as Thomas Jackson[69] and Elizabeth Warren[70] developed and published novel theories of business bankruptcy. Bankruptcy and insolvency became a more mainstream topic in legal discourse and popular news coverage, especially as the United States and Canada entered the recession of the early 1980s and as Chapter 11 filings increased. American companies even began to use Chapter 11 strategically, in order to deal with mass tort claims or troublesome unions.[71] Bankruptcy under Chapter 11 thus became a tool for corporate management to cut costs and streamline operations – a way to improve the corporate bottom line in a competitive marketplace.

Of further note, the American reforms were followed by bankruptcy amendments in England in 1986, which similarly included a company restructuring component.[72] Several bankruptcy reform bills were also introduced in Canada in the 1970s and through the 1980s; however, Canada did not enact substantial bankruptcy reforms until 1992.[73]

In Canada, the 1970 *Tassé Report*, commissioned by parliament, provided the most comprehensive history of Canadian bankruptcy and insolvency law at the date of writing, and made recommendations for substantial bankruptcy law reform. Tassé noted a growing trend among secured creditors in terms of carrying out self-help remedies outside bankruptcy and insolvency law, such as receivership, with few regulatory checks and balances.[74] Tassé's recommendations that receiverships be subject to a baseline level of regulation indicate that by this point there was discomfort with the practice of relying totally on secured creditors' representatives to look out for the interests of junior and unsecured claims holders.[75] For instance, Tassé proposed that the indenture trustee not be permitted to act also as receiver, and that all receivers be licensed trustees under the *Bankruptcy Act*.[76] As this historical account shows, abrogation of junior creditor claims in bondholder reorganizations and sharp practice by indenture trustees acting as receivers have a history at least as long as the CCAA. It is therefore noteworthy that it was not until the 1970s that concerns about this sort of behaviour led to concrete recommendations for legislative reform.

Interestingly, there is little concern in the *Tassé Report* about potential abuses that might be carried out by debtor companies.[77] In 1933, Lewis Duncan voiced concerns about the potential use of the CCAA by debtors to the detriment of their creditors.[78] By 1970, however, the abuse of bankruptcy and insolvency law by debtors, while certainly something to be discouraged,[79] was no longer a reason to prohibit corporate restructuring altogether. Tassé proposed repealing the CCAA and recommended adding general business reorganization provisions to the *Bankruptcy Act*,[80] which is indicative of changing ideas around corporate reorganization; Tassé recognized that the original purpose of the CCAA was to patch over defects in trust deeds and serve as a bondholder remedy, rather than provide a general business restructuring statute.[81] Accordingly, this recommendation was not merely designed to consolidate existing insolvency statutes under a single act – it represented an effort to add a meaningful business restructuring component to Canadian insolvency law and policy.

In the space of several decades, while formal bankruptcy law changed very little, attitudes and outlooks concerning secured creditor remedies and business reorganization shifted markedly. Growing consideration for the rights of unsecured and junior creditors may be linked to the rise of new interest groups, such as organized labour. Concern for the fate of the debtor company itself also appears to have increased during this period and, in many cases, became entwined with the interests of other stakeholders or creditor groups, such as labour and the wider community in which the company operated. New legislation surrounding labour and environmental claims, for instance, meant that these (involuntary) creditors could not simply be disregarded, as in earlier bondholder reorganizations. And the advent of bankruptcy theories centred on stakeholder interests helped give voice to these new constituencies in business insolvencies. The rights of secured creditors remained powerful, but faced greater public scrutiny if exercised to the significant detriment of weaker groups and claimants. This last development was probably facilitated in part by the growth of the business press and increased coverage of bankruptcy and insolvency matters in the mainstream news media, particularly from the 1980s recession onward.

The 1960s and 1970s were, accordingly, a period of formal stasis in terms of the CCAA itself, while significant formal and informal changes took place, largely incrementally, in related areas of politics, law, and finance. Similar to the financing changes of the 1910s and 1920s, these developments helped lay the groundwork for another critical juncture in Canadian business reorganization practices. The failure of secured creditor remedies, particularly in corporate restructuring, to keep up with the significant changes in secured lending practices created conditions that were ripe for another restructuring crisis.

The recessions of the 1980s and 1990s brought to light the inadequacies of existing corporate restructuring mechanisms. As in the 1930s, this precipitated a new cycle of legal change and punctuated the former equilibrium. Much like the 1930s, what made this juncture particularly critical was that inadequate secured creditor remedies (the lack of effective mechanisms to carry out full company reorganizations) coincided with deep economic downturns. Many companies, including large Canadian concerns such as Dome Petroleum, Daon Development, and Olympia and York, encountered financial difficulty. Echoing the 1930s, the 1980s and 1990s recessions called attention to the inadequacy of existing statutory law and financing agreements to effect going-concern reorganizations,[82] especially for the benefit of large, secured lenders. These events thus converged to create another restructuring crisis for Canadian companies and, more significantly, for the large financial institutions that supplied much of their debt financing.

In some instances, the size of the losses incurred by Canadian financial institutions led to concern about the financial soundness and stability of the institutions themselves.[83] Unprecedentedly, three Canadian life insurance companies failed.[84] Provincial and federal regulators wound up a number of smaller financial institutions,[85] along with two chartered banks.[86] In terms of financial institution failures,[87] Canada appears to have fared worse during the 1980s and 1990s recessions than during the Great Depression.[88] This underscores the importance of considering the role of lenders and lender perspectives when studying the means by which restructuring crises, particularly in the 1980s and 1990s, were ultimately resolved.

Like life insurance companies without majority provisions during the Great Depression, chartered banks in the 1980s and 1990s found they had, in many cases, inadequate tools with which to restructure debtor companies, and this potentially put their own solvency in jeopardy. This is notwithstanding the fact that Canada had a central bank by this time, which did not exist during the worst days of the Great Depression. It was in large part due to the failures of financial institutions in the 1980s and 1990s that the federal government subsequently established the Office of the Superintendent of Financial Institutions (OSFI) to oversee the Canadian financial sector, including chartered banks and life insurance companies.[89] Solvency issues affecting financial institutions during this period probably also contributed to the refusal by the government of Prime Minister Jean Chrétien (Liberal) to allow bank mergers among Canada's Big Five banks in the 1990s and early 2000s – mergers which would have further concentrated the Canadian banking sector, where any one of the Big Five banks were arguably already too big to fail.[90]

The CCAA's endurance on the statute books (due to stalled bankruptcy reform efforts) was an important factor in the way subsequent events unfolded. As a parchment institution, the act provided an historical precedent for company reorganization – an existing set of institutional arrangements around which future actors could potentially coordinate. The CCAA provided a benchmark against which other business restructuring provisions, such as the 1992 amendments to the BIA, would ultimately be evaluated.

As in the 1930s, how Canada resolved the issue of facilitating corporate reorganizations for the benefit of financial institutions in the 1980s and 1990s would have potentially long-lasting implications for the law and practice of corporate restructuring. Whatever approach was adopted to effect corporate reorganizations was likely to generate a significant amount of positive feedback, as companies and some of their major creditors moved to effect large reorganizations. Unlike in the 1930s, however, at this new critical juncture, a legislative solution in the form of enabling legislation or bankruptcy amendments was not immediately forthcoming. Constitutional concerns over the ability of federal law to adjust secured claims were absent from public discourses. Moreover, as illustrated by bankruptcy developments in the United States and by the *Tassé Report* in Canada, a number of new ideas about bankruptcy and restructuring were circulating among parliamentarians, scholars, and practitioners by the time of the 1980s and 1990s recessions. These ideas would, accordingly, influence responses to the restructuring crisis. Therefore, the solution to the reorganization crisis of the 1980s and 1990s was likely to look different from the approach taken in the 1930s, and put corporate restructuring on a new trajectory.

4 Conclusion

Rather than responding to restructuring incentives established by insolvency law, large secured creditors resorted to receivership or insolvency law to effect reorganizations that were not possible through other means. Commercial incentives drove lender-led restructuring efforts, as did lender solvency concerns in some cases. Bank-supported restructurings ended up under the CCAA for a number of reasons. They included the possibility of a court-ordered stay, which blocked other, usually junior, creditors from enforcing their claims; the ability to bind third-parties to a restructuring plan; and the national scope of the act, which was used to coordinate restructurings under multiple pieces of legislation. Restructuring through insolvency legislation often proved a more powerful and effective method of conducting company reorganization for firms that fell within the act's ambit.

This differs somewhat from developments in other countries as well as conventional narratives surrounding Canadian business reorganization. For instance, in their discussion of bankruptcy reform in the United States and England, Halliday and Carruthers note that banks' strong legal rights translated into relatively weak influence in the polity of law reform in both countries.[91] In Canada, banks proved quite successful at managing the public relations aspects of corporate insolvencies by framing the lender remedy of reorganization as having wider public interest benefits, for example. Canadian courts picked up on this theme in their CCAA decisions. The demonstrable commitment of Canadian secured lenders to reorganizing debtors through insolvency law (which could provide knock-on benefits for other constituencies) aided their success in the polity.

By the time of the 1992 bankruptcy reforms, banks were relatively immune from the criticism that they pursued their own self-interest to the detriment of all other parties. The fact that Canadian developments primarily occurred in the courts benefitted large lenders. As repeat players, banks were better positioned than most other parties in an insolvency to influence case law developments.[92] The fact that courts are usually limited to existing legal architectures when effecting legal change[93] also helps explain why a DIP reorganization regime was built onto an existing secured creditor remedy. Unlike American and British banks that saw their legal rights diminished by statutory reforms, Canadian banks managed to maintain fairly strong legal rights in the 1980s and 1990s cases that characterized the CCAA as a DIP reorganization regime.

The success of Canadian banks in the polity stems in part from the fact that rather early in Canadian history constitutional constraints forced secured lenders into the more public sphere of court-appointed receivership and insolvency law to effect full corporate reorganizations. Additionally, in the 1980s and 1990s, Canadian banks spearheaded a number of high-profile restructurings in the courts. In England, the fact that bank efforts to restructure corporate debtors tended to take place in the more private space of the boardroom may help explain why they were less successful at convincing the British public that they did not oppose restructuring in principle.[94] A public track record for reorganizations went a long way toward securing favourable developments in reorganization law for large Canadian lenders. If more streamlined enabling legislation had been possible earlier in Canadian history, as it was in England, Canadian banks may not have proved so successful in the polity.

Debtors that did not have the support of their largest secured creditors, and thus little chance of completing a restructuring, also resorted to insolvency law. In this and in later periods, such debtor-led efforts form the basis of conventional DIP restructuring narratives, which borrowed from American narratives surrounding Chapter 11. But the CCAA itself neither created an incentive, nor forced majority secureds, to accept a plan against their economic interests. In this regard, the act remains an enabling statute. Incentives to restructure, which do not arise from the insolvency scenario itself – the type of incentives that may tip the scales in favour of restructuring – may, however, come from outside of insolvency law altogether, in the form of government concessions or plan funding, for instance.[95]

External factors were thus important to individual reorganizations, and the development of CCAA law more broadly. This underscores the significance of the broader social, political, legal, and historical context in which restructuring takes place. It forms the (subconscious) lens through which courts, practitioners, politicians, and scholars approach and interpret the CCAA. This context is dynamic. It continues to evolve and change, with implications for ideas about corporate reorganization, and this in turn influences the way various actors approach the statute. This perspective helps explain why some actors, such as the government and the judiciary, have taken different views of the act at different times. The federal government's hands-off approach to many CCAAs in the Great Depression is at odds with Canada's offers of plan funding for certain CCAAs during the 1980s and 1990s. The Canadian judiciary's approach to the act follows a similar pattern. The relatively hands-off approach in the 1930s and 1940s is in marked contrast to more activist styles of judging in CCAA cases in the 1980s, 1990s, and beyond. Broader changes in the social, political, and legal terrain surrounding the CCAA contributed to changing ideas about corporate reorganization, which in the 1980s and 1990s prompted greater governmental and judicial involvement.

7

Purposive Interpretation and Pro-Active Judging, 1980s–1990s

Proceedings under the C.C.A.A. are a prime example of the kind of situations where the court must draw upon [inherent jurisdiction] to "flesh out" the bare bones of an inadequate and incomplete statutory provision in order to give effect to its objects.[1]

B.D. Macdonald J., *Re Westar Mining Ltd., 1992*

1 Introduction

This chapter examines *how* the CCAA was re-interpreted and deployed by courts in the 1980s and 1990s in light of earlier commercial and legal changes. Several scholars identified a key role for public interest concerns in bankruptcy theories that developed during this period, illustrating how contextual factors such as environmental and labour issues worked their way into insolvency law scholarship. This chapter highlights the role of changing societal factors in the outward reinterpretation and repurposing of the act from a bondholder remedy into a DIP remedy. It also shows how these changes informed the public interest narrative that developed around the CCAA, and how this narrative was read back into the origins of the statute. Accordingly, this chapter is concerned with this dissonance between conventional interpretations of the act and its early history.

Reinventing the CCAA as a DIP restructuring mechanism involved overcoming several technical hurdles. Other authors have documented the progression of cases that fleshed out the anemic CCAA in terms of substantive law and procedure,[2] and have provided a chronology of the cases that transformed the CCAA into a modern DIP restructuring statute. This chapter sheds light on the deeper influences underlying these practical and legal developments. Why did lawyers and courts view qualifying criteria such as the trust deed requirement as obstacles? Whose interests did a corporate rehabilitation statute (purportedly) serve? Who propagated the idea that the CCAA advanced the public interest and stakeholder rights, and why? What prompted outward transformation of the CCAA from a secured creditor remedy into a DIP restructuring regime?

Commentators historically justified secured creditor remedies of seizure and receivership on the basis of the creditor's proprietary interest in the collateral, and made little effort beyond that to normatively defend the priority of secured creditors and their powerful recovery mechanism.[3] As late as 1985, for example, John R. Varley noted:

> The legal justification for the secured creditor's superior position is that such was bargained for, and the secured creditor should be as entitled to enforce its contractual rights under the bargain as is the borrower.[4]

Changes in stakeholder rights that occurred between the 1930s and the 1980s and 1990s, however, led to increasing concern about how junior creditors fared in insolvencies and receiverships.[5] In 1970, Tassé linked these concerns with Canada's bifurcated system of dealing with secured and unsecured claims, and stalled efforts to unite these systems under a new bankruptcy law.[6] He noted that even within the field of receivership, a number of potential issues arose that could act detrimentally to the interests of junior creditors.

Unfairness to junior creditors at the hands of large secureds in receiverships probably existed at least as far back as the 1920s. But earlier commentators recorded few complaints about issues of fairness. Instead practitioners such as Fraser regarded efforts by junior creditors to try to exploit opportunities to improve their priority vis-à-vis bondholders as a nuisance.[7] By the 1980s, however, high profile cases called attention to these issues and led to different results. This points to the rise of other considerations, such as the development of stakeholders' rights and political voice, which ultimately lent traction to longstanding issues of unfairness in business insolvencies.

Debtors' use of the CCAA in the 1980s and 1990s as a shield against secured creditor remedies in receivership or bankruptcy was also a newly acceptable phenomenon and required a fresh justification. In this regard as well, concern for stakeholder rights played an important role. The public interest narrative that developed around stakeholder rights in insolvency focused corporate reorganization debates around sympathy-evoking stakeholder groups, instead of unsympathetic images of large secured creditors, inept or self-serving managers, or shareholders who stood only to lose their investments. This provided a convenient gloss for large creditors and large companies insofar as it helped marshal support for reforms. Had the CCAA instead been cast as a secured creditor remedy, it is doubtful that the news media and legal literature would have received its revival as warmly.[8] It is also unlikely courts would have been as keen to give a large and liberal interpretation to a private, secured creditor remedy. The public interest thus provided a policy rationale for expansive statutory interpretation. At the same time, widespread support for the CCAA was explained with the notion that it advanced the wider public interest. Courts, counsel, and scholars used public interest concerns as guideposts for reinterpreting the act.

2 Reinterpreting the CCAA

Confronted with CCAA applications in the 1980s, courts approached the interpretation of the act against a much-changed socio-political backdrop and with a new principle of statutory interpretation in hand. Relying on Driedger's 1974 "modern principle of statutory interpretation,"[9] courts applied purposive statutory interpretation in CCAA cases.[10] For example, in *Norcen Energy Resources Ltd.* v *Oakwood Petroleums Ltd.*, Forsyth J. held:

> In construing a statute, one must always keep in mind the objects that the piece of legislation is designed to achieve. This principle is emphasized in Driedger:
>
> The comprehension of legislation is, in a sense, the reverse of the drafting process. The reader begins with the words of the Act as a whole and, from a reading of these words in their setting, deduces the intention of Parliament as a whole, the legislative scheme, and the object of the Act, and then makes construction of the particular enactment harmoniously with the words, framework and object of the Act. [Citations omitted.][11]

In the bankruptcy case *Re Rizzo & Rizzo Shoes Ltd.*, Iacobucci J. elaborated:

> [Driedger] recognizes that statutory interpretation cannot be founded on the wording of the legislation alone. At p. 87 he states:
>
> "Today there is only one principle or approach, namely, the words of an Act are to be read in their entire context and in their grammatical and

ordinary sense harmoniously with the scheme of the Act, the object of the Act, and the intention of Parliament." [Citations omitted.][12]

The federal *Interpretation Act* complemented this approach by providing that every act of parliament was to be "deemed remedial, and … given such fair, large and liberal construction and interpretation as best ensures the attainment of its objects."[13] Although the federal *Interpretation Act* has contained a provision to this effect from as early as 1927,[14] earlier reported decisions under the CCAA did not bear out the "large and liberal" interpretation now associated with Canadian statutory interpretation, and the CCAA in particular.

According to judicial decisions from the 1980s and 1990s, the use of the CCAA to address firm failures further underscored the remedial nature of the legislation. In *Elan Corp.* v *Comiskey (Trustee of)* Doherty J.A., dissenting in part, opined:

> The legislation is remedial in the purest sense in that it provides a means whereby the devastating social and economic effects of bankruptcy- or creditor-initiated termination of ongoing business operations can be avoided while a court-supervised attempt to reorganize the financial affairs of the debtor company is made.[15]

Furthermore, in *Re Lehndorff General Partner Ltd.*, Farley J. held that the act is "remedial legislation entitled to a liberal interpretation" because it is meant "to facilitate compromises and arrangements between companies and their creditors as an alternative to bankruptcy."[16]

In the later case *Bell ExpressVu Ltd. Partnership* v *Rex*, the SCC specifically identified the supporting role of section 12 of the *Interpretation Act* in Driedger's interpretive approach. In this case, the court noted that it frequently cited the modern principle of statutory interpretation as its preferred approach to statutory interpretation, and that this principle was "buttressed" by section 12 of the *Interpretation Act* in the case of federal legislation.[17]

Taken together, cases such as these provided a new framework for interpreting the CCAA, which differed dramatically from the strict and narrow approach evident in case law from the 1930s and 1940s.

Yet the emphasis in the modern approach to statutory interpretation on the purposes or objects of legislation posed a crucial difficulty with respect to the CCAA. Recall that the purpose of the act – to serve as a secured creditor remedy – was deliberately downplayed in the

1930s due to concerns that this was a constitutionally invalid purpose of a federal bankruptcy and insolvency statute. Furthermore, by the 1980s and 1990s courts and practitioners saw the CCAA as obscure and antiquated.[18] The text of the statute was skeletal and did not contain a preamble or other statement of its purposes. Little published writing on insolvency law and the CCAA existed that could shed light on the original objects of the act[19] and, read in isolation, materials such as Edwards's journal article, parliamentary debates, and reported cases tended to be misleading. Material that could have helped elucidate the act's objects often fell under non-insolvency law subject headings, which do not appear to have been consulted.[20] Yet in order to interpret the CCAA according to Driedger's principle, courts had to *begin* with the policy underlying the act. This they did, although the purposes the courts attributed to the act differed from its original objects.

Judicial decisions in the 1980s and 1990s conceived of the CCAA as a stand-alone insolvency statute, instead of a branch of company or receivership law. Conceptually separating the CCAA from these other areas of law meant that courts were relatively free in, and reliant on, their discretion to analogize and distinguish CCAA law from other receivership and restructuring precedents. This opened up the possibility of developing unique practices and procedures under the act according to its new objects.

The CCAA's new purposes thus entailed great room for the exercise of judicial discretion and inherent jurisdiction. In cases such as *Norcen*, the court, after affirming that Driedger's principle was sound, stated:

> The authorities are of some assistance in arriving at a determination of the purpose of the C.C.A.A. Illustrative are the words of Wachowich J. in *Meridian Dev. Inc. v. T.D. Bank*:
>
> The legislation is intended to have wide scope and allows a judge to make orders which will effectively maintain the status quo for a period while the insolvent company attempts to gain the approval of its creditors for a proposed arrangement which will enable the company to remain in operation for what is, hopefully, the future benefit of both the company and its creditors.[21]

Courts based their exercise of judicial discretion or inherent jurisdiction in part on the skeletal nature of the act, noted in numerous decisions.[22]

> Proceedings under the C.C.A.A. are a prime example of the kind of situations where the court must draw upon such powers [inherent jurisdiction] to "flesh out" the bare bones of an inadequate and incomplete statutory provision in order to give effect to its objects.[23]

The large and liberal approach to statutory interpretation augmented misconceptions about the CCAA's purposes, as courts used section 12 of the federal *Interpretation Act* to flesh out the statute according to its new objects. A growing body of case law affirmed, reaffirmed, and elaborated on initial misconceptions about the CCAA. Not only did this validate the new objects of the act, it contributed to the legitimacy of a normative policy of promoting business reorganization through Canadian insolvency law.

The CCAA represented the *only* Canadian insolvency law to facilitate complete company reorganizations until 1992, which also influenced judicial decision-making during this period. The act's capacity for binding secured creditors was essential for carrying out corporate reorganizations. The 1980s and 1990s recessions created compelling commercial reasons for debtors and secured creditors to try to use the CCAA to achieve restructurings that could not be effected through other means.[24] The adverse impact of large corporate insolvencies on stakeholders (public interest considerations) represented an additional rationale to attempt restructurings. Reported decisions from this period illustrate judicial sensitivity to this factor in reorganization efforts.[25] Interestingly it seems few (if any) lawyers, courts, or commentators questioned the normative desirability of corporate reorganization by this time. This underscores how much ideas surrounding corporate failure had changed in the decades since the Great Depression, and even since the 1970s.[26] Not coincidentally, this period also roughly coincides with the advent of theoretical inquiry into the question of corporate insolvency by legal scholars.[27] With DIP corporate reorganization widely seen as acceptable, and even desirable, the only remaining issue facing courts, counsel, and scholars was how to justify debtor-led reorganization for consumption by both the public and the legal community.

Insolvency Law

The few reported decisions on the CCAA that existed by the early 1980s reinforced earlier judicial characterization of the act as primarily insolvency law rather than insolvency law out of necessity. Reported cases, especially the brief decisions of the 1930s and 1940s, illustrate judicial confusion about the CCAA's true objects and usually dealt narrowly with the act as an insolvency law statute.[28] In the *CCAA Reference*, for example, the SCC's judgment did not substantively address the main constitutional issue that the act raised concerning secured creditor rights.[29] Nevertheless, a number of reported cases from the 1980s cited passages from the CCAA constitutional reference as an indication of the act's original purposes.[30] For example, in *Meridian Developments Inc.* v *Toronto Dominion Bank*, the Alberta Court of Queen's Bench wrote:

In the words of Duff C.J.C. who spoke for the court [*Reference re Companies' Creditors Arrangement Act*]:

> ... the aim of the Act is to deal with the existing condition of insolvency in itself to enable arrangements to be made in view of the insolvent condition of the company under judicial authority which, otherwise, might not be valid prior to the initiation of proceedings in bankruptcy ... [Citations omitted.][31]

The fact that the CCAA was largely disconnected from the legislative, economic, and political context that surrounded its enactment influenced how courts approached the act. The CCAA had remained frozen in time, which contributed to its obscurity by the 1980s. Recall that the act enshrined majority provisions into legislative form and, in so doing, responded to the possibility of financial institution failures amid the Great Depression, but only to a limited extent due to constitutional controversy over secured creditor rights. Constitutional and corporate insolvency law discourses, on the other hand, had progressed greatly in the decades following the 1930s.[32]

The fact that practitioners and courts in the 1980s viewed the CCAA as primarily insolvency law, rather than insolvency law out of necessity, underscores the tremendous shift that took place. By extending receivership remedies for secured creditors into insolvency law, the CCAA and FCAA legitimized the adjustment of secured creditor rights as a valid part of Canadian bankruptcy and insolvency law. They did this so successfully that secured creditor rights were a non-issue in the 1980s and 1990s, constitutionally speaking.[33] Insolvency law discourses, particularly surrounding corporate reorganization, also advanced significantly leading up to the 1980s. Most notably, a period of bankruptcy reform in the United States during the 1970s culminated in the enactment of inter alia Chapter 11 in 1978.[34] Chapter 11 quickly became a popular DIP reorganization regime among American corporations, and a model for many other countries contemplating bankruptcy reform in order to facilitate reorganizations.[35] Chapter 11 also promoted and legitimized going-concern reorganizations as a normative policy goal for corporate insolvency legislation. Canadian and American commentators and theorists promoted this idea as well, whereas this view represented just one of two competing ideals of corporate bankruptcy half a century earlier.[36]

Historical conceptions of secured creditors as progenitors of restructuring were notably absent from Canadian restructuring discourses during the 1980s and 1990s. These were supplanted by new public interest narratives that cast secureds in a more minor, supporting role.

This contrasts with the English experience. Leading up to the 1970s and 1980s, English banks remained major providers of corporate financing, which they still secured using floating charges. In 1977, Prime Minister James Callaghan's Labour government issued a report that pushed to subject floating charge holders to a bankruptcy law-restructuring regime.[37] This report was followed by significant reforms to English insolvency law in the 1980s. In Canada, on the other hand, new institutions entered the corporate lending market in the 1960s and 1970s. During this period Canadian banks overtook life insurance companies as major providers of long-term corporate loans. Furthermore, Canadian banks tended to take security for corporate loans under the *Bank Act* or PPSAs, rather than under trust deeds. By the 1980s and 1990s, the Canadian secured lending landscape looked quite different than it had in the 1930s, when parliament enacted the CCAA. The major lenders had changed and so had the preferred form of taking security. As a result, Canadian reorganization developments again diverged from those in England, despite similar legal origins. This in turn proved significant for Canadian corporate restructuring narratives.

In light of this new corporate insolvency law paradigm, and the fading political, economic, and legal factors that framed the CCAA's enactment, lawyers, courts, and commentators in the 1980s and 1990s regarded the act as primarily an insolvency law statute. This reaffirmed earlier judicial mischaracterization of the act, evident in cases such as the *CCAA Reference*. The contemporary perception was that the CCAA represented a stand-alone restructuring regime, instead of a part of a larger body of law and practice concerning secured financing and receivership reorganizations.

Debtor Remedy

Several factors help explain the courts' characterization of the CCAA as a debtor remedy during this period. First, debtors, not creditors, often made CCAA applications,[38] and media reports usually described the act as a debtor remedy along the lines of Chapter 11,[39] amid growing popularity and legitimization of the American bankruptcy code as a DIP restructuring mechanism.[40] Furthermore, in 1970 the *Tassé Report* had recommended improving the operation of compromise or arrangements under bankruptcy and insolvency law. This showed that views on DIP reorganization were changing within Canada as well.[41] Evidently debtor or manager abuse of corporate reorganization provisions was no longer the overarching concern it once was. In view of these considerations, as well as developments in stakeholder rights and statutory interpretation, courts saw the policy of the CCAA as helping debtors and their creditors attempt restructurings in order to avoid liquidation and winding up.

The fact that a secured creditor remedy was presumed to be a debtor remedy demonstrates the equivocal nature of the act's few provisions. It calls attention to the fact that the CCAA's new purposes came from sources other than the act itself. The skeletal CCAA of the 1980s lacked clear policy guidance, and its few substantive provisions were often ambiguous. For instance, either the debtor or one of its creditors could make an application under the act.[42] In other words, both debtors and creditors had unilateral recourse to the statute, producing indeterminate policy guidance as to whom the statute was intended to help. In contrast, Chapter 11, which the US Congress intended principally as a remedy for debtors, contains separate, little used provisions for creditor-initiated applications, known as "involuntary petitions."[43]

Canadian interpretations of the CCAA as a debtor remedy were interrelated with several other ideas. Chief among these was the notion that secured creditors conventionally did not resort to bankruptcy or insolvency law[44] and did not seek to restructure insolvent firms. This construction of secured creditor preferences drew implicitly on American and British experiences with enacting corporate restructuring legislation under the heading of "insolvency law" in the 1970s and 1980s.[45] But this framing of secured creditor preferences is poorly suited to the Canadian context in view of the demonstrable commitment of large secured creditors to restructuring debtors both inside and outside insolvency law. It is especially inapt with respect to secured creditor remedies such as CCAA and FCAA. While large secured lenders in Canada were probably no more eager to resort to conventional insolvency legislation than their American or British counterparts, from an early date the practical outcome of the Canadian division of powers made insolvency law their best option in certain cases. Nevertheless, lenders may be more inclined to restructure large companies, as opposed to small ones, and in any event the restructuring must make commercial sense for the lending institution.

The well-publicized actions of large Canadian banks with respect to farm foreclosures in the 1980s likely contributed to the view that large secureds preferred to pursue liquidation rather than debt restructuring.[46] Vocal bank opposition to certain debtor-led CCAAs probably compounded this view.[47] Due to the financial resources that are necessary to participate in a court-driven process, however, banks were arguably among the few stakeholders in a position to challenge the interpretation or application of the CCAA, especially in 1980s cases.

This probably further contributed to the perception that large secureds generally objected to debtor reorganization, and preferred to pursue other remedies, though this perception flew in the face of bank support for other large reorganizations in this period.

Going-Concern Reorganization

The idea that the CCAA was intended to facilitate going-concern reorganizations is related to perceptions that the act was a debtor remedy.[48] While creditor remedies generally seek to maximize creditor returns, a corporate debtor remedy suggests that there is at least a chance that the debtor will continue to exist. If going-concern reorganizations were not a possible goal of restructuring regimes such as the CCAA, they probably would not be characterized as debtor remedies.

In keeping with the impression that the CCAA was a debtor remedy, numerous reported cases from the 1980s and early 1990s articulated going-concern reorganizations as a main objective of the act.[49] For example, in *Northland Properties* the court stated:

> There can be no doubt about the purpose of the C.C.A.A. It is to enable compromises to be made for the common benefit of the creditors and of the company, particularly to keep a company in financial difficulties alive and out of the hands of liquidators ...[50]

Such statements of the CCAA's purposes aligned with stakeholder-centred theories of business bankruptcy, since they presumed a more stakeholder-inclusive theory of the corporation (at least at the point of insolvency) than the shareholder primacy model. The courts' remaking of the CCAA into a more stakeholder-friendly reorganization regime followed its reinterpretation of Canadian corporate governance along similar lines.[51] The transformation of the CCAA occurred as academics began incorporating stakeholder interests into formal theories and accounts of business bankruptcy, and rehabilitating the debtor accordingly took on wider importance.[52]

Earlier reported decisions also influenced the going-concern reorganization object of the act. For example, in *D. W. McIntosh Ltd.* the court noted:

> I am well aware of the fact that *The Companies' Creditors Arrangement Act* has been held to be bankruptcy legislation but the object of that Act is to keep companies going and not particularly to sell all the assets and divide the proceeds among the creditors.[53]

The court in *In re Avery Construction* stated:

> To my mind *The Companies' Creditors Arrangement Act, 1933*, is designed to keep the company in business, and is not to be used as a means of winding up the company ...[54]

In some cases courts quoted from Stanley Edwards's 1947 article in support of the going-concern reorganization objective of the CCAA. In the *Quintette* case, for instance, the court excerpted and relied on several passages from Edwards's article, to expound the "historic and continuing purposes of the act: Its object, as one Ontario court has stated in a number of cases, is to keep a company going despite insolvency."[55]

Nevertheless, continuation of the debtor company is better described as a common feature of CCAAs, rather than the act's main objective. At the outset of his thesis Edwards states: "One of the main *features* of a reorganization ... is that the business of the company is allowed to continue."[56] This issue is often moot because the debtor company continues as a going-concern after CCAA proceedings.

Recall that the CCAA (and bondholder reorganizations) facilitated going-concern reorganizations because liquidation was often unviable or suboptimal as a secured creditor remedy.[57] According to Edwards, reorganization was primarily a commercial response to a business problem, which in some cases overlapped with a situation of firm insolvency.[58] Secured creditors pursued (and still pursue) debt restructuring because of inadequacies or failures in the market for liquidations.[59] Contemporary scholars such as Jérôme Sgard have highlighted the necessity of functioning markets for liquidation to effectively operate as a creditor remedy.[60] So one can argue in favour of company reorganization on the basis that liquidation is an inadequate secured creditor remedy. But this is distinct from arguments that promote corporate reorganization because it is perceived to be more politically or socially desirable than liquidation.

Edwards's thesis confronted the problem of how to facilitate reorganizations under existing Canadian legislation in order to benefit creditors and shareholders without unduly sacrificing their rights.[61] In his thesis and journal article he advocates an insolvency law-restructuring regime to facilitate corporate reorganizations, and outlines suggestions for how courts might promote this under the CCAA *without* legislative amendment. Edwards presents the possibility of wider public interest benefits of reorganization for stakeholders, such as employees, as a potential additional rationale in support of corporate restructurings, but these arguments are ancillary to its purpose as a creditor remedy.[62]

Although large portions of Edwards's thesis and article *advocate* for going-concern reorganization, Canadian courts later established going-concern reorganization as the principal object of the CCAA. In so doing, they drew from the 1933 parliamentary debates, early reported decisions, and Edwards's 1947 article. The broad, public interest at stake in company insolvencies informed and justified this practical objective. Edwards's arguments may have held particular sway with courts because they dovetailed with what courts could do in terms of effecting legal change.[63] Read in their historical context, however, Edwards's parameters for effecting bold policy change in corporate reorganizations are rather contrived. It is unclear why Edwards did not instead suggest legislative reform of Canadian bankruptcy and insolvency law.

Public Interest

Incorporating public interest considerations into corporate reorganization discourses helped legitimize and garner public approval for the judicial repurposing of the CCAA. The fact that the public interest came to form a key part of CCAA considerations in the 1980s and 1990s represented a substantial reframing of the constituencies (stakeholders, weaker creditors) that comprised the corporation. Canadian debates about corporate reorganization shifted away from concerns about potential abuse of process by managers or shareholders[64] and from traditional contentment with leaving large secureds to decide the fate of insolvent firms (and junior creditors) through receivership. Contemporary CCAA narratives came to centre instead on stakeholders (labour, the community, tort victims) and the public interest benefits of keeping debtor firms in operation. This helped create a positive public image for corporate reorganization and public support for novel interpretations of the CCAA.

According to Canadian courts, the many constituencies involved in corporate insolvency meant that the public interest involved in a company insolvency generally weighed in favour of attempting a restructuring.[65] Lawyers and courts brought this public interest paradigm to bear in their reading of the CCAA and the scant material on the enactment and history of the statute.[66] For example, the court stated in *Sklar-Peppler*:

> The proposed plan exemplifies the policy and objectives of the Act as it proposes a regime for the court-supervised re-organization of the applicant company intended to avoid the devastating social and economic effects of a creditor-initiated termination of its ongoing business operations and

enabling the company to carry on its business in a manner in which it is intended to cause the least possible harm to the company, its creditors, its employees and former employees and the communities in which it carries on and carried on its business operations.[67]

Courts drew on Edwards's article in spite of the quite different policy purposes underlying the CCAA and the fact that his arguments were advocacy, not history.[68] In setting out his arguments in favour of a general corporate restructuring regime based on the public interest, Edwards drew mainly on US precedents and literature,[69] and specifically advocated that Canadian courts change course and adopt an approach more along US lines.[70] He favoured the post-*Chandler Act* (1938) version of US corporate reorganization, which incorporated significant public interest safeguards. In demonstrating the public interest character of this approach, Edwards noted inter alia that the US *Bankruptcy Act* expressly provided that the SEC play a supervisory role in company restructurings.[71] So, it is noteworthy that neither the CCAA nor its American analogue (section 77B, enacted in 1934) included such provisions.[72] Nevertheless, Edwards essentially argued that Canadian courts should assume the role of guardian of the public interest in CCAAs.[73] Yet he stated elsewhere that courts have only two points at which to deal with the CCAA plan,[74] so it is unclear how courts could play a role similar to the SEC.

To support a public interest view of the CCAA, commentators and the courts in the 1980s and 1990s also gave considerable weight to the brief 1933 parliamentary debates[75] and even to the full title of the act,[76] which they thought captured the purposes of the statute succinctly. In point of fact, a bondholder remedy view of the CCAA also accords with the long title of the act, and historical sources, such as Edwards, provided an incomplete picture of the CCAA even at the date of their writing.[77] Since the text of the CCAA stayed more or less the same for fifty years, interpretation of the act as a debtor remedy actually showcases the transformation of ideas surrounding corporate reorganization over that period.

Although the CCAA makes no mention of the public interest, it does expressly address the interests of creditors:

Scope of Act

8. *This Act is in extension and not in limitation of the provisions of any instrument now or hereafter existing governing the rights of creditors or any class of them* and has full force and effect notwithstanding anything to the contrary contained in any such instrument. [Emphasis added.][78]

This study did not locate any reported decisions that substantively address the italicized portion of this provision, despite the fact that it dates back to the CCAA's original enactment; it remains in the current version of the act and has been little changed since 1933.[79] Neither Edwards's thesis nor his article address this provision.[80] Inexplicably, the provision titled "Scope of Act" is missing from discussions about the scope of the CCAA.[81]

A number of cases consider the latter part of section 8 in terms of the court's power to restrain the exercise of creditors' rights under "other instruments" in the course of CCAA proceedings.[82] Courts have relied on this section almost exclusively to justify the staying of creditor-initiated proceedings, such as creditor remedies under the *Bank Act*[83] or those specified in contract.[84]

On its face this appears to serve as the type of limitation that this section prohibits. Yet reported cases do not reconcile this inconsistency. Judicial reasoning in cases such as *Chef Ready* fell back on "the broad public policy objectives of the CCAA" instead as a sort of counter-balance to a limitation (in the form of the stay) of creditor remedies such as seizure and receivership.[85] This seems to imply that insolvency law must curtail the rights of creditors (usually secured creditors) to some extent (if only through a delay on realization[86]) in order to preserve the possibility that a "greater good" might be achieved through reorganization.[87] In other words, it is the debtor, or a broad constituency of stakeholders, whose interests are extended, and not limited, by the act.

On the other hand, viewing the CCAA as a bondholder remedy reconciles the two statements contained in section 8. The CCAA *extended*, and *did not limit*, the provisions of an instrument governing the rights of bondholders by providing a statutory restructuring mechanism for their benefit that built on existing practices under majority provisions. Nevertheless, this section did not compel bondholders to use the act if instead they preferred to use the majority provisions in their trust deed only, which many did.[88] The portion of the provision that reads "any instrument now or hereafter existing" also speaks to the fact that the CCAA was enacted to address two specific problems: cover drafting defects in existing trust deeds, and provide for the possibility of compliance with new listing requirements on the New York Stock Exchange.

According to a bondholder-remedy understanding of the CCAA, the latter half of section 8 prohibited contracting out of the act's ambit, and arguably also prohibited contracting around the purpose of the statute as expressed in the first part of the provision. Historically, the CCAA probably had to contain a provision against contracting out of its scope in order to satisfy US listing requirements.[89] This was likely necessary to underscore the fact that the act was "not in limitation" of instruments governing creditors' rights in order to distinguish the act from majority provisions and allay American concerns.[90]

Section 8 was the most appropriate starting point for determining the purposes of the CCAA. When this provision was read in light of the trust deed provision, and the definitions of "company" and "debtor company," it established that the policy behind the act was to facilitate reorganizations of companies for the benefit of their bond-holders, and could only be applied when used as such. Although Edwards presented interesting policy arguments in his 1947 article, the 1953 trust deed amendment (initially) frustrated the possibility of courts taking up his suggestions. Remarkably, these same policy arguments later guided judicial repurposing of the act in the 1980s and 1990s.

Summary

Judicial interpretations of the CCAA's underlying policy in the 1980s and 1990s incorporated a significant public policy element. Pro-DIP restructuring narratives circulating by the 1980s, particularly thanks to the popularity of Chapter 11, influenced the way parties approached the skeletal CCAA. The lack of a clear written policy rationale for the CCAA compounded the act's obscurity. In contrast to the 1930s, lawyers and courts in the 1980s approached the act without serious reservations about the normative desirability of DIP reorganization, or the constitutionality of restructuring secured claims through insolvency law. They regarded the act on its face as a Canadian Chapter 11. Accordingly, they saw reorganization as both the practical outcome and the policy objective of the act.

Purposive interpretations of the CCAA adopted in the 1980s and 1990s usually boiled down to a policy goal of effecting DIP company reorganizations, within the few strictures of economic considerations, statutory voting requirements, and judicial approval of the plan. To do this would require removing the one barrier that made the act the preserve of bondholders – the trust deed amendment – and this is examined in the next chapter. Since parliament designed the CCAA to operate under the architecture of receivership, this brief statute would also require significant fleshing out by the courts in order to function as a DIP remedy. Public interest considerations helped legitimate and popularize corporate reorganization, and so formed an important touchstone for judicial development of CCAA law.

These case-driven changes in CCAA law raise fundamental questions about the role of Canadian courts and legislatures: Where was parliament when these developments were taking place? How is it that courts brought about significant changes to statutory law *without* parliamentary involvement? Parliament's neglect of bankruptcy and insolvency reform throughout much of the latter part of the twentieth century helps, at least somewhat, to explain why courts intervened as they did. Due to the inaction of parliament, courts believed they were forced into deciding whether to fill a gap in the legislative framework or allow large corporations to fail, with possible knock-on effects for Canadian financial institutions. An explanation, however, differs from a justification. This courts' framing of the decision before them in the 1980s and 1990s seems like a fool's choice because remedying defects in legislation is the purview of the legislature. In point of fact, the restructuring crisis of the 1930s *was* resolved through new legislation. By stepping in, courts diffused political pressure on parliament, which otherwise could have spurred it into action. Courts and the legislature appeared to have reversed roles, creating a distinctive dynamic of legal change that has become endemic of contemporary CCAA law.

3 Historical Institutionalism and Recursivity of Law

The 1980s and 1990s marked another period of significant change in Canadian corporate restructuring law and practice. These changes primarily took place in Canadian courts, in direct response to attempts to restructure specific companies. Accordingly, these developments may be described as (initially) semi-formal in nature, as they lacked the formality of legislative reform, and yet they were not as informal as purely private arrangements. Moreover, since CCAA law largely developed on a case-by-case basis, these changes came about incrementally. Restructuring practice, and law trickled up from ad hoc restructuring attempts in a given case, to the court of first instance, and occasionally to appellate courts. The precedential value and formality of the law increased with each advancement. Ultimately, many of these case law developments were enshrined in legislation through later statutory amendments. Taken together over roughly two decades, case law developments revived and fundamentally changed judicial interpretations and applications of the CCAA, and in so doing reshaped the law and practice of Canadian corporate reorganization.

In the recessions of the 1980s and 1990s, large secured creditors and corporate debtors turned to the CCAA for several reasons. First, financial institution solvency issues were a key driver of restructuring efforts in respect of large corporate debtors. The recessions were the first significant economic downturns chartered banks faced in the role of major long-term secured lenders. Canadian banks found that traditional remedies, such as seizure and liquidation, were not necessarily adequate or optimal in the context of a general market downturn when many corporate clients, including some of the banks' largest clients, encountered financial difficulty. Facing large and widespread losses, financial institutions, including chartered banks, actively supported a number of the largest, often ad hoc, corporate restructurings during the 1980s and 1990s, through the CCAA and other mechanisms. The support of these large secured creditors was usually essential for carrying out successful reorganizations due, for instance, to the majority voting requirements contained in the CCAA. In some cases banks sought and obtained special permission from regulatory authorities to implement debt-for-equity exchanges as part of restructuring plans.

The success of large secureds in this regard, and in the court cases that repurposed the CCAA, bears out the idea that sophisticated repeat players (such as banks) are better able to advance their interests through lawmaking and adjudication than one-time players (such as debtors or labour unions), and in this way they help shape law in a manner favourable to their interests.[91] Debtors, on the other hand, predictably turned to restructuring – particularly a stay of proceedings under the act – as an attempt at self-preservation or to minimize large, impending liabilities. It is worth noting that within the context of insolvency, debtors are not usually an organized interest group.

A second factor that contributed to the revival of the CCAA relates to changing ideas about company reorganization. In large part due to the influence of US ideas about bankruptcy law, the concept of DIP going-concern reorganization had gained greater acceptance, and even some popularity, in the press and among practitioners by the 1980s and 1990s. Unlike the attitudes of the 1930s, DIP reorganizations were not regarded as necessarily abusive of creditor rights. Rather, facilitating DIP reorganization was increasingly seen as a desirable normative goal of bankruptcy and insolvency legislation.[92] In the context of the 1980s and 1990s, corporate restructuring was seen as an alternative to liquidation and winding up, and had a role in saving jobs, with knock-on benefits for the wider community. This appears to be the first time that company restructuring was broadly associated with job retention in Canada. During the Great Depression, restructuring was so closely associated with job losses that important employers, like the CNR and Algoma Steel, were not allowed to restructure, either privately or under the CCAA. Instead, the federal government nationalized or subsidized such corporations to ensure ongoing employment for workers.[93] The Algoma Steel reorganizations under the CCAA in the 1990s and 2000s, however, were both justified in part on the argument that restructuring would help *save* jobs, and different levels of government contributed funding to both restructurings on primarily these grounds.[94]

This points to changes in the public relations surrounding large firm reorganizations (restructuring results in jobs lost versus jobs saved) as well as approaches to dealing with firm insolvencies (nationalization versus government-supported private reorganization), rather than changes in the *outcome* – the fate of the firm – which in both periods was to preserve important enterprises as going concerns. The other notable constant has been the support of large secured lenders for such reorganizations and their influence in terms of shaping law. So the practical outcome (for workers and large secured lenders) of bondholder reorganizations or the nationalization of important firms in the 1930s is probably little different from the contemporary CCAA reorganization of companies such as Algoma Steel. The most significant distinction between the two periods is that the 1980s and 1990s witnessed the application of a public interest gloss to a century-old bondholder remedy.

Changing ideas around reorganization accordingly influenced responses to situations of corporate insolvency. Borrowing from ideas in Chapter 11, restructuring came to be regarded as a possible solution to firm insolvency in Canada as well. In a highly recursive fashion, this de novo legal concept helped frame the way parties and judges approached the issue of firm insolvency. Most notably, this new paradigm influenced how the skeletal CCAA was read and interpreted. Going-concern reorganizations, for the wider public good, were regarded as the main policy purpose of the act, which lacked a preamble or other policy statement. What little of the legislative and historical context was apprehended – enacted during the Great Depression; purportedly to save jobs, according to Hansard; limited in application to insolvent companies with outstanding trust deeds – was seen to affirm the policy goal of going-concern reorganizations of large companies.[95] Much subsequent case law, including exercises of judicial discretion and inherent jurisdiction, was decided in view of this implicit policy goal. This view of CCAA law lined up much better with a number of American theories of business bankruptcy then in circulation. Reported cases, news coverage, and academic literature from this period gave less attention to the use of the CCAA as a remedy for large creditors, although it was still employed as such. Ideas had changed considerably about company reorganization, helping to shape practical and conceptual approaches to dealing with firm insolvency during the 1980s and 1990s, including those carried out under the CCAA.

New ideas in respect of company insolvency and reorganization were also influenced by stakeholder groups, which were not major actors in early twentieth-century company reorganizations. Concern for employees, the environment, and wider communities in which companies operated assumed significant roles in corporate insolvencies and wider academic debates in the 1980s and 1990s.[96] Bankruptcy theorists, and even judges, justified going-concern reorganizations in part on the basis of the benefits that would accrue to such stakeholders. Accordingly, stakeholders that previously had no say in corporate restructuring matters assumed central roles in both theoretical discussions and actual corporate reorganizations. These groups provided a publicly appealing face for corporate reorganizations, which also advanced the interest of less sympathy-evoking constituencies, such as large secured creditors, debtor management, and shareholders. Later, Canadian judges accordingly received as dictum the ancillary and somewhat far-fetched (for their time) policy arguments suggested by Stanley Edwards in 1947, concerning the benefits of going concern-reorganizations for workers. Edwards's recommendations for a novel policy approach to company reorganization to be largely overseen by judges (rather than parliament) – which appears to have held no sway in 1947, and which was mooted in any event by the 1953 trust deed amendment – effectively became guide posts for the contemporary development of CCAA law and policy. Although large secured creditors essentially dropped out of the legal and public justification for effecting reorganizations at this point, they remained major drivers and beneficiaries of large corporate restructurings.

4 Conclusion

In terms of practical outcomes, modern CCAA law is not that different from the bondholder and CCAA reorganizations of the early twentieth century. The key distinction is that contemporary reorganization discourses applied a public relations gloss to large corporate restructurings under the umbrella of the public interest. The legitimization and normative desirability of DIP reorganization, however, is relatively new to Canadian insolvency law policy. These developments also obscured the origins and ongoing operation of Canadian corporate restructuring as a secured creditor remedy.

Broader socio-political changes in Canada leading up to the 1980s informed subsequent CCAA developments, and other areas of corporate law also reflected these contextual changes.[97] Changing ideas about corporate rescue were linked to changing ideas and attitudes about the corporate form. Under a strict shareholder primacy view of the corporation, it would be difficult to justify DIP reorganization as being in the public interest – this would essentially be a shareholder remedy. In this regard, the public interest narrative implicitly rests on a more stakeholder-friendly view of the corporation.

American bankruptcy developments and ideas in circulation by the 1980s and 1990s influenced the way parties in Canada approached the CCAA. Contemporary discourses lent legitimacy to the notion of considering the public interest in firm insolvencies, as Edwards had advocated in 1947. Ideas propounded in more recent discourses on bankruptcy theory and policy also help explain the selective way in which courts applied ideas from Edwards and other early CCAA materials when interpreting the act: counsel, courts, and scholars drew from Edwards and other historical sources with a view to finding historical support for contemporary conceptions of corporate bankruptcy.

New approaches to judging and statutory interpretation played an integral role in case-driven CCAA developments. Modern, policy-conscious courts brought purposive statutory interpretation to bear on the arcane and skeletal Act. Courts incorporated contemporary socio-political concerns and bankruptcy discourses into their reading of the statute. Instead of giving voice to the original policy purposes of the act, courts drew on material to apply a public interest gloss to an antiquated bondholder remedy. This gloss was probably necessary to help legitimize going-concern reorganizations in the late twentieth century – particularly those facilitated by the courts rather than parliament. A strict application of early twentieth-century bondholder reorganization practices to the 1980s and 1990s context would likely have affronted modern Canadian laws and policies concerning organized labour, stakeholder concerns, and the more nebulous idea of the public interest. This might have generated protest to the process of judicial decision-making that was fleshing out the CCAA, and thrown the legitimacy of case-driven developments into question. Nevertheless, despite the new legitimacy narrative surrounding the act, the underlying architecture of the CCAA still functioned as an effective remedy for large secured creditors.

8

Judicial Sanction of Tactical Devices

It is the duty of the court to give effect to legislation, not to emasculate it. The plain language of s. 3 offers no other conclusion than that it was enacted to exclude certain companies from the benefits of the Act. No company is excluded if all that is required is an "entrance fee" in the form of a trust deed created not to raise capital, but simply to gain access to a legal remedy not otherwise available. I cannot think that the legislation was intended to be interpreted in a way that permits this. In my opinion, s. 3 contemplates the existence of securities characterized by genuineness in the sense that they were issued to raise capital or secure existing indebtedness and not, as here, to achieve an oblique purpose. To hold otherwise would fail to give effect to the spirit and intent of the legislation.[1]

Wimmer J., *Re Norm's Hauling Ltd., 1991*

1 Introduction

The CCAA represented the *only* Canadian insolvency law to facilitate complete company reorganizations until 1992, which influenced judicial decision-making during this period. The 1980s and 1990s recessions created compelling commercial reasons for debtors and secured creditors to use the CCAA to achieve restructurings that could not be effected through other means. In *Re Philip's Manufacturing Ltd.*, for instance, the British Columbia Supreme Court held:

The bankruptcy proposal procedures are quite impractical for the average company because they do not bind secured creditors ... While that deficiency appears to have been recognized, based on the bankruptcy amendments presently proposed [referring to the 1992 amendments to the *Bankruptcy Act*], the Act [CCAA] now forms the only practical means of avoiding liquidation in the event of insolvency. That means, and access to it by the greatest number of potential debtors, should be preserved. The practice of gaining access to the Act by the "entry fee" of an instant trust deed is by no means new. It has been condoned by this and other courts on numerous occasions in the past. *If that is judicial legislation, so be it* [emphasis added].[2]

Judicial sanction of instant trust deeds marked a pivotal point in the CCAA's transformation. An "instant" trust deed refers to a last-minute loan obtained by the company in the form of bonds or debentures issued under a trust deed and running in favour of a trustee. The amount borrowed was usually nominal since the purpose of the loan was simply to bring a debtor company within the ambit of the CCAA. By affirming the legitimacy of instant trust deeds, courts effectively interpreted away the trust deed requirement. More broadly, allowing this tactical device made the text of the CCAA instrumental in achieving its new policy objectives. Courts went on to interpret the act's provisions in a large and liberal or strict and narrow fashion accordingly. The sanction of instant trust deeds thus ushered in and affirmed the ad hoc use of the act to facilitate restructurings. Through judicial discretion or inherent jurisdiction, courts repurposed the act and "put flesh on bones."[3]

From the time of its enactment, the skeletal CCAA generated confusion among courts charged with interpreting and applying the act and this led to unintended outcomes. In both periods of legal change examined in this book, DIP restructuring emerged as an unintended consequence of the CCAA. In the 1930s, the courts' strict and narrow interpretation of the act allowed debtor-led CCAAs, which ultimately led to the 1953 trust deed amendment. In the 1980s and 1990s, however, characterization of the statute as a debtor remedy led to the effective repeal of the trust deed requirement. While purposive statutory interpretation in the latter period gave effect to the CCAA's new objects, courts, paradoxically, tended to interpret the trust deed requirement in a strict and narrow fashion. In some cases courts expressly placed more importance on commercial expediency than on discerning the underlying purpose of the trust deed provision.[4] So even within the courts' new framework of purposive interpretation, one can critique their treatment of the trust deed requirement.

2 Instant Trust Deeds

In the early 1980s the trust deed provision read as follows:

Application

3. This Act does not apply in respect of a debtor company unless
   (a) the debtor company has outstanding an issue of secured or unsecured bonds, debentures, debenture stock or other evidence of

indebtedness of the debtor company or of a predecessor in title of the debtor company issued under a trust deed or other instrument running in favour of a trustee, and

(b) the compromise or arrangement that is proposed under section 4 or section 5 in respect of the debtor company includes a compromise or arrangement between the debtor company and the holders of an issue referred to in paragraph (a).[5]

The trust deed provision thus preserved the act as a bondholder remedy and prevented its use in cases not involving bondholders. As the 1938 committee minutes show, parliament intended this provision to protect junior creditors from debtor-led reorganizations, which lacked receiver or trustee oversight.

Tactical Devices

Case law from the 1980s and 1990s illustrates that courts either did not fully apprehend this purpose of the trust deed provision and its bearing on the framers' original intent for the CCAA, or else afforded it little weight. The appellate decisions in *Re United Maritime Fishermen* (*UMF*) and *Elan* are illustrative.

In *UMF*, the New Brunswick Court of Queen's Bench heard arguments from opposing counsel that drew attention to the intended impact of the 1953 trust deed amendment. Counsel stressed that although the CCAA (1933) applied to all companies, the trust deed amendment introduced a significant change to the scope of the act.[6] The court summarized counsel's arguments as follows:

It is submitted that "the purpose of the amendment was to prevent *any* insolvent incorporated company from making application under the *Act* and to severely restrict the operation of the *Act* by limiting the availability of the *Act* to companies which have outstanding issues of bonds, stocks or other evidences of indebtedness, issued under a trust deed and running in favour of a trustee." In favour of its submission, counsel cites from debates of the House of Commons and Senate, in 1952, when the amendment was introduced, and in particular relies on the following passage of the then Minister of Justice the Honourable Mr. Garson, who said:

With the passage of this Bill, it will leave companies that have *complex financial structures, and a large number of investor creditors*, able to use the *Companies' Creditors Arrangement Act* for the purpose of reorganization. Moreover, they will be able to use it efficiently; because, as a rule, the terms of their own trust deed provide for a trustee of the creditors whose business it will be to look after their interests properly, a provision which is almost invariably absent in the case of mercantile creditors. (Emphasis added.)

In other words what counsel is saying is that the Act is, since 1952, only available to "companies with complex financing and which have outstanding bona fide trust deeds."[7]

It seems that opposing counsel in this and subsequent cases[8] conflated the purpose and effect of the trust deed provision. Relying on the brief 1952–3 parliamentary debates, counsel argued that the *purpose* of the amendment was to restrict the scope of the act to companies with complex financial structures. Historical evidence shows this was just a probable *effect* of the trust deed restriction.[9] The court had to decide on this basis whether to interpret the trust deed provision strictly and narrowly or purposively with a view to the supposed intention of parliament.

Although the lower court in *UMF* acknowledged that parliament meant for section 3 to serve as a restriction, it looked at the strict wording of the trust deed provision only[10] and noted:

While the words "complex financial structures" and "a large number of investor creditors" have been used by the then Minister of Justice in debate, those words do not appear in s. 3. Nevertheless, should counsel be correct in his submission, I would then conclude, from the following abstracts from Ex. R-1, that U.M.F./Bluenose [the debtor companies] do have "complex financial structures and a large number of investor creditors".[11]

The New Brunswick Court of Appeal held that this provision "severely restricted" the scope of the act, but then undermined that restriction by allowing for the possibility of instant trust deeds.[12] The New Brunswick Court of Appeal noted the reasons behind the trust deed amendment, as submitted by counsel, which it described as "mischief," but the court ultimately limited its analysis to the text of the provision.[13] The appellate decision in *UMF* thus adopted a literal interpretation of the trust deed requirement and limited its inquiry to whether or not the debtor met the criteria set out in the provision.

This approach is somewhat at odds with the modern principle of statutory interpretation set out by Driedger, which incorporates a restricted version of the former mischief rule.[14] Driedger states: "The courts still look for the 'mischief' and 'remedy,' but now use what they find as aids to discover the meaning of what the legislature has said rather than to change it." Since, in the court's view, parliament intended the trust deed amendment to remedy certain "mischief," this fact would seem to be important to interpreting and applying that provision "harmoniously with the scheme of the act, the object of the act, and the intention of parliament."[15]

The Ontario *Elan* case affirmed the reasoning in *UMF* but took its analysis one step further. In that case the debtors issued an instant trust deed expressly for the purpose of gaining access to the CCAA.[16] Farley J. initially refused the application on the grounds that they had only one outstanding debenture, and the wording of section 3 required more than one debenture.[17] So the debtors each issued two more debentures and returned to court the same day to re-apply under the CCAA, whereupon Farley J. granted an order under the act.[18] At first blush one versus three debentures seems like a pointless distinction. But this strict interpretation was probably a necessary step in the judicial repurposing of the CCAA because judges are limited to existing legal frameworks when effecting change.[19]

In *Elan* the court based its reasons for allowing instant trust deeds on statements of the CCAA's policy purposes in the 1933 parliamentary debates, as filtered through judicial decisions such as *Chef Ready* and Edwards's 1947 article.[20] The majority made no mention of the 1953 trust deed amendment. Doherty J.A., dissenting in part, dismissed opposing counsel's submission concerning the 1953 debates and amendment because he found them unilluminating and "[t]he interpretation of words found in a statute, by reference to speeches made in parliament at the time legislation is introduced, has never found favour in our Courts."[21] Opposing counsel's argument from the *UMF* case is apposite:

> The court was misled by the presentation to it of precedents and articles which either dealt with the intent of the Act and its applicability prior to the amendment of 1952 or that these precedents and articles, if written after 1952 have all missed the significant change brought about by the introduction of s. 3.[22]

So where were courts supposed to look to discern the policy objectives of the skeletal, preamble-less CCAA?

The lack of a clear policy rationale for why the CCAA was supposedly limited to large, complex companies was probably a key reason for the little judicial weight given to the 1952–3 debates. In this way ambiguity helped create the possibility for legal change.[23] Courts and counsel relied on materials, such as the 1933 parliamentary debates (indirectly) and Edwards's article, which they believed captured the policy underlying the act. Additionally, courts, such as in *Elan*, relied on developing practices under the CCAA to inform their interpretation of the trust deed provision.[24]

The dissent in the Ontario Court of Appeal decision in *Elan* became an influential precedent endorsing the use of tactical devices to gain access to the act. Yet in this decision the court restricted its analysis of the trust deed provision to the text itself.[25] Remarkably the one substantive amendment to the CCAA up to the 1990s elicited little scrutiny, despite the fact that courts were interpreting the act purposively. The lack of clarity concerning the trust deed's underlying policy seems like an unsatisfactory reason to rely instead on the policy of the CCAA *prior to* the trust deed amendment. Whatever the original purposes of the CCAA were, purposive interpretation would suggest that they be interpreted in light of the changes made to the act in 1953.

"Sham" Creditors

At least one court did interpret the trust deed requirement in a purposive fashion. In its reasons, the Saskatchewan Court of Queen's Bench, in *Norm's Hauling*, emphasized the significance of the trust deed provision in terms of its impact on the scope of the act.[26] The court noted that this restriction would not serve as a restriction at all if the court recognized instant trust deeds:

> It is the duty of the court to give effect to legislation, not to emasculate it. The plain language of s. 3 offers no other conclusion than that it was enacted to exclude certain companies from the benefits of the Act. No company is excluded if all that is required is an "entrance fee" in the form of a trust deed created not to raise capital, but simply to gain access to a legal remedy not otherwise available. I cannot think that the legislation was intended to be interpreted in a way that permits this. In my opinion, s. 3 contemplates the existence of securities characterized by genuineness in the sense that they were issued to raise capital or secure existing indebtedness and not, as here, to achieve an oblique purpose. To hold otherwise would fail to give effect to the spirit and intent of the legislation.[27]

The Saskatchewan Court of Queen's Bench accordingly held that instant trust deeds did not bring the debtor within the ambit of the act. The court further held that the debtor in question was not a large, complex company of the type that parliament ostensibly had in mind when it introduced the trust deed provision.[28] The court also noted the difficulty of reconciling the idea of instant trust deeds as an entry fee

with any reasonable parliamentary intention behind the trust deed provision. Presumably only non-commercial creditors would be interested
in purchasing such securities. In this case, as well as in *Elan* and *UMF*,
relatives or managers rather than commercial creditors purchased the
instant trust deeds that were used to gain access to the act.[29]

Judicial Discretion

In their interpretations of section 3, the courts in *UMF* and *Elan* did
not attempt to restrict the act to large companies with complex capital
structures. In the *Elan* dissent Doherty J.A. stated:

> Attempts to qualify those words [of section 3] are not only contrary to the
> wide reading the Act deserves, but can raise intractable problems as to
> what qualifications or modifications should be read into the Act … It must
> be remembered that qualification under s. 3 entitles the debtor company
> to nothing more than consideration under the Act. Qualification under s. 3
> does not mean that relief under the Act will be granted. The circumstances
> surrounding the creation of the debt needed to meet the s. 3 requirement
> may well have a bearing on how a court exercises its discretion at various
> stages of the application, but they do not alone interdict resort to the Act.[30]

Doherty J.A. paired a strict reading of section 3 with the balancing function of judicial discretion. This suggested a greater role for judicial discretion based on allowing instant trust deeds than would be necessary
if courts had refused to recognize such instruments by interpreting that
provision purposively.

A strict interpretation of the act probably necessitated at least the
prospect of greater use of judicial discretion in order to avoid obvious
problems it raised in terms the act's other provisions. Subsection 12(3)
[formerly numbered 11(2), presently numbered 20(2)] is a case in point.
Recall that this provision provided that a debtor could admit claims for
voting purposes and retain the right to contest liability for those claims
later on.[31] Ernest Bertrand's original concerns surrounding the possible fraud that this provision appeared to invite, which were alleviated
in part by the trust deed provision, resurface under strict and narrow
interpretations of the statute's provisions that eliminated the presence
of a receiver or trustee.

Creditor Classification

Allowing instant trust deeds also raised the question of how to clas-
sify instant debt for voting purposes. Subsection 3(b) specified that any

compromise or arrangement *had to* include debt issued under this qualifying instrument or else the act could not be applied at all.[32] This study uncovered no reported decisions that substantively deal with this classification issue. Perhaps counsel did not raise the issue before the court. In *Elan*, however, the majority noted that the debtor placed the "sham" creditors in their own class, and the lower court approved this classification for voting purposes.[33] Doherty, J.A., however, would have put the sham creditors in a class with two other secured creditors.[34]

Putting instant debt holders in their own class potentially gives them veto over the proposed plan, which seems absurd on its face. Admittedly it is difficult to see why these debt holders would vote against a plan, since they bought securities in an insolvent undertaking without any expectation of being repaid.[35] If their support is guaranteed, their vote is ceremonial, which is difficult to reconcile with the parliamentary intention behind the trust deed provision.

On the other hand, grouping instant debt holders with any other creditors is problematic because these claims holders are distinct from genuine debt holders.[36] Their support for the plan stems from something other than their claim. So it is unclear how these creditors can be grouped with genuine creditors based on having the same interests, as intended under section 4.[37] Instant debt holder support for the plan appears to stack the deck of the class in which these claims holders are placed. To avoid this, and the possibility of an effective veto, these creditors would need to be placed in a class where their vote would be inconsequential, which again raises the issue of parliamentary intention.

The practical scenario that unfolds from recognizing instant trust deeds raises further doubts about the courts' interpretation of this requirement. This is particularly the case when contrasted with the original intention of the provision, which was to limit CCAA reorganizations to those involving bondholders. By contrast, the classification issues that arise in pure capital restructurings are relatively minor.

Expanding Judicial Discretion

It is ironic that in adopting a strict interpretation of the trust deed provision, courts thought they were keeping matters simple by avoiding "intractable problems as to what qualifications or modifications should be read into the Act."[38] Courts actually complicated matters by introducing legitimate DIP reorganizations into Canada under the auspices of a bondholder remedy. This put courts, counsel, debtors, shareholders, and creditors in uncharted territory. Instant trust deeds and the fact that this tactical device allowed companies and creditors to use the

CCAA as a general restructuring statute gave rise to many new issues. Since the act did not speak to any of these issues, they were left, by default, to the discretion of the court to decide, thereby amplifying judicial discretion.

It is difficult to reconcile the court's strict interpretive approach in cases like *UMF* and *Elan* with later cases such as *Stelco*. These later cases expressly adopted a large and liberal approach when interpreting equally straightforward provisions, such as the requirement that the debtor be insolvent at the time of application.[39] On the other hand, in the third-party asset-backed commercial paper (ABCP) restructuring, the court again held to a strict and narrow interpretation of "company" in allowing ineligible debtors to be converted into eligible companies on the eve of application, for the express purpose of gaining access to the CCAA.[40] In the Montréal, Maine & Atlantique Canada Co. insolvency, the Quebec Superior Court essentially qualified the exclusion of railway companies from the scope of the act by implying that the prohibition only applied if railway companies had access to other complete restructuring legislation.[41] The result is that the railway company restriction in section 2 of the CCAA is not a restriction at all.[42]

The supposed silence of the act produced by a strict and narrow interpretation of a given provision often leads to the exercise of judicial discretion in a manner that appears to override one of the few matters on which the statute is *not* silent. The exercise of judicial discretion in this way disables statutory restrictions. In other words, courts adopt such a narrow view of the act's prohibitions that the supposed prohibitions do not operate as prohibitions at all, and serve as an entry point for the exercise of judicial discretion. Instant trust deeds,[43] instant incorporation documents,[44] and the interpretations of "railway company"[45] and "insolvency"[46] are all examples where arguments from silence have eroded the boundaries of the CCAA's scope.

Reported cases vacillate between strict and narrow and large and liberal approaches to the interpretation of specific provisions, with the common theme of expanding the scope of the act to encompass debtors that would otherwise not qualify for CCAA protection. This line of cases suggests that any type of enterprise can potentially be brought within the act's purview, notwithstanding its purported restrictions. A common thread in these decisions is a policy of ensuring wide access to the CCAA, and the policy justification is the intrinsic public interest benefits of CCAA reorganizations. These cases affirm the ability of courts to bend the text of the act to achieve these ends. A large and liberal interpretation, however, does not equate to giving the CCAA wide scope, nor is a wide scope the object of the act.

The theme of expanding the CCAA's scope points to the significance of the role reversal between the courts and the legislature. Inaction on the part of parliament, and its tendency to memorialize case law developments into statutory form (for example, removing the trust deed requirement), allowed CCAA courts to function much like a modern-day Court of Chancery. Courts used their discretion and creative interpretations of legislation to go beyond the law as enshrined in statute, which encouraged parties to seek further such rulings that amplified judicial jurisdiction. Although courts purportedly interpreted the CCAA in pursuit of equitable ends, the supposed recipients of these equitable remedies were often absent from the court-driven process due to the considerable financial, geographic, and even legal barriers to participation (for example, due to ex parte applications).

Increased judicialization in CCAA law seems to have eroded the rule of law and the role of precedent, leading to an ad hoc style of judging in which commercial pragmatism was the overarching objective. As legal philosophers such as Ronald Dworkin have noted, pragmatism as a guiding principle cannot offer a coherent policy direction.[47] A socio-legal analysis shows that the case-by-case decisions that result serve only to entrench the pattern of ad hoc decision-making. Taken together, a jurisprudence oriented around "doing what makes sense under the circumstances" (assuming there is agreement about what that is[48]) produces apparently conflicting individual outcomes that seem principle-less in the whole. CCAA case law is an example of the standard pragmatist's dilemma: articulating a particular goal by which to gauge when things are "better" undermines the pragmatist's claim because that goal cannot be justified without arguing in a circle.[49] So the supposed policy goal of effecting going-concern restructurings, for instance, has no power to restrain liquidating CCAAs so long as liquidation "makes sense under the circumstances."

Therefore, while commercial pressures help *explain* why, as a matter of history, courts approached CCAA interpretation as they did, they provide an unsatisfactory *justification* for these changes. Notwithstanding the importance one attaches to commercial pragmatism as a method of interpreting the CCAA, it does not offer a rationale for overriding express statutory language, nor does it provide a justification for the role reversal between the courts and parliament.

Trustee to Monitor

In tandem with these developments, a new role evolved within CCAA proceedings for an entity known as the "monitor." The CCAA monitor is a unique feature of Canadian insolvency law that developed on an ad hoc basis alongside the DIP restructuring regime.[50] The monitor's role was intended to help protect creditors against the risks of allowing incumbent management to stay in control of the debtor company. In this sense, the monitor role patched the gap in debtor oversight that was created by interpreting away the trust deed requirement. Recall that the purpose of the trust deed requirement was to ensure the presence of a trustee in all CCAAs, and often this trustee would serve as a receiver in the context of restructuring efforts. In contemporary CCAAs, the monitor was supposed to ameliorate potential conflicts of interest faced by incumbent management by serving as a watchdog who would sound the alarm if the debtor did something that was offside.[51] The main beneficiaries of the monitor's actions were creditors. The court was another intended beneficiary, as the monitor's office supposedly provided an impartial third-party to report on the debtor's actions and affairs. Thus, the monitor was supposed to be an integral part of the DIP regime, which provided an important check and balance on the risks involved with allowing the debtor to remain in possession.

The evolution of the monitor followed a similar pattern to other CCAA developments in this period. The office of the monitor originated in the 1980s at the discretion of CCAA judges.[52] Early on this office was sometimes referred to as an "interim receiver" highlighting the parallels between the roles of receivers and the CCAA monitor in acting as a check on debtor behaviour, protecting the interest of creditors, and serving as an officer of the court.[53] As a court officer the monitor's fees were protected, receiving priority over the claims of existing creditors.[54] Over time the appointment of the monitor, although still discretionary, became commonplace, and by the mid-1990s it was regarded as standard practice.[55] In 1997 the case law consensus was institutionalized in amendments to the CCAA, which made the appointment of a monitor a mandatory part of proceedings under the act.[56]

The importance placed on flexibility in CCAAs, including in the monitor's role, has meant that the duties of the office evolved over time, often in response to commercial concerns.[57] Although some responsibilities are now standard, others remain case-specific and are set out as part of the initial (and any subsequent) orders by a CCAA judge.[58] Like other aspects of CCAA law, certain changes in practice concerning this oversight role foreran legislative reforms.[59] For instance, some debtor companies attempted to co-opt the monitor role by requesting that their accounting firm be named to fulfill this function in the CCAA proceedings.[60] The company's accounting firm tended to be familiar with the business and financials, which could create commercial efficiencies and weighed in favour of their appointment as a watchdog.[61] Some courts acceded to this request, resulting in the monitor being less arm's length than originally intended.[62] In other cases courts found that the company's accounting firm would not be independent enough,[63] and the optics of the debtor's accounting firm serving as monitor undermined the idea of a check on incumbent management.[64] This development led to legislative amendments in the 2000s that prohibited this practice except with the permission of the court.[65] The legislative change aimed to establish a new standard practice for such appointments, without sacrificing flexibility to appoint the debtor's accounting firm should the circumstances warrant it.

The CCAA monitor position, which essentially replaced the trustee under the trust deed requirement, must now be filled by a licensed insolvency trustee, ensuring oversight by the OSB and addressing concerns that arose as early as the 1930s and 1940s about the lack of trustee oversight.[66] The invention and evolution of this new role, however, did not alter the ethic of commercial pragmatism that is at the heart of CCAA law. This left large, secured creditors well-positioned, by virtue of their commercial power relative to other parties, to advance their interests through the monitor's office, much as they had through the trustee's office in 1930s and 1940s restructurings. The invention of the CCAA monitor was in effect a contemporary gloss on an existing CCAA concept. Despite significant efforts at judicial innovation, the new system for overseeing the debtor looks very similar to the old one.

Contingencies and Changing Ideas

Since courts relied in part on the act's (supposed) silence to justify arguments in favour of instant trust deeds and similar tactical devices, it is surprising that they seem not to have considered potentially helpful insolvency materials. The *Tassé Report*, published in 1970, sheds light on origins and purposes of insolvency legislation such as the CCAA. Tassé's coverage of the CCAA provides more insight into the history of the act than do the parliamentary debates. The *Report* identifies the statute as a bondholder remedy and describes the reasons for the trust deed amendment.[67] So this parliamentary report could have shed light on the "brief" and "unilluminating" debates from 1933 and 1953. It also could have helped contextualize early CCAA cases by showing that, for the most part, these debtor-led restructurings were the abuse that the trust deed provision was meant to prevent. This study found no reported CCAA cases that mention the *Tassé Report*.[68] The same is true for a 1952 practice note on the CCAA from the *Canadian Bankruptcy*

Reports, which discussed a number of undesirable practices under the act, many of which the trust deed amendment effectively addressed.[69] It is surprising that counsel did not come across this practice note when searching for CCAA case law in the *Canadian Bankruptcy Reports*, yet quite a number of reported decisions reference early case law from it as well as Edwards's 1947 journal article.[70] Courts and opposing counsel had good reasons to refer to Tassé and the 1952 practice note, as well as the issues these documents raise.[71] So it appears that counsel may not have consulted all the relevant insolvency law documents on the CCAA, which helped perpetuated misapprehensions about the act as a standalone restructuring statute for the benefit of debtor companies. This in turn seems to have contributed to the perception that there are gaps in the act that judges must fill, using their discretion or inherent jurisdiction, when in fact parliament merely intended for the CCAA to patch over defects in trust deeds.[72]

In the result, Edwards's 1947 article had a greater impact on the development of CCAA law after the 1970s than either the 1953 trust deed amendment or the *Tassé Report*. Yet the courts' articulation of the potentially large role of judicial discretion under the CCAA and the flexible court-driven nature of the act are at odds with Edwards's writing on these points. According to Edwards, the court only had two opportunities to deal with a CCAA plan – on application and at the sanction hearing – and it had limited powers at both stages.[73] He also took issue with the practice of ex parte applications under the statute, as did other commentators,[74] since a hearing of all interested parties at the point of application would, in his view "aid the court in avoiding errors and will assist it in obtaining as full a knowledge as possible of the company's affairs, which will be very valuable to it in exercising its discretion."[75] Nevertheless, contemporary courts allow ex parte applications by debtors under the CCAA, provided the applicant makes full and fair disclosure of all relevant facts.[76] Professor Roderick J. Wood notes that ex parte applications may be useful if there is a threat of creditors initiating enforcement remedies against the debtor.[77] Earlier commentators, however, specifically identified ex parte orders as problematic and potentially abusive.[78] This shift in opinion appears to be in keeping with changing ideas about the CCAA, which now suggest that the debtor needs protection under the auspices of the act.

The strict and narrow approach to interpreting section 3 and other supposed obstacles to using the act are also at odds with Driedger's modern principle of statutory interpretation in some respects. This approach instead sounds like a partial return to the mischief rule of statutory construction insofar as courts concern themselves more with the "spirit" than the text of the act. As described by Driedger:

> Judges paid more attention to the "spirit" of the law than to the letter. Having found the mischief they proceeded to make mischief with the words of the statute. They remodeled the statute, by taking things out and putting things in, in order to fit the "mischief" and "defect" as they had found them.[79]

In CCAA case law, courts did not seek to remedy mischief, but rather supposed gaps or statutory silence, which they filled in view of the new policy purposes they ascribed to the act. The focus of courts on the spirit of the CCAA and reliance on judicial discretion demoted the text of the act to a supporting role in deciding many boundary-pushing CCAA cases. Courts interpreted the text strictly and narrowly if it interfered with the act's supposed purposes, and granted it a large and liberal construction if it seemed to give effect to the spirit of the legislation. Courts thereby molded the CCAA to fit its purported policy objective. In this process they ignored (section 8) or overrode (section 3) provisions that did not fit with their conception of the act. In so doing it appears courts gave relatively little weight to Driedger's guideline that "the words of an act are to be read in their entire context and in their grammatical and ordinary sense harmoniously with the scheme of the act."[80] Courts replaced the act's restrictions with judicial discretion, yet in practice judges seldom (if ever) deploy their discretion as a restriction in CCAA cases.[81]

Although commentators lauded the judicial fleshing out of the CCAA as an achievement of purposive statutory interpretation,[82] there are also weaknesses in this approach to statutory construction. For instance, it comes with certain costs in terms of compromising predictability and the rule of law. In seeking to expand the parameters of the act, courts actually eroded those parameters without exercising their discretion to add meaningful safeguards. By its silence, parliament lent its tacit approval to this process.

Inherent Jurisdiction and Judicial Discretion

In contemporary CCAA law there is a line of cases and commentary that draws a distinction between the concepts of inherent jurisdiction and judicial discretion as bases for judicial action when the statute itself is silent. The two concepts are often applied interchangeably and confused with each other. The blurring of the concepts has been criticized, and the more contemporary view seems to be that the distinction between jurisdiction and discretion is vital and must always be observed. Some judges and commentators have argued that this distinction is crucial to justifying judge-driven changes in CCAA law.[83] The argument advanced in favour of distinguishing inherent jurisdiction from judicial discretion is essentially this: While statutory law puts limits on judicial discretion, there is theoretically no limit on a judge's inherent jurisdiction provided that the statute does not deal with all or part of the issues. Therefore, inherent jurisdiction provides much greater scope for judicial innovation. As the distinction between these two concepts forms part of the narrative justification for contemporary CCAA law, a brief description and analysis of inherent jurisdiction and judicial discretion is necessary.

It is first worth mentioning that the central argument of this book does not hinge on a distinction between inherent jurisdiction and judicial discretion. The book advances the argument that beginning in the 1980s and 1990s judges became far more active in developing CCAA law in response to commercial pressures, forerunning statutory changes in many cases, such that the locus of change was often the courts instead of parliament. Judicial innovation was not limited to points on which the statute was silent, and included creatively overriding express limitations contained in the act. Whether this judicial activity is classified as inherent jurisdiction or judicial discretion does not alter the broader point presented in this book. The author takes the view that judges relied on their discretion to innovate in the area of CCAA law for the conceptual reason that the broad discretion afforded to judges under the statute leaves little or no room for them to exercise inherent jurisdiction. Nevertheless, from a socio-legal perspective, the fact that some judges thought they were relying on inherent jurisdiction is probably significant to an explanatory account of these legal changes. This belief likely contributed to the willingness of judges to flesh out an anemic statute. Query whether a court *not* endowed with inherent jurisdiction – a statutory court such as the Federal Court, for instance – would have acted so boldly or creatively to put flesh on the bones of a skeletal statute?

Inherent jurisdiction is an English common law doctrine that provides that a superior court has the ability to hear any matter that comes before it, subject to specific enumerated restrictions.[84] The powers of the superior court are said to be inherent rather than derived from statute, as the underlying foundation for court power is the common law. Although inherent jurisdiction may theoretically be deployed in a wide range of circumstances, the focus of the doctrine is in allowing the court to control the proceedings brought before it.[85] Canadian courts have adopted the English doctrine of inherent jurisdiction.[86]

At a broad level inherent jurisdiction may be limited by express wording in a statute that limits judicial authority or by an exclusive grant of jurisdiction to another adjudicative body (for example, a statutory court).[87] More specifically, inherent jurisdiction cannot be exercised in a manner that conflicts with a statute or rule.[88] Judges cannot rely on their inherent jurisdiction to negate an unambiguous expression of legislative will.[89] Finally, as a special and extraordinary power, inherent jurisdiction should be exercised sparingly and in a clear case.[90] As inherent jurisdiction is limited by legislation, the growth of statutes as a source of law over the nineteenth and twentieth centuries has arguably limited the range of circumstances in which a judge might be called upon to exercise their inherent jurisdiction. Thus, the boundary line between inherent jurisdiction and legislation is, in many instances, essentially that between the judicial and parliamentary branches of government.

Judicial discretion, on the other hand, provides that judges have the authority to make some decisions according to their discretion. Unlike inherent jurisdiction, judicial discretion is not an independent source of judicial authority. Rather it is a mechanism that provides some flexibility in the application of the law such that a judge may decide certain matters within a range of possible outcomes. The governing law determines whether and how much discretion is accorded to judges. Highly prescriptive provisions or tests may leave little or no room for judicial discretion, whereas laws that are more open-ended tend to leave considerable space for exercises of judicial discretion, and may even require a judge to exercise their discretion in order to apply broad principles to specific situations. Therefore, judicial discretion provides some flexibility in the application of the law, while inherent jurisdiction provides a basis for judicial action, geared toward matters of procedure, in the absence of an applicable statutory law.

Based on these descriptions of inherent jurisdiction and judicial discretion, consider this question: When a judge makes an order in a CCAA case pursuant to section 11 of the Act, is it an exercise of inherent jurisdiction or judicial discretion? (Section 11 provides that a court may make "any order it thinks fit.") It is submitted that such an order is an exercise of judicial discretion because the source of authority for making the order is derived from a statutory provision that specifically grants judges the jurisdiction to make orders. The jurisdiction exercised is therefore statutorily granted.[91] Judicial discretion is exercised in crafting a section 11 order as a necessary condition of translating a judge's broad ability to grant "any order" into granting a specific order in a specific insolvency.

Some readers may disagree with this analysis and the primary objection is addressed below. At this juncture, however, the reader is invited to engage in a thought experiment to illustrate the point: Suppose a statutory court that heard a CCAA matter did *not* have inherent jurisdiction and had to rely only on section 11. Would this constrain judging under the CCAA? In theory, the answer must be "no" by virtue of section 11. This section conveys broad powers on the court to make "any order it thinks fit" in CCAA proceedings. It therefore appears to draw the universe of potential court orders needed to control those proceedings within statutory purview and expressly adds them to the jurisdiction of the court hearing a CCAA matter. As a practical matter, it is therefore unnecessary to revert to inherent jurisdiction, while as a matter of law it is improper to do so.[92] If, on the other hand, there were no section 11, a statutory court would arguably lack jurisdiction to carry out the mandate of the act. Section 11 would appear to convey jurisdiction to CCAA judges as a matter of statute, and the implementation of section 11 necessitates judicial discretion in the crafting of specific orders. If this is so, then inherent jurisdiction as a basis for orders made under the CCAA is pre-empted by section 11 as a matter of both law and logic.[93]

The primary objection likely to be raised in response to the view that CCAA judges exercise discretion, as opposed to inherent jurisdiction, is this: The CCAA was a skeletal statute which provided almost no legislative guidance on the myriad questions – both substantive and procedural – that arise in large, complex reorganizations. Therefore judges had to resort to inherent jurisdiction in order to give effect to legislative intent with respect to the overall purpose of the act. The substantive weaknesses of this argument have been discussed in this chapter and the previous chapter. Here it is worth evaluating this argument from a conceptual standpoint.

When asserting that the CCAA is silent, judges and commentators typically point to the lack of specific statutory guidance on a range of procedural matters, and then use these "gaps" to support their argument in favour of relying on section 11 and inherent jurisdiction to fill the gaps. CCAA decisions such as *Westar Mining Ltd.*, *Dylex*, and *Royal Oak Mines* appear to be tacitly premised on this idea.[94] But the very presence of section 11 contemplates the myriad range of orders that a court might need to make in order to give effect to legislative purpose. If a bona fide case for exercising inherent jurisdiction relies on a legislative deficiency and the legislation has specifically granted judges jurisdiction to make orders to address any potential circumstance, then a situation in which a judge would need to rely on their inherent jurisdiction would depend on section 11 being deficient, which appears to be virtually impossible based on the broad wording of that section.

So, the unstated premise of arguments in favour of developing CCAA law based on inherent jurisdiction is that *section 11* is somehow deficient. It seems that judges resort to inherent jurisdiction, not to fill gaps in the act overall but – bewilderingly – in section 11 in particular. Theoretically there could be a circumstance in which section 11 is deficient, which would necessitate a judge resorting to inherent jurisdiction to give effect to the purposes of the CCAA. It is submitted that such a circumstance would be very rare, however, as the constraints around section 11 tend to be express limits imposed by that section or other provisions of the statute.[95] Since statutory limits constrain both inherent jurisdiction and judicial discretion, they serve not as legislative deficiencies but rather as boundaries within which parliament has determined judges should act. Although it is not impossible, it is hard to imagine a situation in which section 11 is truly deficient in a way which would justify resort to inherent jurisdiction without contravening other parts of the CCAA. As far this study has been able determine, during the twentieth century no reported case pointed to this kind of situation as a basis for exercising inherent jurisdiction in CCAA proceedings.[96] Therefore, it is submitted that the argument based on the distinction between inherent jurisdiction and judicial discretion is actually a question-begging argument based on the tacit interpretation of the act as excluding section 11. This is an illogical argument. Its proponents purport to rely on both inherent jurisdiction and judicial discretion under section 11 to make judicial orders under the CCAA, when it must be one or the other.

In any event, whether one adopts the view that courts exercise inherent jurisdiction or judicial discretion, in all cases the starting point for a judge hearing a CCAA matter is the interpretation of the statute itself.[97] The concepts of judicial discretion and inherent jurisdiction only come into play if the statute provides room for judicial discretion or if the statute is silent, respectively. An argument advanced in this book is that beginning in the 1980s and 1990s CCAA judges began to go beyond established principles of statutory interpretation, and this trend helped facilitate a much greater role for judicial creativity, whether that creativity is properly termed inherent jurisdiction or judicial discretion. In several notable instances, judicial innovation overrode points on which the statute was actually *not* silent. If this critique about the errors in the interpretation of the CCAA is correct, then whether judges were purporting to exercise inherent jurisdiction or their discretion is beside the point. The issue is one of statutory interpretation and the proper roles of legislatures and courts. In the evolution of CCAA law, parliament and the courts appear to have switched roles at certain times.

3 Historical Institutionalism and Recursivity of Law

Contingency characterized court-driven CCAA developments in the 1980s and 1990s. The very fact that the act was largely converted into a debtor-remedy was not a predictable development before the 1980s. For instance, early on in this period, reported decisions reflected different approaches to the validity of instant trust deeds issued to gain access to the CCAA, as judges grappled with how to resolve the obscurity and ambiguity around this provision. Ultimately, Doherty J.A.'s dissent in the 1990 *Elan* decision became (and remains) a touchstone authority for the use of instant trust deeds and other tactical devices to gain access to the act. Recognizing the validity of instant trust deeds ensured, in turn, that the act could not operate as a bondholder remedy as intended, and was a critical factor in the outward conversion of the act into a debtor remedy. From the vantage point of 1953, however, future judicial sanction of such instruments was not foreseeable, as these would have completely undermined the trust deed restriction added to the statute in that year. Dissents do occasionally become influential over time. However, which dissents will prove influential, and when they will become influential, is hard to predict. The *Elan* dissent rather quickly became an influential authority in the interpretation of trust deeds, but Doherty J.A.'s assessment of the provision was (initially) one of several possible ways of understanding that section. As Doherty J.A.'s reasoning was increasingly adopted, however, it became harder to shift to another interpretation, even a better one.[98] Self-reinforcement through the use of precedent, positive feedback and path dependence locked in Doherty J.A.'s explication of section 3, with ongoing ramifications for judicial analyses of other tactical devices in the CCAA context. Accordingly this line of cases marked a major shift in approaches to Canadian corporate reorganization under insolvency law.

Unlike earlier bondholder reorganizations, in the 1980s and 1990s parties often exclusively relied upon the skeletal act to effect full company reorganizations, usually in an ad hoc fashion. This effectively made contemporary CCAA reorganizations even more court-driven than those carried out by bondholders in the 1930s. Earlier receivership reorganizations relied to a great extent on the trustee's or receiver's power under the governing trust deed – documents which commonly reached 300 pages in length – and accordingly the court-driven processes under the CCAA or similar provincial legislation were merely supplemental. Without a similar private architecture for effecting reorganizations, however, later parties turned to the CCAA as the core framework for reorganizing companies. This development necessitated a much greater role for judges in CCAA lawmaking since the act, by design, did not contain much in the way of restructuring guidelines.

4 Conclusion

As a tactical device, instant trust deeds became standard practice for many debtors seeking recourse to the act until parliament repealed the trust deed requirement in 1997.[99] As in the 1930s, without any effective legislative provision to bar debtor companies from accessing the act, debtor applications soon formed the bulk of CCAA applications. Lawyer Richard B. Jones recorded that following recognition of instant trust deeds, the CCAA "became a favourite of debtors' counsel, and the number of applications grew rapidly."[100]

Judicial recognition of instant trust deeds was a critical development in the CCAA's outward transformation into a debtor remedy. Recognizing instant trust deeds was tantamount to the repeal of this requirement because it allowed the CCAA (once again) to facilitate DIP restructurings, which did not necessarily entail trustee or receiver oversight. This conceptually separated CCAA reorganization from receivership. Although the act's harmonizing provisions could still be used to effect receivership reorganizations, the institution of receivership proceedings was no longer necessary to the operation of the CCAA. While the CCAA can still be used as a secured creditor remedy (and probably cannot effectively be used to the detriment of large secureds) it is no longer *only* a secured creditor remedy since there is nothing to prevent a CCAA compromise solely in respect of unsecured and trade debts.

While the trust deed provision originally made the act the preserve of bondholders, and gave effect to parliamentary intention in this regard, subsequent judicial treatment paradoxically made section 3 the touchstone of the CCAA's new purposes and operation. Without judicial sanction of such tactical devices, as a method by which to give effect to the new policy purposes of the act, courts probably could not have outwardly repurposed the statute. In a stroke of irony, purposive interpretation by Canadian courts undermined and further obscured the original policy objectives of the act, and paved the way for a new DIP reorganization regime. Courts played a central role in this process of legal change, which came about on a case-by-case basis.

Nevertheless, interpreting away the trust deed provision also benefited large secured lenders. By the 1980s and 1990s, Canadian banks relied far less on trust deed-style financing, meaning that the trust deed provision also restricted their access to the CCAA. As discussed in chapter 6, banks and other large secureds had commercial incentives to restructure certain firms, and in the Canadian context they generally could not carry out full corporate reorganization outside of bankruptcy and insolvency law. Eliminating the trust deed requirement once again gave large secured lenders (banks) full access to the CCAA as a creditor remedy.

Unlike secured lenders in the context of formal US and English bankruptcy reforms, the court-driven developments of the 1980s and 1990s did not substantially limit the (strong) legal rights of Canadian banks. The forum of the courts gave these large lenders a unique advantage to help shape legal changes vis-à-vis other parties. Several court-based developments illustrate their influence, such as the appointment of a monitor to oversee the debtor's affairs. This achieved much the same outcome for banks as having their own receiver in that secureds (and other creditors) could get the opinion of a third party on the state of the debtor's affairs.[101] In the formal statutory reforms of 1997, parliament lowered the CCAA's majority requirement from three-fourths to two-thirds.[102] This left only the largest creditors with an effective veto, and potentially made it easier for large creditors to push through a plan against the wishes of smaller creditors. Judicial sanction of "convenience classes" to buy off junior creditors further took small creditors out of the equation in terms of plan voting.[103] And parliament did not add any provisions similar to involuntary proceedings or "cram down" to the act.[104]

9

Formalizing a Modern Debtor-in-Possession Restructuring Narrative

The purpose of the CCAA – Canada's first reorganization statute – is to permit the debtor to continue to carry on business and, where possible, avoid the social and economic costs of liquidating its assets.
...

Early commentary and jurisprudence also endorsed the CCAA's remedial objectives. It recognized that companies retain more value as going concerns while underscoring that intangible losses, such as the evaporation of the companies' goodwill, result from liquidation. Reorganization serves the public interest by facilitating the survival of companies supplying goods or services crucial to the health of the economy or saving large numbers of jobs. Insolvency could be so widely felt as to impact stakeholders other than creditors and employees.[1]

Marie Deschamps J., *Century Services Inc v Canada (AG)*, 2010

1 Introduction

By taking matters before the courts, major insolvency parties circumvented stalled bankruptcy reform efforts. Courts and major parties were therefore in a prime position to shape law on the ground in response to real-time insolvency developments.[2] Much CCAA law developed on a case-by-case basis, away from Ottawa and the interest groups that are typically involved with formal law reform.[3] Courts accordingly molded CCAA law to fit contemporary circumstances in ways that proved quite useful for reorganizing large companies on an ad hoc basis. This helped immunize the act from further repeal attempts, and established the status quo against which any formal reform efforts would have to face off.

Parliament lent support for redevelopment of CCAA law along these lines. Far from intervening to rein in the courts, Ottawa and some provincial governments offered plan funding in several notable cases.

Furthermore, the federal bank regulator made concessions allowing banks to facilitate a number of high-profile reorganizations involving debt-for-equity swaps in 1980s and 1990s restructurings. In the 1992 bankruptcy reforms, parliament retained the CCAA essentially as is and took repeal off the agenda. By facilitating reorganizations under the CCAA in these ways, parliament also helped advance the interests of banks.

The potential public interest benefits of going-concern reorganizations did not prompt large secureds, shareholders, or management to attempt restructurings. These groups already had incentives to reorganize firms when there was a reasonable chance of turning the business around. Rather, debtors, lenders, counsel, courts, and academics spun the public interest narrative around the interests of weaker creditor and stakeholder groups. This narrative included stakeholders that were not participants in early CCAAs, such as employees. Including these groups in contemporary CCAAs may have helped garner plan funding in the form of compromising junior creditor claims in a publicly palatable way – for instance, by convincing employees to take wage cuts as part of a reorganization attempt.[4] A public interest approach to CCAA law also helped attract wider public support for reorganizations when news of such activities was disseminated through the press. So despite obscuring the operation of the act as a secured creditor remedy, the role of the public interest narrative is important for understanding how the act was outwardly refashioned into a DIP remedy during the 1980s and 1990s.

This is not to suggest that reorganizations never benefit creditors and interest groups other than large secureds, but these benefits are usually trickle-down in nature, or have been tacked on to the CCAA. They do not stem from the original purposes or operation of the act. In this respect, the recent history of the CCAA is a continuation of early practices under the act and a century-old tradition of secured creditors spearheading corporate restructuring efforts in Canada. Specific exceptions to this phenomenon come from fairly recent legislative protections – although even contemporary commentators question whether these go far enough in protecting the interests of unsecured and involuntary creditors.[5]

CCAA developments in the 1980s and 1990s were the product of a unique Canadian fact pattern that made the act ripe for change. Due to the degree of contingency surrounding these events, it is difficult to conceive of similar circumstances arising spontaneously elsewhere and leading to comparable results – although this is not impossible. Certainly, in the 1970s and 1980s, the development of corporate reorganization law in the United States and England occurred along quite different trajectories. While the corporate reorganization regimes in those countries are functionally similar to the CCAA,[6] this study reveals some of the distinct mechanisms through which CCAA law developed. A comparison of these mechanisms across jurisdictions arguably goes further in explaining the resulting corporate reorganization regimes. This approach accordingly lends itself to a deeper understanding of CCAA law developments within Canada, especially vis-à-vis broadly similar regimes in countries like the United States and England.

2 Historical Institutionalism and Recursivity of Law

Judges and Courts

Canadian courts underwent significant changes during the period in which the CCAA was little used. As a result, courts were well-placed by the 1980s and 1990s to revive the CCAA, using their inherent jurisdiction or judicial discretion. First, overseas appeals to the judiciary in England ended in 1949, making the SCC the court of last resort and freeing it from the obligation to follow JCPC precedents. Second, from the 1960s to the 1980s, the Supreme Court of Canada, especially due to the influence of Bora Laskin, was transformed into a modern, policy-conscious institution. The SCC assumed a far greater role in developing Canadian law rather than merely settling disputes.[7] The *Canadian Charter of Rights and Freedoms* also came into effect in the early 1980s, which led to a notable increase in judicial review in Canada.[8]

On a related note, legal education, especially in Ontario, similarly underwent a dramatic transformation leading up to this point. Preparation for a career as a lawyer went from being an apprenticeship-type program with a heavy practical bent, under the tutelage of the Law Society of Upper Canada, to being primarily an academic, university-based degree program, followed by a period of practical training (articling or clerking).[9] This influenced how future lawyers approached the legal issues they confronted in their practice. It also directly impacted on judicial decision making, particularly in the SCC, which, under Chief Justice Laskin, significantly grew its law student clerking program. Through their clerks, Supreme Court judges had their finger on the pulse of many of the newest ideas from academia, and these increasingly made their way into judicial decisions.

The Canadian bench of the 1980s and 1990s, even at the lower court level, was therefore far more imaginative and policy-conscious – even activist in some instances – than that of the 1920s and 1930s. This proved significant in subsequent CCAA law developments. A less imaginative bench that was unconcerned with policy would have been an unlikely institution to breathe new life into a dead letter act. This highlights the significant role of legal institutions such as courts in mediating the interpretation and application of law on the books into law in practice. Moreover, it illustrates that in the regenesis of the CCAA, courts have not just mediated law, but exerted such influence, in many instances, as to create substantive new law. In the area of CCAA law, Canadian courts have had, in some respects, an even greater role than parliament.

Although judicial rulings conceptually separated DIP insolvency under the act from receivership, DIP reorganizations functioned like receivership reorganizations in some important ways. For instance, a debtor-remedy view characterizes the act as a "debtor in possession" restructuring regime, yet being "in possession" is something that large secured creditors actually want to avoid.[10] Whether a debtor company is in receivership, winding-up proceedings, or under CCAA protection, it is "in possession" in the legal sense that the assets remain vested in the debtor. In receivership or winding-up proceedings, however, large secureds generally exercise formal control through a receiver or administrator.[11] In a CCAA restructuring, on the other hand, management usually has formal control of the debtor's affairs. But to the extent that management wishes to see the company reorganized, large secureds can exert considerable influence over decision-making, since their support is usually essential for a restructuring plan to succeed. For instance, in contemporary cases control is sometimes formalized when secureds negotiate a pre-packaged CCAA plan or stipulate terms as a condition of DIP financing. Thus, CCAA negotiations usually take place between debtor management and large secured creditors. While large secureds do not exercise formal control of a company under CCAA protection, the strength of their legal rights inside and outside of insolvency law and their commercial power give them substantial "soft power"[12] to shape and direct restructuring efforts. The strength of their influence in this regard is like an informal type of control. Accordingly, in the shift to a primarily DIP CCAA regime, large secureds have not lost as much control of proceedings as it might at first appear. The act still serves as a secured lender remedy, although it is no longer exclusively used as such.

Contingency, Sequencing, Ambiguity

A significant measure of contingency surrounded the development of the CCAA into a modern DIP restructuring regime. From the vantage point of the 1940s, these developments were unpredictable and unlikely. Had any one of a number of events unfolded otherwise, the results may have been very different. For example, had the *Canadian Bar Review* gone out of print, as the *Fortnightly Law Journal* did, it is unlikely that lawyers or scholars in the 1980s and 1990s would have come across Edwards's 1947 article, just as they failed to find Harold Ernest Manning's CCAA articles in the latter journal. Or had contemporary actors looked instead to the more recent *Tassé Report* to illuminate the history of the CCAA, opposing counsel may well have persuaded judges to reject instant trust deeds on the grounds that they were antithetical to the underlying policy purposes of the act. In the event, however, neither of these alternatives materialized.

Another major factor that contributed to the revival of the CCAA during this period was the fact that there was not yet a general business restructuring law that could facilitate full company reorganizations. In other words, there was no obvious legal mechanism to deal with the restructuring crisis at hand. For largely constitutional reasons, an effective federal statute of this nature would need to come through bankruptcy and insolvency legislation. Until 1992, however, the *Bankruptcy Act* did not provide for complete company reorganization. Its biggest defect was that it did not compulsorily bind secured claims – the type of claims usually held by banks and other powerful creditors. Due to the 1930s constitutional references, provincial legislative responses were powerless to effect arrangements when the company in question was insolvent. With pressure to reorganize large, insolvent companies on a going-concern basis, the CCAA was rediscovered and pressed into service because it was essentially the only piece of existing legislation that could facilitate such reorganizations. A secured creditor remedy rooted in receivership thus formed the basis for Canadian DIP reorganization law and practice.

The resilience of the CCAA to withstand attempts at formal change (such as repeal) thus contributed to the possibility of informal changes to the law in the form of institutional conversion or layering. In other words, the CCAA's endurance on the statute books during a period of formal stasis contributed to the possibility that it could be reinterpreted and repurposed as a debtor- rather than a bondholder-remedy. By the 1980s, since the CCAA was still the only corporate insolvency statute that could bind secured creditors to a plan of arrangement, banks and other actors coordinated around the institutional arrangements enshrined in the act. Asset specificity and positive feedback from CCAA case law affirmed and reaffirmed a few early judicial interpretations of the act as a general corporate restructuring law,[13] thereby contributing to path dependence.

This in turn underscores the importance of sequencing in the unfolding of events. For example, had parliament added general business reorganization provisions to bankruptcy and insolvency law *prior to* the 1980s recession, that approach to reorganizing debtor companies would likely have taken hold instead. Positive feedback through successful reorganizations and case law precedent – particularly during an economic downturn – meant that whatever approach to corporate reorganization was initially adopted in the 1980s was likely to generate a lot of positive feedback, as many companies attempted restructurings. Early approaches to restructuring companies under the stand-alone, skeletal CCAA thus became entrenched rather quickly. By the time similar provisions were added to the BIA in 1992, the CCAA was already the preferred means – both by debtors and large secureds – of restructuring large enterprises in Canada. Thus sequencing and positive feedback help account for the path dependence of CCAA reorganizations from the 1980s onward, including its resilience to survive repeal efforts as well as failed attempts to unify the CCAA and BIA under a single act.

When the CCAA was initially rediscovered, ambiguity surrounding some of its provisions and underlying policy purposes helped drive the new cycle of legal change. Seeking clarity on ambiguous or vague aspects of CCAA law, actors brought these queries before the courts for judicial rulings, in a process known as "settling".[14] By the 1980s and 1990s, the original policy purposes of the trust deed provision did not even feature in reported CCAA decisions, indicating a significant degree of obscurity around the trust deed provision in particular, and the CCAA more generally. Ambiguity thus facilitated new judicial interpretations of the act's underlying policy purposes, which were influenced by relatively new ideas about corporate reorganization then in circulation. Had the policy behind the act and trust deed provision been clear, it is doubtful that the CCAA could have been refashioned by the courts into a DIP restructuring statute. In marked contrast to the way ambiguity facilitated a CCAA revival, the unambiguous, restrictive provision of the FCAA prevented a similar revival of that act through novel judicial interpretations. Ambiguity created the possibility and the courts provided the legal mechanism for effecting substantive legal change.

The Influence of Ideas

This study shows that ideas have the potential to influence legal developments, and accordingly factor into explanatory accounts of legal change. In the context of CCAA law, Edwards's 1947 journal article, which proposed going-concern reorganization as a normative goal for insolvency law, as well as a large role for judicial discretion in CCAAs, was a latent, but ultimately successful, piece of advocacy. Despite a restrictive amendment in 1953, which (in the short term) precluded the possibility of judicial implementation of Edwards's suggestions, in the 1980s and 1990s judges cited policy arguments made by Edwards to justify novel interpretations of the act – including interpreting away the 1953 amendment. The willingness of Canadian judges to adapt the CCAA in this manner was due in part to changing ideas and attitudes about business bankruptcy in the United States and Canada following enactment of the 1978 US *Bankruptcy Code*. Edwards's proposed conception of CCAA law also formed a foundation for further Canadian theoretical work in this area, notably in Janis Sarra's public interest theory of CCAA law. Sarra's theory in turn influenced later case law and substantive legislative amendments to bring the CCAA into greater conformity with these normative theoretical ideas.

Ideas about the CCAA propounded by academics like Edwards and Sarra have thus produced tangible and profound changes in the way the act is applied by judges, and influenced substantive statutory amendments.[15] Accordingly, theories and ideas about business bankruptcy law are important for understanding stability and change in CCAA law over time. The role of ideas from academia in CCAA law development underscores the influence of legal concepts (such as going-concern reorganization), including those that are adopted from other jurisdictions. This relates to a recursivity of law framework, which highlights the important role of legal concepts and legal actors, including academics, on both the implementation and lawmaking sides of the recursive loop.[16] Drawing on ideas from historical institutionalism and recursivity of law, this study offers an explanatory account of how and why these ideas about business bankruptcy law influenced and shaped legal developments.

The process by which ideas have influenced CCAA law displays a high degree of recursivity. Ideas often percolated upwards from the minds of academics and practitioners, to judges, and ultimately to parliament, whereupon they were sometimes enshrined into legislation. Instances in which novel changes in CCAA law flowed from the books into practice are relatively few. The recursive loop of CCAA developments entails a significant degree of judicialization, where judges, through their decisions, assumed a prominent role in lawmaking on the ground. The operation of *stare decisis* in Canadian case law generated positive feedback for this process, such that the judicialization of CCAA law, left to its own devices, essentially became a self-reaffirming concept – an axiom of Canadian corporate reorganization under the act.

Interestingly parliament often responded to "judicial legislation" under the CCAA by enshrining case law precedents into statute. Parliament passed over the opportunity to rein in judge-made law. This generated further positive feedback for the phenomenon of judicialization. The traditional lawmaking process was inverted in a recursive loop that is consistently reaffirmed by Canadian judges and parliament. It is therefore not only the institution of the CCAA that has proven resilient to change over time; the inverted process of CCAA lawmaking has proven to be a resilient set of institution arrangements in and of itself.

Situating the main centre of CCAA lawmaking in the courts carries important ramifications for the role of normative ideas about business bankruptcy law in terms of legal change. Using individual restructuring cases as the basis for effecting legal change provides multiple opportunities for novel and evolving ideas of business bankruptcy.[17] Arguments that do not hold sway under one set of facts may be successfully marshaled in a subsequent case. There is no prejudice for unsuccessful ideas. This is demonstrated by the tremendous influence of Edwards's 1947 journal article more than forty years after its publication.

Once an idea succeeds, it has the potential to revamp CCAA law such that it applies even in those types of cases where it previously failed to hold sway. One way this can occur is through appellate decisions, which may usher in new interpretations and ideas around business reorganization that become binding or persuasive precedent for lower courts. Thus, chronic reproduction, positive feedback and path dependence may reinforce and entrench certain ideas in CCAA law – even if the initial adoption of these ideas is random, suboptimal, or incongruous with existing precedents or practices. To block a new idea from taking hold it must be dismissed in essentially every case in which it is argued. In contrast, an idea need only succeed once – presumably at the appellate level – to transform CCAA law and practice along new lines.[18] Accordingly, CCAA law is perpetually dynamic in the sense that new cases continually create possibilities for legal change that may throw existing interpretations of the act back into flux. Although existing interpretations of CCAA law constitute institutional equilibria at certain times, these interpretations are susceptible to changing conditions.[19]

Thus, there is significant scope for new ideas to infiltrate and influence CCAA law developments via case law rather than through the relatively rare instances of formal insolvency law reform in Canada. Normative views of corporate bankruptcy expressed in case law are accordingly important for historical and explanatory accounts of CCAA law developments.

Path Dependence, Institutional Resilience, Recursivity of Law

Over time, positive feedback and asset specificity have contributed to path dependence in terms of the ad hoc, court-driven approach to CCAA reorganizations. It makes sense that large secureds – as one of the few groups of sophisticated, repeat players in business insolvencies – are content to keep the locus of legal change in the courts, a forum in which they are well-placed to influence legal change as compared to other parties. This phenomenon was further bolstered by chronic reproduction of case law precedents. Restructuring guidelines provided by courts have tended to respond to restructurings on a case-by-case basis as well as to reinforce the court-driven nature of CCAA proceedings. One way courts did this was by granting orders that required parties to report back to the court ("come back" clauses).[20] In addition, the appointment of a receiver or monitor in CCAAs was initially at the discretion of the court, as it was a concept found nowhere in the statute itself. This process accordingly involved a hearing before the supervising judge. Despite subsequent statutory amendments, which have made the appointment of a monitor an essential component of CCAA proceedings[21] (formalizing arrangements that had by that time become standard practice), the appointment process itself still takes place through the court rather than through a summary or administrative procedure.

The creation of the monitor role in CCAAs gave rise to new actors who had a professional interest in ongoing court-driven proceedings under the act. Accordingly, interest groups can spring up around institutional arrangements, like court-driven CCAA proceedings, which may make those arrangements even more resilient to change in the future. This in turn helps explain the endurance of court-driven approaches to CCAA restructurings. Such an approach was initially adopted because the parties were attempting to use an antiquated and skeletal statute to restructure insolvent companies. However, subsequent events have perpetuated this approach to CCAA reorganizations, despite substantial amendments to the act and a large body of case law. The ad hoc, court-driven nature of many CCAAs was originally an *effect* of an economic downturn and lack of restructuring mechanisms in the 1980s and 1990s. Over time, however, this *effect* has assumed a self-perpetuating quality through positive feedback and the self-reinforcement of case law precedents. [22] The ad hocery of CCAA restructurings has itself become a path dependent characteristic of this area of law.

Actors and interest groups that have formed around the heavily court-driven restructuring proceedings help to explain the path dependence and resilience of this approach to corporate reorganization, as well as the endurance of the CCAA in the face of more recent repeal efforts. Where actors such as insolvency professionals have coordinated around institutional arrangements like the CCAA, asset specificity suggests that they will be inclined to oppose institutional change, since they have developed assets that are specific to the existing set of institutional arrangements. In the context of the CCAA, this has been borne out both in the ongoing, ad hoc, court-driven approach to individual insolvencies as well as the preservation of the CCAA on the statute books after its revival in the 1980s. Parliament has not proposed repealing the CCAA since 1992, when the proposal was taken off the bankruptcy reform agenda due to how useful the act had proven to be in practice. Insolvency professionals have played a large and influential role in bankruptcy amendments from 1992 onward.

As insolvency scholars have noted, a recent round of bankruptcy reform has resulted in duplicative amendments to the CCAA and the BIA, despite persuasive efficiency arguments for consolidating both statutes into a single act.[23] The specificity of actor and interest group assets in restructurings under the CCAA accordingly helps account for the ongoing resilience of this stand-alone corporate restructuring statute, despite parallel business restructuring provisions under the BIA.

The formal institutional resilience of the CCAA statute itself, combined with less formal, ongoing changes to CCAA law through case law produces an interesting dynamic in terms of legal developments. The act provides strong, formal authority for judicial lawmaking due to its status as a federal statute, its express provision that empowers courts to decide CCAA matters, and (until recently) its brevity. In other words, it was in part the lack of regular or lengthy formal amendments to the act that provided considerable scope for judicial lawmaking. In contrast, a more lengthy, codified, or frequently updated statute, such as the BIA, is generally seen to convey commensurately less judicial authority in this regard.[24] So the more codified and specific the law, the less room or need for substantive judicial interpretation. The strength and legitimacy of judge-made law depends to some extent on the source of its authority, such as a statute or precedent on which a judge can draw in terms of establishing new interpretations, tests, or rules. In the case of the CCAA, formal institutional resilience and even stasis in respect of a skeletal act – which by virtue of its brevity did more to empower, than constrain judicial lawmaking – effectively provided the means (through judges) for effecting less formal, timely changes to law in practice. These changes could be highly responsive to evolving conditions on the ground, such as those concerning corporate financing practices.

Much like Halliday and Carruthers's recursivity of law theory in respect of formal bankruptcy law reform, CCAA law thus has two poles that hold a recursive loop in dynamic tension. At one end is the statute (law on the books), which is subject to relatively infrequent change through formal statutory amendments. At the other pole is CCAA law in practice, largely overseen by provincial superior courts. CCAA law, accordingly, represents a microcosm of the recursive loop of formal bankruptcy reform set out by Halliday and Carruthers. See figure 9.1, overleaf.

Since the CCAA is a rather open-ended restructuring statute – and was especially so in the 1980s and 1990s – the parties to corporate insolvencies under the act are relatively free to craft a tailor-made restructuring plan in respect of the debtor company. CCAA case law affirms that arrangements under the act can include anything that can be included in a valid contract.[25] In point of fact, the CCAA provides even greater scope for creativity than conventional contracts, since judicial approval of a plan also serves to bind a minority of dissenters and third-parties. Private parties accordingly have a fairly large say in the case-by-case development of corporate reorganization law. Third parties, on the other hand, may not even have standing in a CCAA court. Since case law developments tend to trickle up into statutory amendments, to effect a change or expansion of CCAA law in the courts can result in potentially significant, overarching legal change at the level of formal law reform as well.

Lauren B. Edelman's recursive theory of endogeneity of law[26] is, thus, quite useful for understanding many significant CCAA law developments from the 1980s onward. This theory captures the ways in which private parties create practical, substantive law in the process of carrying out broad legal policies or mandates. In the case of a skeletal act like the CCAA, the parameters and mechanics of judicially approved restructuring plans serve as tangible examples of law for subsequent restructuring efforts under the act. By virtue of judicial sanction, the law made by private parties in the course of implementing the act tends to be institutionalized in case law over time.

A prime example relates to first-day orders under the act. The statute itself does not provide a detailed framework for carrying out CCAA proceedings, including what are now known as initial or first-day orders: The initial application made under the act.[27] Section

Figure 9.1 Inverted Recursive Cycles of CCAA Lawmaking

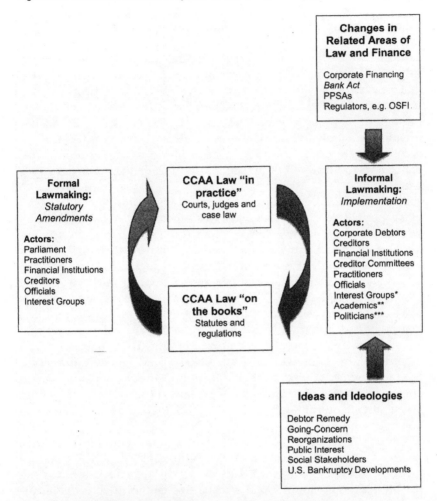

Sources: Adapted from Halliday and Carruthers, "The Recursivity of Law," 1147, and Halliday and Carruthers, *Bankrupt*, 17.

Notes:

*   Interest groups tend not to be involved in individual CCAAs; however, some interest groups have sought and obtained intervener standing in high-profile reorganizations. See e.g., *Re Indalex*, in which the following groups were interveners: Insolvency Institute of Canada; Canadian Labour Congress; Canadian Federation of Pensioners; Canadian Association of Insolvency and Restructuring Professionals; Canadian Bankers Association.

**   The courts have sometimes turned to academic literature in the course of deciding CCAA matters. See esp, Jackson and Sarra, "Selecting the Judicial Tool," 41 [in print] cited *inter alia* in *Re Indalex*.

*** Governments (federal, provincial, etc.) sometimes provide financing for a restructuring.

10 of the CCAA simply provides that applications may be made by "petition or by way of originating summons or notice of motion in accordance with the practice of the court in which the application is made."[28] Furthermore, section 11 gives the court authority to stay any other proceedings against the debtor company, if and as it sees fit.[29] Accordingly, it was largely left to CCAA applicants to decide what to put into their first-day order request and when to put that application before the court.

Debtor's counsel in Canada typically requested a general stay of proceedings against the debtor company as part of its initial application.[30] While the act authorized courts to grant such stays of proceedings, this was not an automatic or compulsory part of restructuring proceedings. Over time, various other requests were added to initial orders: for example, that the debtor maintain possession of the business, that a monitor be appointed (usually the debtor's accounting firm),[31] and that provision be made for DIP financing. None of these concepts originated from the text of the CCAA. Rather, they were suggested by counsel and then approved by judges through numerous ad hoc CCAA decisions, particularly during the 1980s and 1990s.

This is a striking example of Edelman's endogeneity of law theory in action. In their efforts to implement CCAA law, sophisticated private parties formulated various practical measures to carry out reorganizations under the act. In a highly recursive fashion, these practical measures became institutionalized in case law and model CCAA orders[32] over time, such that they now constitute practical CCAA law to many actors involved in corporate reorganizations, as well as to scholars and commentators. Statutory amendments in 2005 added some direction to the material that must accompany initial orders.[33] CCAA amendments in 2009 further enshrined some of these practical measures into legislative form.[34] These statutory amendments complete a recursive cycle that began in the 1980s, with private parties grappling with how to effectively carry out reorganizations under the skeletal CCAA.

Despite notable differences between the restructuring crises of the 1920s–30s and 1980s–90s, one recurring pattern leading to these crises was secured creditor remedies not keeping pace with earlier changes in corporate financing practices. With the onset of economic downturns, large secured lenders wanted to restructure a number of large corporate reorganizations, but lacked the legal tools to do so. In both instances, large secured lenders obtained new law through parliament or the courts to meet this need. This seems to indicate that corporate restructuring may be a particularly necessary or desirable remedy for large secured lenders in times of economic downturn. Perhaps this is because of the size of the losses at stake when a large company defaults or the fact that economic downturns tend to lead to widespread losses as many borrowers face financial difficulty.

It is noteworthy that life insurance companies and chartered banks, which are large, sophisticated, and powerful actors in the Canadian lending environment, were each caught without effective lender remedies in successive recessions. Interestingly, these large lenders were also the architects of their own problems in the sense that it was their omission of majority provisions, and then the switch to non-trust deed-based financing that left them without recourse to bondholder reorganizations and the CCAA, respectively.

These lapses are notable. Perhaps they are due to the fact that the lending agreements and lender remedies in question were both times drawn up in periods of economic growth, with little attention paid to how things might unfold in a mass default scenario, such as in an economic downturn. What is a desirable lender remedy in a strong economy is not necessarily adequate or desirable in a weaker economy. This explanation would certainly fit to the extent that secured creditors favour traditional seizure and liquidation of collateral, since the effectiveness of these actions as lender remedies are tied to market demand and prices – both of which tend to decline in a weak economy when the market may be flooded with similar receivership sales. This phenomenon was recently borne out in the US residential property market, as a result of mass foreclosures stemming from the subprime mortgage crisis. Illiquidity and poor market conditions in turn precipitated the Canadian third-party ABCP crisis, when no new investors could be found for the maturing paper. The failure of traditional secured creditor remedies appears to have prompted reorganization efforts in these instances.

A further factor might be linked to the demonstrable success of large secured creditors in seeing new law introduced to address restructuring crises when they occur. In other words, these parties can fairly reliably get ad hoc legislation or case law precedents to facilitate their preferred lender remedy as the need arises. This may be interrelated with conventional moral hazard concerns. One can question whether the Canadian federal and provincial governments were prepared to allow large, important, financial institutions, such as Canada Life, Sun Life, Canadian Imperial Bank of Commerce, or Caisse de dépôt et placement du Québec, to fail the way they did smaller banks and life insurance companies. The federal and provincial governments have a track record for coming to the aid of large financial institutions as well as much smaller, yet regionally significant firms, to prevent failures of important Canadian companies.

3 Conclusion

Through numerous ad hoc judicial decisions from the 1980s to 2000s, courts gradually repurposed an antiquated bondholder remedy into a modern DIP restructuring statute. Throughout these years, large secured creditors were active participants in helping to shape and direct legal changes through the courts, and public relations in the press. Toward the end of this period, the ideas around debtor restructuring generally, and the role of the CCAA in particular, ossified into a modern DIP restructuring narrative. This narrative assumed the ubiquity of conventional wisdom for CCAA law, and ultimately received the imprimatur of the SCC in the *Century Services* case. This was the first time the SCC was called upon to directly interpret provisions of the CCAA. Reiterating the conventional wisdom in euphonic tones, Deschamps J., writing for the Majority, stated:

> The purpose of the CCAA – Canada's first reorganization statute – is to permit the debtor to continue to carry on business and, where possible, avoid the social and economic costs of liquidating its assets ...
>
> Early commentary and jurisprudence also endorsed the CCAA's remedial objectives. It recognized that companies retain more value as going concerns while underscoring that intangible losses, such as the evaporation of the companies' goodwill, result from liquidation. Reorganization serves the public interest by facilitating the survival of companies supplying goods or services crucial to the health of the economy or saving large numbers of jobs. Insolvency could be so widely felt as to impact stakeholders other than creditors and employees.[35]

Judicial chambers assumed the quality of echo chambers insofar as the original purpose of the CCAA was concerned. Appellate courts served a self-reaffirming function for judicial recharacterization of the act, culminating with the SCC's decision in *Century Services*. The formalization of this modern DIP restructuring narrative marks the end of a cycle of legal change, which began in the 1980s, when the CCAA was rediscovered.

10

Conclusion

For the past twenty-five years the Canadian business insolvency system
has moved ... [toward] reorganization proceedings controlled by the
debtor. Many of the extraordinary powers granted to debtors to effect
such reorganizations were first authorized by the exercise of judicial
discretion ... The courts have shied away from policing the exercise of
those extraordinary powers ...[1]

Andrew J.F. Kent, Wael Rostom, Adam Maerov, and Tushara
Weerasooriya, *Banking and Finance Law Review*

1 Synthesis

In many ways the history of the CCAA is a study in contrasts. On the
surface, the origins and early history of the statute stand juxtaposed
to developments in the 1980s and beyond. A *loi d'exception* became an
entry point for judicial discretion. A bondholder remedy justified on the
strength of property rights and creditor priorities gave way to a debt-
or remedy based on wider public interest concerns. A circumscribed,
private remedy became a malleable and nebulous catch-all for various
public and private issues that happened to intersect with insolvency.
Anxiety about the constitutionality of adjusting secured creditor rights
in cases of insolvency gave way to application of the act to even technically solvent companies. Although parliament originally made the
scope of the CCAA too narrow, later courts held the act was intended
to have wide scope. Contemporary corporate reorganization has thus
proven such an elastic concept[2] that it can be hard to predict where
CCAA law may go next under large and liberal interpretations of its
provisions.[3]

Yet despite all that has changed, some aspects of CCAA law and practice have remained the same. The prominent role of large secureds as protagonists of much corporate reorganization remained consistent over the twentieth-century. Although the identity of the major secureds changed (from life insurance companies to banks), their need for corporate restructuring as a creditor remedy, particularly in economic downturns, did not. This study has thus brought to light the origins of the CCAA as a remedy for large secured creditors, and shown that modern CCAAs continue to advance the interests of this creditor group. It demonstrates that large secured creditors have been major drivers of corporate restructuring developments under the act over the past eighty years. These findings challenge conventional views of the act as a debtor remedy inspired by concern for stakeholder groups, such as labour, and demonstrate the major role played by large secured creditors in corporate restructurings.

This book has offered a theorized interpretation of CCAA history over the twentieth century and contextualized this narrative within the evolving social, economic, political, and legal landscape in Canada from the 1930s and 1940s to the 1980s and 1990s. This period witnessed changes in many areas of Canadian society. The act's forty-year dormancy in the middle of this eighty-year timeframe calls attention to the importance of these contextual changes in terms of evolving ideas about corporate reorganization and the CCAA. It showcases how the act came to be regarded as a debtor remedy that advanced the broader public interest, despite its original purpose as a bondholder-led receivership regime. It also demonstrates how changing views of the CCAA were interrelated with many other changes in Canadian society, such as evolving views of federalism, stakeholder rights, judicial review, and statutory interpretation. Although the text of the CCAA was essentially untouched for forty years, the broad, contextual paradigm shift that took place in Canadian society during that period formed a new lens through which later actors approached the statute. Thus the possibility of the public conceiving of the CCAA as primarily a bondholder receivership remedy in the 1980s and 1990s seems just as unlikely as viewing the act as a debtor remedy for the benefit of stakeholder groups in the 1930s. In other words, actors' understandings of the CCAA in a given time have been significantly shaped by the broader context of their respective place in history. The prolonged disuse of the act during a period of much societal change makes CCAA history a good example of how important contextual factors can be to understanding legal change.

Additionally, this history has brought to light the key mechanisms of legal change that have helped provide answers to the research questions for this study. In 1933 parliament enshrined boilerplate majority provisions into statute, thereby intervening only to the limited extent necessary so that bondholders (financial institutions) could carry on essentially private, self-help remedies. Bondholders, through their trustees or receivers, were key drivers of restructuring developments in this period. On the other hand, strong judicial review and purposive statutory interpretation reflect the legal landscape in Canada by the 1980s and 1990s, which helped make courts agents of more recent changes. Nevertheless, large secureds were well-placed to advance their interests through the courts relative to other parties, and were primary beneficiaries of these changes. Through progressive interpretations of the act, courts granted access to Canada's only insolvency regime capable of facilitating complete company reorganizations, and assumed a prominent role in policy making and lawmaking in this area.

These mechanisms of legal change were products of their respective historical contexts. It is hard to imagine contemporary policy- and results-oriented judging, or the reliance on judge-made law, in the 1930s when bankruptcy statutes were interpreted strictly and narrowly and cases were rarely reported. Furthermore, this sort of reliance on judges would have been unnecessary since bondholders were able to reorganize companies with little regard for junior creditors or stakeholders, and they required only the occasional judicial rubber stamp to give their arrangements the force of law. On the other hand, given the marked changes in these two areas over time, the approach taken in the 1930s to judging and interpreting the CCAA would have been out of place in the 1980s and 1990s. Contemporary judges had to interpret the CCAA in light of a much-changed legal, political, economic, and social backdrop. For instance, contemporary judges have been confronted with the issue of whether environmental liability should be considered a claim under the CCAA.[4] Consider the 2012 case of *Re AbitibiBowater Inc.*, for instance – the concept of environmental liability, the provincial statute, and even the province in question all post-date the CCAA by one or more decades.[5]

In the two periods of legal change examined in this book, changes tended to come from the ground up rather than flowing from statute into practice. Expansive judicial interpretations of the act now raise concerns about perpetual ad hocery and compromising the rule of law,[6] although historical evidence suggests that bondholder reorganizations were also ad hoc. But unlike contemporary CCAA decisions, historical bondholder reorganizations did not generally have precedential value. Echoing Fraser's comment from 1927, perhaps the ad hoc nature of corporate reorganization stems from the fact that it is (still) difficult to distil these practices down to a set of general principles.[7] Contemporary commentators and courts tend to convey this by emphasizing the uniqueness of individual boundary-pushing cases, which in turn justifies the case-by-case and solutions-oriented nature of many CCAA developments.[8] Maybe this means that effective law on corporate reorganization must be merely enabling. In other words, the more facilitatory, rather than prescriptive, that reorganization law becomes, the more useful and relied upon it is likely to be in practice. This might help explain why enabling legislation like the CCAA (and earlier majority provisions) have proven flexible to cover a wide range of circumstances, in marked contrast with some other Canadian bankruptcy and insolvency statutes.[9] The discretion or inherent jurisdiction of contemporary CCAA judges augments the statute's flexibility, especially when coupled with the tendency of progressive judicial interpretation to disable the act's few restrictive provisions. As noted by several insolvency lawyers in 2008:

> For the past twenty-five years the Canadian business insolvency system has moved ... [toward] reorganization proceedings controlled by the debtor. Many of the extraordinary powers granted to debtors to effect such reorganizations were first authorized by the exercise of judicial discretion ... The courts have shied away from policing the exercise of those extraordinary powers ...[10]

As a result, the boundaries of CCAA law tend to be fluid. Nevertheless modern CCAA law, and historic bondholder reorganizations, have been efficacious precisely because they facilitate reorganizations that make commercial and political sense by taking their cue from practices on the ground, rather than relying on parliament to prescribe restructuring principles or policies. The elasticity of corporate restructuring under majority provisions, and now the CCAA, is a hallmark of this area of law.

This raises an interesting question about whether the essence of these restructuring regimes has less to do with their practical outcomes than with the way these outcomes are brought about. This interpretation would fit with the broad character of both regimes in that it is hard to distil general principles of restructuring that are common to all bondholder reorganizations or CCAAs when one focuses on outcomes. But one does find some consistency when examining methods of restructuring under each. For example, consider common descriptions of the CCAA, such as: It is "intended to have wide scope" and it gives judges much room to exercise their discretion. On their own these two statements convey little about what the act is intended to achieve, but they provide an indication of the mechanisms by which resolutions will be brought about (even though they have little predictive power). The same is true for the utilitarian majority provisions of historical trust deeds.

This interpretation of bondholder reorganizations and CCAA law accords with the central argument of this book about the prominent role of large secureds, since they are usually the most powerful parties in an insolvency context and in the best position to influence individual outcomes. Large creditors have an incentive to keep the locus of legal change in the courts. The wide range of possible outcomes in case-driven developments can work to their advantage, since they can often pursue the outcome that best advances their interest in a given case, without having to make the ex ante trade-offs that picking one outcome over another (as it applies in all cases) would entail (such as liquidation over reorganization.) In other words, lenders can advocate a specific outcome in one case, but leave their options open about how potential future cases might be resolved. This gives them a good chance at achieving an optimal resolution in most cases in which they are involved. They may still lose in an individual case, but they are unlikely to be on the losing side of a legal rule change.[11]

The process of legal change at play in modern CCAA law is also an example of Arthur Stinchcombe's observation that "an effect created by causes at some previous period [can become] ... *a cause of that same effect in succeeding periods.*"[12] The exercise of judicial discretion went from being a means of carrying out restructurings under an antiquated act, to a de facto policy objective for how CCAA reorganizations should be conducted. This in turn might help account for the tendency of courts to exercise judicial discretion in a way that breaks down statutory restrictions and broadens the act's scope, as well as parliament's relatively hands-off approach to CCAA lawmaking.

One effect of the way courts deploy judicial discretion in CCAAs is that one instance of it tends to beget another. As discussed in chapter 8, the acceptance of instant trust deeds led to further exercises of judicial discretion in order to flesh out[13] majority provisions into a DIP restructuring regime. Commentators may voice concerns about the implications this raises for the rule of law and the notion that statutes should convey clear expectations,[14] but these critiques might miss a more significant point. Perhaps the key issue is that judicial discretion has itself become a policy objective for conducting CCAA law. Broadening the act's scope – by recognizing instant trust deeds, applying the act to a solvent company, and so on – is a manifestation of this objective. This phenomenon, as well as the typical (but vague) policy statements that the act is "intended to have wide scope,"[15] has the quality of a self-fulfilling prophecy because the means of giving life to the act's dead provisions (judicial discretion) has essentially become the reason for doing so (to exercise judicial discretion). This flows from roughly thirty years of case law that has interpreted the court's order making power under section 11 as if that provision was the guiding policy of the act. In effect, the act is an instrumental legal regime within which judges may assist restructuring efforts. Therefore, a better query might be to ask *whether* and *why* it is necessary, as a matter of normative policy, to continue to rely so heavily on judicial discretion in CCAAs.

The role of judicial discretion in CCAA law relates to studying cycles of legal change because of the particular way it affects reform efforts. Usually the political impetus to reform or repeal bankruptcy law arises during or after economic recessions, when many debtors avail themselves of insolvency law, and such activity highlights deficiencies of existing legislation. In Canada, bankruptcy reform has historically been a rare event. At one point this led to a situation where "the very old and tottery"[16] *Bankruptcy Act* from the 1930s was being relied on to address over-indebtedness problems arising as late as the 1980s and early 1990s.[17] (Amendments to the BIA and CCAA in 2005 added a requirement that the statute at least be reviewed again in five years' time.[18]) Stalled bankruptcy reform efforts were accordingly a significant factor in CCAA developments in the 1980s and 1990s.[19] Since that time courts have consciously and consistently adopted progressive interpretations of the act in order to provide satisfactory outcomes in individual CCAA cases. One by-product of this approach is that courts avoid contributing to the dissatisfaction that could help create political pressure for formal legal reforms. It is hard to see how the political impetus for formal changes to CCAA law can ever build to a critical juncture in a way that punctuates the current equilibrium of broad judicial discretion and expansive statutory interpretation. The body of modern CCAA case law instead demonstrates how courts can pre-empt the need for legislative reforms. This is in keeping with the general tendency of increased judicial review to be a "one-way street."[20]

Another facet of the phenomenon of judicialization relates to debates over ex ante versus ex post approaches to theorizing bankruptcy law. Perpetual ad hocery under a more codified bankruptcy statute or an ex ante structuring vision of bankruptcy would lend more weight to concerns about predictability and the rule of law. But these seem like far less important concerns under a regime like the CCAA that is seen as expressly concerned with effecting satisfactory ex post solutions on a case-by-case basis.[21] Provided the CCAA achieves this objective and judicial interpretation is seen as progressive rather than arbitrary, it will likely remain immune to calls for repeal or to curtail judicial discretion on broad policy grounds. Ex ante approaches to theorizing bankruptcy, and the usual criteria for evaluating these approaches, do not fit with modern CCAA law, which is decidedly ex post and ad hoc in its policy and practical orientation.

An interesting corollary is that the ex post approach of CCAA law shines in response to the unanticipated events that tend to expose the deficiencies and outmodedness of more codified bankruptcy laws. Flurries of restructuring activity (economic downturns) generate satisfaction with, and justify, progressive interpretations of CCAA law. Conversely, these same events tend to produce dissatisfaction with rigid interpretations of codified bankruptcy regimes, and so underscore the need for formal legal reforms. This occurred with respect to the Canadian *Bankruptcy Act* and FCAA in the 1980s and 1990s, for instance. The way in which a bankruptcy regime is perceived to respond to these sorts of situations (flurries of activity or significant, unanticipated failures) can help create either inertia against, or momentum for, formal legal reforms.

The CCAA escaped repeal in the 1980s and 1990s precisely because the act proved to be useful and satisfactory for resolving large corporate insolvencies in practice. In contrast, the CCAA has been most vulnerable to repeal or substantive reform during periods of economic prosperity when there was very little bankruptcy activity. The act escaped early repeal efforts because key interest groups presented evidence to parliament that attested to the need for the act as a backup bondholder remedy. But even when the act did not have many defenders (in the 1970s, for instance), there was still not enough momentum in reform efforts to overcome the inertia of being on the statute books. These later bills, which included reforms of the *Bankruptcy Act*, never made their way into law.

Thus the longevity and success of contemporary CCAA law – and the bondholder reorganizations on which it was based – are tied to the fact that it is seen to excel when other bankruptcy laws tend to come up short, thanks in large part to progressive judging. As a result, CCAA law runs counter to typical cycles of legal change in bankruptcy law by stymieing the usual impetuses (deficiencies in existing law) and mechanisms (parliamentary action) for legislative reform. The factors that tend to prompt formal bankruptcy reform efforts tend to reinforce CCAA approaches to corporate reorganization, thereby generating ongoing positive feedback. Since reform efforts seldom arise during periods of stasis, it is hard to see how this pattern could be broken in a way that would lead to fundamental reform. Modern approaches to CCAA law appear to represent a deep equilibrium in this respect, making change seem unlikely.[22] But of course unlikely is not the same as impossible.

This analysis does not suggest that there are *no* arguments to which CCAA law is vulnerable. Many of the critiques of interpretive pragmatism offered by Dworkin appear to apply to contemporary approaches to CCAA law.[23] These critiques aim at the circularity of the reasoning of the pragmatic approach to legal interpretation and the propensity of pragmatism to self-destruct.[24] Such arguments challenge the logic underlying CCAA developments since the 1980s by evaluating these changes on their own terms and purporting to show how they come up short. With the right confluence of factors such arguments could gain the traction needed to lead to a critical juncture moment that could usher in fundamental reforms.[25] If and when that might happen, however, is of course hard to predict.

2 Historical Institutionalism and Recursivity of Law

From the perspective of the 1920s, very little of this historical narrative unfolded the way one might have expected. The history of CCAA law includes a sequence of unpredictable events and unintended consequences. But despite their unpredictability and unlikelihood looking forward, these events are important for an explanatory account of CCAA history and legal change. Ideas from historical institutionalism such as critical junctures, positive feedback, and path dependence help explain how unlikely or even accidental events factor into legal developments over time, and a recursivity of law analysis illustrates the mechanisms that contribute to these phenomena. These concepts help explain how and why events unfolded the way they did, and illustrate the power of ideas to refashion old institutions.

Although change was probably inevitable to address the restructuring crisis of the 1930s, the specific way events unfolded was not. The outcomes of the SCC and JCPC reference cases on point looked implausible to commentators and lawyers in the early 1930s, for example. Nevertheless the sequence of the events that did transpire is important for understanding the trajectory of CCAA law over time.

Furthermore, the fact that the act was essentially a dead letter by the early 1980s made it look like it would be repealed in the next round of bankruptcy reforms. But its technical presence on the statute books led to its regenesis, and it became a major part of modern Canadian bankruptcy and insolvency law.

Twice over the course of the CCAA's history debtor-led reorganizations emerged as an unintended consequence of the legislation. In the 1930s and 1940s, this abuse of the legislation led to calls to repeal the act and eventually prompted parliament to enact the trust deed restriction. In the 1980s and 1990s, however, courts, counsel, and parliament regarded debtor-led restructurings as the intended purpose of the statute and minimized the restrictiveness of the trust deed provision to facilitate debtor access to the act. A much-changed societal landscape in Canada by the 1980s and 1990s finally lent traction to earlier ideas about the normative desirability of corporate restructuring as a debtor remedy.

Another theme that arises in this narrative is how the steps that were taken to bring Canadian corporate lending practices more in line with American norms made it difficult or impossible to rely on existing restructuring mechanisms, which were rooted in historical English practices. One might think that the importance of foreign investment or American influence would lead a country like Canada to embrace more fully the US approaches to corporate financing and restructuring; or a legal origins analysis might suggest that English approaches would prevail and facilitate a greater role for British investment in Canada. The way historical events unfolded, however, was more complex and nuanced. Canadian companies removed provisions in financing instruments that US investors found objectionable in the 1920s and 1930s, and in so doing (inadvertently) eliminated their ability to restructure as well. The Canadian government responded to this problem by enshrining majority provisions into legislative form (the CCAA) in order to facilitate company restructurings by bondholders. The act also ensured ongoing access to American debt markets, since the US *Trust Indenture Act of 1939* formally barred bonds governed by Canadian majority provisions from the New York Stock Exchange. Yet most Canadian companies used the CCAA to reinsert majority provisions into their trust deeds – effectively opting out of access to US debt markets. Canadian rather than British investors represented nearly 100 per cent of purchasers of new Canadian corporate bonds for the next fifteen years. Although American influence and legal origins represent two significant factors, they are only part of a larger, multifaceted story.

Then in the 1980s and 1990s, Canadian corporate restructuring increasingly came to outwardly resemble American approaches under Chapter 11, but in practice reorganizations in Canada still maintained much in common with historical English bondholder reorganizations. Contemporary CCAA law is a hybrid of English schemes and receivership, with influences from Chapter 11. While comparative legal analyses tend to describe the CCAA as a functional equivalent to Chapter 11 (which is broadly true),[26] this characterization belies the distinct origins and development of the former act. The most unique aspect of the act to date – the feature that makes the CCAA, "the CCAA" – is the paradoxical way in which it has remained true to its original function as a remedy for large secured creditors (financial institutions) *despite* and *because of* new, and quite different, judicial interpretations of the statute to suit an evolving societal landscape. This characterization applies to earlier bondholder reorganizations to a certain extent as well. In both cases, limited parliamentary intervention helps to facilitate this process. The result is an area of law that draws on historical English and contemporary US approaches, and yet is distinctive from both. In neither of those two countries do the mechanisms of (and justifications for) legal change rely so heavily, overtly, and in such a sustained way on judge-made law concerning corporate reorganization.[27]

This historical account of the CCAA bears out the theory that institutions – particularly parchment institutions – tend to be highly resilient in the face of change or abolishment.[28] The CCAA survived at least three repeal bills introduced between 1933 and 1992, in addition to other, unrelated recommendations for repeal by practitioners and at least one parliamentary committee.[29] A socio-legal and recursivity of law analysis demonstrates that the act itself was a continuation of the long-standing practice of bondholder reorganizations in Canada and England, which developed under floating charges in the mid-nineteenth century. The enshrining into legislation of a secured creditor remedy developed under nineteenth-century trust deeds has effectively preserved a bondholder remedy from a period when trust deeds were a primary method of securing long-term financing, despite the significant expansion and development of new forms of lending and secured creditor remedies in the latter half of the twentieth century. The trust deed restriction was then done away with in the 1980s and 1990s – first through use of instant trust deeds, and then formal repeal – once large secureds shifted to other methods of taking security. Accordingly, this development is consistent with the central argument of this book that large, long-term secured creditors have been major drivers of developments in corporate reorganization law in Canada – inside and outside insolvency law – from the late nineteenth century to the present day.

In the result, institutional resilience, path dependence, and the process of statutory reinterpretation led to substantial (outward) institutional conversion of the CCAA in the 1980s and 1990s rather than outright repeal. In this process, historical and institutional factors played a large and arguably more significant role than the interest group politics surrounding specific instances of law reform. One particular difficulty that this transformation raises in the legal context, especially in view of the large role of judges in expanding the act on a case-by-case basis, is that this process of adaptation seems to go against the idea that statutes convey clear expectations, as well as the operation of the rule of law in the commercial restructuring context. Flexibility appears to be more important to both normative and functional conceptions about CCAA law than legal certainty or the rule of law.

As a twentieth-century history, this book has referred to twenty-first-century changes only briefly. At this juncture, these developments are still too fresh for an historical analysis. In time, however, they will ripen into prime material for historical study, opening up new avenues for scholars to build upon this work by carrying forward and improving the analysis in this book. A goal of this book has been to help elevate scholarship on CCAA law by using a theoretical frame that brings to light the role of institutions and social dynamics in this unique legal practice area. It opens up new scholarly terrain for advancing the field of knowledge in CCAA law in particular, and in commercial law more generally. Further such study has the potential to enrich Canadian commercial law scholarship. It is a task that calls for a scholarly dialogue that helps advance knowledge by probing disconnections between legal practice and legislation, and interrogating pat answers. It is sincerely hoped that, in the years to come, more scholars will take up this important work.

For now, this book can offer some preliminary thoughts on twenty-first-century developments and trends, drawing on the foregoing analysis.

Looking Forward

A fairly comprehensive series of amendments to the act came into force in 2009 and enshrined much of the preceding thirty years of case law into legislation. These amendments have been interpreted as a parliamentary affirmation of the re-purposing of the statute, and probably demarcate the end of this cycle of change, in terms of introducing a formal (if temporary) equilibrium in CCAA law and practice.[30] Perhaps judges will take these amendments as encouragement to continue developing judicial legislation under the act, possibly even circumventing the new statutory provisions if they think the circumstances so warrant. Alternatively, the amendments could usher in a more restrained approach to judicial discretion and inherent jurisdiction on points of law or procedure that the act now addresses.

In at least one recent case it appears that judges are following the former approach.[31] Given the history of the act, especially over the past thirty years, path dependence and institutional resilience suggest that this is the more likely outcome. At this point, it is unlikely that any textual provision of the CCAA – whether it is an anachronism or a recent addition by parliament – will substantially curtail the use of judicial discretion or inherent jurisdiction. To reverse this trend parliament would probably need to send the courts a much stronger signal, such as repealing the CCAA and replacing it with a new act. The fact that courts have, in some instances, affirmed older case law tests instead of new legislation on point appears to highlight how entrenched the inverted process of lawmaking under the act has become over the past thirty years.

The start of the newest cycle of change in CCAA law appears to be the recent trend toward liquidating plans. The public interest aspects of the going-concern reorganization object of the act do not account for or justify the use of the CCAA to effect liquidations. It is possible that the increase in liquidating plans may lead to layering within the law, whereby the act may be deployed to effect company liquidations in addition to going-concern restructurings. The legitimacy narrative surrounding the act may be modified to account for this new purpose, or liquidating CCAAs may represent a parallel and potentially subversive institutional track within CCAA law.[32] The fact that the act's conventional policy goal of facilitating going-concern restructurings has been powerless against the adoption of liquidating plans demonstrates the extent to which commercial pragmatism guides CCAA interpretation.[33]

Recent discussions on liquidating plans highlight the role of vulture funds, distressed debt traders, and hedge funds in corporate insolvencies.[34] While the identity and interests of claimholders in a given CCAA case may go some way to explaining the supposed rise of liquidating plans, this study demonstrates that vulture funds and distressed debt traders were active in CCAAs and bondholder reorganizations in the early twentieth century as well. Since no formal records were kept on CCAAs until 2009, it is difficult to say whether liquidating plans are actually on the rise, or just attracting more attention. In any event, the phenomenon of liquidating plans is consistent with the central argument of this book, as they expressly utilize the act as a lender- rather than a debtor-remedy.

Despite all that has changed, the major role of large secureds in corporate restructurings has remained a consistent feature of developments under this act. This in turn helps account for the CCAA's resilience in the face of repeated repeal efforts. The intended beneficiaries of the act are relatively strong and systemically important actors in the Canadian setting. Although approaches to the act and interpretations of the CCAA have evolved over time, they have continued to meaningfully advance the interests of large secureds relative to other groups.

The historical use of separate statutory remedies for large secureds versus unsecured creditors in cases of debtor insolvency also helps to fill in the bigger historical picture of Canadian bankruptcy and insolvency law and its relationship to receivership. This may help explain why the CCAA continues to exist separately from the BIA, with little support outside of academia[35] for combining these statutes into a single act. The fact that the first insolvency statute to facilitate complete company restructuring was grounded in receivership demonstrates that binding secured claims was necessary for a company reorganization statute to be effective. As this study shows, parliament *adopted* secured creditor remedies into federal law, rather than using bankruptcy and insolvency law merely to *limit* secured creditor rights (as those existed under provincial legislation). Parliament later went on to add receivership provisions to bankruptcy and insolvency legislation, which suggests that the CCAA may be part of a broader trend of transitioning some secured creditor rights from provincial to federal law. Note, however, that federal legislation does not necessarily imply greater power for secureds. For instance, a significant drawback of the CCAA in 1933 was that it only applied to insolvent companies, whereas majority provisions applied to solvent and insolvent companies. Along similar lines, the federal receivership provisions in the BIA restrict receivers in some ways.[36] Nevertheless, it is possible that there is now a growing commercial need for more uniformity concerning secured claims in insolvency,[37] much as Telfer noted that there was an increasing commercial need for a federal bankruptcy statute to deal with unsecured claims by 1919.[38]

Courts and the Legislature

The parallels between contemporary CCAA courts and the former English Court of Chancery may suggest a way forward, which could restore courts and the legislature to their respective roles. The end of the Chancery Courts provides an historic precedent for reining in judges,[39] which, combined with a call for parliament to re-assert itself, could provide a route to return to a legislature-led process of lawmaking in corporate reorganization.

The importance of returning to a legislative approach is underscored by comparing the track records of parliament and the courts with respect to CCAA law. Through much of the twentieth-century parliamentary enquiries into CCAA law have produced accurate and detailed accounts of the act's original purpose and sound recommendations for reform. This is exemplified in the discussions of the parliamentary committees tasked with reviewing early CCAA repeal bills in the 1930s and 1940s and the *Tassé Report* published in 1970. Courts, on the other hand, have demonstrated a sense of confusion about the CCAA's purposes and made errors in its interpretation. Thus, in addition to the democratic argument that legislative reform is properly the purview of the legislature, in the area of CCAA law this has bolstered a poor track record on the part of courts. The intrinsically reactive nature of the judicial process, which is confined to responding to legal issues that arise on a case-by-case basis, seems like a poor venue for farsighted policy-making. One would hope and expect that public policy in bankruptcy and insolvency law – as in other areas – would be pursued systematically and not in an ad hoc manner. The current method of judicial discretion is arguably an unsuitable instrument through which to achieve broad public policy goals connected with corporate restructuring. To the extent that public policy rationales have been relied upon to support expansive interpretations of CCAA law, they perhaps provide an even more compelling justification for returning to a parliamentary approach.

3 Conclusion

Over the past eighty years, evolving understandings of Canadian federalism alongside many other societal changes have facilitated novel and progressive interpretations of the CCAA, such that contemporary interpretations of the act now extend far beyond the expectations of its framers. One cannot help but wonder how earlier commentators would have reacted to modern CCAA law. In 1935, Harold Ernest Manning declared the CCAA unconstitutional for purporting to adjust secured creditor claims in cases of insolvency.[40] What would he think of its application to secured claims when the debtor is still solvent? Formal stasis of federal insolvency law and significant changes in many other areas of Canadian law and society help explain how receivership was added to the purview of parliament in cases of corporate insolvency (or near-insolvency). The active role of large secured creditors as protagonists of corporate reorganization provides a common thread and a reason for these gradual yet rather spectacular changes.

Appendices

Appendix 1 – Dominion Companies in Bankruptcy or Liquidation

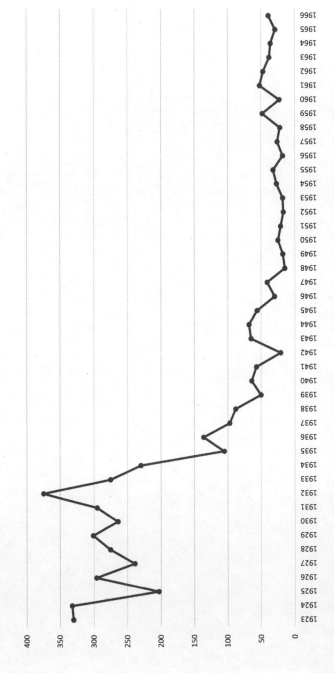

Note: Chart data is compiled from the Department of the Secretary of State, *Annual Reports of the Secretary of State of Canada* (Ottawa: King's Printer, 1924–1967).

Appendix 2 – Commercial Failures

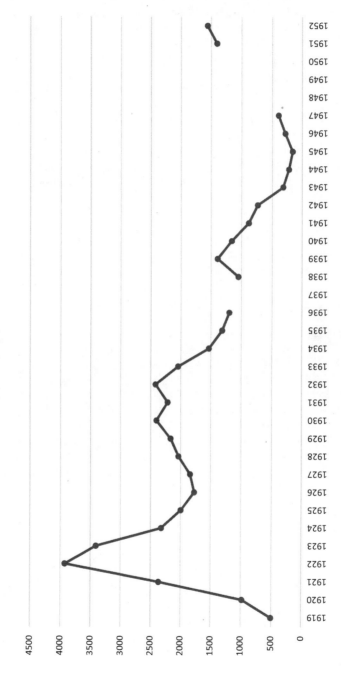

Note: Data gathered from Reports of the Dominion Bureau of Statistics: *Twelve Years of the Economic Statistics of Canada by Month and Years, 1919–1930* (Issued as a Supplement to the *Monthly Review of Business Statistics*, November 1931) (Ottawa: King's Printer, 1931), 12–13 (Commercial Failures as reported by Bradstreets); *Recent Economic Tendencies in Canada, 1919–1934* (Issued as a Supplement to the *Monthly Review of Business Statistics* June, 1935) (Ottawa: King's Printer, 1935), 39–40; *Monthly Review of Business Statistics*, vols. 9–21 (Ottawa: King's Printer, 1934–1946), data set described as "Commercial Failures as reported by Bradstreets" until 1930, simply "Commercial Failures" until 1937, and thereafter "Canadian Failures," as reported by Dun's Statistical Review; *Canadian Statistical Review*, *January and February 1953* (Ottawa: Queen's Printer, 1954). None of these terms were defined.

Appendix 3 – CCAA Usage, 1933 to 2017

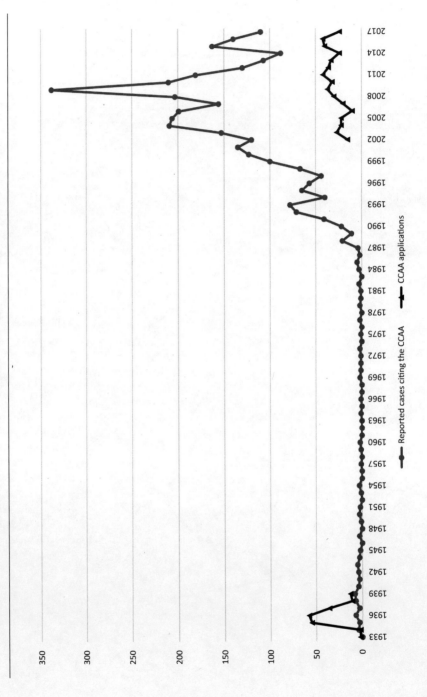

Reported cases citing the CCAA — CCAA applications

Note: Data for cases citing the CCAA comes from the print version of the Canadian Statute Citations and Supplements up to the end of 2017.

See "Canadian Statute Citations: September 2015" in Jilean Bell et al., eds, *Carswell Car to Constitution Act, 1982 Preamble* (Toronto: Thomson Reuters Canada Limited, 2015), 327–86; "Canadian Statute Citations: October 2015 – September 2018" in Jilean Bell et al., eds, *Carswell Ce to Co* (Toronto: Thomson Reuters Canada Limited, 2018), 34–48.

Data for CCAA applications is not complete for the years prior to 2010. The Office of the Superintendent of Bankruptcy began tracking CCAA filings from mid-September 2009, therefore statistics were taken from the OSB website from this point to the end of 2017; see "CCAA Records List" (last visited 5 October 2019), online: *Office of the Superintendent of Bankruptcy* <ic.gc.ca/eic/site/bsf-osb.nsf/eng/h_br02281.html> [perma.cc/9VQQ-2RPD]. Filing data for the 1930s only concerns CCAA applications filed in Montreal, and comes from data compiled by the Montreal Board of Trade from trade publications and presented to a parliamentary committee, where the figures were uncontested; see H.S.T. Piper, *1938 Minutes*, 2.

In the 1990s there was briefly a rule under the CCAA that facilitated record keeping. Whenever the court made an order under section 4 or 5 of the act the party that requested the order was required to send a copy of the order to the Superintendent of Bankruptcy; see SOR/92–580, s 3. This rule was repealed, ostensibly due to constitutional concerns. The specifics of the constitutional concerns were not noted. See Jacob S. Ziegel, "Repeal of the *Companies' Creditors Arrangement Act* Rule PC 1999–1072" (1999) 10 CBR (4th) 222.

Notes

1 Historical Institutionalism and the Recursivity of Law

1 Arthur L. Stinchcombe, *Constructing Social Theories* (New York: Harcourt, Brace and World, 1968), cited in Paul Pierson, *Politics in Time: History, Institutions, and Social Analysis* (Princeton, NJ: Princeton University Press, 2004), 46 [emphasis in original].

2 *Companies' Creditors Arrangement Act*, SC 1933, c 36 [*CCAA* 1933].

3 E.J. Lemaire (Clerk of the Privy Council), Minute of a Meeting of the Committee of the Privy Council (23 January 1934) PC 117 in Supreme Court of Canada fonds, LAC (RG 125, vol. 661); *Reference re Companies' Creditors Arrangement Act (Canada)*, 1934 SCR 659, [1934] 4 DLR 75 [*CCAA Reference*].

4 *British Columbia (AG) v Canada (AG)*, [1936] SCR 384, [1936] 3 DLR 610 [*FCAA Reference SCC*], reviewing *Farmers' Creditors Arrangement Act*, SC 1934, c 53.

5 *Companies' Creditors Arrangement Act*, RSC 1952, c C-54, s 2A, as am SC 1953 c 3, s 2. The bonds or debentures could be secured or unsecured.

6 Changes to the *Farmers' Creditors Arrangement Act* in 1935 and 1938 limited the applicability of the statute. The repeal and replacement of the act in 1943 narrowed the act's scope, ultimately rendering it useless to adjust secured debts, although the act remained on the statute books until 1988. See Stephanie Ben-Ishai and Virginia Torrie, "Farm Insolvency in Canada" (2013) 2 IIC Journal 33, 36–51; *Farmers' Creditors Arrangement Act Amendment Act*, SC 1935, c 20; *An Act to Amend the Farmers' Creditors Arrangement Act*, SC 1938, c 47; *Farmers' Creditors Arrangement Act*, SC 1943–1944, c 26, esp Preamble, s 7. See further Virginia Torrie, "Federalism and Farm Debt During the Great Depression: Political Impetuses for the *Farmers' Creditors Arrangement Act, 1934*" (2019) 82:2 Sask L Rev 207.

7 *United States Bankruptcy Code*, 11 USC (1978).

8 Janis Sarra, *Creditor Rights and the Public Interest* (Toronto: University of Toronto Press, 2003).

9 Janis Sarra, *Rescue! The Companies' Creditors Arrangement Act*, 2nd ed (Toronto: Carswell, 2013). See also David E. Baird, *Baird's Practical Guide to the Companies' Creditors Arrangement Act* (Toronto: Carswell, 2009) and John D. Honsberger and Vern W. DaRe, *Debt Restructuring: Principles and Practice* (Toronto: Thomson Reuters, 2008).

10 A 2014 article provides an overview of the legislative history of the CCAA based on Roger Tassé et al., *Bankruptcy and Insolvency: Report of the Study Committee on Bankruptcy and Insolvency Legislation* (Ottawa: Information Canada, 1970): Alfonso Nocilla, "The History of the *Companies' Creditors Arrangement Act* and the Future of Restructuring Law in Canada" (2014) 56:1 CBLJ 73.

11 Douglass C. North, *Institutions, Institutional Change, and Economic Performance* (Cambridge: Cambridge University Press, 1990), 1, on why "history matters."

12 This definition is found in *Bankruptcy and Insolvency Act*, RSC 1985, c B-3 [*BIA*], s 2 "bankruptcy," Part II "Bankruptcy Orders and Assignments."

13 Ibid., s 2, "insolvent person."

14 See Clémentine Sallée and David Tournier, "Reorganization: A Commercial Concept Juridicially Defined" (2009) 88:1 Can Bar Rev 87.

15 *Companies' Creditors Arrangement Act*, RSC 1985, c C-36 [*CCAA* 1985]; *BIA*, Part III, Division 1, "Commercial Proposals."

16 *Canada Business Corporations Act*, RSC 1985, c C-44 [*CBCA*], s 192.

17 Receivership is predominantly used by secured creditors, but is occasionally used by unsecured creditors. See Virginia Torrie, "Should Paramountcy Protect Secured Creditor Rights?: *Saskatchewan v Lemare Lake Logging* in Historical Context" (2017) 22.3 Rev Const Stud 405, 410.

18 In 1992 parliament added a receivership provision to the BIA: *BIA*, Part XI "Secured Creditors and Receivers," ss 243–252 as am SC 1992, c 27; SC 2005, c 47; SC 2007, c 36. See further Torrie, "Should Paramountcy Protect Secured Creditor Rights?," 412.

19 Janis Sarra, *Rescue! The Companies' Creditors Arrangement Act*, 1st ed (Toronto: Thomson Carswell, 2007); Sarra, *Rescue!*, 2nd ed; *Century Services Inc. v Canada (AG)*, 2010 SCC 60, [2010] 3 SCR 379, paras 15 and 18, per Deschamps J., McLachlin C.J. and Binnie, LeBel, Charron, Rothstein and Cromwell JJ. Concurring, citing Stanley Edwards, "Reorganizations Under the Companies' Creditors Arrangement Act" (1947) 25:6 Can Bar Rev 587, 593.

   Several American bankruptcy scholars have argued that corporate insolvency law should include a rescue component. See e.g. Karen Gross,

Failure and Forgiveness: Rebalancing the Bankruptcy System (New Haven: Yale University Press, 1997); Karen Gross, "Taking Community Interests into Account in Bankruptcy: An Essay" (1994) 72:3 Wash Univ LQ 1031; Karen Gross, "On the Merits: A Response to Professors Girth and White" (1999) 73:2 Am Bankr LJ 485; Marjorie Girth, "Rethinking Fairness in Bankruptcy Proceedings" (1999) 73:2 Am Bankr LJ 449.

20 Majority creditor support is required by the following statutes: *CCAA* 1985, s 6(1); *BIA*, ss 2 "ordinary resolution," 50(1.8), 115, for commercial proposals; *CBCA*, s 192; Industry Canada, Policy Statement 15.1 "Policy concerning arrangements under Section 192 of the 'Canada Business Corporations Act'" (Ottawa: Industry Canada, 4 January 2010), 3.10, requiring a two-thirds majority support. The two-thirds threshold remains the same in the current version of the policy: "Policy on arrangements – *Canada Business Corporations Act*, section 192" (last modified 8 January 2014), online: *Corporations Canada* <https://corporationscanada.ic.gc.ca /eic/site/cd-dgc.nsf/eng/cs01073.html> [perma.cc/75K7-3UTE].

21 The "collective action problem" refers to the organizational and cost barriers that can obstruct action by a group of creditors for their common benefit.

22 The "common pool" in this context refers to the value of the debtor company, and the "problem" is that of getting creditors to maximize the value of the common pool for their mutual benefit, rather than just seeking to recover their individual claims against the company.

23 See Thomas H. Jackson, *The Logic and Limits of Bankruptcy Law* (Cambridge, MA: Harvard University Press, 1986), chaps. 1 and 2; Thomas H. Jackson and Robert E. Scott, "On the Nature of Bankruptcy: An Essay on Bankruptcy Sharing and the Creditors' Bargain" (1989) 75:2 Va L Rev 155, 160–2.

24 *Trust Indenture Act of 1939*, 53 Stat 1173 (1939); 15 USC 1940; De Forest Billyou, "Corporate Mortgage Bonds and Majority Clauses" (1947–1948) 57:4 Yale LJ 595, 596–7. The thumbnail sketch of US majority provisions (also called "collective action clauses") with which many American readers are familiar is that these provisions were widely used leading up to 1939, at which point they were outlawed by the *Trust Indenture Act of 1939*. However, the use and regulation of majority provisions in the US was actually more complex. Even prior to the *Trust Indenture Act of 1939* majority provisions were not widely used in the United States due to several factors, including the reluctance of the New York Stock Exchange to list bonds subject to such clauses.

25 Bruce G. Carruthers and Terence C. Halliday, *Rescuing Business: The Making of Corporate Bankruptcy Law in England and the United States* (Oxford: Oxford University Press, 1998); Terence C. Halliday and Bruce G. Carruthers, *Bankrupt: Global Lawmaking and Systemic Financial Crisis* (Stanford: Stanford University Press, 2009).

26 Iain D.C. Ramsay, *Personal Insolvency in the 21st Century: A Comparative Analysis of the US and Europe* (Oxford: Hart Publishing, 2017).

27 David A. Skeel Jr, *Debt's Dominion: A History of Bankruptcy Law in America* (Princeton: Princeton University Press, 2001), 13–14.

28 For instance, scholars have adopted an historical institutionalism approach to the study of developments in health policy, federalism, labour movements, sovereignty and democracy. See Jacob S. Hacker, "The Historical Logic of National Health Insurance: Structure and Sequence in the Development of British, Canadian and U.S. Medical Policy" (1998) 12:1 Stud in Am Polit Develop 57; Ronald L. Watts, "The American Constitution in Comparative Perspective: A Comparison of Federalism in the United States and Canada" (1987) 74:3 J of Am Hist 769, cited in Pierson, *Politics in Time*, 164; Ruth Berins Collier and David Collier, *Shaping the Political Arena: Critical Junctures, The Labor Movement, and Regime Dynamics in Latin America* (Notre Dame: University of Notre Dame Press, 2002), cited in Pierson, *Politics in Time*, 134; Arend Lijphart, *Patterns of Democracy: Government Forms and Performance in Thirty-Six Countries* (New Haven: Yale University Press, 1999), cited in Pierson, *Politics in Time*, 158–9.

Some bankruptcy scholars have also used ideas from historical institutionalism. See Jérôme Sgard, "Bankruptcy Law, Majority Rule, and Private Ordering in England and France (Seventeenth–Nineteenth Century)" (2010) OXPO Working Paper (last visited 5 October 2019), online: <hal-sciencespo.archives-ouvertes.fr/hal-01069444> [perma. cc/XR84-D9KD]; Ramsay, *Personal Insolvency*; Halliday and Carruthers, *Bankrupt: Global Lawmaking*, 17, citing Wolfgang Streeck and Kathleen Thelen, "Introduction: Institutional Change in Advanced Political Economies," in Wolfgang Streeck and Kathleen Thelen, eds, *Beyond Continuity: Institutional Change in Advanced Political Economies* (New York: Oxford University Press, 2005).

29 Pierson, *Politics in Time*.

30 Skeel, *Debt's Dominion*.

31 Thomas G.W. Telfer, "The Canadian Bankruptcy Act of 1919: Public Legislation or Private Interest?" (1994–1995) 24:3 CBLJ 357; Thomas G.W. Telfer, "A Canadian 'World without Bankruptcy': The Failure of Bankruptcy Reform at the End of the Nineteenth Century" (2004) 8:1 Austl J Legal Hist 83; Thomas G.W. Telfer, *Ruin and Redemption: The Struggle for a Canadian Bankruptcy Law, 1867–1919* (Toronto: Osgoode Society for Canadian Legal History and University of Toronto Press, 2014).

See also Thomas G.W. Telfer and Bruce Welling, "The Winding-Up and Restructuring Act: Realigning Insolvency's Orphan to the Modern Law Reform Process" (2008) 24:1 BFLR 233.

32 Pierson, *Politics in Time*, 17–18.

33 See Alan Watson, "Legal Change: Sources of Law and Legal Culture" (1982–1983) 131:5 Univ Penn L Rev 1121, 1123, cited in Telfer, "A Canadian 'World Without Bankruptcy,'" 85.

34 Margaret Levi, "A Model, a Method, and a Map: Rational Choice in Comparative and Historical Analysis," in Mark I. Lichbach and Alan S. Zuckerman, eds, *Comparative Politics: Rationality, Culture, and Structure* (Cambridge: Cambridge University Press, 1997), 28, cited in Pierson, *Politics in Time*, 20.

35 Pierson, *Politics in Time*, 45.

36 Ibid. [emphasis in original].

37 Stinchcombe, *Constructing Social Theories*, cited in Pierson, *Politics in Time*, 46.

38 Pierson, *Politics in Time*, 142.

39 Ibid., 143.

40 Kathleen Thelen, "How Institutions Evolve: Insights from Comparative Historical Analysis," in James Mahoney and Dietrich Rueschemeyer, eds, *Comparative Historical Analysis in Social Sciences* (Cambridge: Cambridge University Press, 2003), 226, cited in Pierson, *Politics in Time*, 137.

41 Pierson, *Politics in Time*, 137.

42 Thelen, "How Institutions Evolve," cited in ibid., 138.

43 Pierson, *Politics in Time*, 148, citing James E. Alt et al., "The Political Economy of International Trade: Enduring Puzzles and an Agenda for Inquiry" (1996) 29:6 Comp Polit Stud 689; David A. Lake, *Entangling Relations: American Foreign Policy in Its Century* (Princeton: Princeton University Press, 1999).

44 Pierson, *Politics in Time*, 148, citing Peter Alexis Gourevitch, "The Governance Problem in International Relations," in David A. Lake and Robert Powell, eds, *Strategic Choice and International Relations* (Princeton: Princeton University Press, 1999), 144–5.

45 Kathleen Thelen, "Historical Institutionalism in Comparative Politics" (1999) 2 Annual Rev Poli Sci 369; Thelen, "How Institutions Evolve"; Stephen D. Krasner, "Sovereignty: An Institutional Perspective" in James A. Caporaso, ed., *The Elusive State: International and Comparative Perspectives* (Newbury Park, CA: Sage, 1989); Collier and Collier, *Shaping the Political Arena*; all cited in Pierson, *Politics in Time*, 134–5.

46 Pierson, *Politics in Time*, 135.

47 Hacker, "Historical Logic of National Health Insurance," 78 [emphasis in original].

48 Thelen, "Historical Institutionalism"; Thelen, "How Institutions Evolve"; both cited in Pierson, *Politics in Time*, 135.

49 See e.g. Carruthers and Halliday, *Rescuing Business*; Halliday and Carruthers, *Bankrupt: Global Lawmaking*; Terence C. Halliday and Bruce G.

Carruthers, "The Recursivity of Law: Global Norm Making and National Lawmaking in the Globalization of Corporate Insolvency Regimes" (2007) 112:4 Am J of Sociology 1135.

50 Halliday and Carruthers, *Bankrupt: Global Lawmaking*, 53.
51 Halliday and Carruthers, "The Recursivity of Law," 1146.
52 Ibid.
53 Ibid.
54 Ibid.
55 See Frank Baumgartner and Bryan D. Jones, *Agendas and Instability in American Politics* (Chicago: University of Chicago Press, 1993).
56 Carruthers and Halliday, *Rescuing Business*, 16–17.
57 Ibid., citing historical institutionalist scholars Streeck and Thelen, *Beyond Continuity*.
58 Carruthers and Halliday, *Rescuing Business*.
59 Ibid., citing Streeck and Thelen, *Beyond Continuity*.
60 Halliday and Carruthers, "The Recursivity of Law," 1142–3.
61 See e.g. Carruthers and Halliday, *Rescuing Business*, chap. 2 "Professional Innovation and the Recursivity of Law."
62 Halliday and Carruthers, "The Recursivity of Law," 1142.
63 Ibid., 1143.
64 Ibid., 1142.
65 Ibid.
66 Ibid.
67 Ibid., based on examples of nineteenth-century English Factory Acts.
68 Ibid., 1144, citing Ryken Grattet and Valerie Jenness, "The Birth and Maturation of Hate Crime Policy in the United States" (2001) 45:4 Am Behav Scientist 668; Ryken Grattet and Valerie Jenness, "Examining the Boundaries of Hate Crime Law: Disabilities and the Dilemma of Difference" (2001) 91:3 J of Crim L and Criminology 653; Ryken Grattet, "Structural Contradictions and the Production of New Legal Institutions: The Transformation of Industrial Accident Law Revised," in William J. Chambliss and Marjorie Zatz, eds, *Making Law: The State, the Law, and Structural Contradictions* (Bloomington: Indiana University Press, 1993).
69 Halliday and Carruthers, "The Recursivity of Law," 1144, citing Jeb Barnes, *Overruled? Pluralism, Court–Congress Relations and Legislative Overrides* (Stanford, CA: Stanford University Press, 2004).
70 Lauren B. Edelman, "Legal Ambiguity and Symbolic Structures: Organizational Mediation of Civil Rights Law" (1992) 97:6 Am J Sociology 1531; Lauren B. Edelman, "Legality and the Endogeneity of Law," in R. Kagan, M. Krygier and K. Winston, eds, *Legal and Community: On the Intellectual Legacy of Philip Selznick* (Lanham, MD: Rowman & Littlefield, 2002); Lauren B. Edelman, "Law at Work: An Endogenous Approach to

Civil Rights," in Laura Beth Nielsen and Robert L. Nelson, eds, *Handbook of Employment and Discrimination Research: Rights and Realities* (The New York: Springer, 2008).
71 Halliday and Carruthers, "The Recursivity of Law," 1144.
72 Ibid., 1144–5.
73 Ibid., 1143.
74 Gregory C. Shaffer, "Transnational Recursivity Theory: Halliday and Carruthers' *Bankrupt*" (2011) 9:71 Socioeconomic Rev 371; (2011) Minnesota Legal Studies Research Paper No. 11–38, 4 (last visited 5 October 2019), online: <ssrn.com/abstract=1926830> [perma.cc/E4EK-2ZFC].
75 Sgard, "Bankruptcy Law, Majority Rule," 9–11.
76 See Sallée and Tournier, "Reorganization: A Commercial Concept Juridicially Defined."

2 Corporate Restructuring as a Bondholder Remedy

1 Fred R. MacKelcan, "Canadian Bond Issues" (1952) 30:4 Can Bar Rev 325, 326–7.
2 Sgard, "Bankruptcy Law, Majority Rule," 9–10.
3 Ibid., 9–11.
4 W. Kaspar Fraser, "Reorganization of Companies in Canada" (1927) 27:8 Colum L Rev 932.
5 Baron Bowen (Charles S. Christopher), "Progress on the Administration of Justice during the Victorian Period," in *Select Essays in Anglo-American Legal History*, vol. 1 (Boston: Little, Brown and Company, 1907), cited in Sgard, "Bankruptcy Law, Majority Rule," footnote 31.
6 Sgard, "Bankruptcy Law, Majority Rule," 11.
7 *Companies Act 1862* (UK), 25 and 26 Vict, c 89, see Part IV, esp s 136. The term "creditor" referred to both secured and unsecured creditors.
8 See e.g., *Companies Act 2006* (UK), c 46, s 283 "special resolutions"; *CBCA*, s 2(1) "special resolution."
9 *Joint Stock Companies Arrangements Act 1870* (UK), 33 and 34 Vict, c 104.
10 Ibid., s 4. Also see *Companies Act 1867* (UK), 30 and 31 Vict, c 131, under which companies could also have recourse to the *Joint Stock Companies Arrangements Act 1870* (UK); *Re Alabama, New Orleans, Texas and Pacific Junction Railway Company Limited* (1890), [1891] 1 Ch 213, [1890] 12 WLUK 62, per Fry J.
11 See W.K. Fraser, representing the Dominion Mortgage and Investments Association (DMIA), House of Commons Standing Committee on Banking and Commerce, *Minutes of Proceedings and Evidence Respecting the Companies Creditors' Arrangement Act, No. 1, 7 June 1938* (Ottawa: King's Printer, 1938) [*1938 Minutes*], 18–19.

12 See *Re Alabama*, per Lindley L.J.

13 *Companies Act, 1929* (UK), 19 and 20 Geo 5, c 23, s 153.

14 Fraser, "Reorganization of Companies," 956, citing "The Rights and Remedies of the Bondholder under Corporate Bonds and Indentures: I" (1927) 27:4 Colum L Rev 433; "The Rights and Remedies of the Bondholder under Corporate Bonds and Indentures: II" (1927) 27:5 Colum L Rev 579.

15 Hon. C.H. Cahan (Conservative), *Debates of the House of Commons of Canada* (9 May 1933) 17th Parl, 4th Sess (Ottawa: King's Printer, 1933), 4724.

16 *Companies Act*, RSC 1927, c 79. See further "Corporate Reconstructions by Arrangements with Shareholders or Creditors" (1949) 62:3 Harv L Rev 468, 468–9, footnote 3, describing the CCAA as a Canadian counterpart to English schemes of arrangement under the *Companies Act, 1948*, 11 and 12 Geo 6, c 38, s 206.

Contemporary CCAA practice bears out its English roots in a number of ways. For example, third-party releases may be used under a CCAA plan, emulating English schemes. See e.g., *ATB Financial v Metcalfe & Mansfield Alternative Investments II Corp.*, 2008 ONCA 587, 92 OR (3d) 513, para 48; and discussion in Virginia Torrie, "Analyzing the Canadian Third-Party ABCP Liquidity Crisis and Restructuring through the Lenses of Securities and Insolvency Law" (LLM Thesis, Osgoode Hall Law School of York University, 2010) [unpublished], 118–20; Paul Halpern et al., *Back from the Brink: Lessons from the Canadian Asset-Backed Commercial Paper Crisis* (Toronto: University of Toronto Press, 2016), 91-92; Jennifer Payne, *Schemes of Arrangement: Theory, Structure and Operation* (Cambridge: Cambridge University Press, 2014), 23–4. Whereas third-party releases under Chapter 11 are the subject of conflicting case law. See Stephen J. Lubben, *American Business Bankruptcy: A Primer* (Cheltenham, UK: Edward Elgar, 2019), 171.

17 France has included business compositions in bankruptcy law for centuries: Sgard, "Bankruptcy Law, Majority Rule."

On Canadian bondholders reorganizations, see e.g. G.F.H., "Case Note on the Ontario case of *O'Brien v British American Nickel Corporation and National Trust Co.*" (1925) 3:8 Can Bar Rev 498; *M. J. O'Brien Ltd. v Br. Am. Nickel Corp. Ltd.*, [1925] 4 DLR 455, 57 OLR 536 (CA), (W.K. Fraser representing the defendant company, National Trust Co.), citing several English decisions on point, including: *North-West Transportation Co. v Beatty*, [1887] UKPC 39, LR 12 App Cas 589, (appealed from the SCC); *Goodfellow v Nelson Line (Liverpool) Ltd.*, [1912] 2 Ch 324, [1912] WLUK 76.

See also Winslow Benson, *Business Methods of Canadian Trust Companies*, 1st ed (Toronto: Ryerson Press, 1949); Fred R. MacKelcan, "Canadian Bond Issues."

18 See e.g., the following English texts by Paul Fredrick Simonson: *The Law Relating to the Reconstruction and Amalgamation of Joint-Stock Companies: Revised and Largely Rewritten*, 3rd ed (London: Sweet and Maxwell, 1919); *The Debenture and Debenture Stock Holders' Legal Handbook, with Appendix*

Containing Forms (London: Effingham Wilson, 1920); *The Law Relating to the Reduction of the Share Capital of Joint-Stock Companies*, 2nd ed (London: Sweet and Maxwell, 1924); *The Law Relating to the Reconstruction and Amalgamation of Joint-Stock Companies: Together with Forms and Precedents*, 4th ed (London: Jordan and Sons, 1931); *The Law Relating to the Reduction of the Share Capital of Joint-Stock Companies*, 3rd ed (London: Jordan and Sons, 1932).

19 Fraser, "Reorganization of Companies," 933; William Kaspar Fraser and Hugh Williamson MacDonnell, *Handbook on Companies with Appendix and Forms* (Toronto: Carswell, 1922).

20 Fraser, "Reorganization of Companies," 934.

21 Payne, *Schemes of Arrangement*, 8, citing *Re Dominion of Canada Freehold Estate and Timber Co Ltd* (1886), 55 LT 347, para 351, per Chitty J.

22 Payne, *Schemes of Arrangement*, 36, noting the (principally historical) importance of the form of notice of class meetings because it may be the only way to notify certain groups (e.g., holders of bearer bonds) about the proposed arrangement.

23 In the 1988 restructuring of Dome Petroleum, the debtor had a number of outstanding bearer bonds: Simon B. Scott, Timothy O. Buckley and Andrew Harrison, "The Arrangement Procedure under Section 192 of the *Canada Business Corporation Act* and the Reorganization of Dome Petroleum Limited" (1990) 16:3 CBLJ 296, 310–11.

24 Fraser, "Reorganization of Companies," 936–7.

25 Ibid., 937, citing an example of court intervention in *Re New York Taxicab Co. (sub nom Seguin v The Company)* (1912), [1913] 1 Ch 1, 107 LT 813.

26 MacKelcan, "Canadian Bond Issues," 329; G.F. Curtis, "The Theory of the Floating Charge" (1941–1942) 4:1 UTLJ 131, 145.

27 William D. Moull, "Security under Sections 177 and 178 of the Bank Act" (1986) 65:1 Can Bar Rev 242, 242–4.

28 Michael Bliss, *Northern Enterprise: Five Centuries of Canadian Business* (Toronto: McClelland and Stewart, 1989), 431–2.

29 Robert R. Pennington, "The Genesis of the Floating Charge" (1960) 23:6 Mod L Rev 630, 630.

30 MacKelcan, "Canadian Bond Issues," 341, cited in Jean Pierre Garant, "The Floating Charge in Canadian Bond Market" (PhD Dissertation in Finance, University of Illinois at Urbana-Champaign, 1971) [unpublished], 69–70.

31 MacKelcan, "Canadian Bond Issues," 329.

32 Curtis, "Theory of the Floating Charge," 145–146; Fraser, "Reorganization of Companies," 933.

33 Fraser, "Reorganization of Companies," 933; Curtis, "Theory of the Floating Charge," 133–40, 145–6, citing *Re Panama, New Zealand, and Australian Royal Mail Co.* (1870), LR 5 Ch App 318, the foundational case upholding the floating charge, which was affirmed in *Salomon v Salomon and Co. Ltd.* (1897), [1896] UKHL 1, [1897] AC 22, para 49. See judicial

characterizations of the floating charge in: *Governments Stock and Other Securities Investment Co Ltd v Manila Rly Co* (1896), [1897] AC 81, 86, per Lord Macnaghten, 75 LT 553 (HL); *Re Yorkshire Woolcombers Association, Limited* (*sub nom Houldsworth v Yorkshire Woolcombers Association Ltd*), [1903] 2 Ch 284, 295, per Romer L.J., 88 LT 811; *Illingworth v Houldsworth*, [1904] AC 355, 358, per Lord Macnaghten, 73 LJ Ch 739 (HL); *Evans v Rival Granite Quarries Ltd*, (1910) 2 KB 979, 999, per Buckley L.J., 79 LJKB 970 (CA).

See also, Pennington, "The Genesis"; Roy Goode, *Legal Problems of Credit and Security*, 4th ed (London: Sweet and Maxwell, 2008), chaps. 4 and 5; Robert R. Pennington, *Company Law*, 8th ed (London: Butterworths, 2001), 539–41; Eilís Ferran, *Principles of Corporate Finance Law* (Oxford: Oxford University Press, 2008), 368–84.

34 Garant, "The Floating Charge," 66–70.

35 Ibid., 67, citing Fraser, "Reorganization of Companies," 934.

36 Moull, "Security Under Sections 177 and 178," 242–4.

37 E.P. Neufeld, *The Financial System of Canada: Its Growth and Development* (Toronto: Macmillan of Canada, 1972), 110–11.

38 Moull, "Security Under Sections 177 and 178," 242–4.

39 Douglas R. Johnson, "Accounts Receivable Financing in Canada: Nature of the Charge and Rights of Priority" (1981) 15:1 UBC Law Rev 87, 121–33.

40 MacKelcan, "Canadian Bond Issues," 331–2; Curtis, "Theory of the Floating Charge," 149; Benson, *Business Methods*, 165, citing Fred R. MacKelcan, "The Position of Holders of Industrial Bonds," (no further bibliographic details available); *Dom. Iron and Steel Co. v Can. BK. Commerce*, [1928] 1 DLR 809, per Mellish J., 1928 CarswellNS 98 (NSSC).

41 Curtis, "Theory of the Floating Charge," 149, citing *Wallace v Universal Automatic Machines Co.*, [1894] 2 Ch 547, 554, per Kay L.J. [1891–94] All ER Rep 1156 (CA); Benson, *Business Methods*, 163.

42 J.L. Stewart and Laird Palmer, eds, *Fraser and Stewart Company Law of Canada*, 5th ed (Toronto: Carswell, 1962), 436, cited in Garant, "The Floating Charge," 61.

43 Ibid.

44 See e.g., *Personal Property Security Act*, RSO 1990, c P.10, s 16.

45 Benson, *Business Methods*, 121; Curtis, "The Theory of the Floating Charge," 133–40, 145–6, citing *Re Panama*; *Salomon v Salomon*, para 49.

46 See Roderick J. Wood, "The Floating Charge in Canada" (1988–1989) 27:2 Alta L Rev 191, 199–201, citing *inter alia Evans v Rival Granite Quarries*; E. Manson, "The Reform of Company Law" (1895) 11 LQR 346, 352; E. Manson, "The Growth of the Debenture" (1897) 13 LQR 418.

47 John R. Varley, "Receivership: The Contest Between Secured and General Creditors," in M.A. Springman and Eric Gertner, eds, *Debtor-Creditor Law: Practice and Doctrine* (Toronto: Butterworths 1985), 497. Note that execution creditors do not acquire a property interest in the debtor's assets, but the process of execution binds the debtor's assets. See further Tamara M.

Buckwold, "The Reform of Judgment Enforcement Law in Canada: An Overview and Comparison of Models for Reform" (2017) 80:1 Sask L Rev 71, 94–5, making the point in relation to present-day judgment enforcement law.

48 Fraser, "Reorganization of Companies," 943–4.

49 MacKelcan, "Canadian Bond Issues," 329; Benson, *Business Methods*, 1st ed, 172.

50 Sarra, "Creditor Rights," 42; Carruthers and Halliday, *Rescuing Business,* 244.

51 Fraser, "Reorganization of Companies," 934.

52 E.g., *Re Canadian Red Cross Society* (1998), 5 CBR (4th) 299, 81 ACWS (3d) 932, (Ont Ct (Gen Div)) applied the "Soundair Factors" from *Royal Bank of Canada v Soundair Corp.* (1991), 83 DLR (4th) 76, 7 CBR (3d) 1 (CA), a receivership case. These factors were originally laid out in *Crown Trust Co. v Rosenberg* (1986), 60 OR (2d) 87, 39 DLR (4th) 526 (SC (HCJ)), also a receivership case. See Alfonso Nocilla, "Asset Sales Under the Companies' Creditors Arrangement Act and the Failure of Section 36" (2011–2012) 52:2 CBLJ 226, 227–8.

53 See *Re Dairy Corporation of Canada Limited*, [1934] OR 436, [1934] 3 DLR 347 (SC (HCJ)) concerning a shareholder restructuring under *Companies Act*, RSO 1927, c 218, s 64a, considered in early CCAA cases such as *Re Wellington Building Corporation Limited*, [1934] OR 653, [1934] 4 DLR 626 (SC) and cited in the Canadian Encyclopedic Digest 4th (online), *Companies' Creditors Arrangement Act*, "Approval of Plan of Arrangement: Sanction of Plan by Court: General" (XVIII.2.(a)), § 966; *Re Alabama*, per Lindley L.J.

54 Garant, "The Floating Charge," 68.

55 Ibid., citing Benson, *Business Methods*, 1st ed, 326.

56 Garant, "The Floating Charge," 68.

57 Fraser, "Reorganization of Companies," 936. This situation prevailed in England into the 1980s; see Kenneth Cork et al., *Report of the Review Committee on Insolvency Law and Practice*, 1982 Cmnd 855; Carruthers and Halliday, *Rescuing Business*, 202–3, 209–10, 339–46.

58 Fraser, "Reorganization of Companies," 936.

59 See Curtis, "The Theory of the Floating Charge," 145–8; MacKelcan, "Canadian Bond Issues," 343.

60 MacKelcan, "Canadian Bond Issues," 343.

61 Curtis, "The Theory of the Floating Charge," 147; Benson, *Business Methods*, 1st ed, 164–5, 169. See *Bank Act*, RSC 1927, c 12, s 88; *Bank of Montreal v Guaranty Silk Dyeing and Finishing Co.*, [1934] OR 625, [1934] 4 DLR 394 (SC (HCJ)); *Dom. Iron and Steel Co. v Can. BK. Commerce*; Moull, "Security Under Sections 177 and 178," 242–4.

62 Benson, *Business Methods*, 1st ed, 164–5, 169.

63 "George F. Curtis, OC, OBC, QC" (last visited 5 October 2019), online: *Peter A. Allard School of Law, the University of British Columbia* <historyproject.

allard.ubc.ca/law-history-project/profile/george-f-curtis-oc-obc-qc>
[https://perma.cc/B7H8-2Q2L]; Curtis, "The Theory of the Floating
Charge," 147–149, citing *Robson v Smith*, [1895] 2 Ch 118, 64 LJ Ch 457;
Brunton v Electrical Engineering Co., [1892] 1 Ch 434, 61 LJ Ch 256; *Biggerstaff
v Rowell's Wharf Ltd.*, [1896] 2 Ch 93, 65 LJ Ch 536; *Wilson v Kelland*, [1910] 2
Ch 306, 79 LJ Ch 580; *Re Connolley Bros.*, [1912] 2 Ch 25, 81 LJ Ch 517.

64 Fraser, "Reorganization of Companies," 942, citing *Statute Law Amendment
Act*, SO 1917, c 27, s 17, amending certain provisions of the Ontario
Judicature Act, RSO 1917, c 56, s 106(5) pertaining to bondholders. See also
Bulk Sales Act, SO 1917, c 33.

65 See Roderick J. Wood, "The Regulation of Receiverships" 2009
ANNREVINSOLV 9 (Westlaw).

66 Fred R. MacKelcan, "A Philosophy of Trust Management that Packs a
Wallop," (1943) *Pamphlet Published by National Trust Co.*, 14 (no pagination
in original pamphlet).

67 Garant, "The Floating Charge," 65.

68 See e.g., MacKelcan, "Canadian Bond Issues," 347–8; Fraser, "Reorganization
of Companies," 942–3.

69 Diane M. Hare and David Milman, "Debenture Holders and Judgment
Creditors – Problems of Priority" (1982) LMCLQ 57, 66–67, footnote
79, discussing "equitable execution" under English Judicature Acts; *Re
Shepherd* (1889), 43 Ch D 131, 137, per Bowen L.J., 59 LJ Ch D 131.

70 *Judicature Act* 1917 (Ontario).

71 See *BIA*, Part X "Secured Creditors and Receivers," s 46. On common-law
appointments see *Gaskell v Gosling*, [1896] 1 QB 669, 691–2, per Rigby,
L.J., 65 LJQB 435 (CA), cited in Wood, "The Regulation of Receiverships,"
footnote 5.

72 A recent Canadian example is the third-party ABCP insolvency, which
was a quasi pre-packaged bankruptcy carried out under the CCAA;
see Torrie, "Analyzing the Canadian Third-Party ABCP. See further
Vanessa Finch, *Corporate Insolvency Law: Perspectives and Principles*, 2nd ed
(Cambridge: Cambridge University Press, 2009), chap. 10 "Pre-packaged
administrations"; Cork, *Report of the Review Committee*, paras 232, 914, 917,
919.

73 Fraser, "Reorganization of Companies," 933, 957.

74 *Benedict v Ratner*, 268 US 353 (1925); Grant Gilmore, *Security Interests in
Personal Property*, vol. 1 (Boston: Little Brown, 1965), 253–61.

75 MacKelcan, "Canadian Bond Issues," 332–4; Curtis, "The Theory of the
Floating Charge," 135; Fraser (DMIA), *1938 Minutes*, 18–19; Benson,
Business Methods, 1st ed, 169; for an overview of the American receivership
reorganizations practices of the 1920s and 1930s, see Skeel, *Debt's
Dominion*, chaps. 2–4. Also see Jacob S. Ziegel, "The Privately Appointed

Receiver and Enforcement of Security Interests: Anomaly or Superior Solution?" in Jacob S. Ziegel, ed, *Current Developments in International and Comparative Corporate Insolvency Law* (Oxford: Clarendon Press, 1994), 466–7, noting that private receiverships were not adopted in the United States.

76 MacKelcan, "Canadian Bond Issues," 332–4; P.J.J. Martin (Liberal), *1938 Minutes*; Skeel, *Debt's Dominion*, 73–4.

77 Fraser, "Reorganization of Companies," 950, citing *Re Bailey Cobalt Mines Ltd.* (1920), 47 OLR 13, 51 DLR 589 (CA), which concerned proceedings under *Winding-up Act*, RSC 1906, c 144.

78 *Winding-up Act*, RSC 1927, c 213, ss 63–4, cited in Fraser, "Reorganization of Companies," 949.

79 Fraser, "Reorganization of Companies," 950.

80 Ibid.; John Armour and Sandra Frisby, "Rethinking Receivership" (2001) 21:1 Oxford J Leg Stud 73.

81 Fraser, "Reorganization of Companies," 950.

82 *Bankruptcy Act of 1919*, SC 1919, c 36, ss 2(k) (definition of corporation), 2(o) (definition of debtor), 13 (composition procedure), and discussion in Telfer, "Bankruptcy Act of 1919," 391–3, citing Tassé, *Report of the Study Committee*, 19. See also Telfer, *Ruin and Redemption*, 172.

83 Telfer, "Bankruptcy Act of 1919," 391–3.

84 Sgard, "Bankruptcy Law, Majority Rule," 9–10. See also Carruthers and Halliday, *Rescuing Business*, 109–10, 136, 272, 525, discussing the "Phoenix Syndrome."

85 Fraser, "Reorganization of Companies." See also *Companies Act*, SC 1934, c 33, ss 122–4.

86 Fraser, "Reorganization of Companies," 953–4.

87 Ibid., 955, citing SO 1921, c 138 in relation to Goodyear Tire and Rubber Company of Canada Limited.

88 H.S.T. Piper (Montreal Board of Trade), *1938 Minutes*, 2–6. Also see the reasons of the court in *Re Wellington*.

89 See H.E. Manning, "Company Reorganization, Part 4" (1932–1933) 2 Fortnightly LJ 192; Edwards, "Reorganizations."

90 *The British North America Act, 1867* (UK), 30 and 31 Vict c 3, ss 91(21), 92(13). [Now titled *Constitution Act, 1867*].

91 Ibid., ss 91(2), 92(11).

92 H.E. Manning, "Company Reorganization, Part 1" (1932–1933) 2 Fortnightly LJ 139, 139; H.E. Manning, "Company Reorganization, Part 2" (1932–1933) 2 Fortnightly LJ 158, 158.

93 *CCAA Reference; FCAA Reference SCC*, aff'd *British Columbia (AG) v Canada (AG)*, [1937] UKPC 10, [1937] AC 391 [*FCAA Reference JCPC*]: reviewing *FCAA 1934*.

94 Neufeld, *The Financial System of Canada*, 490.

95 Ibid.
96 Ibid.
97 Ibid., 492–3.
98 Ibid.
99 Tassé, *Report of the Study Committee*, 19.
100 Fraser (DMIA), *1938 Minutes*, 19; Billyou, "Corporate Mortgage
    Bonds and Majority Clauses," 597. See further Francis Lynde Stetson,
    *Preparation of Corporate Bonds, Mortgages, Collateral Trusts, and Debenture
    Indentures, in Some Legal Phases of Corporate Financing, Reorganization
    and Regulation* (New York: Macmillan, 1917), 71; "Effect of Deeds of
    Trust on the Negotiability of Corporate Bonds" (1928) 42:1 Harv L Rev
    115; "Negotiable Instruments. Corporate Bonds. Effect of Reference
    to Mortgage on Negotiability" (1929) 29:3 Colum L Rev 365; "Bonds.
    Negotiability. Effect of Incorporation of Trust Indenture in Corporate
    Bonds" (1929) 42:5 Harv L Rev 700; "Negotiable Instruments. Bonds.
    Negotiability. Reference to Deed of Trust." (1928–1929) 38:6 Yale LJ
    825; "Negotiability of Corporate Bonds, Recent New York Legislation"
    (1930–1931) 40:2 Yale LJ 261; "Effect of Tax Exemption and Tax Refunding
    Provisions on the Negotiability of Corporate Bonds" (1930) 29:1 Mich L
    Rev 77; R.T. Steffen and H.E. Russell, "The Negotiability of Corporate
    Bonds" (1931–1932) 41:6 Yale LJ 799; S. Locker, "Negotiability of
    Corporate Bonds" (1932–1933) 7:2 St John's Rev 306.
101 MacKelcan, "Canadian Bond Issues," 330–1, citing e.g., the *Trust Indenture
    Act of 1939*, 53 Stat 1173 (1939), ss 316(a)(1), 316(a)(2). See also Fraser
    (DMIA), *1938 Minutes*, 19.
102 Billyou, "Corporate Mortgage Bonds," footnotes 17, 18, citing Stetson,
    Preparation of Corporate Bonds; Steffen and Russell, "The Negotiability of
    Corporate Bonds."
103 Billyou, "Corporate Mortgage Bonds," 597, footnote 19, with exceptions
    such as *Indenture, United States Steel Corp, Art 7* (1903) and the listed
    bonds described in *Chalmers v Nederlandsch Amerikaansche*, 36 NYS2d 717
    (City Ct 1942).
104 Graham D. Taylor and Peter A. Baskerville, *A Concise History of Business in
    Canada* (Toronto: Oxford University Press, 1994), 312.
105 Benson, *Business Methods*, 1st ed, 169.
106 See Canadian Department of Trade and Commerce, *Census of Industry:
    The Pulp and Paper Industry, 1925* (Ottawa: King's Printer, 1927), 10.
        See also Eugene A. Forsey, "The Pulp and Paper Industry" (1935) 1:3 Can
    J Econ Polit Sci 501; Taylor and Baskerville, *A Concise History*, 305–6, 381.
107 Bliss, *Northern Enterprise*, 420.
108 Barry E.C. Boothman, "Night of the Longest Day: The Receivership of
    Abitibi Power and Paper" (Paper delivered at Administrative Sciences

Association of Canada, 1992) [unpublished], 22. See also, Hon. Charles
Patrick McTague et al., *Report of the Royal Commission Inquiring into
the Affairs of Abitibi Power and Paper Company, Limited* (Toronto: Royal
Commission Inquiring into the Affairs of Abitibi Power and Paper
Company, 1941), report submitted to the Lieutenant-Governor of Ontario.
Taylor and Baskerville, *A Concise History*, 312: Abitibi was the fourth
largest non-financial company in Canada in 1929 (ranked by assets).

109 Boothman, "Night of the Longest Day," 26.

110 Ibid.

111 Ibid.

112 Ibid.

113 Ibid.

114 Ibid., 24, 26, citing *Judicature Amendment Act*, SO 1935, c 32; *Montreal
Trust Co. v Abitibi Power and Paper Co.*, [1938] OR 81, 19 CBR 179 (SC), per
McTague J., aff'd [1938] OR 589, [1938] 4 DLR 529 (CA).

115 E.g., the trust deed for Great Lakes Paper bonds did not provide for
calling bondholder meetings or selling assets for non-cash consideration;
see *National Trust Co. v Great Lakes Paper Co.*, [1936] 1 DLR 718, [1936]
OWN 13 (HCJ) rev'd [1936] 2 DLR 239, [1936] OWN 113 (CA).

116 Some provinces did enact such legislation during the Depression; see e.g.,
Judicature Amendment Act 1935 (Ontario), s 15(i).

117 H.E. Manning, "Company Reorganization, Part 3" (1932–1933) 2 Fortnightly
LJ 176, 176–7; Manning, "Company Reorganization, Part 4," 192–3.

118 In the early 1930s, the Canadian government came close to defaulting on
its bonds. Bliss, *Northern Enterprise*, 417–18.

119 Taylor and Baskerville, *A Concise History*, 378–80, noting the establishment
of the Bank of Canada in 1935.

120 E.g., by 1931 Sun Life was insolvent. Bliss, *Northern Enterprise*, 416–17,
citing Memorandum for Rt. Hon. Mr. Bennett from G.D. Finlayson,
Superintendent of Insurance, "RE: Sun Life Assurance Co. of Canada" (19
September 1931).

121 See e.g., Fraser (DMIA), *1938 Minutes*, 10; Dominion Mortgage and
Investments Association, *Yearbook 1934* (Toronto: DMIA, 1935), 13. See
also H.E. Manning, "Companies Reorganization and the Judicature
Amendment Act 1935, Part 1" (1935–1936) 5 Fortnightly LJ 23, 23.

122 Manning, "Company Reorganization, Part 1," 139 citing *Companies Act,
1929* (UK), ss 153–5.

123 Manning, "Companies Reorganization and the Judicature Amendment
Act 1935, Part 1," 23.

124 Ibid.

125 See e.g., Fraser (DMIA), *1938 Minutes*; Manning, "Company
Reorganization, Part 1."

126 Alfred F. Topham, Alfred Robert Taylour, and A.M.R. Topham, *Palmer's Company Precedents*, 14th ed (London: Stevens & Sons, Ltd., 1933), 158 cited in Billyou, "Corporate Mortgage Bonds," 595.

3 Enshrining a Bondholder Remedy in Federal Legislation

1 *Re Wellington*, para 18, per Kingstone J.
2 Hon. C.H. Cahan (Conservative), *Debates of the House of Commons of Canada*, (20 April 1933) 4th Sess, 17th Parl (Ottawa: King's Printer, 1933), 4090–1.
3 Rt. Hon. A. Meighen (Conservative), *Debates of the Senate of Canada* (9 May 1933) 4th Sess, 17th Parl (Ottawa: King's Printer, 1933), 474.
4 *CCAA* 1933, ss 3–4.
5 Ibid., ss 3–4, 8–9.
6 Ibid., s 2(a) "court." Although the Northwest Territories was not mentioned in this subsection of the act, in 1947 the Deputy Minister of Justice Canada gave the opinion that the CCAA was in force in the territory and an application under the act could be made to the Provincial Court. See F.P. Varcoe (Deputy Minister of Justice Canada) to R.A. Gibson (Deputy Commissioner, Administration of the Northwest Territories) (10 November 1947) in Northwest Territories and Yukon Branch Files, LAC (RG 85-C-1-a, vol. 1020, reel T13997, file 18388).
  The definition of "court" first expressly included mention of courts in the Northwest Territories in 1970: *Companies' Creditors Arrangement Act*, RSC 1970, c C-25, s 2 "court." Unusually, this change seems to first appear in RSC 1970, rather than in an amending act. Despite careful checking, no corresponding amending act could be found for this change in the definition of "court."
7 *CCAA* 1933, s 19.
8 Ibid., ss 10, 18, 20; *Bankruptcy Act*, RSC 1927, c 11; *Winding-up Act*, 1927.
9 H.F. Gordon (Department of Finance) to the Hon. E.N. Rhodes (Minister of Finance) (10 September 1935) in Bennett Papers, LAC (MG26-K, reel M-959), 1–2. H.F. Gordon reported that he believed smaller debtor companies were having "harsh settlements" forced on them by some lawyers. He noted that under the CCAA informal reference to a judge was made only after the parties had come to an agreement, and that in many cases the judge approved the arrangement "without full knowledge of the circumstances under which the arrangement was reached."
10 Ibid.; *CCAA* 1933, s 5.
11 See *Debates of the House of Commons of Canada*, (20 April 1933) 4th Sess, 17th Parl (Ottawa: King's Printer, 1933), 4090–1, in the same volume see also: (24 April 1933), 4194–5, (9 May 1933), 4722–4; *Debates of the Senate of Canada*, (9 May 1933) 4th Sess, 17th Parl (Ottawa: King's Printer,

1933), 467, in the same volume see also: (10 May 1933), 4747–4745, (11 May 1933), 484.

12 Boothman, "Night of the Longest Day," 26; Bliss, *Northern Enterprise*, 406.

13 Boothman, "Night of the Longest Day," 26.

14 Bliss, *Northern Enterprise*, 415; Louis A. Knafla, "Richard 'Bonfire' Bennett: The Legal Practice of a Prairie Corporate Lawyer, 1898 to 1913" in Carol Wilton, ed, *Beyond the Law: Lawyers and Business in Canada, 1830 to 1930*, vol. 4 (Toronto: Butterworths for the Osgoode Society, 1990), 325; Taylor and Baskerville, *A Concise History*, 372–3.

15 Knafla, "Richard 'Bonfire' Bennett," 328.

16 P.B. Waite, *In Search of R.B. Bennett* (Montreal and Kingston: McGill Queen's University Press, 2012), 23–4. See also "History" (last visited 5 October 2019), online: *Bennett Jones LLP* <bennettjones.com/history> [perma.cc/9ADM-NR9E].

17 Waite, *In Search of R.B. Bennett*, 71. See also "Past CBA Presidents" (last visited 5 October 2019), online: *Canadian Bar Association* <cba.org/Who-We-Are/Governance/Board-of-Directors/Past-CBA-Presidents> [perma.cc/9JSN-GYSX].

18 Knafla, "Richard 'Bonfire' Bennett," 329. See also Waite, *In Search of R.B. Bennett*.

19 Manning, "Companies Reorganization and Judicature," 23; Ian M. Drummond, "Canadian Life Insurance Companies and the Capital Market, 1890–1914" (1962) 28:2 Can J Econ Polit Sci 204, 207–8, noting that life insurance companies held significant investments in the Canadian bond and mortgage markets.

20 On the CCAA see, Manning, "Companies Reorganization and Judicature," 23. On the FCAA see, Rt. Hon. R.B. Bennett (Conservative), *Debates of the House of Commons of Canada*, (3 June 1934) 5th Sess, 17th Parl (Ottawa: King's Printer, 1934), 3638.

21 J.R. Mallory, *Social Credit and the Federal Power in Canada* (Toronto: University of Toronto Press, 1954), 101, citing (19 September 1936) *Financial Post*.

22 On the unique case of Saskatchewan see, Torrie, "Federalism and Farm Debt," 213.

23 Mallory, *Social Credit*, 95–6, citing an interview with Mr. Jules Fortin, Secretary, Dominion Mortgage and Investments Association (Toronto, 27 May 1946).

24 Torrie, "Federalism and Farm Debt," 208–9, citing W.T. Easterbrook and Hugh G.J. Aitken, *Canadian Economic History* (Toronto: Macmillan Company of Canada, 1956, reprinted Gage Publishing Ltd, 1980), 493; Taylor and Baskerville, *A Concise History*, 373; Bliss, *Northern Enterprise*, 414–15; Gregory P. Marchildon, "The Prairie Farm Rehabilitation

Administration: Climate Crisis and Federal-Provincial Relations during the Great Depression" (2009) 90:2 Cdn Historical Rev 275, 283.

25 On the negotiation of farm debt under federal legislation see, Virginia Torrie, "Farm Debt Compromises during the Great Depression: An Empirical Study of Applications made under the *Farmers' Creditors Arrangement Act* in Morden and Brandon, Manitoba" (2018) 41:1 Manitoba LJ 377, 383–92.

26 Torrie, "Federalism and Farm Debt," 223–4.

27 Robert Bryce, *Maturing in Hard Times: Canada's Department of Finance through the Great Depression* (Kingston and Montreal: McGill-Queen's University Press, 1986), 161.

28 Dominion Mortgage and Investments Association, *Yearbook 1933* (Toronto: DMIA, 1934), 15–16.

29 *Yearbook 1934*, 13.

30 Ibid.

31 Ibid.; *Yearbook 1933*, 16.

32 *Yearbook 1933*, 43. This language came from the provision titled "Scope of Act," see *CCAA* 1933, s 7.

33 H.S.T. Piper, *1938 Minutes*, 2–10.

34 H.F. Gordon (Department of Finance) to the Hon. E.N. Rhodes (Minister of Finance) (10 September 1935) in Bennett Papers, LAC (MG26-K, reel M-959), 1. Gordon reported that regulations were only beginning to be drafted two years after the CCAA was enacted.
    Larry A. Glassford, *Reaction and Reform: The Politics of the Conservative Party under R.B. Bennett 1927–1938* (Toronto: University of Toronto Press, 1992), 146. Glassford records that the CCAA was given little administrative support by the department charged with its administration, the Secretary of State under C.H. Cahan.

35 *Bankruptcy Act*, 47 Stat 1474 (1933). MacKelcan, "Canadian Bond Issues," 341–7. See also Skeel, *Debt's Dominion*, 73–4, chaps. 2 and 3.

36 *CCAA* 1933, s 7; see also s 19.

37 See *FCAA* 1934.

38 Bryce, *Maturing in Hard Times*, 159–62.

39 *Century Services*, para 15, per Deschamps J., McLachlin C.J. and Binnie, LeBel, Charron, Rothstein and Cromwell JJ. concurring.

40 Ibid., para 18, citing Edwards, "Reorganizations Under the CCAA," 593.

41 Sarra, *Creditor Rights*, 13.

42 Benson, *Business Methods*, 1st ed, 172.

43 Edwards, "Reorganizations Under the CCAA"; Stanley E. Edwards, "Protection of the Rights of Creditors in the Reorganization of Insolvent Canadian Companies" (LLM Thesis, Harvard Law School, Harvard University, 1947) [unpublished], 32–3.

44 Ben-Ishai and Torrie, "Farm Insolvency in Canada."

45 *CCAA* 1933, s 2(b) "company"; *CCAA* 1985, s 2 "company." In 2018, parliament removed the prohibition against railway companies filing under the CCAA see, *Transportation Modernization Act*, SC 2018, c 10, s 89, amending *CCAA* 1985, s 2(1) "company."

46 Lewis Duncan, "The Bankruptcy Act Amendment Act of 1932 – Part II: The Creation of the Office of the Superintendent of Bankruptcy" (1932–1933) 2 Fortnightly LJ 101, 102.

47 Financial institutions generally fell under the *Winding-up Act* in case of insolvency. *Winding-up Act* 1927.

48 See Telfer, *Ruin and Redemption*, chap. 9, "Reform Achieved: The *Bankruptcy Act of 1919.*"

49 Boothman, "Night of the Longest Day," 24, 26, citing *Judicature Amendment Act* 1935 (Ontario).

50 *Montreal Trust Co. v Abitibi Power and Paper Co.* (SC), 19 CBR 179, 188, per McTague J.

51 See *Judicature Amendment Act* 1935 (Ontario).

52 Boothman, "Night of the Longest Day," 24, 26, citing *Judicature Amendment Act* 1935 (Ontario); see also *National Trust Co. v Great Lakes Paper Co.*, where this provision of the *Judicature Act* was used to reorganize Great Lakes Paper.

53 See MacKelcan, "Canadian Bond Issues," 347–8.

54 *Re Comptoir coopératif du combustible Ltée* (1935), 74 Que SC 119, 17 CBR 124.

55 Boothman, "Night of the Longest Day," 26; but see *CCAA* 1933, s 6; *Re Wellington*, para 20.

56 *Minister of National Revenue v Cohen's Co.* (1935), 73 Que SC 291, 17 CBR 143, para 2; *Special War Revenue Act*, RSC 1927, c 179; *Minister of National Revenue v Roxy Frocks Manufacturing Co.* (1936), 62 Que KB 113, 18 CBR 132 (In Appeal), paras 13–14, 38–40; *R v Kussner*, [1936] Ex CR 206, 18 CBR 58, para 29, citing *Interpretation Act*, RSC 1927, c 1, s 16 which states: "No provision or enactment in any Act shall affect, in any manner whatsoever, the rights of His Majesty, his heirs or successors, unless it is expressly stated therein that His Majesty shall be bound thereby." The court noted that the CCAA did not contain an express provision binding the Crown. See further Statements in Defence of Defendant A. Kussner (6 March 1935), Statement in Defence of Defendant E.J. Kussner (6 March 1935), Reply to Statement of Defence (1 June 1936), in Exchequer Court Records (BANQ).

In 1933 Deputy Minister of Justice, C.P. Plaxton opined in correspondence with the Commissioner of Excise that the CCAA was inapplicable to Crown claims in respect of unpaid tax debts owed by the debtor Geo. Everal Co. Ltd. The Deputy Minister advised the Commissioner of Excise to take the position that Crown claims were not bound by the CCAA, but acknowledged that there was some doubt that this was correct for Crown claims arising *after* the coming into force of the statute. C.P. Plaxton (Deputy Minister of Justice) to Commissioner of Excise (4 August 1933; 23 August 1933), Commissioner of Excise to Deputy Minister of Justice (17 August 1933), and Departmental Solicitor for the Commission of Excise to the Deputy Minister of Justice (26 August 1933) in Department of Justice Papers, LAC (RG 13, vol. 387, file 1933–1077).

In the 1939 CCAA restructuring of Brock Manufacturing Company Ltd. the proposed plan of arrangement would have treated Crown claims (consisting of debts owed to the Receiver General of Canada, Province of Quebec, and City of Montreal) as privileged claims. The plan would have provided for repayment in full of all privileged claims prior to paying ordinary unsecured creditors 50 cents on the dollar. A Notice of Meeting of Creditors, Plan of Arrangement, Balance Sheet, Lists of Privileged and Unsecured Claims, and Voting Proxy were forwarded to the Superintendent, Excise Tax Collections (Department of National Revenue, Excise Division). It is unclear what position the Superintendent took with respect to the treatment of Crown claims as privileged claims under the CCAA. See David M. Johnson (Deputy Minister of Finance) to Wm. B. Stuart (Superintendent, Excise Tax Collection, Department of National Revenue) (19 December 1939) Department of Finance Papers, LAC (RG 19, vol. 296, file 101–53–96). The *Bankruptcy Act* in force at the time provided that a debtor's bankruptcy did not interfere with the collection of tax debts: *Bankruptcy Act* 1927, ss 125, 188. See further *Re West & Co.* (1921), 50 OLR 631, 2 CBR 3 (SC (In Bankruptcy)), para 22; *Re D. Moore Co.* (1927), 61 OLR 434, [1928] 1 DLR 383 (SC (App Div)); *Re General Fireproofing Co. of Canada*, [1936] OR 510, 17 CBR 371 (CA), paras 4–6, 13.

57 Boothman, "Night of the Longest Day."
58 *Re Wellington*, para 20.
59 *CCAA* 1933, s 2(c) "debtor company."
60 See *Re Stelco Inc.* (2004), 48 CBR (4th) 299, 129 ACWS (3d) 1065 (Ont SCJ), see esp paras 21, 22; leave to appeal to Ontario Court of Appeal refused, [2004] OJ No 1903 (Lexis); leave to appeal to SCC refused [2004] SCCA No. 336 (Lexis).
61 *Re Lehndorff General Partner Ltd.* (1993), 17 CBR (3d) 24, 37 ACWS (3d) 847 (Ont Ct J (Gen Div, Comm List), para 5, per Farley. J.
62 Algoma Plan Sanctioning Hearing, [2001] OJ No 4630 (Ont SCJ), Court File No 01-CL-4115 (Lexis); Endorsement Order, 19 December 2001; *Re Algoma Steel Inc.* (2002), 30 CBR (4th) 1, 111 ACWS (3d) 401 (Ont SCJ (Comm List)), para 8, per LeSage, C.J.S.C., cited in Sarra, *Creditor Rights*, 157.
63 There were exceptions, however. In the insolvency of the New Brunswick firm F.W. Daniel & Company, the debtor initially made an assignment into bankruptcy under the *Bankruptcy Act*. The Canadian Credit Men's Trust Association was appointed trustee, and under its trusteeship facilitated a plan of arrangement under the CCAA, which was approved by the court

in an order that simultaneously annulled the bankruptcy proceedings. See *Re Daniel & Co.* (1934), 16 CBR 21, 1934 CarswellNB 1 (NBSC (KB Div, In Bankruptcy)). See further "Order Sanctioning Compromise and Annulling Bankruptcy (7 February 1934) (NBSC (KB Div, In Bankruptcy)), in Court of Queen's Bench Bankruptcy Records, Provincial Archives of New Brunswick (RS53-N) (File 806).

64 Telfer, "Canadian Bankruptcy Act of 1919," 391–3, citing Tassé, *Report of the Study Committee*, 19, on the disabling of the composition provisions of the *Bankruptcy Act 1919* in 1923.

65 *Re Wellington*, para 18.

66 Ibid., paras 19, 21.

67 *Roxy Frocks; R v Kussner; R v Miss Style Inc.* (1936), 61 Que KB 283, 18 CBR 20 (In Appeal); *Parisian Cleaners & Laundry Ltd. v Blondin* (1938), 66 Que KB 456, 20 CBR 452 (In Appeal).

68 See e.g., *Blondin*, ibid.

69 See e.g., David Milman, "Receivers as Agents" (1981) 44 Mod L Rev 658; Armour and Frisby, "Rethinking Receivership." For an overview of the Canadian context see Stephanie Ben-Ishai and Thomas G.W. Telfer, eds, *Bankruptcy and Insolvency Law in Canada: Cases, Materials, and Problems* (Toronto: Irwin Law 2019), chap. 17, "Receiverships."

70 See e.g., *Re Bilton Brothers Ltd.*, [1939] 4 DLR 223, 21 CBR 79 (Ont SC); *1938 Minutes*.

71 See generally, *1938 Minutes*.

72 *An Act to Amend the Companies' Creditors Arrangement Act, 1933*, SC 1952–1953, c 3, s 2.

73 H.F. Gordon (Department of Finance) to the Hon. E.N. Rhodes (Minister of Finance) (10 September 1935) in Bennett Papers, LAC (MG26-K) (reel M-959), 1. Gordon remarked that the CCAA was "little known throughout Canada." The present study shows that while the CCAA was little known by the general public (especially when contrasted with the FCAA), it was known within financial circles.

See Glassford, *Reaction and Reform*, 146. Drawing at least in part on the Gordon Memorandum, Glassford erroneously concluded that "the Companies' Creditors Arrangement Act ... sat on the shelf and had little real impact."

74 Fraser, "Reorganization of Companies."

75 The Dominion Bureau of Statistics was established by the *Statistics Act*, SC 1918, c S-19.

76 Fraser, "Reorganization of Companies," 943.

77 See e.g., "Bankruptcy Reforms" (1932–1933) 2 Fortnightly LJ 196, 196; Duncan, "Bankruptcy Act Part II," 101.

78 But see *Blondin*, reversing *Blondin v Parisian Cleaners & Laundry* (28 May 1938), Quebec City No. 35322 (Que Sup Ct) [unreported]. See further materials filed

in the *Blondin* appeal: Factum de l'intime (17 November 1938), Appellant's Factum (22 November 1938), Appendice conjoint, all held in Superior Court Records (BANQ). On appeal the court held that the manager's claim to salary and commissions was an unsecured claim under the CCAA.

79 Gad Horowitz, *Canadian Labour in Politics* (Toronto: University of Toronto Press, 1968), chap. 2, "First Steps."

80 Ibid., 58–66.

81 Ibid., 80–4.

82 See e.g., Manning, "Companies Reorganization and Judicature, Part 1"; H.E. Manning, "Companies Reorganization and the Judicature Amendment Act 1935, Part 2" (1935–1936), 5 Fortnightly LJ 40; Lewis Duncan and William John Reilly, *Bankruptcy in Canada*, 2nd ed (Toronto: Canadian Legal Authors Limited, 1933), 1107–8. The third edition of this text does not mention the CCAA: Lewis Duncan and John D. Honsberger, *Bankruptcy in Canada*, 3rd ed (Aurora: Canada Law Book, 1961). The fourth and fifth editions include brief references to the CCAA: John D. Honsberger and Vern W. DaRe, *Bankruptcy in Canada*, 4th ed (Aurora: Canada Law Book, 2009), 18, 27, 110, 114, 117–19, 190; John D. Honsberger and Vern W. DaRe, *Honsberger's Bankruptcy in Canada*, 5th ed (Toronto: Thomson Reuters, 2017), 23, 33–4, 126, 135–6, 215.

83 Duncan and Reilley, *Bankruptcy in Canada*, 1107–8.

84 Ibid.

85 MacKelcan, "Canadian Bond Issues," 343–4; Curtis, "Theory of the Floating Charge," 147.

86 MacKelcan, "Canadian Bond Issues," 343–4.

87 Fraser, "Reorganization of Companies," 936.

88 Hon C.H. Cahan (Conservative), *Debates of the House of Commons of Canada*, (9 May 1933) 4th Sess, 17th Parl (Ottawa: King's Printer, 1933), 4724.

89 Pierson, *Politics in Time*, 143

90 H.S.T. Piper (Montreal Board of Trade), *1938 Minutes*, 2: 206 CCAA applications were filed in the city of Montreal up to 31 May 1938.

91 See Ben-Ishai and Torrie, "Farm Insolvency in Canada," 57: indicating a total of 301 filings from 2000 to 2012, citing: Keith Pritchard, "Analysis of Recent Cases Under the Companies' Creditors Arrangement Act" (2004) 40:1 CBLJ 116, 119; Alfonso Nocilla, "Is 'Corporate Rescue' Working in Canada?" (2013) 53:3 CBLJ 382; Janis Sarra, "Development of a Model to Track Filings and Collect Data for Proceedings Under the CCAA" (March 2006) Final Report to the OSB (last visited 5 October 2019), online: *Innovation, Science and Economic Development Canada* <strategis.ic.gc.ca/ eic/site/bsf-osb.nsf/vwapj/Sarra-2006-ENG.pdf/$FILE/Sarra-2006-ENG. pdf> [perma.cc/74G5-BAHS]; "CCAA Records List" (last visited 5 October 2019), online: *Office of the Superintendent of Bankruptcy* <ic.gc.ca/eic/site/ bsf-osb.nsf/eng/h_br02281.html> [perma.cc/9VQQ-2RPD].

92 See e.g., Roderick J. Wood, "Rescue and Liquidation in Restructuring Law" (2013) 53:3 CBLJ 407; Nocilla, "Is 'Corporate Rescue' Working"; Sarra, "Development of a Model."

4 Constitutional References and Changing Conceptions of Federalism

1 Manning, "Company Reorganization, Part 1," 140.
2 See e.g., Brooke Claxton, "Social Reform and the Constitution" (1935) 1:3 Can J Econ Polit Sci 409, 411–13; Manning, "Company Reorganization, Part 1," 139; Manning, "Company Reorganization, Part 2," 158; Manning, "Company Reorganization, Part 3," 176; Manning, "Company Reorganization, Part 4," 192; Manning, "Companies Reorganization and Judicature, Part 1," 23; Manning, "Companies Reorganization and Judicature, Part 2," 40; Factum on behalf of the Attorney-General for Quebec, filed with the Supreme Court of Canada (Ottawa: King's Printer, 1934) (SCC, Records Centre), 3–4, submitted in the *CCAA Reference*.
3 Manning, "Companies Reorganization and Judicature, Part 1," 23.
4 Factum on behalf of the Attorney-General for Canada, filed with the Supreme Court of Canada (Ottawa: King's Printer, 1934) (SCC, Records Centre), para 12.
5 See e.g., *Judicature Amendment Act* (Ontario), s 15(i); *Debt Adjustment Act*, SA 1923, c 43; *Debt Adjustment Act*, SA 1937, c 79; *Debt Adjustment Act*, SS 1931, c 59; *Reduction and Settlement of Land Debts Act*, SA 1937, c 27; *Debt Adjustment Act*, SM 1931, c 7.
6 See *Yearbook 1933*, 15–16.
7 Claxton, "Social Reform," 411–13.
8 "Companies Reorganization and Judicature, Part 1," 23.
9 Ben-Ishai and Torrie, "Farm Insolvency in Canada," 34, citing Marchildon, "The Prairie Farm Rehabilitation," 282.
10 Department of the Secretary of State, *Sessional Paper No. 165* (3 March 1938) [unpublished], returning an order of the House of Commons, dated 28 February 1938, 12–15.
11 Taylor and Baskerville, *A Concise History*, 325–6, 381–2.
12 Bliss, *Northern Enterprise*, 421.
13 Ibid., 422; Taylor and Baskerville, *A Concise History*, 285.
14 Taylor and Baskerville, *A Concise History*, 325; Bliss, *Northern Enterprise*, 422–3.
15 Bliss, *Northern Enterprise*, 422–3; Bryce, *Maturing in Hard Times*, 151–2.
16 Taylor and Baskerville, *A Concise History*, 411.
17 See e.g., Dominion Mortgage and Investments Association, *Yearbook 1932* (Toronto: DMIA, 1933), 18, 48, 175–6, as well as other years in the 1920s and 1930s.

18 Taylor and Baskerville, *A Concise History*, 380–1; Joseph Sirois et al., *Report of the Royal Commission on Dominion-Provincial Relations* (Ottawa: King's Printer, 1940), Book I, 160, and related discussion in Mallory, *Social Credit and the Federal Power*, chap. 7, "Public Finance and the Public Debt."

19 H. Blair Neatby, *William Lyon Mackenzie King, 1924–1932: The Lonely Heights* (Toronto: University of Toronto Press, 1963), 312.

20 Ibid.

21 Marchildon, "The Prairie Farm Rehabilitation," 282, citing e.g., Jakob B. Madsen, "Agricultural Crisis and the International Transmission of the Great Depression" (2001) 61:2 J of Econ Hist 327; A.E. Safarian, *The Canadian Economy in the Great Depression* (Toronto: McLelland and Stewart, 1970); E.W. Stapleford, *Report on Rural Relief due to Drought Conditions and Crop Failures in Western Canada, 1930–1937* (Ottawa: Minister of Agriculture, 1939).

22 See e.g., W.A. Carrothers, "Problems with Canadian Federalism" (1935) 1:1 Can J Econ Polit Sci 26; V.W. Bladen, "The Economics of Federalism" (1935) 1:3 Can J Econ Polit Sci 348; Norman McL Rogers, "The Political Principles of Federalism" (1935) 1:3 Can J Econ Polit Sci 337; R. McQueen, "Economic Aspects of Federalism: A Prairie View" (1935) 1:3 Can J Econ Polit Sci 352; J.A. Corry, "The Federal Dilemma" (1941) 7:2 Can J Econ Polit Sci 215; F.R. Scott, "The Special Nature of Canadian Federalism" (1947) 13:1 Can J Econ Polit Sci 13; D.C. Rowat, "Recent Developments in Canadian Federalism" (1952) 18:1 Can J Econ Polit Sci 1; Donald V. Smiley, "Two Themes of Canadian Federalism" (1965) 31:1 Can J Econ Polit Sci 80; F.R. Scott, "The Privy Council and Mr. Bennett's 'New Deal' Legislation" (1937) 3:2 Can J Polit Sci 234.

23 W.J. Waines, "Dominion-Provincial Financial Arrangements: An Examination of Objectives" (1953) 19:3 Can J Econ Polit Sci 304, 304–7; David Schneiderman, "Harold Laski, Viscount Haldane, and the Law of the Canadian Constitution in the Early Twentieth Century" (1998) 48:4 UTLJ 521, esp. 521–2. See generally, John T. Saywell, *The Lawmakers: Judicial Power and the Shaping of Canadian Federalism* (Toronto: University of Toronto Press for the Osgoode Society for Canadian Legal History, 2004).

24 F.R. Scott, "The Consequences of the Privy Council Decisions" (1937) 15:6 Can Bar Rev 485, 488–9.

25 See e.g., Horowitz, *Canadian Labour in Politics*; Carrothers, "Problems with Canadian Federalism"; Bladen, "The Economics of Federalism"; Rogers, "The Political Principles of Federalism"; McQueen, "Economic Aspects of Federalism"; Corry, "The Federal Dilemma"; Scott "The Special Nature"; Rowat, "Recent Developments"; Smiley, "Two Themes of Canadian Federalism."

26 See e.g., Eugene Forsey, "Disallowance of Provincial Acts, Reservation of Provincial Bills, and Refusal of Assent by Provincial Lieutenant-Governors

since 1867" (1938) 4:1 Can J Econ Polit Sci 47; Eugene Forsey, "Disallowance of Provincial Acts, Reservation of Provincial Bills, and Refusal of Assent by Lieutenant-Governors, 1937–47" (1948) 14:1 Can J Econ Polit Sci 94.

27 Torrie, "Federalism and Farm Debt," 222–3.

28 See e.g., J.R. Mallory, "Disallowance and the National Interest" (1948) 14:3 Can J Econ Polit Sci 342, citing, *Reference re the Power of Disallowance and the Power of Reservation (Canada)*, [1938] SCR 71, [1938] 2 DLR 8.

See further W. Christian and C. Campbell, *Political Parties and Ideologies in Canada: Liberals, Conservatives, Socialists, Nationalists* (Toronto: McGraw-Hill Ryerson, 1974), 95–6.

29 *Natural Products Marketing Act*, SC 1934, c 57; *FCAA 1934*; *Limitation of Hours of Work Act*, SC 1935, c 63; *Weekly Rest in Industrial Undertakings Act*, SC 1935, c 14; *Minimum Wages Act*, SC 1935, c 44; Section 498A of the *Criminal Code*, SC 1935, c 56, s 9; *Dominion Trade and Industry Commission Act*, SC 1935, c 59; *Employment and Social Insurance Act*, SC 1935, c 38.

30 (3 January 1935) *Winnipeg Free Press*, 1 cited in Alvin Finkel, *Business and Social Reform in the Thirties* (Toronto: James Lorimer and Company, Publishers, 1979), 36.

31 See e.g., Claxton, "Social Reform," 409.

32 See e.g., Christian and Campbell, *Political Parties*, 96; and see generally, Finkel, *Business and Social Reform*; Taylor and Baskerville, *A Concise History*, 374.

33 Finkel, *Business and Social Reform*.

34 Ben-Ishai and Torrie, "Farm Insolvency in Canada," 39, citing Rt. Hon. R.B. Bennett (Conservative), *Debates of the House of Commons of Canada* (3 June 1934) 5th Sess, 17th Parl (Ottawa: King's Printer, 1934), 3638–9; Torrie, "Federalism and Farm Debt," 224–5.

35 *Debates of the House of Commons of Canada* (14 February 1938) 3rd Sess, 18th Parl (Ottawa: King's Printer, 1938), 395, 587; *FCAA 1934*, Preamble. See generally Ben-Ishai and Torrie, "Farm Insolvency in Canada;" Torrie, "Federalism and Farm Debt," 225.

36 W.T.L. Lucas (United Farmers of Alberta), *Debates of the House of Commons of Canada* (18 June 1934) 5th Sess, 17th Parl (Ottawa: King's Printer, 1934), 4054–55; *Bankruptcy Act 1927*, s 7.

37 E.g., *Debt Adjustment Act 1923* (Alberta) and discussion in Mallory, *Social Credit*, 98–101; *Drought Area Relief Act*, SA 1922, c 43; *Debt Adjustment Act 1931* (Manitoba).

38 Rt. Hon. A. Meighen (Conservative), *Debates of the Senate of Canada* (9 May 1933) 4th Sess, 17th Parl (Ottawa: King's Printer, 1933), 474.

39 See e.g., H.S.T. Piper (Montreal Board of Trade), *1938 Minutes*, 2–6; E. Bertrand (Liberal), *Debates of the House of Commons of Canada* (22 February 1938) 3rd Sess, 18th Parl (Ottawa: King's Printer, 1938), 680.

40 See the New Deal legislation, and academic commentary: Scott, "The Privy Council"; Claxton, "Social Reform"; William McConnell, "The Judicial Review of Prime Minister Bennett's 'New Deal'" (1968) 6:1 OHLJ 39; Finkel, *Business and Social Reform*; Carrothers, "Problems with Canadian Federalism"; Bladen, "The Economics of Federalism"; Rogers, "The Political Principles of Federalism"; McQueen, "Economic Aspects of Federalism"; Corry, "The Federal Dilemma"; Scott "The Special Nature"; Rowat, "Recent Developments"; Smiley, "Two Themes of Canadian Federalism"; Raphael Tuck, "Social Security: An Administrative Solution to the Dominion-Provincial Problem" (1947) 13:2 Can J Econ Polit Sci 256.

Contrast with a handful of scholarly writing on the CCAA and Bankruptcy Act Amendments: Manning, "Company Reorganization, Part 1"; Manning, "Company Reorganization, Part 2"; Manning, "Company Reorganization, Part 3"; Manning, "Company Reorganization, Part 4"; "Protective Committees" (1940–1941) 10 Fortnightly LJ 183; Edwards, "Reorganizations"; Duncan and Reilley, *Bankruptcy in Canada*; "Bankruptcy Act Proclaimed" (1932–1933) 2 Fortnightly LJ 118.

The FCAA 1934 received relatively widespread attention among the bankruptcy and insolvency statutes, as noted in Ben-Ishai and Torrie, "Farm Insolvency in Canada," 46, footnote 75.

41 See *BIA* 1985, ss 2 "property," 71.

42 See Telfer, *Ruin and Redemption*, chap. 9 "Reform Achieved: The *Bankruptcy Act of 1919*," 145–73.

43 There are a few notable exceptions which are subject to federal jurisdiction; e.g., the *Bank Act* governs lending relationships between banks and borrowers.

44 On negative implication see, W.R. Lederman, "The Concurrent Operation of Federal and Provincial Laws in Canada" (1963) 9:3 McGill LJ 185, 191. On the FCAA see, Torrie, "Federalism and Farm Debt," 255.

45 Manning, "Companies Reorganization, Part 1"; Manning, "Companies Reorganization: Part 2."

46 Factum on behalf of the Attorney-General for Canada, filed with the Supreme Court of Canada (Ottawa: King's Printer, 1934) (SCC, Records Centre), submitted with respect to the *CCAA Reference*, para 2; Lemaire, "Minute of a Meeting," approved by his Excellency the Governor General (23 January 1934) PC 117.

47 Lemaire, "Minute of a Meeting."

48 Factum on behalf of the Attorney-General for Quebec, filed with the Supreme Court of Canada (Ottawa: King's Printer, 1934) (SCC, Records Centre), paras 3–5.

49 Ibid., paras 4–5.

50 Ibid., para 5.

51 Factum on behalf of the Attorney-General for Canada, filed with the Supreme Court of Canada (Ottawa: King's Printer, 1934) (SCC, Records Centre), paras 27–31.

52 Ibid., paras 15–20.

53 Ibid., para 31.

54 Ibid.

55 Ibid., para 32.

56 *Reference re Securities Act*, 2011 SCC 66, [2011] 3 SCR 837.

57 *Reference re Provincial Company Legislation*, [1913] 48 SCR 331, 15 DLR 332; *Bonanza Creek Gold Mining Co. v The King*, [1916] UKPC 11, [1916] 1 AC 566 (Ont); *Constitution Act, 1867*. See also discussion in Bruce Welling, Lionel Smith and Leonard I. Rotman, *Canadian Corporate Law: Cases, Notes and Materials*, 4th ed (Markham, ON: LexisNexis, 2010), 60–6

58 See *Companies Act* 1927, ss 112A, 112B as am *The Companies Act Amending Act, 1923*, SC 1923, c 39, s 4; A similar provision has long been a part of provincial corporate law statutes as well. See e.g., *Companies Act* 1927 (Ontario), s 64(a), and discussion in *Re Dairy Corporation*.

59 *Companies Act* 1927, ss 126–8, as am SC 1934, c 33, ss 122–4.

60 *CCAA Reference*, para 1, per Duff, C.J.C., para 17, per Cannon J.

61 Ibid., paras 3–4, per Duff C.J.C.

62 Ibid., para 7.

63 Ibid., para 5.

64 I.A. Humphries (Deputy Attorney General, Ontario) to Charles Lanctot (Deputy Attorney General, Quebec) (7 June 1934) in Attorney General Central Registry Criminal and Civil Files, Archives of Ontario (RG 4–32).

65 Charles Lanctot (Deputy Attorney General, Quebec) to I.A. Humphries (Deputy Attorney General, Ontario) (11 June 1934) in Attorney General Central Registry Criminal and Civil Files, Archives of Ontario (RG 4–32).

66 Following the SCC's decision in the *CCAA Reference*, Manning called the office of the Attorney General for Ontario to ask whether the province would appeal the decision to the JCPC. A solicitor for the Attorney General for Ontario replied by letter, indicating that Ontario was not planning an appeal, nor was it likely that Quebec would appeal the decision: Joseph Sedgwick (Solicitor, Attorney General's Department, Ontario) to H.E. Manning (25 September 1934) in Attorney General Central Registry Criminal and Civil Files, Archives of Ontario (RG 4–32).

67 Manning, "Companies Reorganization, Part 1"; Manning, "Companies Reorganization, Part 2."

68 Edwards LLM, "Protection of the Rights of Creditors," 32–3. But see *Lemare Lake Logging Ltd. v 3L Cattle Company Ltd.*, 2014 SKCA 35, 467 Sask R 1. The Saskatchewan Court of Appeal's decision has since been overturned by the SCC: *Saskatchewan (AG) v Lemare Lake Logging Ltd.*, 2015 SCC 53, [2015] 3 SCR 419. See Torrie, "Should Paramountcy Protect Secured Creditor Rights?"

69 The dissent is not discussed here since it is not relevant to a study of the CCAA. See Ben-Ishai and Torrie, "Farm Insolvency in Canada," 43–4.
70 *FCAA Reference SCC*, para 15.
71 Ibid., para 11.
72 *L'Union St. Jacques de Montreal v Bélisle* (1874), LR 6 PC 31, CR [7] AC 154 (Que JCPC), para 36, per Lord Selborne.
73 *FCAA Reference SCC,* para 19.
74 Ibid., para 25.
75 Ibid., para 18.
76 *Reference re Assignments & Preferences Act, s. 9*, [1894] UKPC 8, [1894] AC 189, para 20.
77 *L'Union St. Jacques.*
78 *Reference re Assignments & Preferences Act, s. 9*, para 27.
79 *FCAA Reference SCC*, para 12.
80 Ibid., paras 28, 31 citing *Re Silver Brothers, Limited*, [1932] UKPC 6, [1932] AC 514, 519–21.
81 *BIA* 1985, s 86, as am SC 1992 c 27, s 39. See further L.W. Houlden and G.B. Morawetz, *Houlden and Morawetz Bankruptcy and Insolvency Analysis*, F§191 – Crown Interests (accessed 28 January 2020). See further Lloyd W. Houlden, Geoffrey B. Morawetz and Janis P. Sarra, *The 2015 Annotated Bankruptcy and Insolvency Act* (Toronto: Carswell, 2015), 535–40; Honsberger and DaRe, *Honsberger's Bankruptcy in Canada*, 5th ed, 469.
   In 1997 parliament added a provision to the CCAA which binds the Crown: *CCAA* 1985, s 21 as am SC 1997, c 12, s 126. This provision is now enshrined in s 40.
82 Bliss, *Northern Enterprise*, 392.
83 *FCAA Reference JCPC*, paras 14–15.
84 See *Reference re The Weekly Rest in Industrial Undertakings Act, Minimum Wages Act and The Limitation of Hours of Work Act*, [1937] UKPC 6, [1937] AC 326; *Reference re The Employment and Social Insurance Act, 1935*, [1937] UKPC 7, [1937] AC 355; *British Columbia (Attorney General) v Canada (Attorney General)*; *Reference re Natural Products Marketing Act, 1934 (Canada)*, [1937] UKPC 9, [1937] AC 377; *FCAA Reference* JCPC; *Reference re The Dominion Trade and Industry Commission Act, 1935*, [1937] UKPC 11, [1937] AC 405.
85 See e.g., Scott, "The Privy Council"; Scott, "The Consequences of the Privy Council Decisions;" Scott, "The Consequences," 491–2. Except for reorganizations under the federal *Companies Act*.
86 In the case of insolvent companies, see e.g., *Montreal Trust Co. v Abitibi Power & Paper Co.* In the case of insolvent farmers, see Torrie, "Federalism and Farm Debt," 255–6.
87 See e.g., C.M. Herbert, "The Month in Canada: 'New Deal' Legislation – Help for the Farmer" (30 July 1934) *Barron's* 20; "Aid Farmers on Debts: Canadian Boards Seek Compromises with Creditors" (6 January 1935)

New York Times N2; "Canadian Debt Refund Urged by Mr. Bennett. Lower Interest Rates for Dominion Holders. Reconstruction of Entire System Foreshadowed." (11 September 1935) *Financial Times* 7; "Social Laws of Canada. Decision Sought on Validity. Powers of Parliament Questioned." (6 November 1936) *Financial Times* 10; "Canada's Relief for Farmers. Last Hearing Begun in 'New Deal' Series." (27 November 1936) *Financial Times* 9; "Canadian 'New Deal' Appeals Ended. Act to Keep Farmers on the Land. Judgment Reversed in Every Case." (28 November 1936) *Financial Times* 9; "Canada's Economic Position" (9 February 1935) *The Economist* 301; "Canada" (18 July 1936) *The Economist* 116.

88 See e.g., Vincent C. MacDonald, "The Canadian Constitution Seventy Years After" (1937) 15:6 Can Bar Rev 401, 411, where the *FCAA Reference* is covered in three brief paragraphs.

89 A. Berriedale Keith, "The Privy Council Decisions: A Comment from Great Britain" (1937) 15:6 Can Bar Rev 428, 434; Scott, "The Privy Council," 241; Scott, "The Consequences," 492–3; Saywell, *The Lawmakers*, 216. But see R.J. Burns, "Recent Depression Legislation" (1934–1936) 1 Alta LQ 16; D. McLaws, "The Farmers' Creditors Arrangement Act" (1936–1938) 2 Alta LQ 239; J.E.A. MacLeod, "The Farmers' Creditors Arrangement Act" (1936–1938) 2 Alta LQ 167.

90 On the CCAA see e.g., Manning, Company Reorganization, Part 1"; Manning, "Company Reorganization, Part 2"; Manning, "Company Reorganization, Part 3"; Manning, "Company Reorganization, Part 4"; Manning, "Companies Reorganization, Part 1"; Manning, "Companies Reorganizations, Part 2"; Duncan and Reilley, *Bankruptcy in Canada*, 1107–8; *Yearbook 1934*, para 13; W.J. Reilley (Superintendent of Bankruptcy), *1938 Minutes*, para 28.

91 In the Canadian context, see e.g., R.C.C. Cuming, "Canadian Bankruptcy Law: A Secured Creditor's Heaven" (1994–1995) 24:1 CBLJ 17; David B. Light, "Involuntary Subordination of Security Interests to Charges for DIP Financing under the Companies' Creditors Arrangement Act" (2002) 30 CBR (4th) 245; Anthony Duggan, "The Status of Unperfected Security Interests in Insolvency Proceedings" (2008) 24:1 BFLR 103; Roderick J. Wood, "The Definition of Secured Creditor in Insolvency Law" (2010) 25:3 BFLR 341; Roderick J. Wood, "The Structure of Secured Priorities in Insolvency Law" (2011) 27:1 BFLR 25.

92 J. Murray Ferron, "The Constitutional Impairment of the Rights of Secured Creditors in Canada and the United States" (1986) 60 CBR 146, 161–7, and discussion in Ben-Ishai and Torrie, "Farm Insolvency in Canada," 47.

93 See *Montreal Trust Co. v Abitibi Power & Paper Co* (SC), per McTague J., aff"d [1938] OR 589, [1938] 1 DLR 548 (CA).

94 *Reference re The Orderly Payment of Debts Act, 1959 (Alta.)*, [1960] SCR 571, 1 CBR (NS) 207.

95 Halliday and Carruthers, "The Recursivity of Law," 1142.

5 Efforts to Repeal the CCAA

1 Hon. Stuart S. Garson (Minister of Justice, Liberal), *Debates of the House of Commons* (23 January 1953) 7th Sess, 21st Parl (Ottawa: King's Printer, 1953), 1269.
2 H.S.T. Piper (Montreal Board of Trade), *1938 Minutes*, 2–6.
3 Bill No. 26, *An Act to Repeal The Companies' Creditors Arrangement Act, 1933*, 3rd Sess, 18th Parl, 1938.
4 Skeel, *Debt's Dominion*, 129–84. Benson, *Business Methods*, 1st ed, 133, citing the work of William Douglas and the SEC, which led to the enactment of the *Trust Indenture Act of 1939*, 15 USC 1939.
5 Benson, *Business Methods*, 1st ed, 133–42.
6 Hon. C.H. Cahan (Conservative), *Debates of the House of Commons* (8 March 1938) 3rd Sess, 18th Parl (Ottawa: King' Printer, 1938), 1139–42.
7 Edward J. Chambers, "The 1937–8 Recession in Canada" (1955) 21:3 Can J Econ Polit Sci 293; Bryce, *Maturing in Hard Times*, 64–6, citing Safarian, *The Canadian Economy*.
8 Chambers, "The 1937–8 Recession in Canada," 306–8.
9 H.S.T. Piper (Montreal Board of Trade), *1938 Minutes*, 2.
10 H.F. Gordon (Department of Finance) to the Hon. E.N. Rhodes (Minister of Finance) (10 September 1935) in Bennett Papers, LAC (MG26-K, reel M-959), 1–2. Gordon suggested that responsibility of the CCAA be transferred from the Secretary of State to the Department of Finance. The Department of Finance oversaw the FCAA (as well as the *Bankruptcy Act*), and Gordon felt that the offices of the registrars of the Boards of Review could handle CCAA applications in collaboration with the judges who served as chairs of the Boards of Review in each province. He thought this would benefit smaller debtor companies which, it was believed, were having "harsh settlements" forced on them by some lawyers. Gordon further noted that under the CCAA informal reference to a judge was made only after the parties had come to an agreement, and that in many cases the judge approved the arrangement "without full knowledge of the circumstances under which the arrangement was reached." Gordon recommended that whatever department oversaw the CCAA should charge a fee of $100 per application to make oversight "self-funding."

Gordon became the second director of the FCAA. See Bryce, *Maturing in Hard Times*, 162.

Adjusted for inflation, $20,000 in 1935 dollars would amount to roughly $360,500 in 2018 dollars, "Inflation Calculator" (last visited 5 October 2019), online: *Bank of Canada* <bankofcanada.ca/rates/related/inflation-calculator/> [perma.cc/9ERU-34LV].

11 W.J. Reilley (Superintendent of Bankruptcy), *1938 Minutes*, 28.

12 Ibid., 3–4.

13 Ibid. See also Duncan and Reilley, *Bankruptcy in Canada*, 1107–8.

14 *1938 Minutes*, 6.

15 Claxton, "Social Reform," 409–10; Scott, "The Privy Council."

16 Claxton, "Social Reform," 409–10.

17 Ibid., 429–34.

18 Ibid.; Rogers, "The Political Principles of Federalism," 339. McConnell, "The Judicial Review."

19 Claxton, "Social Reform," 411–13.

20 Ibid.

21 Ibid., 409–10.

22 Ibid., 431–3.

23 See *1938 Minutes*.

24 Tassé, *Report of the Study Committee*, 20.

25 G.H. Stanford, *To Serve the Community: The Story of the Toronto Board of Trade* (Toronto: University of Toronto Press for the Toronto Board of Trade of Metropolitan Toronto, 1974).

26 H.S.T. Piper (Montreal Board of Trade), *1938 Minutes*, 2–10.

27 J. Gerard Kelley (Toronto Board of Trade), *1938 Minutes*, 10–18.

28 Ibid., 7–8, 27, see also 16–18.

29 H.S.T. Piper (Montreal Board of Trade), *1938 Minutes*, 2–3.

30 J. Gerard Kelley (Toronto Board of Trade), *1938 Minutes*, 10.

31 Taylor and Baskerville, *A Concise History*, 252–4; Bliss, *Northern Enterprise*, 270–8, 393–4.

32 Taylor and Baskerville, *A Concise History*, 253, noting that of the ten leading financial institutions in Canada in 1929, six were headquartered in Toronto (Canadian Bank of Commerce, Bank of Nova Scotia, National Trust Co., Toronto General Trust Co., Canada Life Assurance Co., and Dominion Bank), and four were headquartered in Montreal (Royal Bank of Canada, Bank of Montreal, Royal Trust Co., and Public Utility Investment Co.)

33 Drummond, "Canadian Life Insurance Companies," 205–6.

34 Bliss, *Northern Enterprise*, 416–17.

35 Ibid.

36 Dominion Mortgage and Investments Association, *Yearbook 1938* (Toronto: DMIA, 1939), 21.

37 Ibid.

38 Ibid.

39 W.K. Fraser (DMIA), *1938 Minutes*, 10.

40 Ibid.

41 Ibid., 19.

42 Ibid. See also Benson, *Business Methods*, 1st ed, 164.

43 W.K. Fraser (DMIA), *1938 Minutes*, 19.

44 *Bankruptcy Act*, 47 Stat 1474 (1933) (codified prior to repeal at *United States Bankruptcy Code*, 11 USC, s 77B); Skeel, *Debt's Dominion*, 107–9.

45 W.K. Fraser (DMIA), *1938 Minutes*, 19.

46 Ibid.

47 Rt. Hon. A. Meighen (Conservative), *Debates of the Senate of Canada* (9 May 1933) 4th Sess, 17th Parl (Ottawa: King's Printer, 1933), 474.

48 Chambers, "The 1937–8 Recession in Canada," 307.

49 Lee A. Kelley (CCMTA), *1938 Minutes*, 27–8.

50 Ibid., 27.

51 Ibid.

52 Ibid., 28.

53 Thomas G.W. Telfer, "The New Bankruptcy 'Detective Agency'? The Origins of the Superintendent of Bankruptcy in Great Depression Canada" [unpublished manuscript].

54 W.J. Reilley (Superintendent of Bankruptcy), *1938 Minutes*, 28.

55 Ibid.

56 A 1946 effort to consolidate Canadian bankruptcy and insolvency law and repeal the CCAA failed, see Tassé, *Report of the Study Committee*, 20; Thomas G.W. Telfer, "Canadian Insolvency Law Reform and 'Our Bankrupt Legislative Process" 2010 ANNREVINSOLV 21 (Westlaw); Ziegel, "Canada's Dysfunctional Insolvency Reform Process and the Search for Solutions" (2010) 26:1 BFLR 63. Note that in the 2000s the OSB gained jurisdiction over the CCAA, see *CCAA* 1985, ss 26–31 as am SC 2005, c 47, s 131; SC 2007, c 36, ss 73–5.

57 *1938 Minutes*, 28. In 2014 Industry Canada conducted a statutory review of the CCAA and BIA but excluded the *Winding-up and Restructuring Act*, RSC 1985, c W-11 and *Wage Earner Protection Program Act*, SC 2005, c 47, s 1. See "Statutory Review of the *Bankruptcy and Insolvency Act* and the *Companies' Creditors Arrangement Act*" (last visited 5 October 2019), online: *Industry Canada* <ic.gc.ca/eic/site/cilp-pdci.nsf/eng/h_cl00870.html> [perma. cc/3LGQ-YRTF].

58 Manning, "Companies Reorganization and Judicature," 23.

59 Edwards, "Protection of the Rights of Creditors," 13.

60 Ibid.

61 Neufeld, *The Financial System of Canada*, 490–3.

62 Benson, *Business Methods*, 1st ed, 164; MacKelcan, "Canadian Bond Issues," 341–8; Billyou, "Corporate Mortgage Bonds," 597.

63 See e.g., *Companies Act* 1934, ss 144–5; *CCAA* 1933, s 19.

64 MacKelcan, "Canadian Bond Issues," 326–7.

65 E. Bertrand (Liberal), *1938 Minutes*, 19–20.

66 *CCAA* 1933, s 11(2). Now enumerated in *CCAA* 1985, s 20(2).

67 E. Bertrand (Liberal), *1938 Minutes*, 20.

68 W.K. Fraser (DMIA), *1938 Minutes*, 19–20.

69 Now enshrined in *CCAA* 1985, s 20(2). The entry for this subsection in *Houlden and Morawetz's Bankruptcy and Insolvency Analysis* contains no citations to case law or academic literature. See *Houlden and Morawetz Bankruptcy and Insolvency Analysis*, N§146 – Debtor Right to Reserve Right to Contest Claim (accessed 25 September 2019). In contrast, subsection 20(1) is the subject of a long entry citing a number of cases, see N§145 – Determination of Amount of Claims (accessed 25 September 2019). See Houlden, Morawetz and Sarra, *The 2015 Annotated Bankruptcy and Insolvency Act*, 1356–9. One reported case cites this provision but does not discuss it in great detail see, Virginia Torrie and Vern W. DaRe, "The Participation of Social Stakeholders in CCAA Proceedings" 2020 ANNREVINSOLV 9 (Westlaw), footnote 66, citing *Re 8640025 Canada Inc.*, 2018 BCCA 93, para 34, 58 CBR (6th) 257.

70 Telfer, "The Canadian Bankruptcy Act of 1919," 393.

71 See e.g., *Re Wellington; ATB Financial v Metcalfe & Mansfield Alternative Investments II Corp.* (2008), 43 CBR (5th) 269, 47 BLR (4th) 74 (Ont SCJ (Comm List)), para 22.

72 "Protective Committees." The details provided about the company suggest that it was likely the receivership and reorganization of Wellington Building Corp.

73 See Benson, *Business Methods*, 1st ed, 192, praising the CCAA and stating that abuses of reorganization proceedings such as those uncovered in the United States by the SEC had not arisen in Canada.

74 See e.g., Jeffrey B. Gollob, "Distressed Debt Lenders and their Impact on Restructurings and Workouts in Canada" 2004 ANNREVINSOLV 5 (Westlaw); Janis Sarra, "Judicial Exercise of Inherent Jurisdiction under the CCAA" (2004) 40:2 CBLJ 280, 290; Jason Harris, "Enhancing the Role of Creditors' Committees in Corporate Rescue Laws" 2011 ANNREVINSOLV 23 (Westlaw); Robert J. Chadwick and Derek R. Bulas, "Ad Hoc Creditors' Committees in CCAA Proceedings: The Result of a Changing and Expanding Restructuring World" 2011 ANNREVINSOLV 5 (Westlaw); Janis Sarra, "Manoeuvring through the Insolvency Maze – Shifting Identities and Implications for CCAA Restructurings" (2011) 27:1 BFLR 155, 158.

In the US context see e.g., Douglas G. Baird and Robert K. Rasmussen, "Antibankruptcy" (2010) 119:4 Yale LJ 648.

75 "Protective Committees," 183–5.

76 Ibid.

77 Ibid.
78 Benson, *Business Methods*, 1st ed, 170.
79 "Protective Committees."
80 Ibid.
81 *CCAA* 1933, s 5. In 1997 the voting provision was amended to the effect that a veto would require 33 1/3 per cent of the claims in a given class, see *CCAA* 1985, s 6(1), as am SC 1997 c 12, s 123.
82 Sarra, "Manoeuvring Through the Insolvency Maze," 158–9.
83 *Wellington*; "Wellington Building" (6 October 1934) *Globe and Mail* 14.
84 *Wellington*.
85 "Protective Committees," 185.
86 Benson, *Business Methods*, 1st ed, 170. Unlike in the US, where the SEC assumed a supervisory role.
87 E.P. Neufeld, *The Financial System of Canada*, 490–3.
88 Pierson, *Politics in Time*, 147, citing Arthur Stinchcombe, "Social Structure and Organizations" in James March, ed, *Handbook of Organizations* (Chicago, Rand McNally, 1965).
89 Pierson, *Politics in Time*, 18–19 citing Baumgartner and Jones, *Agendas and Instability in American Politics*; Collier and Collier, *Shaping the Political*; John Ikenberry, "History's Heavy Hand: Institutions and the Politics of the State" (1994) [unpublished manuscript]; Stephen Krasner, "Sovereignty: An Institutional Perspective."
90 DMIA was defunct by 1970, see Tassé, *Report of the Study Committee*, 20–1.
91 *An Act to Amend the Companies' Creditors Arrangement Act, 1933*, 1952–3, s 2.
92 See e.g., *1938 Minutes*. See also Bill A5, 2nd Sess, 20th Parl, 1946. (No further bibliographic information available). This bill proposed repeal of the CCAA as part of wider bankruptcy reform. Note this was a private member's bill put forward by the Hon. Sen. J. Gordon Fogo (Liberal), cited in Tassé, *Report of the Study Committee*, 20 (This study could not locate a surviving copy of Bill A5 or related Committee Proceedings); and, Bill C-217, *An Act to Amend the Bankruptcy Act (Priority of Claims)*, 2nd Sess, 34th Parl, 1989. This was a private member's bill put forward by Mr. John R. Rodriguez (NDP).
93 Skeel, *Debt's Dominion*, 74, 112–13.
94 Ibid.; Chap. X of the *Chandler Act of 1938*, 52 Stat 840 (1938).
95 Dominion Mortgage and Investments Association, *Yearbook 1939* (Toronto: DMIA, 1940), 16.
96 Ibid.
97 Ibid.
98 See Appendix "Table of Duplicative Provisions in the BIA and the CCAA as added by Statute c. 47" (as of 18 October 2006) in Jacob Ziegel, "The BIA and CCAA Interface" in Stephanie Ben-Ishai and Anthony Duggan, eds,

Canadian Bankruptcy and Insolvency Law (Markham, ON: LexisNexis, 2007), 340–1.

99 See e.g., Ziegel, "The BIA and CCAA Interface," 316–18; Ziegel, "Canada's Dysfunctional Insolvency Reform Process."

6 New Lenders, New Forms of Lending

1 Dunnery Best, "Reluctant Rescuers: Banks Forced to Acquire Shares in Problem Firms" (7 December 1985) *Financial Post*, section 1, page 1.
2 Bliss, *Northern Enterprise*, 481. See also appendices 1 and 2.
3 A notable exception is Atlantic Acceptance Corporation: Hon. S.H.S. Hughes et al., *Report of the Royal Commission Appointed to Inquire into the Failure of Atlantic Acceptance Corporation, Limited* (Toronto: Queen's Printer for Ontario, 1969).
4 See Tassé, *Report of the Study Committee*.
5 SC 1992, c 27.
6 See e.g., *Moratorium Act*, RSS 1953, c 98 (first enacted: SS 1943, c 18); *Orderly Payment of Debts Act*, SA 1959, c 61; *Saskatchewan Farm Security Act*, SS 1988–1989, c S-17.1; *Family Farm Protection Act*, SM 1986–1987, c 6.
7 J.A. Galbraith, *Canadian Banking* (Toronto: The Ryerson Press, 1970), 226; Neufeld, *The Financial System of Canada*, 128–31.
8 See Thomas Walkom, "From Profits to Horrors: MPs' Bank Probe a Peep Show on Economy" (16 June 1982) *Globe and Mail* (Nexis), noting testimony provided at the House of Commons Standing Committee on Finance, Trade and Economic Affairs.
9 Horowitz, *Canadian Labour in Politics*, chap. 7 "The New Party."
10 This affected the structure of *Companies' Creditors Arrangement Act* plans; see e.g., *Re Anvil Range Mining Corporation* (2001), 25 CBR (4th) 1, 104 ACWS (3d) 812 (Ont SCJ (Comm List)), aff'd (2002), 34 CBR (4th) 157, 115 ACWS (3d) 923 (Ont CA), cited in Sarra, *Creditor Rights*, 192–3; *CCAA* 1985, s 11.8, as am SC 1997, c 12, s 124.
11 See also Kennedy, *A Critique of Adjudication*, 113–15.
12 Lijphart, *Patterns of Democracy*, 216, citing Carl Baar, "Judicial Activism in Canada," 53.
13 See Girard, *Bora Laskin*, Part V "The Supreme Court of Canada." Contrast with the pre-Laskin SCC, see Weiler, *In the Last Resort*, Part 1 "On Law in the Supreme Court: A Preliminary View."
14 *The Constitution Act, 1982*, Schedule B to the *Canada Act 1982* (UK), 1982, c 11; Baar, "Judicial Activism," 53, cited in Lijphart, *Patterns of Democracy*, 216.
15 Driedger, *The Construction of Statutes*, 1st ed.
16 Some corporate loans were secured with trust deeds which included a charge on the undertaking, although the general trend was toward General

Security Agreements. See discussion in Stephen D.A. Clark, "Typical Security Taken By Banks" Paper in Proceedings of 1984 Annual Institute of Continuing Legal Education: "Business Law: Borrowing from Banks" (2 February 1984) [unpublished]; James S. Hilton, "Receivership Clauses in Mortgages" Paper in Proceedings of The Canadian Bar Association-Ontario, 1985 Annual Institute on Continuing Legal Education: "Real Property: Mortgage Matters" (9 February 1985) [unpublished].

17 See e.g., "Last Week the Tories Rushed to Pass Tough New Trust Company Legislation" (25 December 1982) *Globe and Mail* (Nexis); Walkom, "From Profits to Horrors."

18 Walkom, "From Profits to Horrors."

19 Ibid.

20 Stephanie Ben-Ishai, "Bank Bankruptcy in Canada: A Comparative Perspective" (2009) 25:1 BFLR 59, 60–1.

21 The only three Canadian life insurance companies to have ever failed did so during this period, in 1992, 1993, and 1994; see "Past Insolvencies" (last visited 5 October 2019), online: *Assuris* <assuris.ca/Client/Assuris/ Assuris_LP4W_LND_WebStation.nsf/page/Past+Insolvencies!OpenDocu ment&audience=policyholder> [perma.cc/4HKL-YQNT].

22 John DeMont, "Bank Collapses Rock Confidence in Alberta Financial Institutions" (21 September 1985) *Financial Post*, section 3, page B9; Tim O'Connor, "Ontario Takes Over Three Trust Companies" (7 January 1983) *United Press International* (Nexis); "New Trust Company Legislation"; Emilio S. Binavince and H. Scott Fairley, "Banking and the Constitution: Untested Limits of Federal Jurisdiction" (1986) 65:1 Can Bar Rev 328, 330, footnote 7

23 The Big Five banks are Royal Bank of Canada, Toronto-Dominion Bank, Canadian Imperial Bank of Commerce, Bank of Nova Scotia, and Bank of Montreal.

24 See e.g., William Poole, "Moral Hazard: The Long-Lasting Legacy of Bailouts" (2009) 65:6 Fin Analysts J 17. See also Kenneth Ayotte and David A. Skeel Jr, "Bankruptcy or Bailouts?" (2010) 35 J Corp Stud 469.

25 E.g., the third-party ABCP restructuring, see Torrie, "Analyzing the Canadian Third-Party ABCP."

26 See Halliday and Carruthers, "The Recursivity of Law," 1144; Mark Tushnet, "Defending the Indeterminacy Thesis" (1996–1997) 16:3 QLR 339, 345.

27 Tushnet, "Defending the Indeterminancy Thesis." See further, Marc Galanter, "Why the 'Haves' Come Out Ahead: Speculations on the Limits of Legal Change" (1974) 9:1 Law and Soc'y Rev 95.

28 Cork, *Report of the Review Committee*, para 1502.

29 Scott Haggett, "Salvation, not Liquidation, Receivers' aim" (16 June 1992) *Financial Post*, section 1, page 33.

30 Richard B. Jones, "The Evolution of Canadian Restructuring: Challenges for the Rule of Law" 2005 ANNREVINSOLV 18 (Westlaw), 492 (in print).

31 See e.g., Peter P. Farkas, "Why Are There so Many Court-Appointed Receiverships?" (2003) 20:4 Nat Insolv Rev 37; Jeffrey C. Carhart, "Appointing a Receiver and Seizing Equipment" (2005) 22:6 Nat Insolv Rev 53.

32 Dennis Slocum, "Merger of Dome Petroleum felt possible" (9 October 1986) *Globe and Mail* B7; "Dome Can't Meet Debt Obligations" (3 September 1982) *Associated Press* (Nexis).

33 "Dome Petroleum Discloses Refinancing Proposal From Creditor" (23 September 1982) *Associated Press* (Nexis).

34 Jennifer Lewington, "Ottawa guarantees: $100 million loan to cash-poor Dome" (26 June 1982) *Globe and Mail* (Nexis); "Dome Offered Plan to Reschedule Debt" (24 September 1982) *New York Times* D4.

35 Lewington, "Ottawa guarantees"; "Dome Offered Plan to Reschedule Debt."

36 On how legal concepts may gain legitimacy see, Tushnet, "Defending the Indeterminacy Thesis."

37 See e.g., Gord McIntosh, "Dome Petroleum Eyes New Defence Strategy against Liquidation" (25 September 1986) *Globe and Mail* B7; David Hatter, "Dome's Fate on Agenda in Europe" (4 October 1986) *Financial Post*, section 2, page 18; Canadian Press, "Recalcitrant Dome Lender Urged to Hold Firm" (12 November 1986) *Globe and Mail* B16; Eric Reguly, "Swiss Put Dome Back on Brink" (9 February 1987) *Financial Post*, section 1, page 2.

38 Slocum, "Merger of Dome Petroleum."

39 Ibid. See also Paul Brent, "Peoples Acted to Head Off Bank" (31 December 1992) *Financial Post*, section 2, page 1.

40 See e.g., Duncan and Reilley, *Bankruptcy in Canada*, 1107–8.

41 "Amoco Canada Completes Purchase of Dome" (12 September 1988) *Oil and Gas Journal* 31. See also Sarra, *Creditor Rights*, 18, citing *inter alia*: *Policy Statement of Director of CBCA* (1994) 17 OSCB 4853; Simon Scott, "The Acquisition of Dome Petroleum Limited by Amoco Corporation" in Jacob S. Ziegel and David Baird, eds, *Case Studies in Recent Canadian Insolvency Reorganizations* (Toronto: Carswell, 1997), 300, citing unreported judgment (28 January 1988), 311, 313.

42 This interpretation of parliamentary power with respect to bankruptcy and insolvency and federally incorporated companies may be changing, with a view to limiting use of the CBCA for debt restructurings where the CCAA may more properly apply. See *In the Matter of a Proposed Arrangement Involving 9171665 Canada Ltd. and Connacher Oil and Gas Limited* (2 April 2015), Calgary 1501–00574 (Alta QB); Kevin J. Zych et al., "Case Note: Important Restrictions Placed on Use of CBCA for Debt Restructurings" (2015) 32:1 BFLR 197.

43 Dome had outstanding issues of securities issued under a trust deed and running in favour of a trustee within the meaning of the CCAA trust deed requirement. See Scott, Buckley and Harrison, "The Arrangement Procedure," 310–11; *CCAA* 1985, s 3.

44 Sarra, *Creditor Rights*, 18.

45 See discussion of the Dome reorganization in Scott, Buckley and Harrison, "The Arrangement Procedure," 309–18.

46 Sarra, *Rescue!*, 2nd ed, 13, citing *inter alia Re Algoma Steel Inc.* (2002), para 8, LeSage C.J.C.S.; *Re Sammi Atlas Inc.* (1998), 3 CBR (4th) 171, 173–4, 78 ACWS (3d) 10 (Ont Ct J (Gen Div) (Comm List)); *Re Fracmaster Ltd.*, 1999 ABQB 379, 11 CBR (4th) 204, per Paperny J., aff'd in 1999 ABCA 178, 11 CBR (4th) 230, paras 18–23.

47 See e.g., Nocilla, "Is 'Corporate Rescue' Working."

48 Best, "Reluctant Rescuers."

49 Martin Mittelstaedt, "Bailout Plans Swell Banks' Shareholdings" (19 May 1984) *Globe and Mail* (Nexis).

50 Ibid.; Bliss, *Northern Enterprise*, 554; Galbraith, *Canadian Banking*, 18.

51 Mittelstaedt, "Bailout Plans."

52 Best, "Reluctant Rescuers."

53 This restructuring ultimately failed; see Arthur O. Jacques, "United Co-operatives of Ontario" in Jacob S. Ziegel, ed, *Case Studies in Recent Canadian Insolvency Reorganizations* (Toronto: Carswell, 1998), 595 *et seq*, cited in Jones, "The Evolution," 491 (in print), footnote 25.

54 Pritchard, "Analysis of Recent Cases."

55 Oliver Bertin, "UCO Remains Optimistic Despite Setbacks" (29 August 1984) *Globe and Mail* (Nexis).

56 The Intair reorganization is one example; see e.g., Ann Gibbon, "Creditors' Vote Keeps Intair Flying" (14 December 1990) *Globe and Mail* (Nexis); Ann Gibbon, "Intair Confident Creditors Will Accept Rescue Proposal: Carrier Plans to Offer 20 Cents on the Dollar to Some Suppliers" (29 November 1990) *Globe and Mail* (Nexis).

57 Anthony McCallum, "Ailing Nu-West Group Files Debt-Restructuring Plan" (23 March 1984) *Globe and Mail* (Nexis).

58 See Sarra, *Creditor Rights*, chap. 5 "Algoma Steel Corporation: Recognition of Human Capital Investments," chap. 6 "Judicial Recognition of 'Social Stakeholders' in *CCAA* Proceedings: Anvil Range Mining Corporation."

59 Michael Crawford, "'War Zone' of Bankruptcy Battles Is Getting Bigger and More Profitable: As Business Is Shot Down, Insolvency Cases Skyrocket" (13 December 1990) *Financial Post*, section 1, page 18.

60 Sarra, *Creditor Rights*, 16.

61 But see *Wage Earner Protection Program Act* 2005, as am SC 2007, c 36, s 93 [in force 7 July 2008, see SI/2008–78]. For a discussion of labour claims in business insolvencies under the *Wage Earner Protection Program*, see David

E. Baird and Ronald B. Davis, "Labour Issues" in Ben-Ishai and Duggan, *Canadian Bankruptcy and Insolvency Law*. The most recent amendments to the *Wage Earner Protection Program* enhance the priority of worker wage claims in employer insolvencies: *Budget Implementation Act, 2018, No. 2*, SC 2018, c 27, ss 626–53. Most notably, the maximum benefit payable under the program is increased and the program is extended to include BIA proposals, CCAA proceedings, and foreign proceedings recognized under the BIA by Canadian courts. See Jennifer Sokal, "Recent Developments in Canadian Bankruptcy and Insolvency Law" (2019) 34:2 BFLR 267, 270–3.

62 *Unemployment Insurance Act*, SC 1940, c 44.

63 The NDP was formed in 1961: Horowitz, *Canadian Labour*, chap. 7 "The New Party."

64 *Pension Benefits Amendment Act*, SO 1980, c 80, s 7. The applicable provisions are now contained in the *Pension Benefits Act*, RSO 1990, c P-8, ss 82–6.

65 Sarra, *Creditor Rights*, 178.

66 See discussion of PBGF in Algoma's 2001 insolvency in ibid., 178–9.

67 Court-appointed and private receiverships do not necessarily provide a mechanism for binding recalcitrant creditors to the restructuring plan. See generally Farkas, "Why Are There So Many Court-Appointed Receiverships?"

68 See Carruthers and Halliday, *Rescuing Business*; Skeel, *Debt's Dominion*, Part 3 "The Revitalization of Bankruptcy."

69 See e.g., Jackson and Scott, "On the Nature of Bankruptcy," 160; Jackson, *The Logic and Limits*.

70 See e.g., Elizabeth Warren, "Bankruptcy Policy" (1987) 54:3 U Chic L Rev 775.

71 Kevin J. Delaney, *Strategic Bankruptcy* (Berkeley and Los Angeles: University of California Press, 1998), chap. 3 "The Manville Corporation: Solving Asbestos Liability through Bankruptcy," chap. 4 "Continental Airlines: Using Bankruptcy to Abrogate Union Contracts."

72 Carruthers and Halliday, *Rescuing Business*, 3.

73 SC 1992, c 27, s 61(2).

74 Tassé, *Report of the Study Committee*, chap. 3 "Liquidation Outside of Bankruptcy."

75 Ibid., see 57, 63–72 "IV – Liquidation Outside Bankruptcy, Recommendations," 181.

76 Ibid., 35.

77 Ibid., 57–60.

78 Duncan and Reilley, *Bankruptcy in Canada*, 1107–1108.

79 See Tassé, *Report of the Study Committee*, 7–59, 87–88.

80 Ibid., 175, esp "II – Measures to Facilitate the Payment of Debts, Recommendations," 3–4.

81 Ibid., 19–22.
82 Excepting the CBCA for federal companies, see Janis Sarra, *Creditor Rights*, 18, citing *inter alia*: *Policy Statement of Director of CBCA* (1994) 17 OSCB 4853.
83 See e.g., "New Trust Company Legislation"; Walkom, "From Profits to Horrors."
84 See "Past Insolvencies."
85 See e.g., Binavince and Fairley, "Banking and the Constitution," 330, footnote 7; O'Connor, "Ontario Takes Over Three Trust Companies."
86 Ben-Ishai, "Bank Bankruptcy in Canada," 59–61. The two banks wound up in the 1980s were Northland Bank (1985) and Canadian Commercial Bank (1985).
87 The term "failure" is used to indicate an instance in which a financial institution collapsed, resorted to bankruptcy legislation, or was wound-up by a regulator.
88 Chris C. Nicholls, *Financial Institutions: The Regulatory Framework* (Toronto: LexisNexis, 2008), 16; Neufeld, *The Financial System of Canada*, 243.
89 OSFI was established in 1987; see "Our History" (last visited 5 October 2019), online: *Office of the Superintendent of Financial Institutions* <osfi-bsif.gc.ca/Eng/osfi-bsif/Pages/hst.aspx> [perma.cc/GMR2-YQAR].
90 See Letter from the Competition Bureau to the Royal Bank and the Bank of Montreal (11 December 1998), online: <competitionbureau.gc.ca/eic/site/cb-bc.nsf/eng/01612.html> [perma.cc/7H5Y-DWVQ]; Letter from the Competition Bureau to the CIBC and TD Bank (11 December 1998), online: <competitionbureau.gc.ca/eic/site/cb-bc.nsf/eng/01601.html> [perma.cc/KSB2-DZQG]; Statement by the Honourable Paul Martin, Minister of Finance, on the Bank Merger Proposals (14 December 1998), online: <webarchive.bac-lac.gc.ca:8080/wayback/20131002020411/http://www.collectionscanada.gc.ca/webarchives/20071122063125/http://www.fin.gc.ca/news98/98-124e.html> [perma.cc/7FKX-V8SN] all cited in Mark Katz, Anita Banicevic and Jim Dinning, "Antitrust in a Financial Crisis – A Canadian Perspective" (April 2009) *The Antitrust Source* (last visited 5 October 2019), online: *DWVP* <dwpv.com/~/media/Files/PDF_EN/2014-2007/Antitrust_in_a_Financial_Crisis_-_A_Canadian_Perspective.ashx> [perma.cc/5R3V-AT2A], footnotes 10, 11.
91 Carruthers and Halliday, *Rescuing Business*, 154–7.
92 See Galanter, "Why the 'Haves' Come Out Ahead," 101–2, 137.
93 Ibid.
94 See Carruthers and Halliday, *Rescuing Business*, chap. 4 "Weakening the Strong: Banks and Secured Lenders."
95 E.g., the financial support offered by Pierre Trudeau's (Liberal) government to Dome, see Lewington, "Ottawa Guarantees"; "Dome Offered Plan to Reschedule Debt."

7 Purposive Interpretation and Pro-Active Judging

1 *Re Westar Mining Ltd.* (1992), 70 BCLR (2d) 6, 14 CBR (3d) 88 (SC), para 23, per Macdonald J.

2 See e.g., David H. Goldman, "Reorganizations under the *Companies' Creditors Arrangement Act* (Canada)" (1985) 55 CBR (NS) 36; David H. Goldman, David E. Baird and Michael A. Weinczok, "Arrangements Under the *Companies' Creditors Arrangement Act*" (1991) 1 CBR (3d) 135; Jones, "The Evolution."

3 John R. Varley, "Receivership," in Springman and Gertner, eds, *Debtor-Creditor Law*, 433–9, citing some examples such as R.M. Goode, "Is the Law Too Favourable to Secured Creditors?" (1983–1984) 8:1 CBLJ 53; C.R.B. Dunlop, *Creditor-Debtor Law in Canada* (Toronto: Carswell, 1981), 436.

4 Varley, "Receivership," in Springman and Gertner, eds, *Debtor-Creditor Law*, 435.

5 Tamara M. Buckwold, "The Treatment of Receivers in the Personal Property Security Acts: Conceptual and Practical Implications" (1998) 29:2 CBLJ 277, 283–90.

6 Tassé, *Report of the Study Committee*, 56–7.

7 Fraser, "Reorganization of Companies," 950. For instance, junior creditors sometimes tried to challenge bondholders' security on technical grounds, such as a defect in the registration.

8 See e.g., Anne Fletcher, "Little Known Law Saves a Business" (17 September 1990) *Financial Post*, section 4, page 36; Heather D. Whyte, "Canada's Chapter 11 Is Suddenly a Hit" (20 May 1991) *Financial Post*, section 1, page 3.

9 Driedger, *Construction of Statutes*, 1st ed.

10 For an overview of case law on this point see e.g., *Bell ExpressVu Ltd. Partnership v Rex*, 2002 SCC 42, [2002] 2 SCR 559, paras 26–7, citing ibid.; *Stubart Investments Ltd. v R*, [1984] 1 SCR 536, 578, 10 DLR (4th) 1, per Estey J.; *Québec (Communauté urbaine) c Notre-Dame de Bonsecours (Corp.)*, [1994] 3 SCR 3, 63 QAC 161, para 17; *Re Rizzo & Rizzo Shoes Ltd.*, [1998] 1 SCR 27, 106 OAC 1, para 21; *R v Gladue*, [1999] 1 SCR 688, 171 DLR (4th) 385, para 25; *R v Araujo*, 2000 SCC 65, [2000] 2 SCR 992, para 26; *R v Sharpe*, 2001 SCC 2, [2001] 1 SCR 45, para 33, per McLachlin C.J.; *Chieu v Canada (Minister of Citizenship & Immigration)*, 2002 SCC 3, [2002] 1 SCR 84, para 27; *Interpretation Act*, RSC 1985, c I-21, s 12; John Willis, "Statute Interpretation in a Nutshell" (1938) 16:1 Can Bar Rev 1, 6; *R v Ulybel Enterprises Ltd.*, 2001 SCC 56, [2001] 2 SCR 867, para 52; *Murphy v Welsh*, [1993] 2 SCR 1069, 1079, 106 DLR (4th) 404; *Pointe-Claire (Ville) c S.E.P.B., Local 57*, [1997] 1 SCR 1015, 46 Admin LR (2d) 1, para 61, per Lamer C.J.

    The SCC upheld this approach to interpreting the CCAA in *Re Indalex Ltd.*, 2013 SCC 6, JE 2013–185, para 136.

11 *Norcen Energy Resources Ltd. v Oakwood Petroleums Ltd.* (1988), 92 AR 81, 72 CBR (NS) 1 (QB), paras 58–9, citing Driedger, *Construction of Statutes*, 1st ed, 74.

12 *Rizzo & Rizzo*, paras 21–2, citing Driedger, *Construction of Statutes*, 1st ed, 87.

13 *Interpretation Act* 1985, s 12, cited in *Quintette Coal Ltd. v Nippon Steel Corp.* (1990), 2 CBR (3d) 303, 51 BCLR (2d) 105 (CA), para 14, as part of the court's interpretation of the CCAA.

14 *Interpretation Act* 1927, s 15; *Interpretation Act*, RSC 1952, c 158, s 15. Note that this provision was shortened and renumbered in 1967: *Interpretation Act*, SC 1967, c 7, s 11.

15 *Elan Corp. v Comiskey (Trustee of)* (1990), 1 OR (3d) 289, 41 OAC 282, para 57 [dissenting in part].

16 *Re Lehndorff General Partner Ltd.*, para 5, per Farley J.

17 *Bell ExpressVu*, para 26. Note this was not a bankruptcy or insolvency case.

18 See e.g., "Dome Pete finds obscure law for defence against Swiss creditors" (25 September 1986) *Toronto Star* E3; Fletcher, "Little Known Law"; Laura Ramsay, "Troubled Firms Seek Protection under Once-Forgotten 1933 Law" (13 June 1991) *Financial Post* 16; Konrad Yakabuski, "Obscure Canadian Law Helped O&Y" (18 May 1992) *Toronto Star* B2.

19 E.g., Edwards, "Reorganizations"; Tassé, *Report of the Study Committee*, 19–22, but this study did not find any reported CCAA decisions that reference this report.

20 E.g., W.K. Fraser, *Handbook on Canadian Company Law with Forms*, 4th ed (Toronto: Carswell, 1945), 274, 282–4, 290–2; Stewart and Palmer, eds, *Fraser & Stewart Company Law of Canada*, 468–76; Benson, *Business Methods*, 1st ed, 163–73, esp 170; Winslow Benson, *Business Methods of Canadian Trust Companies*, 2nd ed (Toronto: Ryerson Press, 1962), 196; MacKelcan, "Canadian Bond Issues," esp 346–7; Edwards, "Protection of the Rights of Creditors"; Garant, "The Floating Charge."

21 *Norcen*, paras 60–1, citing *Meridian Dev. Inc. v Nu-West Ltd.* (1984), 53 AR 39, 52 CBR (NS) 109 (QB), 114.

22 See e.g., *Re Westar*, para 23, per Macdonald J., cited *inter alia* in *Re Stelco Inc.* (2005), 75 OR (3d) 5, 253 DLR (4th) 109 (CA), para 32.

23 Ibid.

24 See e.g., *Re Philip's Manufacturing Ltd.* (1991), 9 CBR (3d) 1, 60 BCLR (2d) 311 (SC), para 34.

25 See e.g., Algoma Plan Sanctioning Hearing, 1992, *Algoma Steel Corporation*, Court File Doc. No. B62191-A (Ont Ct [Gen Div]); Algoma Plan Sanctioning Hearing, 2001; Algoma Endorsement Order 2001; *Re Algoma Steel Inc.* (2002), para 8, per LeSage, C.J.S.C., cited in Sarra, *Creditor Rights*, 157.

26 See e.g., John D. Honsberger, "Insolvency and the Corporate Veil in Canada" (1972) 15 CBR (NS) 89; Tassé, *Report of the Study Committee*, 88.

27 See e.g., Jackson, *The Logic and Limits*; Jackson and Scott, "On the Nature of Bankruptcy"; Warren, "Bankruptcy Policy"; Donald Korobkin, "Contractarianism and the Normative Foundations of Bankruptcy Law" (1992–1993) 71:3 Tex L Rev 541; Gross, *Failure and Forgiveness*; Sarra, *Creditor Rights*.

28 See e.g., *Re Avery Construction Co.* (1942), 24 CBR 17, 1942 CarswellOnt 86 (Ont Sup Ct [in Chambers]; *Re Arthur W. Flint Co.* (1944), 25 CBR 156, [1944] OWN 325 (Sup Ct (in Bankr)), cited in Goldman, "Reorganizations," cited in turn in cases such as *Banque commerciale du Canada c Station du Mont Tremblant Inc.* (1985), JE 85–378, 1985 CarswellQue 544, para 26; *Elan*, para 56 [dissenting in part].

29 Edwards "Protection of the Rights of Creditors," 12–14, citing Manning, "Company Reorganization, Part 1"; Manning, "Company Reorganization, Part 2"; Manning, "Company Reorganization, Part 3"; Manning, "Company Reorganization, Part 4"; Manning, "Companies Reorganization and Judicature, Part 1"; Manning, "Companies Reorganization and Judicature, Part 2." Note that these sources are not mentioned in Edwards, "Reorganizations Under the CCAA."

30 *CCAA Reference*.

31 *Meridian Dev. Inc. v Nu-West Ltd.* See also e.g., *Icor Oil & Gas Co. v Cdn. Imperial Bank of Commerce* (1989), 102 AR 161, 1989 CarswellAlta 693 (QB); *Diemaster Tool Inc. v Skvortsoff* (Trustee of) (1991), 3 CBR (3d) 133, 1991 CarswellOnt 169 (Ont Ct), para 37; *Re Norm's Hauling Ltd.* (1991), 6 CBR (3d) 16, 91 Sask R 210 (QB), para 3.

32 See e.g., Tassé, *Report of the Study Committee*, chap. 1 "Bankruptcy in a Changing Society"; Skeel, *Debt's Dominion*, chap. 5 "Raising the Bar with the 1978 Bankruptcy Code"; Carruthers and Halliday, *Rescuing Business*, 194–201, 264.

33 But see Ferron, "The Constitutional Impairment," 161–7.

34 Skeel, *Debt's Dominion*, chap. 5, "Raising the Bar with the 1978 Bankruptcy Code."

35 Ibid., 241–2.

36 See Roger S. Foster, "Conflicting Ideals for Corporate Reorganization" (1934–1935) 44:6 Yale LJ 923, cited in Edwards "Protection of Creditor Rights," 29.

37 Carruthers and Halliday, *Rescuing Business*, 194–201.

38 See e.g., *Station Mont-Tremblant Inc. c Banque commerciale du Canada* (1984), 54 CBR (NS) 241, 1984 CarswellQue 37 (Que SC); *Re Victoria Mortgage Corp.* (1985), 57 CBR (NS) 157, 1985 CarswellBC 477 (BC SC); *Re Canadian Bed & Breakfast Registry Ltd.* (1986), 65 CBR (NS) 115, 1986 CarswellBC 504 (BC

SC). See further, Dow Jones Service, "Creditors of Forex accept plan" (21 March 1985) *Globe and Mail* (Nexis); Dow Jones Service, "Investment News: Page Petroleum" (14 March 1986) *Globe and Mail* B6; Dow Jones Service, "Lochiel Gets Staying Order" (16 April 1986) *Globe and Mail* B11; McIntosh, "Dome Petroleum"; Dow Jones Service, "Company Receives Stay of Proceedings" (9 February 1987) *Globe and Mail* (Nexis), referring to Trans-Canada Resources Ltd of Calgary; Kevin Cox, "Sale of $50 Bonds Aids Principal Units" (11 July 1987) *Globe and Mail* (Nexis); "Investment News: Mux Lab" (19 November 1987) *Globe and Mail* (Nexis).

39 See e.g., Whyte, "Canada's Chapter 11"; Lawrence J. Crozier, "Good Faith and the *Companies' Creditors Arrangement Act*" (1989) 15:1 CBLJ 89, 89, footnote 2, citing Ronald N. Robertson, "Legal Problems on Reorganization of Major Financial and Commercial Debtors' Canadian Bar Association Seminar: 'Mega-International Insolvencies'" (1983) [unpublished]; Arthur O. Jacques, "Creditor Arrangements" Canadian Bar Association Seminar: "Corporate Loan Workouts" (1985) [unpublished].

40 Delaney, *Strategic Bankruptcy*.

41 Tassé, *Report of the Study Committee*, 81, 175.

42 *CCAA* 1985, ss 4, 5 (as it stood up to the 1997 amendments).

43 "Voluntary petitions" are those filed by the debtor. "Involuntary petitions" in respect of the debtor may be filed by creditors, subject to certain (more stringent) criteria, see 11 USC, ss 301, 303; Charles R. Sterbach, "Anatomy of an Involuntary Corporate Bankruptcy" (2004) 13 J Bankr L & Prac 1 Art 1, 2.

44 Until 1992, the BIA applied only to unsecured claims, although secured creditors could opt in. This reflects the Act's origins as an unsecured creditor remedy, see Tassé, *Report of the Study Committee*, 16; Telfer, *Ruin and Redemption*, chap. 9 "Reform Achieved: The *Bankruptcy Act of 1919*."

45 Carruthers and Halliday, *Rescuing Business*, 206; Pen Kent, "The London Approach" (1 March 1993) Q1 *Bank of England Quarterly Bulletin* 110 (last visited 5 October 2019), online: *Bank of England* <bankofengland.co.uk/-/media/boe/files/quarterly-bulletin/1993/the-london-approach> [perma.cc/V8WM-ATFB]; Jay Lawrence Westbrook, et al., *A Global View of Business Insolvency Systems* (Leiden: The World Bank and Brill, 2010), chap. 5 "Informal Workouts and Restructurings," esp 175–9.

46 See e.g., Martin Mittelstaedt, "Banks Lobbying to Change Farm Foreclosure Bill" (30 April 1983) *Globe and Mail* B1; Allen Wilford, *Farm Gate Defense: The Story of the Canadian Farmers Survival Association* (Toronto: New Canada Publications, 1985), chap. 6 "Fighting the Banks for Our Farms."

47 See e.g., *Hongkong Bank of Canada v Chef Ready Foods Ltd.* (1990), 4 CBR (3d) 311, 51 BCLR (2d) 84 (CA).

48 But see *Montreal Trust Co. v Atlantic Acceptance Corp.* (1975), 9 OR (2d) 265, 60 DLR (3d) 193 (CA), Appendix A, para 11; Hughes et al., *Report of the Royal Commission into Atlantic Acceptance*; Irvine Duncan Weeks, "The Collapse of Atlantic Acceptance Corporation and its Effect on the Structure of Liabilities and Quality of Reporting of Canadian Finance Companies" (MBA Thesis, Faculty of Commerce and Administration, University of British Columbia, 1968) [unpublished], 21–2.

49 See e.g., *Norcen*, para 74, per Forsyth J.; *Chef Ready*, para 10; *Elan*, para 56 [dissenting in part]; *Re United Maritime Fishermen Co-operative* (1988), 88 NBR (2d) 253, 69 CBR (NS) 161 (CA), para 11 [*UMF CA*].

50 *Northland Properties Ltd. v Excelsior Life Insurance Co. of Canada* (1989), 34 BCLR (2d) 122, 73 CBR (NS) 195 (CA), para 27.

51 See e.g., *Teck Corp. Ltd. v Millar* (1972), 33 DLR (3d) 288, [1973] 2 WWR 385 (BC SC). See further *Peoples Department Stores Inc. (Trustee of) v Wise*, 2004 SCC 68, [2004] 3 SCR 461. But see Jacob S. Ziegel, "Creditors as Corporate Stakeholders: The Quiet Revolution – An Anglo-Canadian Perspective" (1993) 43:3 UTLJ 511.

52 See e.g., Warren, "Bankruptcy Policy"; Donald R. Korobkin, "Rehabilitating Values: A Jurisprudence of Bankruptcy" (1991) 91:4 Columbia L Rev 717; Gross, "Taking Community Interests"; Gross, *Failure and Forgiveness*; Karen Gross, "On the Merits"; Girth, "Rethinking Fairness"; Sarra, *Creditor Rights.*

53 *Re D. W. McIntosh Ltd.* (1939), 20 CBR 234, 251, 1939 CarswellOnt 68 (Ont Sup Ct [in Bankr]), para 58, per Urquhart J., cited in *Re Avery Construction Co.*, para 7, per Urquhart J.

54 *Re Avery Construction Co.*, para 6, cited in *Elan*, para 56 [dissenting in part].

55 *Quintette Coal Ltd. v Nippon Steel Corp.*, para 10, citing Edwards, "Reorganizations," 592.

56 Edwards, "Protection of the Rights of Creditors," 2 [emphasis added].

57 Ibid., 1–3, 12.

58 Ibid., 1–3, 10–13.

59 Edwards, "Reorganizations," 592, citing reasons for promoting reorganization including lack of a buyer for the whole enterprise.

60 Jérôme Sgard, "'Do Legal Origins Matter?' The case of bankruptcy laws in Europe 1808–1914" (2006) 10 European Rev of Econ Hist 389, 394.

61 Edwards, "Protection of the Rights of Creditors," 4. See also Edwards, "Reorganizations," 587, 592.

62 Edwards, "Protection of the Rights of Creditors," 3; Edwards, "Reorganizations," 593.

63 Kennedy, *A Critique of Adjudication*; Galanter, "Why the 'Haves' Come Out Ahead," 137.

64 See e.g., "Protective Committees"; Tassé, *Report of the Study Committee*, 88; Honsberger, "Insolvency and the Corporate Veil." In the US and UK context, see Carruthers and Halliday, *Rescuing Business*, 109–10.

65 *Chef Ready*, para 24, cited in *Elan*, para 60 [dissenting in part]. See also Jones, "The Evolution," 492.

66 See e.g., *Chef Ready*, para 22; Algoma Plan Sanctioning Hearing, 1992; Algoma Plan Sanctioning Hearing, 2001; Endorsement Order 2001; *Re Algoma Steel Inc.* (2002), para 8, per LeSage, C.J.S.C.; all cited in Sarra, *Creditor Rights*, 157.

67 *Sklar-Peppler Furniture Corp. v Bank of Nova Scotia* (1991), 8 CBR (3d) 312, 86 DLR (4th) 621 (Ont Ct (Gen Div)), para 3.

68 Edwards, "Protection of the Rights of Creditors," 12, 23.

69 Edwards, "Reorganizations," 593–4; ibid., 32–4, footnotes 88–97, citing e.g., E. Merrick Dodd Jr., "Fair and Equitable Recapitalizations" (1941–1942) 55:5 Harv L Rev 780; Foster, "Conflicting Ideals"; *Case v Los Angeles Lumber Products Co.*, 308 US 106 (1939); 49 Stat 911 (1935), and 11 USC 1946, s 205; 52 Stat 883 (1938) and 11 USC 1946, ss 572, 665, 665(a), 575, 607; 11 USC 1946, ss 606, 672; 11 USC 1946, s 616 (11); 49 Stat 838 (1935) and 11 USC 1946, s 79.

70 Edwards, "Protection of the Rights of Creditors," 33. See also Edwards, "Reorganizations," 593–4, 596–7, 615, where he argues that CCAA law should also adopt the US absolute priority doctrine. This doctrine provides that, in liquidation proceedings, creditors are paid according to their relative priority. Essentially, high ranking creditors are paid first, followed by junior creditors, and shareholders share the proceeds of any remaining assets.

71 Edwards, "Protection of the Rights of Creditors," 33–4; Edwards, "Reorganizations," 593–4.

72 Skeel, *Debt's Dominion*, 107.

73 Edwards, "Protection of the Rights of Creditors," 33; Edwards, "Reorganizations," 593–4.

74 Edwards, "Reorganizations," 589.

75 As described by Edwards, see e.g., *Chef Ready*, paras 22–3, cited in e.g., *Re Keddy Motor Inns Ltd.* (1992), 13 CBR (3d) 245, 90 DLR (4th) 175 (NS SC), para 9, *Quintette Coal Ltd. v Nippon Steel Corp.*, para 9, and *Citibank Canada v Chase Manhattan Bank of Canada* (1991), 5 CBR (3d) 165, 2 PPSAC (2d) 21 (Ont Ct J (Gen Div)), para 49. See also e.g., Sarra, *Creditor Rights*, 11–14; Edwards, "Reorganizations."

76 Sarra, *Rescue!*, 1st ed, 1, cited in *Re Long Potato Growers Ltd.*, 2008 NBQB 231, 80 CBR (5th) 29, para 40; *Re Tepper Holdings Inc.*, 2011 NBQB 211, 80 CBR (5th) 339, para 27.

77 E.g., Edwards does not mention the 1938 or 1946 repeal bills in his LLM thesis and journal article.

78 *CCAA* 1970, s 8.
79 Formerly enshrined in section 7 of the Act, see *CCAA* 1933, s 7; *CCAA* 1952, s 7; *CCAA* 1970, s 8. Now found in *CCAA* 1985, s 8.
80 Edwards, "Protection of the Rights of Creditors"; Edwards, "Reorganizations."
81 See L.W. Houlden and Geoffrey B. Morawetz, *Bankruptcy Law of Canada*, 3rd ed (Toronto: Carswell, 1989), 2–102, 2–103.
82 L.W. Houlden and Geoffrey B. Morawetz, *Houlden and Morawetz Bankruptcy and Insolvency Analysis*, N§58 – Conflict Between the Act and an Instrument (WL) (retrieved 30 September 2019); Lloyd W. Houlden, Geoffrey B. Morawetz and Janis P. Sarra, *The 2015 Annotated Bankruptcy and Insolvency Act* (Toronto: Carswell, 2015), N§58, 1243–4.
83 See e.g., *Chef Ready,* concerning section 178 *Bank Act* security.
84 See e.g., *Citibank,* paras 45–6, stating that "[s]ection 8 of the CCAA provides that relief under the CCAA is available notwithstanding the terms of any agreement."
85 *Chef Ready,* paras 11, 21–2, esp para 24. See also *Elan,* paras 69, 92–3 [dissenting in part].
86 *Chief Ready,* para 21.
87 Ibid., para 24.
88 Benson, *Business Methods,* 1st ed, 164; MacKelcan, "Canadian Bond Issues," 341–348; Billyou, "Corporate Mortgage Bonds," 597.
89 Ibid.
90 W.K. Fraser (DMIA), *1938 Minutes,* 19.
91 Galanter, "Why the 'Haves' Come Out Ahead."
92 See Tassé, *Report of the Study Committee,* 175–6.
93 Bliss, *Northern Enterprise,* 420–2.
94 See discussion in Sarra, *Creditor Rights,* chap. 5 "Algoma Steel Corporation: Recognition of Human Capital Investments."
95 On how (new) legal propositions can gain acceptance, see further Mark Tushnet, "Defending the Indeterminacy Thesis."
96 See e.g., Gross, *Failure and Forgiveness;* Karen Gross, "Taking Community Interests"; Marjorie Girth, "Rethinking Fairness"; Sarra, *Creditor Rights.*
97 See e.g., *Teck; Peoples.*

8 Judicial Sanction of Tactical Devices

1 *Re Norm's Hauling,* para 7, per Wimmer J.
2 *Re Philip's,* para 34 [citations omitted, emphasis added].
3 *Nu-West,* 219, cited in *Quintette Coal Ltd. v Nippon Steel Corp.,* para 19.
4 See e.g., *Re Philip's,* paras 33–4, referencing *Norm's Hauling,* and *Chef Ready.*
5 *CCAA* 1985, s 3.

6 *Re United Maritime Fishermen Co-operative* (1988), 84 NBR (2d) 415, 67 CBR
   (NS) 44 (QB (Trial Div)) [*UMF QB1*], para 15, varied on reconsideration,
   Re United Maritime Fishermen Co-operative (1988), 87 NBR (2d) 333, 68 CBR
   (NS) 170 (QB) [*UMF QB2*], rev'd on appeal *UMF CA*.

7 *UMF QB1*, paras 15, 17–18 [citations omitted, emphasis in original], varied
   on reconsideration *UMF QB2*, rev'd on appeal *UMF CA*.

8 See e.g., *Elan*, para 81 [dissenting in part]; *Re Stephanie's Fashions Ltd.*
   (1990), 1 CBR (3d) 248, 25 ACWS (3d) 1071 (BC SC), para 4; *Re Philip's*, para
   28; *Re Fairview Industries Ltd.* (1991), 109 NSR (2d) 12, 11 CBR (3d) 43 (SC
   (Trial Div)), paras 56–8.

9 See Billyou, "Corporate Mortgage Bonds," 597; Benson, *Business Methods*,
   1st ed, 164; MacKelcan, "Canadian Bond Issues," 341–8.

10 *UMF QB1*, para 35; *UMF CA*, para 16 (but the court did not deal with this
   question on appeal). See further e.g., *Stephanie's Fashions*, paras 4–5; *Elan*,
   paras 23 [majority], 70, 72, 80 [dissenting in part]; *Fairview*, para 58.

11 *UMF QB1*, paras 15, 17–18 [citations omitted], varied on reconsideration
   UMF QB2, rev'd on appeal *UMF CA*.

12 *UMF CA*, paras 13, 21–4 per Hoyt J.A. (Angers J.A. concurring), citing
   Canadian Bed & Breakfast Registry. The third appellate judge in the *Re United
   Maritime Fishermen* case (Ryan J.A.) would not have provided a decision
   on the appeal since the debtor companies were already in bankruptcy,
   rendering the matter moot. See paras 26–33.

13 *UMF CA*, para 13.

14 Driedger, *Construction of Statutes*, 1st ed, 75.

15 Ibid., 87.

16 *Elan*, para 11 [majority].

17 Ibid., paras 12–13 [majority].

18 Ibid., para 14 [majority].

19 See Galanter, "Why the 'Haves' Come Out Ahead," 137

20 *Elan*, paras 22 [majority] (not citing any authorities), 56–61 [dissenting in
   part], where Doherty J.A. cited: *Re Avery Construction Co.*; *Chef Ready*, 88,
   91; Edwards "Reorganizations," 592–3; Goldman, "Reorganizations," 37–9,
   citing *inter alia Re Avery Construction Co.*, *CCAA Reference*, para 3, and Hon.
   C.H. Cahan (Conservative), *Debates of the House of Commons of Canada*, (20
   April 1933) 4th Sess, 17th Parl (Ottawa: King's Printer, 1933), 4090–1.

21 *Elan*, para 81 [dissenting in part], citing *Reference re Residential Tenancies Act
   (Ontario)*, [1981] 1 SCR 714, 123 DLR (3d) 554, per Doherty J.A.

22 *UMF QB1*, para 17.

23 Halliday and Carruthers, "The Recursivity of Law," 1144, citing
   Grattet and Jenness, "The Birth and Maturation"; Grattet and Jenness,
   "Examining the Boundaries of Hate Crime Law"; Grattet, "Structural
   Contradictions."

24 See e.g., Brian O'Leary, "A Review of the *Companies' Creditors Arrangement Act*" (1987) 4:3 Nat Insolv Rev 38, 39; C. Keith Ham, "'Instant' Trust Deeds Under the C.C.A.A." (1988) 2 Comm Insolv Rep 25; Geoffrey B. Morawetz, "Emerging Trends in the Use of the *Companies' Creditors Arrangement Act*" Proceedings of the First Annual General Meeting and Conference of the Insolvency Institute of Canada (1990) [unpublished], all cited in *Elan*, para 72 [dissenting in part]. See further, Frank J.C. Newbould, Q.C. and Geoffrey B. Morawetz, "Developments and Trends in *Companies' Creditors Arrangement Act* Restructuring" Paper in Proceedings of 1991 Insight Educational Services Conference: "How and When to Use the *Companies' Creditors Arrangement Act (CCAA)*" (4 June 1991) [unpublished], cited in *Fairview*, paras 58, 56.

25 *Elan*, para 93 [dissenting in part].

26 *Norm's Hauling*, para 4.

27 Ibid., para 7.

28 Ibid., para 4.

29 Ibid., para 5; *Elan,* paras 10, 13 [Majority]; *UMF CA*, para 6.

30 *Elan*, para 82 [dissenting in part].

31 At that time, found in: *CCAA* 1985, s 12(3). Formerly enshrined in *CCAA* 1933, s 11(2). Now enshrined in *CCAA* 1985, s 20(2).

32 *CCAA* 1985, s 3.

33 *Elan*, paras 2, 19, 28 [majority].

34 Ibid., para 98 [dissenting in part].

35 Ibid., paras 11, 13 [majority], 71 [dissenting in part].

36 But see ibid., paras 53–4, 97–8 [dissenting in part].

37 Now enshrined in *CCAA* 1985, s 5 "compromises with secured creditors."

38 *Elan*, paras 75, 82 [dissenting in part], citing *UMF QB1*, paras 55–6, varied on reconsideration *UMF QB2*.

39 *Re Stelco* 2004; leave to appeal to Ontario Court of Appeal refused, 2004 CarswellOnt 2936, [2004] OJ No 1903 (CA); leave to appeal to SCC refused [2004] SCCA No. 336, 338 NR 196 (note). See also Vern W. DaRe, "Is Insolvency Still a Prerequisite to Restructuring?" (2004) 49 CBR (4th) 163.

40 See Mario Forte, "*Re Metcalfe*: A Matter of Fraud, Fairness and Reasonableness: The Restructuring of the Third-Party Asset-Backed Commercial Paper Market in Canada" (2008) 17:3 Int Insolv Rev 211, 214–15.

41 See *Re Montréal, Maine & Atlantique Canada Co.*, 2013 QCCS 4039, EYB 2013-225915, paras 1–26, per Martin Castonguay, J.C.S.

42 Note that parliament subsequently removed the restriction that prevented railway companies from filing under the CCAA: *CCAA* 1985, s 2(1) "company" as am *Transportation Modernization Act*, SC 2018, c 10, s 89. See further Ben-Ishai and Telfer, eds, *Bankruptcy and Insolvency Law in Canada*, 519–20.

43 *Elan.*
44 Forte, *"Re Metcalfe."*
45 *Montréal, Maine & Atlantique.*
46 *Re Stelco* 2004.
47 Ronald Dworkin, *Justice in Robes* (Cambridge, Mass.: Harvard University Press, 2006), 91.
48 Dworkin, *Justice in Robes*, 91, see also chap. 1 "Pragmatism and Law."
49 Dworkin, *Justice in Robes*, 91.
50 For an overview see e.g., Peter Farkas, "Defining (and Refining) the Role of the Monitor" (2010) 72 CBR 159; David Mann and Neil Narfason, "The Changing Role of the Monitor" IIC-ART 2008–8 (Westlaw).
51 Andrew J.F. Kent et al., "Canadian Business Restructuring Law: When Should a Court Say 'No'?" IIC-ART 2008–4 (Westlaw), 6.
52 Mann and Narfason, "The Changing Role of the Monitor," 1–2. The term "monitor" was first used in *Re Northland Properties Ltd.* (1988), 29 BCLR (2d) 257, 69 CBR (NS) 266 (SC). See further *Re Northland Properties Ltd.* (1988), 73 CBR (NS) 175, 1988 CarswellBC 558 (SC) aff'd (1989) 34 BCLR (2d) 122, 73 CBR (NS) 195 (CA).
53 Kent et al., "When Should a Court Say 'No'?," 6, citing e.g., ibid., *United Co-Operatives of Ontario*, (August 1984), unreported. On the role of the monitor as an officer of the court see further *Re Bell Canada International Inc.* (2003), 126 ACWS (3d) 790, 2003 CarswellOnt 4537 (Ont SCJ (Comm List)), paras 7–9; *Re Ivaco Inc.* (2006), 83 OR (3d) 108, 25 CBR (5th) 176 (CA), para 55; *Re Pine Valley Mining Corp.*, 2008 BCSC 446, 41 CBR (5th) 49, paras 10–12; *Re Winalta Inc.*, 2011 ABQB 399, 84 CBR (5th) 157, paras 67–8.
    In some jurisdictions CCAA monitors were also appointed as interim receivers under *BIA* 1985, s 47 [as am SC 1992, c 27, s 16]. See e.g., *Re Royal Oak Mines Inc.* (1999), 11 CBR (4th) 122, 1999 CarswellOnt1068 (Ont CJ, Gen Div (Comm List)), appointing the CCAA monitor as interim receiver under *BIA* 1985, s 47 [as am SC 1992, c 27, s 16]. Following amendments to the BIA in the 2000s this practice no longer occurs, see *BIA* 1985, s 47 [as am SC 2005, c 47, s 30; SC 2007, c 36, s 14]. See discussion in Wood, "The Regulation of Receiverships."
54 Kent et al., "When Should a Court Say 'No'?," 6 citing *Re Starcom International Optics Corp.* (1998), 3 CBR (4th) 177, 78 ACWS (3d) 11 (BC SC); *Fairview; Canadian Asbestos Services Ltd. v Bank of Montreal* (1992), 11 OR (3d) 353, 16 CBR (3d) 114 (Ont Ct, Gen Div), add'l reasons at (1993) 13 OR (3d) 291, 10 CLR (2d) 204 (Ont Ct, Gen Div).
55 Mann and Narfason, "The Changing Role of the Monitor," 4.
56 *CCAA* 1985, s 11.7 [as am SC 1997, c 12, s 124]; See discussion in Farkas, "Defining (and Refining) the Role of the Monitor," 1–3; Mann and Narfason, "The Changing Role of the Monitor," 5–7.

57 Mann and Narfason, "The Changing Role of the Monitor," 11. See also
    Farkas, "Defining (and Refining) the Role of the Monitor," 1–3.

58 *CCAA* 1985, s 11.7(3) [as am SC 1997, c 12, s 124], which set out various
    duties and reporting obligations. These responsibilities are now found in
    CCAA 1985, s 23 [as am SC 2005, c 47, s 131; SC 2007, c 36, s 72]. Further
    duties may be assigned to the monitor upon appointment; see e.g.,
    "Initial Order CCAA," (last visited 5 October 2019) online: *Ontario Courts*
    <ontariocourts.ca/scj/files/forms/com/intitial-order-CCAA-EN.doc>
    [perma.cc/G84R-HNW8], 9–12. See also Denis Ferlan, "The Evolving
    Role of the Monitor, Confidential Information and the Monitor's Cross-
    examination, a Québec Perspective" 2011 ANNREVINSOLV 17 (Westlaw).
         The Nortel Networks insolvency is a case in which the court granted
    the monitor expanded powers compared to the typical CCAA case. See *Re
    Nortel Networks Corp.*, 2017 ONSC 673, 44 CBR (6th) 289.

59 Mann and Narfason, "The Changing Role of the Monitor," 9–11; Ferlan,
    "The Evolving Role of the Monitor" Schedule A, 5–18.

60 Kent et al., "When Should a Court Say 'No'?," 6.

61 David P. Bowra, "The Role of the Monitor under the *Companies' Creditors
    Arrangement Act*" IIC-ART 2002-7 (Westlaw), 4. See further Andrew Kent
    and Wael Rostrom, "The Auditor as Monitor in CCAA Proceedings: What
    Is the Debate?" 2003 ANNREVINSOL 7 (Westlaw).

62 The 1997 amendments to the CCAA expressly provided that the debtor's
    auditor could be appointed monitor except as otherwise directed by the
    court. See *CCAA* 1985, s 11.7(2) [as am SC 1997, c 12, s 124].

63 See e.g., *Stokes Building Supplies Ltd.* (1991), 9 CBR (3d) 1, 60 BCLR (2d) 311
    (SC), cited in Mann and Narfason, "The Changing Role of the Monitor," 6.
    Note that the *Stokes* case was decided prior to the 1997 amendments. On a
    monitor's potential conflicts of interest see *Winalta Inc.*

64 For a case in which a monitor was replaced due, at least in part, to the
    appearance of a lack of impartiality, see *Re Nelson Education Ltd.*, 2016
    ONSC 3580, 26 CBR (6th) 161, paras 37–9.

65 SC 2005, c 47, s 129.

66 OSB oversight is provided for by *CCAA* 1985, ss 27–32 [as am SC 2005, c
    46, s 131; SC 2007, c 36, ss 74, 75]. On the 1930s and 1940s concerns about
    trustees see "Protective Committees," 185; Benson, *Business Methods*,
    1st ed, 170. See also recommendations made in Tassé, *Report of the Study
    Committee*, 35.

67 Tassé, *Report of the Study Committee*, 19–22.

68 As of September 29, 2019, this study located only one reported bankruptcy
    or insolvency case which mentions the *Tassé Report*: *Sam Lévy & Associés
    Inc. c Mayrand*, 2005 FC 702, [2006] 2 FCR 543, para 60. This research was
    done using both Westlaw and Quicklaw/LexisAdvance.

69 H.M. Goodman, Q.C., "Practice Note on the *Companies' Creditors Arrangement Act, 1933*" (1952), 32 CBR 227.

70 Cases citing Edwards's 1947 article include e.g., *Chef Ready*, 88, 91 [51 BCLR]; *Re Northland Properties Ltd.* (1988), 73 CBR (NS) 175, paras 47–8, aff'd 73 CBR (NS) 195 (CA), para 22; *Norcen*, paras 30, 40–5; *Elan*, paras 56, 60 [dissenting in part]; *Re NsC Diesel Power Inc.* (1990), 79 CBR (NS) 1, 21 ACWS (3) 55 (NS SC, Trial Div), para 7. Cases citing CCAA cases from the 1930s and 1940s include e.g., *Chef Ready*, para 25; *Re Northland Properties Ltd.*, 73 CBR (NS) 175, paras 13–14, 49–54; *Fairview*, para 34; *Elan*, paras 34, 37 [majority], 56 [dissenting in part]; *Sklar-Peppler*, para 13.

71 A number of cases and press reports referred to the act as "little used" or "obscure." See e.g., *Nu-West*, para 20, cited in e.g., *Re Northland Properties Ltd.* (1988), 69 CBR (NS) 266, para 24; *Re Northland Properties Ltd.* (1988), 73 CBR (NS) 141, para 15; *Quintette Coal Ltd. v Nippon Steel Corp.*, para 19; *Canadian Imperial Bank of Commerce v Quintette Coal Ltd.* (1991), 1 CBR (3d) 253, 53 BCLR (2d) 34 (SC), para 17. See also e.g., *NsC Diesel*, para 3.

See further "Dome Pete Finds Obscure Law"; Fletcher, "Little Known Law"; Ramsay, "Troubled Firms Seek Protection; Yakabuski, "Obscure Canadian Law."

72 See further Richard H. McLaren, *Canadian Commercial Reorganization*, loose leaf, vol. 1 (Aurora: Canada Law Book, 1994), 1–20, cited in Kent et al., "When Should a Court Say 'No'?," 3–4, noting that the CCAA was originally intended to only apply to restructurings of secured debt where a receiver or trustee was present to oversee the debtor.

73 Edwards, "Reorganizations," 589.

74 Goodman, "Practice Note," 227.

75 Edwards, "Reorganizations," 602.

76 Roderick J. Wood, *Bankruptcy and Insolvency Law* (Toronto: Irwin law, 2009), 330, citing *CCAA* 1985, ss 11, 11.02(1) (as am SC 2005, c 47; SC 2007, c 36) [formerly enshrined in s 11]; *Re Hester Creek Estate Winery Ltd.*, 2004 BCSC 345, 50 CBR (4th) 73. Initial orders granting a stay of one month were partly due to the lack or notice, or very short notice (e.g., only a few hours), given to creditors before a debtor's CCAA application, as in cases such as Olympia and York and Eaton's. See e.g., Rod McQueen, "Raising the Dead: Companies like Eaton's Owe Their Lives to a Thin Piece of Legislation and the Elite Group of Insolvency Lawyers Who Manipulate It" (6 September 1997) *Financial Post*, section 1, page 8.

77 Wood, *Bankruptcy and Insolvency Law*, 330.

78 Goodman, "Practice Note," 227. See also Paul Joseph James Martin (Liberal), *1938 Minutes*, 3–4.

79 Driedger, *Construction of Statutes*, 1st ed, 75, referring to judicial approaches to statutory construction around the time of *Heydon's Case*, [1584] 76 ER 637 3 CO REP 7a.

80 Driedger, *Construction of Statutes*, 1st ed, 87.
81 See generally, Kent et al., "When Should a Court Say 'No'?"
82 See e.g., Sarra, *Creditor Rights*; Anthony J. Duggan et al., *Canadian Bankruptcy and Insolvency Law: Cases, Text, and Materials*, 2nd ed (Toronto: Emond Montgomery, 2009), 574. But see also Jones, "The Evolution," 481–2; Kent et al., "When Should a Court Say 'No'?"
83 The argument based on this distinction was championed particularly, but not exclusively, by Justice James Farley of the Ontario Superior Court. See e.g. *Re Westar*; *Re Lehndorff General Partner Ltd.*, 40 [17 CBR (3d)]; *Re Woodward's Ltd.* (1993), 79 BCLR (2d) 257, 17 CBR (3d) 236, 247 (SC); *Re Dylex Ltd.* (1995), 31 CBR (3d) 106, 54 ACWS (3d) 504 (Ont Ct J, Gen Div (Comm List)); *Re T. Eaton Co.* (1997), 46 CBR (3d) 293, [1997] OJ No 6411 (Ont Ct J, Gen Div); *Re Canadian Airlines Corp.* (2000), 19 CBR (4th) 1, [2000] CarswellAlta 622 (Alta QB); *Re Royal Oak Mines* (1999), 7 CBR (4th) 293, [1999] OJ No 864 (Ont Ct J, Gen Div (Comm List)); *Re Air Canada* (2003), 28 CBR (5th) 52, 2003 CarswellOnt 9109 (Ont SCJ (Comm List)), paras 16–17; *Re Stelco Inc.* (2005), 7 CBR (5th) 307, 137 ACWS (3d) 475 (Ont SCJ) (Comm List)), para 24 and (2005) 7 CBR (5th) 310, 137 ACWS (3d) 476, para 24 (rev'd in (2005) 75 OR (3d) 5, 253 DLR (4th) 109 (CA)).
    See also discussion in James P. Dube, "The Stelco Directors Case: Containment of Inherent Jurisdiction in CCAA Proceedings" (2005) 21:1 BFLR 115; Jones, "The Evolution," 481 [in print].
84 *Peacock v Bell and Kendall* (1677), 1 Wms Saund 73, 74, 85 ER 84: "…And the rule for jurisdiction is, that nothing shall be intended to be out of the jurisdiction of a Superior Court, but that which specifically appears to be so; and, on the contrary, nothing shall be intended to be within the jurisdiction of an Inferior Court but that which is so expressly alleged." See further, *Mayor of London v Cox* (1867), 1 E & I App 239, 259 "nothing shall be intended to be out of the jurisdiction of a superior Court, but that which specifically appears to be so," cited in *Board v Board*, [1919] AC 956, 48 DLR 13, 17–18 (JCPC) and *80 Wellesley St. East Ltd. v Fundy Builders Ltd. et al.*, [1972] 2 OR 280, 25 DLR (3d) 386 (CA).
85 See e.g. *Williams and Rees v Local Union No. 1562 of United Mine Workers of America*, [1919] 1 WWR 217, 45 DLR 150, 178 (Alta SC (Trial – App Div)): "That every superior court is the master of its own practice in a proposition laid down by Tindal, C.J. in *Scales v Cheese* (1844), 12 M & W 685, 152 ER 1374, and adopting this, I think that, without any statutory rules of practice, the court can, should a case arise, even though the law be fixed as to the substantial rights of the parties, award such remedies, though they be new, as may appear to be necessary to work out justice between the parties."
    See Halsbury's Laws of Canada (online), *Civil Procedure*, "Courts" (I.4.(5)(a)) at HCV-14 "Presumption of Jurisdiction" (2017 Reissue); Halsbury's

Laws of Canada (online), *Civil Procedure*, "Courts" (I.4.(5)(b)(ii)) at HCV-16 "Inherent Jurisdiction" (2017 Reissue). As commentators such as James P. Dube have noted, although the use of inherent jurisdiction is meant to be procedurally focused, some courts have deployed their inherent jurisdiction to develop substantive law. Thus, even taking for granted that it is proper for the court to rely on inherent jurisdiction in some CCAA matters, their exercise of this jurisdiction is open to criticism on its own terms: Dube, "The Stelco Directors," 118, discussing the use of inherent jurisdiction in Westar to create a superpriority for debtor in possession financing. See *Re Westar*, 14 [70 BCLR (2d)].

86 See e.g. Halsbury's, "Presumption of Jurisdiction"; Halsbury's, "Inherent Jurisdiction"; *Dominion Canners Ltd. v Constanza*, [1923] SCR 46, 61, [1922] SCJ 46; *80 Wellesley St.*; *Re Michie Estate and City of Toronto et al.*, [1968] 1 OR 266, 268–9, 66 DLR (2d) 213 (HCJ).

87 On statutory wording limiting inherent jurisdiction, see e.g. *Re Michie Estate*, 268–9 stating in part: "It appears clear that the Supreme Court of Ontario has broad universal jurisdiction over all matters of substantive law unless the Legislature divests from this universal jurisdiction by legislation in unequivocal terms."

With respect to a grant of jurisdiction to another adjudicative body, the creation of the Federal Court of Canada is a case in point. The Federal Court is a statutory court, which has no jurisdiction except that assigned to it by statute. See e.g. *Ordon Estate v Grail*, [1998] 3 SCR 437, 40 OR (3d) 639, paras 45, 46: (para 45) "Parliament may, within constitutional limits, derogate from the jurisdiction of the provincial courts by conferring jurisdiction upon federal courts constituted by statute pursuant to s. 101 of the *Constitution Act, 1867*." (para 46) "… the complete ouster of jurisdiction from the provincial superior courts in favour of vesting exclusive jurisdiction in a statutory court (rather than simply concurrent jurisdiction with the superior courts) requires clear and explicit statutory wording to this effect." See further *Canada (AG) v TeleZone Inc.*, 2010 SCC 62, [2010] 3 SCR 585; *Douez v Faccebook, Inc.*, 2017 SCC 33, [2017] 1 SCR 751, para 37; *TCR Holding Corp. v Ontario*, 2010 ONCA 233, 69 BLR (4th) 175, para 26; *Kelly v Human Rights Commission (P.E.I.)*, 2008 PESCAD 9, 276 Nfld & PEIR 336, para 8.

88 *Montreal Trust Co. v Churchill Forest Industries (Man.) Ltd.*, [1971] 4 WWR 542, 21 DLR (3d) 75 (MB CA), para 18.

89 *Baxter Student Housing Ltd. v College Housing Co-operative Limited*, [1976] 2 SCR 475, 20 CBR (NS) 240, para 6.

90 *Churchill Forest*, para 18.

91 A number of cases support this view, as discussed by Dube, "The Stelco Directors," 122–3: *Sulphur Corp. of Canada Ltd.*, 2002 ABQB 682, 35 CBR

(4th) 204; *Syndicat national de l'amiante d'Asbestos inc c Mine Jeffrey inc.* (2003), 40 CBR (4th) 95, 35 CCPB 71 (Que CA); *Re Skeena Cellulose Inc.*, 2003 BCCA 344, 43 CBR (4th) 187, per Newbury J.: "The court's use of the term 'inherent jurisdiction' is certainly understandable in connection with a statute that confers broad jurisdiction with few specific limitations. But if one examines the strict meaning of 'inherent jurisdiction', it appears that in many of the cases discussed above, the courts have been exercising their discretion given by the CCAA rather than their inherent jurisdiction ... This is ... discretion given by section 11 ..."; *Re Stelco* (2005), 75 OR (3d) 5, 253 DLR (4th) 109 (CA), paras 32–3, 36, 38, (para 33): "In my opinion ... the better view is that in carrying out his or her supervisory functions under the legislation, the judge is not exercising inherent jurisdiction but rather the statutory discretion provided by s. 11 of the CCAA ..."; *Re Richtree Inc.* (2005), 7 CBR (5th) 294, 10 BLR (4th) 334, para 8 (Ont SCJ, Gen Div (Comm List)).

92 The Ontario Court of Appeal in *Re Stelco* acknowledged the broader implication of this analysis but refused to rule on the issue in general terms: *Re Stelco* (2005), 75 OR (3d) 5, 253 DLR (4th) 109 (CA), para 33: "It is not necessary, for purposes of this appeal, to determine whether inherent jurisdiction is excluded for all supervisory purposes under the CCAA, by reason of the existence of the statutory discretionary regime provided in that Act."

93 A similar argument is made in Jackson and Sarra, "Selecting the Judicial Tool": "Only after exhausting this statutory interpretive function should the court consider whether it is appropriate to assert an inherent jurisdiction. Hence inherent jurisdiction continues to be a valuable tool, but not one that is necessary to utilize in most circumstances."

94 See discussion in *Skeena Cellulose Inc.*, para 45: *Re Westar*, paras 8, 13; *Re Dylex*, para 8; *Re Royal Oak Mines* (1999), 7 CBR (4th) 293, para 4. See further Isaac H. Jacob, Q.C., "The Inherent Jurisdiction of the Court" (1970) 23 Curr Leg Prob 23, 51.

95 The courts' strict, literal interpretation of the trust deed provision is a case in point. Judges effectively "interpreted away" this restriction, such that it did not serve as a restriction at all, based on their view that it was important to ensure wide access to the statute. Although the courts did not necessarily place express reliance on inherent jurisdiction or judicial discretion in so doing, judicial action to effectively eliminate the trust deed provision is open to criticism in either case. See *e.g. Re Philip's*, paras 21–37.

96 The author recognizes that absence of evidence is not the same as evidence of absence. She welcomes input from any reader who is aware of such an instance where this occurred.

97 See Elmer A. Driedger, *The Construction of Statutes*, 2nd ed (Toronto: Butterworths, 1983), 74: "The reader begins with the words of the Act as a whole …"
98 *Re Norm's Hauling.*
99 SC 1997 c 12, s 121, now enumerated in s 3(1) of the present version of the act. The new $5 million debt requirement was intended to limit the scope of the act to large companies. This may have been based on the misapprehended purpose of the trust deed requirement.
100 Jones, "The Evolution," 492.
101 Note that debtors tended to ask the court to appoint their own accounting firm. See generally, Wood, *Bankruptcy and Insolvency Law*, 388–94, esp 392–3.
102 This voting provision was amended by SC 1997 c 12, s 123.
103 Convenience classes are usually made up of small claims that are paid out in full prior to voting on a plan of arrangement. In the third-party ACBP restructuring, small noteholders received compensation up to a $1 million limit, if they voted in favour of the plan of arrangement. These noteholders were thus not a convenience class in a strict sense. See Torrie, "Analyzing the Canadian Third-Party."
104 "Cram down" refers to the ability of a judge to enforce a restructuring plan over the objections of certain classes of creditors, usually secured creditors. See 11 USC, s 1129(b).

9 Formalizing a Debtor-in-Possession Restructuring Narrative

1 *Century Services*, paras 15, 18, per Deschamps J., McLachlin C.J. and Binnie, LeBel, Charron, Rothstein and Cromwell JJ concurring, citing Edwards, "Reorganizations," 593.
2 See Halliday and Carruthers, "The Recursivity of Law," 1143. See also Kennedy, *A Critique of Adjudication*, esp chap. 2 "The Distinction between Adjudication and Legislation."
3 Halliday and Carruthers, "The Recursivity of Law," 1144–5.
4 See e.g., Sarra, *Creditor Rights*, 168–9.
5 See e.g., *Wage Earner Protection Program Act* 2005 [as am SC 2018, c 27, ss 626–53]. But see e.g., David E. Baird and Ronald B. Davis, "Labour Issues" in Ben-Ishai and Duggan, eds, *Canadian Bankruptcy and Insolvency Law*, 73–6. See further Sokal, "Recent Developments," 270–3.
6 See e.g., Simon Djankov et al., "Debt Enforcement around the World" (2008) 116:6 J of Polit Econ 1105.
7 See Girard, *Bora Laskin*, "Part V: The Supreme Court of Canada."
8 *Constitution Act, 1982*; Baar, "Judicial Activism," 53 cited in Lijphart, *Patterns of Democracy*, 216.
9 See e.g., Girard, *Bora Laskin*; on the development of legal education, see more generally, C. Ian Kyer and Jerome E. Bickenbach, *The Fiercest Debate:*

Cecil A Wright, the Benchers, and Legal Education in Ontario 1923–1957 (Toronto: University of Toronto Press for the Osgoode Society, 1987).

10 See *Gaskell v Gosling*, 691–2 [1 QB 669], per Rigby L.J.

Although court appointed receivers are now more commonly used than private receivers in Canada, they were rarely used up until the 1990s; see Wood, "The Regulation of Receiverships," citing Frank Bennett, *Bennett on Receiverships*, 2nd ed (Toronto: Carswell, 1999); Ziegel, "The Privately Appointed Receiver," 453, footnote 7.

11 Wood, "The Regulation of Receiverships," 315–16.

12 The political concept of "soft power" was first set out in Joseph Nye, *Bound to Lead: The Changing Nature of American Power* (New York: Basic Books, 1990), and then elaborated on in Joseph Nye, *Soft Power: The Means to Success in World Politics* (New York: Public Affairs, 2004). "Soft power" refers to the ability to attract and persuade, rather than to coerce.

13 On judicial interpretation, see generally Kennedy, *A Critique of Adjudication*. In the Canadian context (up to the early 1970s), see further Weiler, *In the Last Resort*, esp chapter 1, "The Supreme Court of Canada: Its Structure and Capacities," and chapter 2, "Legal Reasoning in our Highest Court."

14 Halliday and Carruthers, "The Recursivity of Law," 1144, citing Grattet and Jenness, "The Birth and Maturation"; Grattet and Jenness, "Examining the Boundaries of Hate Crime Law"; Grattet, "Structural Contradictions" in Chambliss and Zatz, *Making Law*.

15 The influence of academics on the Canadian bench is a fairly recent phenomenon, which was facilitated in large part by changes that occurred during the 1970s and 1980s in the SCC under Chief Justice Bora Laskin. See Girard, *Bora Laskin*. See also Weiler, *In the Last Resort*, postscript dated January 1974.

16 Halliday and Carruthers, "The Recursivity of Law," 1142.

17 Contrast with opportunities to effect formal bankruptcy reform, which occur rather infrequently, see Ziegel, "Canada's Dysfunctional Insolvency Reform Process"; Stephanie Ben-Ishai, Saul Schwartz and Thomas G.W. Telfer, "A Retrospective on the Canadian Consumer Bankruptcy System: 40 Years after the *Tassé Report*" (2011) 50:1 CBLJ 236.

18 See e.g., Kennedy, *A Critique of Adjudication*, 114.

19 Contrast with "deep" equilibria, see Pierson, *Politics in Time*, 157–8, citing H. Peyton Young, *Individual Strategy and Social Structure: An Evolutionary Theory of Institutions* (Princeton: Princeton University Press, 1998).

20 See e.g., *Houlden and Morawetz' Bankruptcy and Insolvency Analysis*, N§65 – Scope of Order under Initial Application (accessed 30 September 2019); Frank Bennett, *Bennett on Bankruptcy*, 10th ed (Toronto: CCH Canada Limited, 2008), 1151.

21 *CCAA* 1985, s 11.7.

22 Stinchcombe, *Constructing Social Theories* cited in Pierson, *Politics in Time*, 46 [emphasis in original].
23 Ziegel, "Canada's Dysfunctional Insolvency Reform"; Jacob S. Ziegel, chap. 12 "The BIA and CCAA Interface," in Ben-Ishai and Duggan, eds, *Canadian Bankruptcy and Insolvency Law*, 316–18.
24 Ziegel, "Canada's Dysfunctional Insolvency Reform"; Jacob S. Ziegel, chap. 12 "The BIA and CCAA Interface," in Ben-Ishai and Duggan, eds, *Canadian Bankruptcy and Insolvency Law*, 316–18.
25 See e.g., discussion in Fred Myers and Alexa Abiscott, "Asset Backed Commercial Paper: Why the Courts Got It Right" (2009) 25:1 BFLR 5, 19, footnote 49, citing *inter alia ATB Financial* 2008 (CA), leave to appeal refused [2008] SCCA No 337, 257 PAC 400 (note), para 62.
26 Edelman, "Legal Ambiguity."
27 The practice of making initial orders under the CCAA was inspired by the American practice of filing "first–day" motions in tandem with a Chapter 11 application. On the US practice see Lubben, *American Business Bankruptcy*, 101–2.

   The substance of initial CCAA orders was inspired by US bankruptcy law as well. The request for a general stay of proceedings in CCAA orders is a case in point. This request essentially caused the *practice* of Canadian corporate restructuring law to resemble the automatic stay of US Chapter 11. On the automatic stay of proceedings in the US, see Lubben, *American Business Bankruptcy*, 40–2.
28 *CCAA* 1985, s 10 [now in force].
29 Ibid., s 11.
30 See Jones, "The Evolution," esp 490–7.
31 Mann and Narfason, "The Changing Role of the Monitor."
32 See e.g., Frank Bennett, *Bennett on Bankruptcy*, 14th ed (Toronto: CCH Canada Limited, 2012), 1661 "Amended Explanatory Notes for Long Form CCAA Order dated November 18, 2008 and Short Form CCAA Order dated September 12, 2006."
33 See *CCAA* 1985, s 10(2), as am SC 2005, c 47, s 127.
34 See *CCAA* 1985, s 11.7(1) [now in force]; Stephanie Ben-Ishai, *Bankruptcy Reforms 2008* (Toronto: Thomson Carswell, 2008), 61–66, and e.g., 41–42 noting the codification of the CCAA stay of proceedings, now enshrined in *CCAA* 1985, s 11.02.
35 *Century Services*, paras 15, 18, per Deschamps J., McLachlin C.J. and Binnie, LeBel, Charron, Rothstein and Cromwell JJ. concurring, citing Edwards, "Reorganizations," 593.

10 Conclusion

1 Kent et al., "When Should a Court Say 'No'?"
2 See e.g., Fraser, "Reorganization of Companies," 943; Sallée and Tournier, "Reorganization: A Commercial Concept Juridicially Defined."
3 See e.g., *Montréal, Maine & Atlantique*, paras 1–26, per Castonguay, J.C.S.
4 See e.g., *Newfoundland and Labrador v AbitibiBowater Inc.*, 2012 SCC 67, [2012] 3 SCR 443; *Environmental Protection Act*, SNL 2002, c E-14.2.
    See further *Orphan Well Association v Grant Thornton Ltd.*, 2019 SCC 15, 81 Alta LR (6th) 1; *Environmental Protection and Enhancement Act*, RSA 2000, c E-12.
5 Newfoundland joined Canadian Confederation in 1949. Bliss, *Northern Enterprise*, 464–5.
6 See e.g., discussion in Kent et al., "When Should a Court Say 'No'?"
7 Fraser, "Reorganization of Companies."
8 See e.g., W.A. Scott and P.J. Henderson, "Restructuring Canada's ABCP: A Unique, Successful, Private Restructuring" (2009) 28:4 Int'l Fin L Rev [no pagination in original]; Myers and Abiscott, "Asset Backed Commercial Paper," 5, 13, 28–9; *ATB Financial* 2008, (SCJ), aff'd *ATB Financial* 2008 (CA), paras 19 30, 59, 98, 138–9, 145.
9 E.g., *Farmers' Creditors Arrangement* Act, RSC 1952, c 111.
10 Kent et al., "When Should a Court Say 'No'?"
11 See e.g., Galanter, "Why the 'Haves' Come Out Ahead."
12 Stinchcombe, *Constructing Social Theories*, cited in Pierson, *Politics in Time*, 46.
13 See e.g., *Re Westar Mining Ltd.*, para 23, per Macdonald J., cited *inter alia* in *Re Stelco* 2005 (CA), para 32.
14 Kent et al., "When Should a Court Say 'No'?"
15 See e.g., *Norcen*, paras 60–1, citing *Nu-West*. See also Houlden and Morawetz, *Bankruptcy Law of Canada*, 3rd ed, 2–102, 2–103, "The legislation [CCAA] is intended to have wide scope ..." and referencing section 11 of the act, cited in *Elan*, para 102 [dissenting in part].
16 See remarks of Mr. Vic Althouse (NDP), *Debates of the House of Commons of Canada* (20 June 1986) 1st Sess, 33rd Parl (Ottawa: Queen's Printer, 1987), 14793–4. See also Tassé, *Report of the Study Committee.*
17 Jacob S. Ziegel, "Modernization of Canada's Bankruptcy Law in Comparative Context" (1998) 33:1 Tex Int'l LJ 1, 6–7. See also Ben-Ishai, Schwartz and Telfer, "A Retrospective."
18 SC 2005, c 47, s 122, adding Part XIV to *BIA* 1985. See also discussion in Ziegel, "Canada's Dysfunctional Insolvency Reform"; Ben-Ishai and Duggan, *Canadian Bankruptcy and Insolvency Law*. See *BIA* 1985, s 285; *CCAA* 1985, s 63.

19 Ziegel and Baird, eds, *Case Studies*, 6–7.

20 Lijphart, *Patterns of Democracy*, 216, citing Baar, "Judicial Activism," 53.

21 Floodgates arguments tend not to hold sway in CCAA matters. See e.g., *Re Calpine Canada Energy Ltd.*, 2007 ABQB 504, 415 AR 196, para 76, aff'd 2007 ABCA 266, 417 AR 25, para 31. See also *Re Philip's*, para 41.

22 Pierson, *Politics in Time*, 157–8, citing Young, *Individual Strategy and Social Structure*.

23 See Dworkin, *Justice in Robes*, chap. 1 "Pragmatism and Law."

24 Dworkin, *Justice in Robes*, 38, 91.

25 Such factors might include growing dissatisfaction with the costliness of CCAAs (including private fees and costs borne by the public for providing the courts); a sense that most contemporary CCAAs are run-of-the-mill insolvencies which could be administered more summarily; and the recent trend away from CCAA filings in favour of arrangements under *CBCA* 1985, s 192, which are perceived to be more flexible. See e.g., Sean Zweig and Preet K. Bell, "The Expanded Use of the CBCA in Debt Restructurings" 2019 ANNREVINSOLV 27 (Westlaw).

26 See e.g., Ziegel, "The Modernization," 7; Timothy C.G. Fisher and Jocelyn Martel, "Should We Abolish Chapter 11? Evidence from Canada" (1999) 28:1 J Leg Stud 233; Stephanie Ben-Ishai and Stephen Lubben, "Sales or Plans: A Comparative Account of the 'New' Corporate Reorganization" (2010) 56:3 McGill LJ 591, comparing approaches under Chapter 11 and the CCAA. See also discussion in chapter 4.

27 See e.g., *Re Philip's*, para 34, stating in part, "If that is judicial legislation, so be it." See also discussion in chapter 4.

   The term "reorganization" lacks a technical statutory definition. See Sallée and Tournier, "Reorganization: A Commercial Concept Juridicially Defined."

28 Pierson, *Politics in Time*, 143.

29 Tassé, *Report of the Study Committee*, 81, 175.

30 "Probably" because there are some cases which appear to indicate that judges may still be pushing out the boundaries of *CCAA* law, without reference to the new provisions of the act. See e.g., Nocilla, "Asset Sales."

31 See e.g., the following Quebec Superior Court order which holds that a corporation operating a railway is not a "railway company" under the CCAA, and hence is not prohibited from restructuring under the act: *Montréal, Maine & Atlantique*, paras 1–26, per Castonguay, J.C.S. As noted above, parliament subsequently removed the prohibition against railway companies filing under the CCAA: *CCAA* 1985, s 2(1) "company" as am SC 2018, c 10, s 89.

   See also Nocilla, "Is 'Corporate Rescue' Working."

32 One reason for the rise in liquidating CCAAs may have to do with US law or the preferences of US claims holders for having proceedings overseen by a court-appointed or judicially recognized official. In a similar vein, Peter P. Farkas has suggested that US preferences for a court-recognized official in this regard may be part of the reason that court-appointed receiverships are more common than private receiverships in Canada; see Farkas, "Why Are There so Many Court-Appointed Receiverships?"

33 Dworkin, *Justice in Robes*, 91.

34 See e.g., Gollob, "Distressed Debt Lenders"; Sarra, "Judicial Exercise of Inherent Jurisdiction," 290; Harris, "Enhancing the Role of Creditors' Committees"; Chadwick and Bulas, "Ad Hoc Creditors Committees" ; Janis Sarra, "Manoeuvring through the Insolvency Maze," 158.

35 See e.g., discussion in Ziegel, "Canada's Dysfunctional Insolvency Reform"; Jacob S. Ziegel, chap. 12 "The BIA and CCAA Interface,'" in Duggan and Ben-Ishai, eds, *Canadian Bankruptcy and Insolvency Law,* 316–18.

36 See *BIA* 1985, Part XI "Secured Creditors and Receivers," as am SC 1997, c 12; SC 2005, c 47; SC 2007, c 37.

37 PPSAs significantly harmonized provincial secured credit laws in the twentieth-century. See generally, Ronald C.C. Cuming, Catherine Walsh and Roderick Wood, *Personal Property Security Law*, 2nd ed (Toronto: Irwin Law, 2012).

38 Telfer, *Ruin and Redemption*, 147–50, 157–62. See also Virginia Torrie, *Book Review*: Thomas G.W. Telfer, *Ruin and Redemption: The Struggle for a Canadian Bankruptcy Law, 1867–1919*" (Toronto: University of Toronto Press for the Osgoode Society for Canadian Legal History, 2014) (2016) 31:2 BFLR 427.

39 See Michael Lobban, "Preparing for Fusion: Reforming the Nineteenth-Century Court of Chancery, Part I" (2004) 22.2 L and His Rev 389; Michael Lobban, "Preparing for Fusion: Reforming the Nineteenth-Century Court of Chancery, Part II" (2004) 22.4 L and His Rev 565.

40 See e.g., Manning, "Companies Reorganization" and Judicature, Part 1"; Manning, "Companies Reorganization and Judicature, Part 2."

Bibliography

Archival Collections

Bibliothèque et Archives nationales du Québec (Montréal)

Exchequer Court Records
Quebec Superior Court Records

Library and Archives Canada (Ottawa)

R.B. Bennett Papers
Department of Finance Papers
Department of Justice Papers
Northwest Territories and Yukon Branch Files
Supreme Court of Canada Fonds

Provincial Archives of New Brunswick (Fredericton)

Court of Queen's Bench Bankruptcy Records

Archives of Ontario (Toronto)

Attorney General Central Registry Criminal and Civil Files

Supreme Court of Canada Records Centre (Ottawa)

Reference re Companies' Creditors Arrangement Act Case Files

Legislation

Canada

CONSTITUTIONAL STATUTES

The British North America Act, 1867, 30 and 31 Vict, c 3. [Now titled *Constitution Act, 1867*].
The Constitution Act, 1982, Schedule B to the *Canada Act 1982* (UK), 1982, c 11.

STATUTES

Bank Act, RSC 1927, c 12.
Bankruptcy Act of 1919, SC 1919, c 36.
Bankruptcy Act, RSC 1927, c 11.
Bankruptcy and Insolvency Act, RSC 1985, c B-3.
Canada Business Corporations Act, RSC 1985, c C-44.
Companies Act, RSC 1927, c 79.
Companies Act, SC 1934, c 33.
Companies' Creditors Arrangement Act, SC 1933, c 36.
Companies' Creditors Arrangement Act, RSC 1952, c C-54.
Companies' Creditors Arrangement Act, RSC 1970, c C-25.
Companies' Creditors Arrangement Act, RSC 1985, c C-36.
Dominion Trade and Industry Commission Act, SC 1935, c 59.
Employment and Social Insurance Act, SC 1935, c 38.
Farmers' Creditors Arrangement Act, SC 1934, c 53.
Farmers' Creditors Arrangement Act, SC 1943–1944, c 26.
Farmers' Creditors Arrangement Act, RSC 1952, c 111.
Interpretation Act, RSC 1927, c 1.
Interpretation Act, RSC 1952, c 158.
Interpretation Act, SC 1967, c 7.
Interpretation Act, RSC 1985, c I-21.
Minimum Wages Act, SC 1935, c 44.
Natural Products Marketing Act, SC 1934, c 57.
Limitation of Hours of Work Act, SC 1935, c 63.
Special War Revenue Act, RSC 1927, c 179.
Statistics Act, SC 1918, c S-19.
Transportation Modernization Act, SC 2018, c 10, s 89
Unemployment Insurance Act, SC 1940, c 44.
Wage Earner Protection Program Act, SC 2005, c 47, s 1.
Weekly Rest in Industrial Undertakings Act, SC 1935, c 14.

Winding-up Act, RSC 1906, c 144.
Winding-up Act, RSC 1927, c 213.
Winding-up and Restructuring Act, RSC 1985, c W-11.

AMENDING STATUTES

SC 1934, c 33.
SC 1935, c 56.
SC 1953, c 3.
SC 1992, c 27.
SC 1997, c 12.
SC 2005, c 47.
SC 2007, c 36.
SC 1952–1953, c 3.
SC 2018, c 27.
SC 1923, c 39.
SC 1935, c 2.
SC 1938, c 47.

REGULATIONS

SOR/92–580.

BILLS

Bill No. 26, *An Act to Repeal The Companies' Creditors Arrangement Act, 1933*,
     3rd Sess, 18th Parl, 1938.
Bill A5, 2nd Sess, 20th Parl, 1946. (No further bibliographic information
     available).
Bill C-217, *An Act to Amend the Bankruptcy Act (Priority of Claims)*, 2nd Sess,
     34th Parl, 1989.

INTERPRETATION POLICIES

Policy Statement of Director of CBCA (1994) 17 OSCB 4853.
Industry Canada, Policy Statement 15.1 "Policy concerning arrangements
     under Section 192 of the 'Canada Business Corporations Act'" (Ottawa:
     Industry Canada, 4 January 2010).
"Policy on arrangements – *Canada Business Corporations Act*, section 192"
     (last modified 8 January 2014), online: *Corporations Canada* <https://
     corporationscanada.ic.gc.ca/eic/site/cd-dgc.nsf/eng/cs01073.html>
     [perma.cc/75K7-3UTE].

Ontario

STATUTES

Bulk Sales Act, SO 1917, c 33.
Companies Act, RSO 1927, c 218.
Judicature Act, RSO 1917, c 56.
Pension Benefits Act, RSO 1990, c P-8.

AMENDING STATUTES

SO 1935, c 32.
SO 1917, c 27.
SO 1921, c 138.
SO 1980, c 80.

Alberta

STATUTES

Debt Adjustment Act, SA 1923, c 43.
Debt Adjustment Act, SA 1937, c 79.
Drought Area Relief Act, SA 1922, c 43.
Environmental Protection and Enhancement Act, RSA 2000, c E-12.
Orderly Payment of Debts Act, SA 1959, c 61.
Reduction and Settlement of Land Debts Act, SA 1937, c 27.

Saskatchewan

STATUTES

Debt Adjustment Act, SS 1931, c 59.
Moratorium Act, SS 1943, c 18.
Moratorium Act, RSS 1953, c 98.
Saskatchewan Farm Security Act, SS 1988–1989, c S-17.1.

Manitoba

STATUTES

Debt Adjustment Act, SM 1931, c 7.
Family Farm Protection Act, SM 1986–1987, c 6.

Newfoundland and Labrador

STATUTES

Environmental Protection Act, SNL 2002, c E-14.2.

United Kingdom

STATUTES

Companies Act 1862, 25 and 26 Vict, c 89.
Companies Act 1867, 30 and 31 Vict, c 131.
Companies Act 1929, 19 and 20 Geo 5, c 23.
Companies Act 1948, 11 and 12 Geo 6, c 38.
Companies Act 2006, c 46.
Joint Stock Companies Arrangements Act 1870, 33 and 34 Vict, c 104.

United States

STATUTES

47 Stat 1474 (1933).
49 Stat 838 (1935).
49 Stat 911 (1935).
52 Stat 883 (1938).
52 Stat 840 (1938).
53 Stat 1173 (1939)

CODES

11 USC 1933.
11 USC 1946.
11 USC 1978.
15 USC 1940.

Cases

Canada

80 Wellesley St. East Ltd. v Fundy Builders Ltd. et al., [1972] 2 OR 280, 25 DLR
    (3d) 386 (CA).

8640025 Canada Inc. (Re), 2018 BCCA 93, 58 CBR (6th) 257.

9171665 Canada Ltd. and Connacher Oil and Gas Limited (Re) (2 April 2015), Calgary 1501–00574 (Alta QB).

Air Canada (Re) (2003), 28 CBR (5th) 52, 2003 CarswellOnt 9109 (Ont SCJ (Comm List)).

Algoma Steel Inc. (Re) (2002), 30 CBR (4th) 1, 111 ACWS (3d) 401 (Ont SCJ (Comm List)).

Anvil Range Mining Corporation (Re) (2001), 25 CBR (4th) 1, 104 ACWS (3d) 812 (Ont SCJ (Comm List)).

Anvil Range Mining Corporation (Re) (2002), 34 CBR (4th) 157, 115 ACWS (3d) 923 (Ont CA).

Arthur W. Flint Co. (Re) (1944), 25 CBR 156, [1944] OWN 325 (Ont Sup Ct (in Bankr)).

ATB Financial v Metcalfe & Mansfield Alternative Investments II Corp. (2008), 43 CBR (5th) 269, 47 BLR (4th) 74 (Ont SCJ (Comm List)).

ATB Financial v Metcalfe & Mansfield Alternative Investments II Corp., 2008 ONCA 587, 92 OR (3d) 513.

ATB Financial v Metcalfe & Mansfield Alternative Investments II Corp., [2008] SCCA No 337, 257 PAC 400 (note).

Avery Construction Co. (Re) (1942), 24 CBR 17, 1942 CarswellOnt 86 (Ont Sup Ct [in Chambers].

Bailey Cobalt Mines Ltd. (Re) (1920), 47 OLR 13, 51 DLR 589 (CA).

Bank of Montreal v Guaranty Silk Dyeing and Finishing Co., [1934] OR 625, [1934] 4 DLR 394 (SC (HCJ)).

Banque commerciale du Canada c Station du Mont Tremblant Inc. (1985), JE 85–378, 1985 CarswellQue 544.

Baxter Student Housing Ltd. v College Housing Co-operative Limited, [1976] 2 SCR 475, 20 CBR (NS) 240.

Bell Canada International Inc. (Re) (2003), 126 ACWS (3d) 790, 2003 CarswellOnt 4537 (Ont SCJ (Comm List)).

Bell ExpressVu Ltd. Partnership v Rex, 2002 SCC 42, [2002] 2 SCR 559.

Bilton Brothers Ltd. (Re), [1939] 4 DLR 223, 21 CBR 79 (Ont SC).

Blondin v Parisian Cleaners & Laundry (28 May 1938), Quebec City No. 35322 (Que Sup Ct) [unreported].

British Columbia (AG) v Canada (AG), [1936] SCR 384, [1936] 3 DLR 610.

Calpine Canada Energy Ltd. (Re), 2007 ABQB 504, 415 AR 196.

Calpine Canada Energy Ltd. (Re), 2007 ABCA 266, 417 AR 25.

Canada (AG) v TeleZone Inc., 2010 SCC 62, [2010] 3 SCR 585.

Canadian Bed & Breakfast Registry Ltd. (Re) (1986), 65 CBR (NS) 115, 1986 CarswellBC 504 (BC SC).

Canadian Red Cross Society (Re) (1998), 5 CBR (4th) 299, 81 ACWS (3d) 932, (Ont Ct (Gen Div)).

Canadian Airlines Corp. (Re) (2000), 19 CBR (4th) 1, [2000] CarswellAlta 622 (Alta QB)

Canadian Asbestos Services Ltd. v Bank of Montreal (1992), 11 OR (3d) 353, 16 CBR (3d) 114 (Ont Ct, Gen Div).

Canadian Asbestos Services Ltd. v Bank of Montreal (1993), 13 OR (3d) 291, 10 CLR (2d) 204 (Ont Ct, Gen Div).

Canadian Imperial Bank of Commerce v Quintette Coal Ltd. (1991), 1 CBR (3d) 253, 53 BCLR (2d) 34 (SC).

Century Services Inc. v Canada (AG), 2010 SCC 60, [2010] 3 SCR 379.

Chieu v Canada (Minister of Citizenship & Immigration), 2002 SCC 3, [2002] 1 SCR 84.

Citibank Canada v Chase Manhattan Bank of Canada (1991), 5 CBR (3d) 165, 2 PPSAC (2d) 21 (Ont Ct J (Gen Div)).

Companies' Creditors Arrangement Act (Canada) (Reference re), 1934 SCR 659, [1934] 4 DLR 75.

Comptoir coopératif du combustible Ltée (Re) (1935), 74 Que SC 119, 17 CBR 124.

Crown Trust Co. v Rosenberg (1986), 60 OR (2d) 87, 39 DLR (4th) 526 (SC (HCJ)).

D. Moore Co. (Re) (1927), 61 OLR 434, [1928] 1 DLR 383 (SC (App Div)).

D. W. McIntosh Ltd. (Re) (1939), 20 CBR 234, 251, 1939 CarswellOnt 68 (Ont Sup Ct (in Bankr)).

Dairy Corporation of Canada Limited (Re), [1934] OR 436, [1934] 3 DLR 347 (SC (HCJ)).

Daniel & Co. (Re) (1934), 16 CBR 21, 1934 CarswellNB 1 (NBSC (KB Div, In Bankruptcy)).

Diemaster Tool Inc. v Skvortsoff (Trustee of) (1991), 3 CBR (3d) 133, 1991 CarswellOnt 169 (Ont Ct).

Dominion Canners Ltd. v Constanza, [1923] SCR 46, 61, [1922] SCJ 46.

Dom. Iron and Steel Co. v Can. BK. Commerce, [1928] 1 DLR 809, 1928 CarswellNS 98 (NSSC).

Douez v Faccebook, Inc., 2017 SCC 33, [2017] 1 SCR 751.

Dylex Ltd. (Re) (1995), 31 CBR (3d) 106, 54 ACWS (3d) 504 (Ont Ct J, Gen Div (Comm List)).

Elan Corp. v Comiskey (Trustee of) (1990), 1 OR (3d) 289, 41 OAC 282.

Fairview Industries Ltd. (Re) (1991), 109 NSR (2d) 12, 11 CBR (3d) 43 (SC (Trial Div)).

Fracmaster Ltd. (Re), 1999 ABQB 379, 11 CBR (4th) 204.

Fracmaster Ltd. (Re), 1999 ABCA 178, 11 CBR (4th) 230.

General Fireproofing Co. of Canada (Re), [1936] OR 510, 17 CBR 371 (CA).

Governments Stock and Other Securities Investment Co Ltd v Manila Rly Co (1896), [1897] AC 81, 75 LT 553 (HL).

Hester Creek Estate Winery Ltd. (Re), 2004 BCSC 345, 50 CBR (4th) 73.

Hongkong Bank of Canada v Chef Ready Foods Ltd. (1990), 4 CBR (3d) 311, 51 BCLR (2d) 84 (CA).

Icor Oil & Gas Co. v Cdn. Imperial Bank of Commerce (1989), 102 AR 161, 1989 CarswellAlta 693 (QB).

Indalex Ltd. (Re), 2013 SCC 6, JE 2013–185.

Ivaco Inc. (Re) (2006), 83 OR (3d) 108, 25 CBR (5th) 176 (CA)

Keddy Motor Inns Ltd. (Re) (1992), 13 CBR (3d) 245, 90 DLR (4th) 175 (NS SC).

Kelly v Human Rights Commission (P.E.I.), 2008 PESCAD 9, 276 Nfld & PEIR 336.

Lehndorff General Partner Ltd. (Re) (1993), 17 CBR (3d) 24, 37 ACWS (3d) 847 (ON Ct J (Gen Div, Comm List).

Lemare Lake Logging Ltd. v 3L Cattle Company Ltd., 2014 SKCA 35, 467 Sask R 1.

Long Potato Growers Ltd. (Re), 2008 NBQB 231, 80 CBR (5th) 29.

M. J. O'Brien Ltd. v Br. Am. Nickel Corp. Ltd., [1925] 4 DLR 455, 57 OLR 536 (CA).

Meridian Dev. Inc. v Nu-West Ltd. (1984), 53 AR 39, 52 CBR (NS) 109 (QB).

Michie Estate and City of Toronto et al. (Re), [1968] 1 OR 266, 66 DLR (2d) 213 (HCJ).

Minister of National Revenue v Cohen's Co. (1935), 73 Que SC 291, 17 CBR 143.

Minister of National Revenue v Roxy Frocks Manufacturing Co. (1936), 74 Que SC 186, 17 CBR 418.

Minister of National Revenue v Roxy Frocks Manufacturing Co. (1936), 62 Que KB 113, 18 CBR 132 (In Appeal).

Montréal, Maine & Atlantique Canada Co. (Re), 2013 QCCS 4039, EYB 2013-225915, paras 1–26.

Montreal Trust Co. v Abitibi Power and Paper Co., [1938] OR 81, 19 CBR 179 (SC).

Montreal Trust Co. v Abitibi Power and Paper Co., [1938] OR 589, [1938] 4 DLR 529 (CA).

Montreal Trust Co. v Atlantic Acceptance Corp. (1975), 9 OR (2d) 265, 60 DLR (3d) 193 (CA).

Montreal Trust Co. v Churchill Forest Industries (Man.) Ltd., [1971] 4 WWR 542, 21 DLR (3d) 75 (MB CA).

Murphy v Welsh, [1993] 2 SCR 1069, 106 DLR (4th) 404.

National Trust Co. v Great Lakes Paper Co., [1936] 1 DLR 718, [1936] OWN 13 (HCJ).

National Trust Co. v Great Lakes Paper Co., [1936] 2 DLR 239, [1936] OWN 113 (CA).

Nelson Education Ltd. (Re), 2016 ONSC 3580, 26 CBR (6th) 161.

Newfoundland and Labrador v AbitibiBowater Inc., 2012 SCC 67, [2012] 3 SCR 443.

Norcen Energy Resources Ltd. v Oakwood Petroleums Ltd. (1988), 92 AR 81, 72 CBR (NS) 1 (QB).

Norm's Hauling Ltd. (Re) (1991), 6 CBR (3d) 16, 91 Sask R 210 (QB).

Nortel Networks Corp. (Re), 2017 ONSC 673, 44 CBR (6th) 289.

Northland Properties Ltd. (Re) (1988), 29 BCLR (2d) 257, 69 CBR (NS) 266 (SC).

Northland Properties Ltd. (Re) (1988), 73 CBR (NS) 175, 1988 CarswellBC 558 (SC).

Northland Properties Ltd. (Re) (1989), 34 BCLR (2d) 122, 73 CBR (NS) 195 (CA).

Northland Properties Ltd. v Excelsior Life Insurance Co. of Canada (1989), 34 BCLR (2d) 122, 73 CBR (NS) 195 (CA).

NsC Diesel Power Inc. (Re) (1990), 79 CBR (NS) 1, 21 ACWS (3) 55 (NS SC, Trial Div).

Orderly Payment of Debts Act, 1959 (Alta.) (Reference re), [1960] SCR 571, 1 CBR (NS) 207.

Ordon Estate v Grail, [1998] 3 SCR 437, 40 OR (3d) 639.

Orphan Well Association v Grant Thornton Ltd., 2019 SCC 15, 81 Alta LR (6th) 1.

Panama, New Zealand, and Australian Royal Mail Co. (Re) (1870), LR 5 Ch App 318,

Parisian Cleaners & Laundry Ltd. v Blondin (1938), 66 Que KB 456, 20 CBR 452 (In Appeal).

Peoples Department Stores Inc. (Trustee of) v Wise, 2004 SCC 68, [2004] 3 SCR 461.

Philip's Manufacturing Ltd. (Re) (1991), 9 CBR (3d) 1, 60 BCLR (2d) 211 (SC).

Pine Valley Mining Corp. (Re), 2008 BCSC 446, 41 CBR (5th) 49.

Pointe-Claire (Ville) c S.E.P.B., Local 57, [1997] 1 SCR 1015, 46 Admin LR (2d) 1.

Power of Disallowance and the Power of Reservation (Canada) (Reference re), [1938] SCR 71, [1938] 2 DLR 8.

Provincial Company Legislation (Reference re), [1913] 48 SCR 331, 15 DLR 332.

R v Araujo, 2000 SCC 65, [2000] 2 SCR 992.

R v Gladue, [1999] 1 SCR 688, 171 DLR (4th) 385.

R v Kussner, [1936] Ex CR 206, 18 CBR 58.

R v Miss Style Inc. (1936), 61 Que KB 283, 18 CBR 20 (In Appeal).

R v Sharpe, 2001 SCC 2, [2001] 1 SCR 45.

R v Ulybel Enterprises Ltd., 2001 SCC 56, [2001] 2 SCR 867.

Richtree Inc. (Re) (2005), 7 CBR (5th) 294, 10 BLR (4th) 334 (Ont SCJ, Gen Div (Comm List)).

Royal Oak Mines (Re) (1999), 7 CBR (4th) 293, [1999] OJ No 864 (Ont Ct J, Gen Div (Comm List)).

Royal Oak Mines Inc. (Re) (1999), 11 CBR (4th) 122, 1999 CarswellOnt1068 (Ont Ct J, Gen Div (Comm List)).

Residential Tenancies Act (Ontario) (Reference re), [1981] 1 SCR 714, 123 DLR (3d) 554.

Québec (Communauté urbaine) c Notre-Dame de Bonsecours (Corp.), [1994] 3 SCR 3, 63 QAC 161.

Quintette Coal Ltd. v Nippon Steel Corp. (1990), 2 CBR (3d) 303, 51 BCLR (2d) 105 (CA).

Rizzo & Rizzo Shoes Ltd. (Re), [1998] 1 SCR 27, 106 OAC 1.

Royal Bank of Canada v Soundair Corp. (1991), 83 DLR (4th) 76, 7 CBR (3d) 1 (CA).

Sam Lévy & Associés Inc. c Mayrand, 2005 FC 702, [2006] 2 FCR 543.

Sammi Atlas Inc. (Re) (1998), 3 CBR (4th) 171, 78 ACWS (3d) 10 (Ont Ct J (Gen Div) (Comm List)).

Saskatchewan (AG) v Lemare Lake Logging Ltd., 2015 SCC 53, [2015] 3 SCR 419.

Securities Act (Reference re), 2011 SCC 66, [2011] 3 SCR 837.

Skeena Cellulose Inc. (Re), 2003 BCCA 344, 43 CBR (4th) 187.

Sklar-Peppler Furniture Corp. v Bank of Nova Scotia (1991), 8 CBR (3d) 312, 86 DLR (4th) 621 (Ont Ct (Gen Div)).

Station Mont-Tremblant Inc. c Banque commerciale du Canada (1984), 54 CBR (NS) 241, 1984 CarswellQue 37 (Que SC).

Starcom International Optics Corp. (Re) (1998), 3 CBR (4th) 177, 78 ACWS (3d) 11 (BC SC).

Stelco Inc. (Re) (2004), 48 CBR (4th) 299, 129 ACWS (3d) 1065 (Ont SCJ).

Stelco Inc. (Re), 2004 CarswellOnt 2936, [2004] OJ No 1903 (CA).

Stelco Inc. (Re), [2004] SCCA No 336, 338 NR 196 (note).

Stelco Inc. (Re) (2005), 7 CBR (5th) 307, 137 ACWS (3d) 475 (Ont SCJ (Comm List)).

Stelco Inc. (Re) (2005), 7 CBR (5th) 310, 137 ACWS (3d) 476 (Ont SCJ (Comm List)).

Stelco Inc. (Re) (2005), 75 OR (3d) 5, 253 DLR (4th) 109 (CA).

Stephanie's Fashions Ltd. (Re) (1990), 1 CBR (3d) 248, 25 ACWS (3d) 1071 (BC SC).

Stokes Building Supplies Ltd. (1991), 9 CBR (3d) 1, 60 BCLR (2d) 311 (SC).

Stubart Investments Ltd. v R, [1984] 1 SCR 536, 578, 10 DLR (4th) 1.

Sulphur Corp. of Canada Ltd., 2002 ABQB 682, 35 CBR (4th) 204.

Syndicat national de l'amiante d'Asbestos inc c Mine Jeffrey inc. (2003), 40 CBR (4th) 95, 35 CCPB 71 (Que CA).

T. Eaton Co. (Re) (1997), 46 CBR (3d) 293, [1997] OJ No 6411 (Ont CT J, Gen Div).

TCR Holding Corp. v Ontario, 2010 ONCA 233, 69 BLR (4th) 175.

Teck Corp. Ltd. v Millar (1972), 33 DLR (3d) 288, [1973] 2 WWR 385 (BC SC).

Tepper Holdings Inc. (Re), 2011 NBQB 211, 80 CBR (5th) 339.

United Co-Operatives of Ontario, (August 1984), unreported.

United Maritime Fishermen Co-operative (Re) (1988), 84 NBR (2d) 415, 67 CBR (NS) 44 (QB (Trial Div)).

United Maritime Fishermen Co-operative (Re) (1988), 87 NBR (2d) 333, 68 CBR (NS) 170 (QB).

United Maritime Fishermen Co-operative (Re) (1988), 88 NBR (2d) 253, 69 CBR (NS) 161 (CA).

Victoria Mortgage Corp. (Re) (1985), 57 CBR (NS) 157, 1985 CarswellBC 477 (BC SC).

Wellington Building Corporation Limited (Re), [1934] OR 653, [1934] 4 DLR 626 (SC).

West & Co. (Re) (1921), 50 OLR 631, 2 CBR 3 (SC (In Bankruptcy)).
Westar Mining Ltd. (Re) (1992), 70 BCLR (2d) 6, 14 CBR (3d) 88 (SC).
Williams and Rees v Local Union No. 1562 of United Mine Workers of America,
 [1919] 1 WWR 217, 45 DLR 150 (Alta SC (Trial – App Div)).
Winalta Inc. (Re), 2011 ABQB 399, 84 CBR (5th) 157.
Woodward's Ltd. (Re) (1993), 79 BCLR (2d) 257, 17 CBR (3d) 236 (SC).

COURT FILED DOCUMENTS

Algoma Plan Sanctioning Hearing, 1992, *Algoma Steel Corporation*, Court
 File Doc. No. B62191-A (Ont Ct [Gen Div]).
Algoma Plan Sanctioning Hearing, 2001, [2001] OJ No 4630 (Ont SCJ),
 Court File No 01-CL-4115 (Lexis).
Algoma Endorsement Order, 19 December 2001.

United Kingdom

*Alabama, New Orleans, Texas and Pacific Junction Railway Company Limited
 (Re)* (1890), [1891] 1 Ch 213, [1890] 12 WLUK 62.
Assignments & Preferences Act (Reference re), s. 9, [1894] UKPC 8, [1894] AC
 189 (Ont).
Biggerstaff v Rowell's Wharf Ltd., [1896] 2 Ch 93, 65 LJ Ch 536.
Board v Board, [1919] AC 956, 48 DLR 13 (JCPC).
Bonanza Creek Gold Mining Co. v The King, [1916] UKPC 11, [1916] 1 AC 566
 (Ont).
British Columbia (AG) v Canada (AG), [1937] UKPC 10, [1937] AC 391.
Brunton v Electrical Engineering Co., [1892] 1 Ch 434, 61 LJ Ch 256.
Connolley Bros. (Re), [1912] 2 Ch 25, 81 LJ Ch 517.
Dominion of Canada Freehold Estate and Timber Co Ltd. (Re) (1886), 55 LT 347.
Evans v Rival Granite Quarries Ltd, (1910) 2 KB 979, 79 LJKB 970 (CA).
Gaskell v Gosling, [1896] 1 QB 669, 65 LJQB 435 (CA).
Goodfellow v Nelson Line (Liverpool) Ltd., [1912] 2 Ch 324, [1912] WLUK 76.
Heydon's Case, [1584] 76 ER 637 3 CO REP 7a.
Illingworth v Houldsworth, [1904] AC 355, 73 LJ Ch 739 (HL).
New York Taxicab Co. (Re) (sub nom Seguin v The Company) (1912), [1913] 1 Ch
 1, 107 LT 813.
Mayor of London v Cox (1867), 1 E & I App 239.
North-West Transportation Co. v Beatty, [1887] UKPC 39, LR 12 App Cas 589.
Peacock v Bell and Kendall (1677), 1 Wms Saund 73, 85 ER 84.
Robson v Smith, [1895] 2 Ch 118, 64 LJ Ch 457.
Salomon v Salomon and Co. Ltd. (1897), [1896] UKHL 1, [1897] AC 22.

Scales v Cheese (1844), 12 M & W 685, 152 ER 1374.

Silver Brothers, Limited (Re), [1932] UKPC 6, [1932] AC 514.

L'Union St. Jacques de Montreal v Bélisle (1874), LR 6 PC 31, CR [7] AC 154 (Que JCPC).

Wallace v Universal Automatic Machines Co., [1894] 2 Ch 547, [1891-94] All ER Rep 1156 (CA).

Wilson v Kelland, [1910] 2 Ch 306, 79 LJ Ch 580.

Yorkshire Woolcombers Association (Re), Limited (*sub nom Houldsworth v Yorkshire Woolcombers Association Ltd*), [1903] 2 Ch 284, 88 LT 811 (CA).

United States

Benedict v Ratner, 268 US 353 (1925).

Case v Los Angeles Lumber Products Co., 308 US 106 (1939).

Chalmers v Nederlandsch Amerikaansche, 36 NYS2d 717 (City Ct 1942).

Books

Baird, David E. *Baird's Practical Guide to the Companies' Creditors Arrangement Act* (Toronto: Carswell, 2009).

Barnes, Jeb. *Overruled? Pluralism, Court–Congress Relations and Legislative Overrides* (Stanford, CA: Stanford University Press, 2004).

Baumgartner, Frank and Bryan D. Jones. *Agendas and Instability in American Politics* (Chicago: University of Chicago Press, 1993).

Ben-Ishai, Stephanie. *Bankruptcy Reforms 2008* (Toronto: Thomson Carswell, 2008).

Ben-Ishai, Stephanie and Anthony Duggan, eds. *Canadian Bankruptcy and Insolvency Law* (Markham, ON: LexisNexis, 2007).

Ben-Ishai, Stephanie and Thomas G.W. Telfer, eds. *Bankruptcy and Insolvency Law in Canada: Cases, Materials, and Problems* (Toronto: Irwin Law 2019).

Bennett, Frank. *Bennett on Bankruptcy*, 10th ed (Toronto: CCH Canada Limited, 2008).

– *Bennett on Bankruptcy*, 14th ed (Toronto: CCH Canada Limited, 2012).

– *Bennett on Receiverships*, 2nd ed (Toronto: Carswell, 1999).

Benson, Winslow. *Business Methods of Canadian Trust Companies*, 1st ed (Toronto: Ryerson Press, 1949).

– *Business Methods of Canadian Trust Companies*, 2nd ed (Toronto: Ryerson Press, 1962).

Bliss, Michael. *Northern Enterprise: Five Centuries of Canadian Business* (Toronto: McClelland and Stewart, 1989).

Bryce, Robert. *Maturing in Hard Times: Canada's Department of Finance through the Great Depression* (Kingston and Montreal: McGill-Queen's University Press, 1986).

Carruthers, Bruce G. and Terence C. Halliday. *Rescuing Business: The Making of Corporate Bankruptcy Law in England and the United States* (Oxford: Oxford University Press, 1998).

Christian, W., and C. Campbell. *Political Parties and Ideologies in Canada: Liberals, Conservatives, Socialists, Nationalists* (Toronto: McGraw-Hill Ryerson, 1974).

Collier, Ruth Berins and David Collier. *Shaping the Political Arena: Critical Junctures, The Labor Movement, and Regime Dynamics in Latin America* (Notre Dame: University of Notre Dame Press, 2002).

Cuming, Ronald C.C., Catherine Walsh and Roderick Wood. *Personal Property Security Law*, 2nd ed (Toronto: Irwin Law, 2012).

Delaney, Kevin J. *Strategic Bankruptcy* (Berkeley and Los Angeles: U niversity of California Press, 1998).

Driedger, Elmer A. *The Construction of Statutes*, 1st ed (Toronto: Butterworths, 1974).

– *The Construction of Statutes*, 2nd ed (Toronto: Butterworths, 1983).

Duggan, Anthony J., et al. *Canadian Bankruptcy and Insolvency Law: Cases, Text, and Materials*, 2nd ed (Toronto: Emond Montgomery, 2009).

Duncan, Lewis. *The Law and Practice of Bankruptcy in Canada*, 1st ed (Toronto: Carswell, 1922).

Duncan, Lewis and John D. Honsberger. *Bankruptcy in Canada*, 3rd ed (Aurora: Canada Law Book, 1961).

Duncan, Lewis and William John Reilly. *Bankruptcy in Canada*, 2nd ed (Toronto: Canadian Legal Authors Limited, 1933).

Dunlop, C.R.B. *Creditor-Debtor Law in Canada* (Toronto: Carswell, 1981).

Dworkin, Ronald. *Justice in Robes* (Cambridge, Mass.: Harvard University Press, 2006).

Easterbrook, W.T. and Hugh G.J. Aitken. *Canadian Economic History* (Toronto: Macmillan Company of Canada, 1956, reprinted Gage Publishing Ltd, 1980).

Ferran, Eilís. *Principles of Corporate Finance Law* (Oxford: Oxford University Press, 2008).

Finch, Vanessa. *Corporate Insolvency Law: Perspectives and Principles*, 2nd ed (Cambridge: Cambridge University Press, 2009).

Finkel, Alvin. *Business and Social Reform in the Thirties* (Toronto: James Lorimer and Company, Publishers, 1979).

Fraser, W.K. *Handbook on Canadian Company Law with Forms*, 4th ed (Toronto: Carswell, 1945).

Fraser, W.K. and Hugh Williamson MacDonnell. *Handbook on Companies with Appendix and Forms* (Toronto: Carswell, 1922).

Galbraith, J.A. *Canadian Banking* (Toronto: The Ryerson Press, 1970).

Gilmore, Grant. *Security Interests in Personal Property*, vol. 1. (Boston: Little Brown, 1965).

Girard, Philip. *Bora Laskin: Bringing Law to Life* (Toronto: University of Toronto Press for the Osgoode Society for Canadian Legal History, 2005).

Glassford, Larry A. *Reaction and Reform: The Politics of the Conservative Party under R.B. Bennett 1927–1938* (Toronto: University of Toronto Press, 1992).

Gross, Karen. *Failure and Forgiveness: Rebalancing the Bankruptcy System* (New Haven: Yale University Press, 1997).

Halliday, Terence C. and Bruce G. Carruthers. *Bankrupt: Global Lawmaking and Systemic Financial Crisis* (Stanford: Stanford University Press, 2009).

Halpern, Paul et al. *Back from the Brink: Lessons from the Canadian Asset-Backed Commercial Paper Crisis* (Toronto: University of Toronto Press, 2016).

Honsberger, John D. and Vern W. DaRe. *Debt Restructuring: Principles and Practice* (Toronto: Thomson Reuters, 2008).

Honsberger, John D. and Vern W. DaRe. *Bankruptcy in Canada*, 4th ed (Aurora: Canada Law Book, 2009).

Honsberger, John D. and Vern W. DaRe. *Honsberger's Bankruptcy in Canada*, 5th ed (Toronto: Thomson Reuters, 2017).

Horowitz, Gad. *Canadian Labour in Politics* (Toronto: University of Toronto Press, 1968).

Houlden, L.W. and Geoffrey B. Morawetz. *Bankruptcy Law of Canada*, 3rd ed (Toronto: Carswell, 1989).

Jackson, Thomas H. *The Logic and Limits of Bankruptcy Law* (Cambridge, MA: Harvard University Press, 1986).

Kennedy, Duncan. *A Critique of Adjudication* (Cambridge, MA: Harvard University Press, 1997).

Kyer, C. Ian and Jerome E. Bickenbach. *The Fiercest Debate: Cecil A Wright, the Benchers, and Legal Education in Ontario 1923–1957* (Toronto: University of Toronto Press for the Osgoode Society, 1987).

Lake, David A. and Robert Powell, eds. *Strategic Choice and International Relations* (Princeton: Princeton University Press, 1999).

Lijphart, Arend. *Patterns of Democracy: Government Forms and Performance in Thirty-Six Countries* (New Haven: Yale University Press, 1999).

Lubben, Stephen J. *American Business Bankruptcy: A Primer* (Cheltenham, UK: Edward Elgar, 2019).

Mallory, J.R. *Social Credit and the Federal Power in Canada* (Toronto: University of Toronto Press, 1954).

McLaren, Richard H. *Canadian Commercial Reorganization*, loose leaf, vol. 1 (Aurora: Canada Law Book, 1994).

Neatby, H. Blair. *William Lyon Mackenzie King, 1924–1932: The Lonely Heights* (Toronto: University of Toronto Press, 1963).

Neufeld, E.P. *The Financial System of Canada: Its Growth and Development* (Toronto: Macmillan of Canada, 1972).

Nicholls, Chris C. *Financial Institutions: The Regulatory Framework* (Toronto: LexisNexis, 2008).

North, Douglass C. *Institutions, Institutional Change, and Economic Performance* (Cambridge: Cambridge University Press, 1990).

Nye, Joseph. *Bound to Lead: The Changing Nature of American Power* (New York: Basic Books, 1990).

– *Soft Power: The Means to Success in World Politics* (New York: Public Affairs, 2004).

Payne, Jennifer. *Schemes of Arrangement: Theory, Structure and Operation* (Cambridge: Cambridge University Press, 2014).

Pennington, Robert R. *Company Law*, 8th ed (London: Butterworths, 2001).

Pierson, Paul. *Politics in Time: History, Institutions, and Social Analysis* (Princeton, NJ: Princeton University Press, 2004).

Ramsay, Iain D.C. *Personal Insolvency in the 21st Century: A Comparative Analysis of the US and Europe* (Oxford: Hart Publishing, 2017).

Safarian, A.E. *The Canadian Economy in the Great Depression* (Toronto: McLelland and Stewart, 1970).

Sarra, Janis. *Creditor Rights and the Public Interest* (Toronto: University of Toronto Press, 2003).

– *Rescue! The Companies' Creditors Arrangement Act*, 1st ed (Toronto: Thomson Carswell, 2007).

– *Rescue! The Companies' Creditors Arrangement Act*, 2nd ed (Toronto: Carswell, 2013).

Saywell, John T. *The Lawmakers: Judicial Power and the Shaping of Canadian Federalism* (Toronto: University of Toronto Press for the Osgoode Society for Canadian Legal History, 2004).

Simonson, Paul Fredrick. *The Debenture and Debenture Stock Holders' Legal Handbook, with Appendix Containing Forms* (London: Effingham Wilson, 1920).

– *The Law Relating to the Reconstruction and Amalgamation of Joint-Stock Companies: Revised and Largely Rewritten*, 3rd ed (London: Sweet and Maxwell, 1919).

– *The Law Relating to the Reconstruction and Amalgamation of Joint-Stock Companies: Together with Forms and Precedents*, 4th ed (London: Jordan and Sons, 1931).

– *The Law Relating to the Reduction of the Share Capital of Joint-Stock Companies*, 2nd ed (London: Sweet and Maxwell, 1924).

– *The Law Relating to the Reduction of the Share Capital of Joint-Stock Companies*, 3rd ed (London: Jordan and Sons, 1932).

Skeel Jr, David A. *Debt's Dominion: A History of Bankruptcy Law in America* (Princeton: Princeton University Press, 2001).

Springman, M.A., and Eric Gertner, eds. *Debtor-Creditor Law: Practice and Doctrine* (Toronto: Butterworths 1985).

Stanford, G.H. *To Serve the Community: The Story of the Toronto Board of Trade* (Toronto: University of Toronto Press for the Toronto Board of Trade of Metropolitan Toronto, 1974).

Stetson, Francis Lynde. *Preparation of Corporate Bonds, Mortgages, Collateral Trusts, and Debenture Indentures, in Some Legal Phases of Corporate Financing, Reorganization and Regulation* (New York: Macmillan, 1917).

Stewart, J.L. and Laird Palmer, eds. *Fraser and Stewart Company Law of Canada*, 5th ed (Toronto: Carswell, 1962).

Stinchcombe, Arthur L. *Constructing Social Theories* (New York: Harcourt, Brace and World, 1968).

Streeck, Wolfgang and Kathleen Thelen, eds. *Beyond Continuity: Institutional Change in Advanced Political Economies* (New York: Oxford University Press, 2005).

Taylor, Graham D. and Peter A. Baskerville. *A Concise History of Business in Canada* (Toronto: Oxford University Press, 1994).

Telfer, Thomas G.W. *Ruin and Redemption: The Struggle for a Canadian Bankruptcy Law, 1867–1919* (Toronto: Osgoode Society for Canadian Legal History and University of Toronto Press, 2014).

Topham, Alfred F., Alfred Robert Taylour, and AM.R. Topham. *Palmer's Company Precedents*, 14th ed (London: Stevens & Sons, Ltd., 1933).

Waite, P.B. *In Search of R.B. Bennett* (Montreal and Kingston: McGill Queen's University Press, 2012).

Weiler, Paul. *In the Last Resort* (Toronto: Carswell/Methuen, 1974).

Welling, Bruce, Lionel Smith and Leonard I. Rotman. *Canadian Corporate Law: Cases, Notes and Materials*, 4th ed (Markham, ON: LexisNexis, 2010).

Westbrook, Jay Lawrence, et al. *A Global View of Business Insolvency Systems* (Leiden: The World Bank and Brill, 2010).

Wilford, Allen. *Farm Gate Defense: The Story of the Canadian Farmers Survival Association* (Toronto: New Canada Publications, 1985).

Wood, Roderick J. *Bankruptcy and Insolvency Law* (Toronto: Irwin law, 2009).

Young, H. Peyton. *Individual Strategy and Social Structure: An Evolutionary Theory of Institutions* (Princeton: Princeton University Press, 1998).

Ziegel, Jacob S. and David Baird, eds. *Case Studies in Recent Canadian Insolvency Reorganizations* (Toronto: Carswell, 1997).

Essays in Edited Collections

Baar, Carl. "Judicial Activism in Canada" in Kenneth M. Holland, ed, *Judicial Activism in Comparative Perspective* (New York: St. Martin's, 1991), 53–69.

Bowen, Baron (Charles S. Christopher). "Progress on the Administration of Justice during the Victorian Period," in *Select Essays in Anglo-American Legal History*, vol. 1 (Boston: Little, Brown and Company, 1907), 516–557.

Edelman, Lauren B. "Legality and the Endogeneity of Law," in R. Kagan, M. Krygier and K. Winston, eds, *Legal and Community: On the Intellectual Legacy of Philip Selznick* (Lanham, MD: Rowman & Littlefield, 2002), 187–202.

– "Law at Work: The Endogenous Construction of Civil Rights," in Laura Beth Nielsen and Robert L. Nelson, eds, *Handbook of Employment and Discrimination Research* (The New York: Springer, 2008), 337–352.

Gourevitch, Peter Alexis. "The Governance Problem in International Relations," in David A. Lake and Robert Powell, eds, *Strategic Choice and International Relations* (Princeton: Princeton University Press, 1999), 137–164.

Grattet, Ryken. "Structural Contradictions and the Production of New Legal Institutions: The Transformation of Industrial Accident Law Revised" in William J. Chambliss and Marjorie Zatz, eds, *Making Law: The State, the Law, and Structural Contradictions* (Bloomington: Indiana University Press, 1993), 404–420.

Knafla, Louis A. "Richard 'Bonfire' Bennett: The Legal Practice of a Prairie Corporate Lawyer, 1898 to 1913" in Carol Wilton, ed, *Beyond the Law: Lawyers and Business in Canada, 1830 to 1930*, vol. 4 (Toronto: Butterworths for the Osgoode Society, 1990), 320–376.

Krasner, Stephen D. "Sovereignty: An Institutional Perspective" in James A. Caporaso, ed, *The Elusive State: International and Comparative Perspectives* (Newbury Park, CA: Sage, 1989), 69–96.

Levi, Margaret. "A Model, a Method, and a Map: Rational Choice in Comparative and Historical Analysis" in Mark I. Lichbach and Alan S. Zuckerman, eds, *Comparative Politics: Rationality, Culture, and Structure* (Cambridge: Cambridge University Press, 1997), 19–41.

North, Douglass. "In Anticipation of the Marriage of Political and Economic Theory," in James E. Alt, Margaret Levi and Eleanor Ostrom, eds, *Competition and Cooperation: Conversations with Nobelists about Economics and Political Science* (New York: Russell Sage Foundation, 1999), 314–317.

Stinchcombe, Arthur. "Social Structure and Organizations" in James March, ed, *Handbook of Organizations* (Chicago, Rand McNally, 1965), 142–193.

Streeck, Wolfgang and Kathleen Thelen. "Introduction: Institutional Change in Advanced Political Economies," in Wolfgang Streeck and Kathleen Thelen, eds, *Beyond Continuity: Institutional Change in Advanced Political Economies* (New York: Oxford University Press, 2005), 3–39.

Thelen, Kathleen. "How Institutions Evolve: Insights from Comparative Historical Analysis," in James Mahoney and Dietrich Rueschemeyer, eds, *Comparative Historical Analysis in Social Sciences* (Cambridge: Cambridge University Press, 2003), 208–240.

Varley, John R. "Receivership: The Contest Between Secured and General Creditors," in M.A. Springman and Eric Gertner, eds, *Debtor-Creditor Law: Practice and Doctrine* (Toronto: Butterworths 1985), 423–509.

Ziegel, Jacob S. "The Privately Appointed Receiver and Enforcement of Security Interests: Anomaly or Superior Solution?" in Jacob S. Ziegel, ed, *Current Developments in International and Comparative Corporate Insolvency Law* (Oxford: Clarendon Press, 1994), 451–472.

Journal Articles

Alt, James E., et al. "The Political Economy of International Trade: Enduring Puzzles and an Agenda for Inquiry" (1996) 29:6 Comp Polit Stud 689.

Armour, John and Sandra Frisby. "Rethinking Receivership" (2001) 21:1 Oxford J Leg Stud 73.

Ayotte, Kenneth, and David A. Skeel Jr. "Bankruptcy or Bailouts?" (2010) 35 J Corp Stud 469.

Baird, Douglas G. and Robert K. Rasmussen. "Antibankruptcy" (2010) 119:4 Yale LJ 648.

Ben-Ishai, Stephanie. "Bank Bankruptcy in Canada: A Comparative Perspective" (2009) 25:1 BFLR 59.

Ben-Ishai, Stephanie and Stephen Lubben. "Sales or Plans: A Comparative Account of the 'New' Corporate Reorganization" (2010) 56:3 McGill LJ 591.

Ben-Ishai, Stephanie, Saul Schwartz and Thomas G.W. Telfer. "A Retrospective on the Canadian Consumer Bankruptcy System: 40 Years after the *Tassé Report*" (2011) 50:1 CBLJ 236.

Ben-Ishai, Stephanie and Virginia Torrie. "Farm Insolvency in Canada" (2013) 2 IIC Journal 33.

Billyou, De Forest. "Corporate Mortgage Bonds and Majority Clauses" (1948) 57:4 Yale LJ 595.

Binavince, Emilio S. and H. Scott Fairley. "Banking and the Constitution: Untested Limits of Federal Jurisdiction" (1986) 65:1 Can Bar Rev 328.

Bladen, V.W. "The Economics of Federalism" (1935) 1:3 Can J Econ Polit Sci 348.

Bowra, David P. "The Role of the Monitor under the *Companies' Creditors Arrangement Act*" IIC-ART 2002-7 (Westlaw).

Buckwold, Tamara M. "The Reform of Judgment Enforcement Law in Canada: An Overview and Comparison of Models for Reform" (2017) 80:1 Sask L Rev 71.

– "The Treatment of Receivers in the Personal Property Security Acts: Conceptual and Practical Implications" (1998) 29:2 CBLJ 277.

Carrothers, W.A. "Problems with Canadian Federalism" (1935) 1:1 Can J Econ Polit Sci 26.

Chadwick, Robert J. and Derek R. Bulas. "Ad Hoc Creditors' Committees in CCAA Proceedings: The Result of a Changing and Expanding Restructuring World" 2011 ANNREVINSOLV 5 (Westlaw).

Chambers, Edward J. "The 1937–8 Recession in Canada" (1955) 21:3 Can J Econ Polit Sci 293.

Claxton, Brooke. "Social Reform and the Constitution" (1935) 1:3 Can J Econ Polit Sci 409.

Corry, J.A. "The Federal Dilemma" (1941) 7:2 Can J Econ Polit Sci 215.

Crozier, Lawrence J. "Good Faith and the *Companies' Creditors Arrangement Act*" (1989) 15:1 CBLJ 89.

Cuming, R.C.C. "Canadian Bankruptcy Law: A Secured Creditor's Heaven" (1994–1995) 24:1 CBLJ 17.

Curtis, G.F. "The Theory of the Floating Charge" (1941–1942) 4:1 UTLJ 131.

Djankov, Simon et al. "Debt Enforcement around the World" (2008) 116:6 J of Polit Econ 1105.

Dodd, E. Merrick, Jr. "Fair and Equitable Recapitalizations" (1941–1942) 55:5 Harv L Rev 780.

Drummond, Ian M. "Canadian Life Insurance Companies and the Capital Market, 1890–1914" (1962) 28:2 Can J Econ Polit Sci 204.

Dube, James P. "The Stelco Directors Case: Containment of Inherent Jurisdiction in CCAA Proceedings" (2005) 21:1 BFLR 115.

Duggan, Anthony. "The Status of Unperfected Security Interests in Insolvency Proceedings" (2008) 24:1 BFLR 103.

Duncan, Lewis. "The Bankruptcy Act Amendment Act of 1932 – Part II: The Creation of the Office of the Superintendent of Bankruptcy" (1932–1933) 2 Fortnightly LJ 101.

Edelman, Lauren B. "Legal Ambiguity and Symbolic Structures: Organizational Mediation of Civil Rights Law" (1992) 97:6 Am J Sociology 1531.

Edwards, Stanley. "Reorganizations Under the Companies' Creditors Arrangement Act" (1947) 25:6 Can Bar Rev 587.

Farkas, Peter. "Why Are There so Many Court-Appointed Receiverships?" (2003) 20:4 Nat Insolv Rev 37.

Ferlan, Dennis. "The Evolving Role of the Monitor, Confidential Information and the Monitor's Cross-examination, a Québec Perspective" 2011 ANNREVINSOLV 17 (Westlaw).

Ferron, J. Murray. "The Constitutional Impairment of the Rights of Secured Creditors in Canada and the United States" (1986) 60 CBR 146.

Fisher, Timothy C.G. and Jocelyn Martel. "Should We Abolish Chapter 11? Evidence from Canada" (1999) 28:1 J Leg Stud 233.

Fraser, W. Kaspar. "Reorganization of Companies in Canada" (1927) 27:8 Colum L Rev 932.

Forsey, Eugene. "Disallowance of Provincial Acts, Reservation of Provincial Bills, and Refusal of Assent by Provincial Lieutenant-Governors since 1867" (1938) 4:1 Can J Econ Polit Sci 47

– "Disallowance of Provincial Acts, Reservation of Provincial Bills, and Refusal of Assent by Lieutenant-Governors, 1937–47" (1948) 14:1 Can J Econ Polit Sci 94.

– "The Pulp and Paper Industry" (1935) 1:3 Can J Econ Polit Sci 501.

Forte, Mario. "*Re Metcalfe*: A Matter of Fraud, Fairness and Reasonableness: The Restructuring of the Third-Party Asset-Backed Commercial Paper Market in Canada" (2008) 17:3 Int Insolv Rev 211.

Foster, Roger S. "Conflicting Ideals for Corporate Reorganization" (1934–1935) 44:6 Yale LJ 923.

Galanter, Marc. "Why the 'Haves' Come Out Ahead: Speculations on the Limits of Legal Change" (1974) 9:1 Law and Soc'y Rev 95.

Girth, Majorie. "Rethinking Fairness in Bankruptcy Proceedings" (1999) 73:2 Am Bankr LJ 449.

Gollob, Jeffrey B. "Distressed Debt Lenders and their Impact on Restructurings and Workouts in Canada" 2004 ANNREVINSOLV 5 (Westlaw).

Goode, R.M. "Is the Law Too Favourable to Secured Creditors?" (1983–1984) 8:1 CBLJ 53.

Grattet, Ryken and Valerie Jenness. "The Birth and Maturation of Hate Crime Policy in the United States" (2001) 45:4 Am Behav Scientist 668.

Grattet, Ryken and Valerie Jenness. "Examining the Boundaries of Hate Crime Law: Disabilities and the Dilemma of Difference" (2001) 91:3 J of Crim L and Criminology 653.

Gross, Karen. "On the Merits: A Response to Professors Girth and White" (1999) 73:2 Am Bankr L J 485.

– "Taking Community Interests into Account in Bankruptcy: An Essay" (1994) 72:3 Wash Univ LQ 1031.

Hacker, Jacob S. "The Historical Logic of National Health Insurance: Structure and Sequence in the Development of British, Canadian and U.S. Medical Policy" (1998) 12:1 Stud in Am Polit Develop 57.

Halliday, Terence C. and Bruce G. Carruthers. "The Recursivity of Law: Global Norm Making and National Lawmaking in the Globalization of Corporate Insolvency Regimes" (2007) 112:4 Am J of Sociology 1135.

Hare, Diane M. and David Milman. "Debenture Holders and Judgment Creditors – Problems of Priority" (1982) LMCLQ 57.

Harris, Jason. "Enhancing the Role of Creditors' Committees in Corporate Rescue Laws" 2011 ANNREVINSOLV 23 (Westlaw).

Honsberger, John D. "Insolvency and the Corporate Veil in Canada" (1972) 15 CBR (NS) 89.

Ikenberry, John. "History's Heavy Hand: Institutions and the Politics of the State" (1994) [unpublished manuscript].

Jackson, Georgina R., and Janis Sarra. "Selecting the Judicial Tool to get the Job Done: An Examination of Statutory Interpretation, Discretionary Power and Inherent Jurisdiction in Insolvency Matters" 2007 ANNREVINSOLV 3 (Westlaw).

Jackson, Thomas H. and Robert E. Scott, "On the Nature of Bankruptcy: An Essay on Bankruptcy Sharing and the Creditors' Bargain" (1989) 75:2 Va L Rev 155.

Jacob, Q.C., Isaac H. "The Inherent Jurisdiction of the Court" (1970) 23 Curr Leg Prob 23.

Jones, Richard B. "The Evolution of Canadian Restructuring: Challenges for the Rule of Law" 2015 ANNREVINSOLV 18.

Keith, A. Berriedale. "The Privy Council Decisions: A Comment from Great Britain" (1937) 15:6 Can Bar Rev 428.

Kent, Andrew J.F. et al. "Canadian Business Restructuring Law: When Should a Court Say 'No'?" IIC-ART 2008–4 (Westlaw).

Kent, Andrew J.F. and Wael Rostrom. "The Auditor as Monitor in CCAA Proceedings: What Is the Debate?" 2003 ANNREVINSOL 7 (Westlaw).

Korobkin, Donald. "Contractarianism and the Normative Foundations of Bankruptcy Law" (1992–1993) 71:3 Tex L Rev 541.

– "Rehabilitating Values: A Jurisprudence of Bankruptcy" (1991) 91:4 Columbia L Rev 717.

Johnson, Douglas R. "Accounts Receivable Financing in Canada: Nature of the Charge and Rights of Priority" (1981) 15:1 UBC Law Rev 87.

Lederman, W.R. "The Concurrent Operation of Federal and Provincial Laws in Canada" (1963) 9:3 McGill LJ 185.

Locker, S. "Negotiability of Corporate Bonds" (1932–1933) 7:2 St John's Rev 306

Lobban, Michael. "Preparing for Fusion: Reforming the Nineteenth-Century Court of Chancery, Part I" (2004) 22.2 L and His Rev 389.

– "Preparing for Fusion: Reforming the Nineteenth-Century Court of Chancery, Part II" (2004) 22.4 L and His Rev 565.

MacDonald, Vincent C. "The Canadian Constitution Seventy Years After" (1937) 15:6 Can Bar Rev 401.

MacKelcan, Fred R. "Canadian Bond Issues" (1952) 30:4 Can Bar Rev 325.

Madsen, Jakob B. "Agricultural Crisis and the International Transmission of the Great Depression" (2001) 61:2 J of Econ Hist 327.

Mallory, J.R. "Disallowance and the National Interest" (1948) 14:3 Can J Econ Polit Sci 342.

Mann, David and Neil Narfason. "The Changing Role of the Monitor" IIC-ART 2008–8 (Westlaw).

Manning, H.E. "Company Reorganization, Part 1" (1932–1933) 2 Fortnightly LJ 139.

– "Company Reorganization, Part 2" (1932–1933) 2 Fortnightly LJ 158.

– "Company Reorganization, Part 3" (1932–1933) 2 Fortnightly LJ 176.

– "Company Reorganization, Part 4" (1932–1933) 2 Fortnightly LJ 192.

– "Companies Reorganization and the Judicature Amendment Act 1935, Part 1" (1935–1936) 5 Fortnightly LJ 23.

– "Companies Reorganization and the Judicature Amendment Act 1935, Part 2" (1935–1936) 5 Fortnightly LJ 40.

Manson, E. "The Growth of the Debenture" (1897) 13 LQR 418.

– "The Reform of Company Law" (1895) 11 LQR 346.

Marchildon, Gregory P. "The Prairie Farm Rehabilitation Administration: Climate Crisis and Federal-Provincial Relations during the Great Depression" (2009) 90:2 Cdn Historical Rev 275.

McConnell, William. "The Judicial Review of Prime Minister Bennett's 'New Deal'" (1968) 6:1 OHLJ 39.

McQueen, R. "Economic Aspects of Federalism: A Prairie View" (1935) 1:3 Can J Econ Polit Sci 352.

Milman, David. "Receivers as Agents" (1981) 44 Mod L Rev 658.

Moull, William D. "Security under Sections 177 and 178 of the Bank Act" (1986) 65:1 Can Bar Rev 242.

Myers, Fred and Alexa Abiscott. "Asset Backed Commercial Paper: Why the Courts Got It Right" (2009) 25:1 BFLR 5.

Nocilla, Alfonso. "Asset Sales Under the Companies' Creditors Arrangement Act and the Failure of Section 36" (2011–2012) 52:2 CBLJ 226.

– "Is 'Corporate Rescue' Working in Canada?" (2013) 53:3 CBLJ 382.

– "The History of the *Companies' Creditors Arrangement Act* and the Future of Restructuring Law in Canada" (2014) 56:1 CBLJ 73.

Pennington, Robert R. "The Genesis of the Floating Charge" (1960) 23:6 Mod L Rev 630.

Poole, William. "Moral Hazard: The Long-Lasting Legacy of Bailouts" (2009) 65:6 Fin Analysts J 17.

Pritchard, Keith. "Analysis of Recent Cases Under the Companies' Creditors Arrangement Act" (2004) 40:1 CBLJ 116.

Rogers, Norman McL. "The Political Principles of Federalism" (1935) 1:3 Can J Econ Polit Sci 337.

Rowat, D.C. "Recent Developments in Canadian Federalism" (1952) 18:1 Can J Econ Polit Sci 1.

Sallée, Clémentine and David Tournier. "Reorganization: A Commercial Concept Juridicially Defined" (2009) 88:1 Can Bar Rev 87.

Sarra, Janis. "Judicial Exercise of Inherent Jurisdiction under the CCAA" (2004) 40:2 CBLJ 280.

– "Manoeuvring through the Insolvency Maze – Shifting Identities and Implications for CCAA Restructurings" (2011) 27:1 BFLR 155.

Schneiderman, David. "Harold Laski, Viscount Haldane, and the Law of the Canadian Constitution in the Early Twentieth Century" (1998) 48:4 UTLJ 521.

Scott, F.R. "The Consequences of the Privy Council Decisions" (1937) 15:6 Can Bar Rev 485.

– "The Privy Council and Mr. Bennett's 'New Deal' Legislation" (1937) 3:2 Can J Polit Sci 234.

– "The Special Nature of Canadian Federalism" (1947) 13:1 Can J Econ Polit Sci 13.

Scott, Simon B, Timothy O. Buckley and Andrew Harrison. "The Arrangement Procedure under Section 192 of the *Canada Business Corporation Act* and the Reorganization of Dome Petroleum Limited" (1990) 16:3 CBLJ 296.

Scott, W.A. and P.J. Henderson. "Restructuring Canada's ABCP: A Unique, Successful, Private Restructuring" (2009) 28:4 Int'l Fin L Rev [no pagination in original].

Shaffer, Gregory C. "Transnational Recursivity Theory: Halliday and Carruthers' *Bankrupt*" (2011) 9:71 Socioeconomic Rev 371; Minnesota Legal Studies Research Paper No. 11–38 (last visited 5 October 2019), online: <ssrn.com/abstract=1926830> [perma.cc/E4EK-2ZFC].

Sgard, Jérôme. "Bankruptcy Law, Majority Rule, and Private Ordering in England and France (Seventeenth–Nineteenth Century)" (2010) OXPO Working Paper (last visited 5 October 2019), online: <hal-sciencespo .archives-ouvertes.fr/hal-01069444> [perma.cc/XR84-D9KD].

– "'Do Legal Origins Matter?' The case of bankruptcy laws in Europe 1808–1914" (2006) 10 European Rev of Econ Hist 389.

Smiley, Donald V. "Two Themes of Canadian Federalism" (1965) 31:1 Can J Econ Polit Sci 80.

Steffen, R.T. and H.E. Russell. "The Negotiability of Corporate Bonds" (1931–1932) 41:6 Yale LJ 799.

Sterbach, Charles R. "Anatomy of an Involuntary Corporate Bankruptcy" (2004) 13:1 J Bankr L & Prac 1 Art 1.

Telfer, Thomas G.W. "A Canadian 'World without Bankruptcy': The Failure of Bankruptcy Reform at the End of the Nineteenth Century" (2004) 8:1 Austl J Legal Hist 83.

– "Canadian Insolvency Law Reform and 'Our Bankrupt Legislative Process" 2010 ANNREVINSOLV 21 (Westlaw).

– "The Canadian Bankruptcy Act of 1919: Public Legislation or Private Interest?" (1994–1995) 24:3 CBLJ 357.

– "The New Bankruptcy 'Detective Agency'? The Origins of the Superintendent of Bankruptcy in Great Depression Canada" [unpublished manuscript].

Telfer, Thomas G.W. and Bruce Welling. "The Winding-Up and Restructuring Act: Realigning Insolvency's Orphan to the Modern Law Reform Process" (2008) 24:1 BFLR 233.

Thelen, Kathleen. "Historical Institutionalism in Comparative Politics" (1999) 2 Annual Rev Poli Sci 369.

Torrie, Virginia. "Farm Debt Compromises during the Great Depression: An Empirical Study of Applications made under the *Farmers' Creditors Arrangement Act* in Morden and Brandon, Manitoba" (2018) 41:1 Manitoba LJ 377.

– "Federalism and Farm Debt During the Great Depression: Political
  Impetuses for the *Farmers' Creditors Arrangement Act, 1934*" (2019) 82:2
  Sask L Rev 203-257.
– "Should Paramountcy Protect Secured Creditor Rights?: *Saskatchewan v
  Lemare Lake Logging* in Historical Context" (2017) 22:3 Rev Const Stud 405.
Torrie, Virginia and Vern W. DaRe. "The Participation of Social Stakeholders
  in CCAA Proceedings" 2020 ANNREVINSOLV 9 (Westlaw).
Tuck, Raphael. "Social Security: An Administrative Solution to the
  Dominion-Provincial Problem" (1947) 13:2 Can J Econ Polit Sci 256.
Tushnet, Mark. "Defending the Indeterminacy Thesis" (1996–1997) 16:3
  QLR 339.
Waines, W.J. "Dominion-Provincial Financial Arrangements: An
  Examination of Objectives" (1953) 19:3 Can J Econ Polit Sci 304.
Warren, Elizabeth. "Bankruptcy Policy" (1987) 54:3 U Chic L Rev 775.
Watson, Alan. "Legal Change: Sources of Law and Legal Culture" (1982–
  1983) 131:5 Univ Penn L Rev 1121.
Watts, Ronald L. "The American Constitution in Comparative Perspective:
  A Comparison of Federalism in the United States and Canada" (1987) 74:3
  J of Am Hist 769.
Willis, John. "Statute Interpretation in a Nutshell" (1938) 16:1 Can Bar Rev 1.
Wood, Roderick J. "The Definition of Secured Creditor in Insolvency Law"
  (2010) 25:3 BFLR 341.
– "The Floating Charge in Canada" (1988–1989) 27:2 Alta L Rev 191.
– "Rescue and Liquidation in Restructuring Law" (2013) 53:3 CBLJ 407.
– "The Regulation of Receiverships" 2009 ANNREVINSOLV 9 (Westlaw).
– "The Structure of Secured Priorities in Insolvency Law" (2011) 27:1 BFLR 25.
Ziegel, Jacob S. "Canada's Dysfunctional Insolvency Reform Process and
  the Search for Solutions" (2010) 26:1 BFLR 63.
– "Creditors as Corporate Stakeholders: The Quiet Revolution – An Anglo-
  Canadian Perspective" (1993) 43:3 UTLJ 511.
– "Modernization of Canada's Bankruptcy Law in Comparative Context"
  (1998) 33:1 Tex Int'l LJ 1.
Zweig, Sean and Preet K. Bell. "The Expanded Use of the CBCA in Debt
  Restructurings" 2019 ANNREVINSOLV 27 (Westlaw).

Book Reviews, Case Notes, Commentary, and Newsletters

"Bankruptcy Reforms" (1932–1933) 2 Fortnightly LJ 196.
"Bankruptcy Act Proclaimed," (1932–1933) 2 Fortnightly LJ 118.
"Bonds. Negotiability. Effect of Incorporation of Trust Indenture in
  Corporate Bonds" (1929) 42:5 Harv L Rev 700.
"Corporate Reconstructions by Arrangements with Shareholders or
  Creditors" (1949) 62:3 Harv L Rev 468.

"Effect of Deeds of Trust on the Negotiability of Corporate Bonds" (1928) 42:1 Harv L Rev 115.

"Effect of Tax Exemption and Tax Refunding Provisions on the Negotiability of Corporate Bonds" (1930) 29:1 Mich L Rev 77.

"Negotiable Instruments. Bonds. Negotiability. Reference to Deed of Trust." (1928–1929) 38:6 Yale LJ 825.

"Negotiable Instruments. Corporate Bonds. Effect of Reference to Mortgage on Negotiability" (1929) 29:3 Colum L Rev 365.

"Negotiability of Corporate Bonds, Recent New York Legislation" (1930–1931) 40:2 Yale LJ 261.

"Protective Committees" (1940–1941) 10 Fortnightly LJ 183.

"The Rights and Remedies of the Bondholder under Corporate Bonds and Indentures: I" (1927) 27:4 Colum L Rev 433.

"The Rights and Remedies of the Bondholder under Corporate Bonds and Indentures: II" (1927) 27:5 Colum L Rev 579.

Burns, R.J. "Recent Depression Legislation" (1934–1936) 1 Alta LQ 16.

Carhart, Jeffrey C. "Appointing a Receiver and Seizing Equipment" (2005) 22:6 Nat Insolv Rev 53.

DaRe, Vern W. "Is Insolvency Still a Prerequisite to Restructuring?" (2004) 49 CBR (4th) 163.

Farkas, Peter. "Defining (and Refining) the Role of the Monitor" (2010) 72 CBR 159.

Goldman, David H. "Reorganizations under the *Companies' Creditors Arrangement Act* (Canada)" (1985) 55 CBR (NS) 36.

Goldman, David H., David E. Baird and Michael A. Weinczok. "Arrangements Under the *Companies' Creditors Arrangement Act*" (1991) 1 CBR (3d) 135.

Goodman, Q.C., H.M. "Practice Note on the *Companies' Creditors Arrangement Act, 1933*" (1952), 32 CBR 227.

H., G.F. "Case Note on the Ontario case of *O'Brien v British American Nickel Corporation and National Trust Co.*" (1925) 3:8 Can Bar Rev 498.

Ham, C. Keith. "'Instant' Trust Deeds Under the C.C.A.A." (1988) 2 Comm Insolv Rep 25.

Katz, Mark, Anita Banicevic and Jim Dinning. "Antitrust in a Financial Crisis – A Canadian Perspective" (April 2009) *The Antitrust Source* (last visited 5 October 2019), online: *DWVP* <dwpv.com/~/media/Files/PDF_EN/2014-2007/Antitrust_in_a_Financial_Crisis_-_A_Canadian_Perspective.ashx> [perma.cc/5R3V-AT2A].

Light, David B. "Involuntary Subordination of Security Interests to Charges for DIP Financing under the Companies' Creditors Arrangement Act" (2002) 30 CBR (4th) 245.

MacLeod, J.E.A. "The Farmers' Creditors Arrangement Act" (1936–1938) 2 Alta LQ 167.

McLaws, D. "The Farmers' Creditors Arrangement Act" (1936–1938) 2 Alta LQ 239.

O'Leary, Brian. "A Review of the *Companies' Creditors Arrangement Act*" (1987) 4:3 Nat Insolv Rev 38.

Sokal, Jennifer. "Recent Developments in Canadian Bankruptcy and Insolvency Law" (2019) 34:2 BFLR 267.

Torrie, Virginia. *Book Review*: Thomas G.W. Telfer, *Ruin and Redemption: The Struggle for a Canadian Bankruptcy Law, 1867–1919* (Toronto: University of Toronto Press for the Osgoode Society for Canadian Legal History, 2014) (2016) 31:2 BFLR 427.

Ziegel, Jacob S. "Repeal of the *Companies' Creditors Arrangement Act* Rule PC 1999–1072" (1999) 10 CBR (4th) 222.

Zych, Kevin J., et al. "Case Note: Important Restrictions Placed on Use of CBCA for Debt Restructurings" (2015) 32:1 BFLR 197.

Conference Proceedings

Boothman, Barry E.C. "Night of the Longest Day: The Receivership of Abitibi Power and Paper" (Paper delivered at Administrative Sciences Association of Canada, 1992) [unpublished].

Clark, Stephen D.A. "Typical Security Taken by Banks' Paper in Proceedings of 1984 Annual Institute of Continuing Legal Education: 'Business Law: Borrowing from Banks" (2 February 1984) [unpublished].

Hilton, James S. "Receivership Clauses in Mortgages" Paper in Proceedings of The Canadian Bar Association-Ontario, 1985 Annual Institute on Continuing Legal Education: "Real Property: Mortgage Matters" (9 February 1985) [unpublished].

Jacques, Arthur O. "Creditor Arrangements" Canadian Bar Association Seminar: "Corporate Loan Workouts" (1985) [unpublished].

Morawetz, Geoffrey B. "Emerging Trends in the Use of the *Companies' Creditors Arrangement Act*" Proceedings, First Annual General Meeting and Conference of the Insolvency Institute of Canada (1990) [unpublished].

Newbould, Q.C., Frank J.C. and Geoffrey B. Morawetz. "Developments and Trends in *Companies' Creditors Arrangement Act* Restructuring" Paper in Proceedings of 1991 Insight Educational Services Conference: "How and When to Use the *Companies' Creditors Arrangement Act (CCAA)*" (4 June 1991) [unpublished].

Robertson, Ronald N. "Legal Problems on Reorganization of Major Financial and Commercial Debtors' Canadian Bar Association Seminar: 'Mega-International Insolvencies'" (1983) [unpublished].

Theses and Dissertations

Edwards, Stanley E. "Protection of the Rights of Creditors in the
  Reorganization of Insolvent Canadian Companies" (LLM Thesis,
  Harvard Law School, Harvard University, 1947) [unpublished].
Garant, Jean Pierre. "The Floating Charge in Canadian Bond Market"
  (PhD Dissertation in Finance, University of Illinois at Urbana-
  Champaign, 1971) [unpublished].
Torrie, Virginia. "Analyzing the Canadian Third-Party ABCP Liquidity
  Crisis and Restructuring through the Lenses of Securities and Insolvency
  Law" (LLM Thesis, Osgoode Hall Law School of York University, 2010)
  [unpublished].
Weeks, Irvine Duncan. "The Collapse of Atlantic Acceptance Corporation
  and Its Effect on the Structure of Liabilities and Quality of Reporting of
  Canadian Finance Companies" (MBA Thesis, Faculty of Commerce and
  Administration, University of British Columbia, 1968) [unpublished].

Government Documents

Canada

DEBATES AND PARLIAMENTARY DOCUMENTS

Debates of the House of Commons of Canada, 4th Sess, 17th Parl (Ottawa:
  King's Printer, 1933).
Debates of the House of Commons, 7th Sess, 21st Parl (Ottawa: King's Printer,
  1953).
Debates of the House of Commons of Canada, 1st Sess, 33rd Parl (Ottawa:
  Queen's Printer, 1987).
Debates of the Senate of Canada, 4th Sess, 17th Parl (Ottawa: King's Printer,
  1933).
House of Commons Standing Committee on Banking and Commerce.
  *Minutes of Proceedings and Evidence Respecting the Companies Creditors'
  Arrangement Act, No. 1, 7 June 1938* (Ottawa: King's Printer, 1938).
Lemaire, E.J. (Clerk of the Privy Council), Minute of a Meeting of the
  Committee of the Privy Council (23 January 1934) PC 117.

LETTERS AND STATEMENTS

Letter from the Competition Bureau to the Royal Bank and the Bank of
  Montreal (11 December 1998), online: <competitionbureau.gc.ca/eic
  /site/cb-bc.nsf/eng/01612.html> [perma.cc/7H5Y-DWVQ].

Letter from the Competition Bureau to the CIBC and TD Bank (11 December 1998), online: <competitionbureau.gc.ca/eic/site/cb-bc.nsf /eng/01601.html> [perma.cc/KSB2-DZQG].

Statement by the Honourable Paul Martin, Minister of Finance, on the Bank Merger Proposals (14 December 1998), online: <webarchive.bac-lac .gc.ca:8080/wayback/20131002020411/http://www.collectionscanada .gc.ca/webarchives/20071122063125/http://www.fin.gc.ca/news98 /98-124e.html> [perma.cc/7FKX-V8SN].

REPORTS AND PUBLICATIONS

Canadian Department of Trade and Commerce. *Census of Industry: The Pulp and Paper Industry, 1925* (Ottawa: King's Printer, 1927).

Department of the Secretary of State. *Annual Reports of the Secretary of State of Canada* (Ottawa: King's Printer, 1924–1967).

– *Sessional Paper No. 165* (3 March 1938) [unpublished].

Dominion Bureau of Statistics. *Canadian Statistical Review, January and February 1953* (Ottawa: Queen's Printer, 1954).

– *Monthly Review of Business Statistics*, vols. 9–21 (Ottawa: King's Printer, 1934–1946).

– *Recent Economic Tendencies in Canada, 1919–1934* (Issued as a Supplement to the *Monthly Review of Business Statistics*, June 1935) (Ottawa: King's Printer, 1935).

– *Twelve Years of the Economic Statistics of Canada by Month and Years, 1919–1930* (Issued as a Supplement to the *Monthly Review of Business Statistics*, November 1931) (Ottawa: King's Printer, 1931).

Hughes, Hon. S.H.S., et al. *Report of the Royal Commission Appointed to Inquire into the Failure of Atlantic Acceptance Corporation, Limited* (Toronto: Queen's Printer for Ontario, 1969).

McTague, Hon. Charles Patrick, et al. *Report of the Royal Commission Inquiring into the Affairs of Abitibi Power and Paper Company, Limited* (Toronto: Royal Commission Inquiring into the Affairs of Abitibi Power and Paper Company, 1941).

Sarra, Janis. "Development of a Model to Track Filings and Collect Data for Proceedings Under the CCAA" (March 2006) Final Report to the OSB (last visited 5 October 2019), online: *Innovation, Science and Economic Development Canada* <strategis.ic.gc.ca/eic/site/bsf-osb.nsf/vwapj/Sarra-2006 -ENG.pdf/$FILE/Sarra-2006-ENG.pdf> [perma.cc/74G5-BAHS].

Sirois, Joseph, et al. *Report of the Royal Commission on Dominion-Provincial Relations* (Ottawa: King's Printer, 1940).

Tassé, Roger, et al. *Bankruptcy and Insolvency: Report of the Study Committee on Bankruptcy and Insolvency Legislation* (Ottawa: Information Canada, 1970).

Ontario

Stapleford, E.W., *Report on Rural Relief due to Drought Conditions and Crop Failures in Western Canada, 1930–1937* (Ottawa: Minister of Agriculture, 1939).

United Kingdom

Kenneth Cork et al., *Report of the Review Committee on Insolvency Law and Practice*, 1982 Cmnd 855.

Annotations, Encyclopedias and Reference Materials

Canadian Encyclopedic Digest 4th (online) (Westlaw).
Bell, Jilean, et al., eds. *Canada Statute Citator* (Toronto: Thomson Reuters Canada Limited, 2015).
– *Canada Statute Citator* (Toronto: Thomson Reuters Canada Limited, 2018).
Halsbury's Laws of Canada (online) (2017 Reissue) (LexisAdvance).
Houlden, Lloyd W. and G.B. Morawetz. *Houlden and Morawetz's Bankruptcy and Insolvency Analysis* (Westlaw).
Houlden, Lloyd W., Geoffrey B. Morawetz and Janis P. Sarra, *The 2015 Annotated Bankruptcy and Insolvency Act* (Toronto: Carswell, 2015).

Pamphlets, Trade Publications and Indentures

Dominion Mortgage and Investments Association. *Yearbook 1932* (Toronto: DMIA, 1933).
– *Yearbook 1933* (Toronto: DMIA, 1934).
– *Yearbook 1934* (Toronto: DMIA, 1935).
– *Yearbook 1938* (Toronto: DMIA, 1939).
– *Yearbook 1939* (Toronto: DMIA, 1940).
Indenture. United States Steel Corp, Art 7 (1903).
Kent, Pen. "The London Approach" (1 March 1993) Q1 *Bank of England Quarterly Bulletin* 110 (last visited 5 October 2019), online: *Bank of England* <bankofengland.co.uk/-/media/boe/files/quarterly-bulletin/1993/the-london-approach> [perma.cc/V8WM-ATFB].
MacKelcan, Fred R. "The Position of Holders of Industrial Bonds" (No further bibliographic details available).
– "A Philosophy of Trust Management that Packs a Wallop," (1943) *Pamphlet Published by National Trust Co.*

Periodicals and Newspapers

Associated Press
Barron's
The Economist
Financial Post
Financial Times
Globe and Mail
New York Times
Oil and Gas Journal
Toronto Star
United Press International
Winnipeg Free Press

Websites

"CCAA Records List" (last visited 5 October 2019), online: *Office of the Superintendent of Bankruptcy* <ic.gc.ca/eic/site/bsf-osb.nsf/eng /h_br02281.html> [perma.cc/9VQQ-2RPD].

"George F. Curtis, OC, OBC, QC" (last visited 5 October 2019), online: *Peter A. Allard School of Law, the University of British Columbia* <historyproject .allard.ubc.ca/law-history-project/profile/george-f-curtis-oc-obc-qc> [https://perma.cc/B7H8-2Q2L].

"History" (last visited 5 October 2019), online: *Bennett Jones LLP* <bennett jones.com/history> [perma.cc/9ADM-NR9E].

"Our History" (last visited 5 October 2019), online: *Office of the Superintendent of Financial Institutions* <osfi-bsif.gc.ca/Eng/osfi-bsif/Pages/hst.aspx> [perma.cc/GMR2-YQAR].

"Past CBA Presidents" (last visited 5 October 2019), online: *Canadian Bar Association* <cba.org/Who-We-Are/Governance/Board-of-Directors /Past-CBA-Presidents> [perma.cc/9JSN-GYSX].

"Past Insolvencies" (last visited 5 October 2019), online: *Assuris* <assuris.ca /Client/Assuris/Assuris_LP4W_LND_WebStation.nsf/page/Past+ Insolvencies!OpenDocument&audience=policyholder> [perma.cc /4HKL-YQNT].

Index

Page numbers with (f) refer to figures; pages with (t) refer to tables. CCAA refers to *Companies' Creditors Arrangement Act*, and FCAA refers to *Farmers' Creditors Arrangement Act*.